# COCKBURN'S MILLENNIUM

*Frontispiece.* Henry Cockburn in the last year of his life: a photograph taken by J. G. Tunny

# COCKBURN'S MILLENNIUM

Karl Miller

Duckworth

First published in 1975 by
Gerald Duckworth & Co. Ltd.
The Old Piano Factory
43 Gloucester Crescent, London NW1

ISBN 0 7156 0913 0

Printed in Great Britain by
Ebenezer Baylis and Son Ltd.
The Trinity Press, Worcester, and London

# Contents

## Illustrations

# For Jane

*Errata*

Page 28: 'accounted by his kind' should read 'accounted by his kin'. Page 72, footnote 1: James Rutherfurd was Andrew's younger (not 'young') brother. Page 81: footnote 3 refers to the words 'According to Jeffrey'. Page 109 (see also page 118): Gibson-Craig's banquet was held at the new, and not the old, High School. Page 113: 'the mean of "wealth and sense" ' should read 'the men . . .' Page 136: the words 'a gentleman by adoption' refer to John Thomson, and not to Baron Hume. Page 149, footnote 3: the watermark is 1833. Page 154: the point about Cockburn's versification should read: 'The dactyllic metre is much the same.' Page 165: 'he addresses him' should read 'he addresses the Devil.' Page 177: Mrs Cockburn's 'i' my life' should be followed by an exclamation-mark. Page 215: 'One of his early friends was Simpson' should read 'was the son of Simpson'. Page 216: Sylvia Plath's thesis was not a doctoral but an undergraduate thesis. Page 221: 'his discussion should come to rest' should read 'this discussion . . .' Page 233: in Cockburn's account of the Stewart trial, 'from the country' should read 'from the county'. Page 234: 'civil-jury millennium' should read 'jury-trial millennium'. Page 251: in Cockburn's eulogy of John MacFarlane, 'human' should read 'humane'. By way of addendum, rather than erratum: there is no reason to think that the poem 'The Holy Grove', ascribed to Cockburn in Chapter Nine, was modelled on Coleridge's 'Love'.

# *Preface*

There has been no previous book about Henry Cockburn. He was his own biographer, and the quality of his performance may have had a daunting effect on those who might otherwise have wished to attempt his life, though the only person ever to have entertained such designs, so far as I am aware, is his descendant, Claud Cockburn. But there is much that Henry Cockburn does not say about himself, just as there is much that no one can know about himself. I have tried to supplement the account he gives of his life in the *Memorials*, the *Journal* and the *Circuit Journeys*, and, where I could, to avoid reiterating his own testimony. Considered as a biography, the result is a little peculiar, and it is as well to say straight away that it is perhaps less of a biography than a series of arguments and reflections on the subject of his life and works, and on the process of social and cultural change by which they were affected. It is shaped like a hill. It goes up—to the high ground of his enchanted leisure—and it comes down again, returning to the Edinburgh where he worked and did his duty. It is like a hill, too, in affording a succession of views of the biographical facts, including some very distant prospects. It is not, at any rate, the kind of biography which travels, with suitable pauses, from first to last.

There is at least one man in the world who appears to think that there is no need for books on this subject. When I went once to Edinburgh to talk about it, a member of the Cockburn Association was heard to remark: 'There is nothing new to say about Cockburn.' Cockburn should be let alone, rather as a number of things were let alone by the Whig Reformers of the 1830s. But the situation is that practically nothing has been written about him since the early essays and memorabilia, that the published sources which bear on several aspects of his career are far from substantial, that his manuscripts have yet to be edited, though a start may soon be made, and that there exist writings of his which are either published or made generally available for the first time in the present book. For the purposes of the book, I have consulted the manuscript collection of his letters and papers which is held in the National Library of Scotland, and I have assembled a set of poems by him. The journal of his Continental tour, a transcription of which forms part of the Jeffrey papers in the National Library, and which has yet to be published, is discussed here with the intention that there should be extensive quotation: the Venetian section is given almost in its entirety. At the end of the book appears a memorial by Cockburn, sections of which have not been published before, and which concerns the inhabitants of the Outer House of the Court of Session.

Cockburn was a lawyer, and I am not. About certain of his pursuits I can write only as an amateur or layman. My main purpose was to study his work as literature, to concentrate on matters of expression and of the imagination, and on their relation to the successive Scotlands which he dreamt of, described and predicted. In doing so, I commit one or two acts of auto-biography myself, and I think I should say a word about these.

I chose to write about Cockburn because I take delight in him and in his times, and in writing about him there were occasions when I wanted to write also about the Scotland in which I myself grew up, a hundred years after his death. The desire to do this may partly be explained in terms of a shared acquaintance with certain of the institutions and landscapes of the country: chiefly, the High School of Edinburgh and the Pentland Hills. But there is a further coincidence which is worth mentioning. In his early forties, after a period of crisis in his life, and on the verge of a period of hopeful turbulence in the affairs of Scotland, Cockburn turned towards the past, towards his parents, and towards his childhood, and began to write his memoirs. In attempting—at the same age as he then was—to understand what happened to him, I turned towards my own childhood and towards the experience of my parents. And I thought about what it is for a succeeding generation to pass into their forties—conscious of their dead, and of their own deaths. It did not seem unreasonable to allow various tremors of sympathy to enter the book, by way of acknowledgement of this last coincidence.

At certain points I have speculated fairly freely about the nature of Cockburn's psychological development, while seeking to make clear what is speculative and what is not. Cockburn can often resist the 'how he may have felt' of biography, and these hypotheses do not represent an effort to evoke the character of his conscious experience. They represent a model of his imaginative life, of its tendencies and tensions—one to which, as I have also made clear, some of the distinctive themes and presuppositions of recent times have contributed.

In particular, what may appear to be a contradictory attitude to social and political change, on Cockburn's part, is related to his posture of loyalty and disloyalty towards his kin, and to a pattern of aggression and compunction which may have been established early in life. I do not wish to suggest that change requires explanation solely or primarily in terms of the inner lives or psychological idiosyncrasies of its exponents, or that such explanations are especially due when the changes in question fall short of the absolute and unqualified—which is no improvement on the opposing view that revolutionaries need psychiatry. Cockburn had sound reasons of policy and prudence for drawing the line where he did, for blowing hot and cold. His sense of the public interest, of the interests of his kind, and of what was expected of a Scottish Whig, was certainly efficacious in producing what some modern readers might regard as an ambivalent attitude to reform. For all that, I feel that his part in the Reform Bill was very much in character, and deeply acceptable to his inner life.

The *Memorials* and the *Journals* are his best-known works, and in quoting from them I have not always thought it necessary to supply references. The sources for important quotations from both works are supplied in the form of page references or dates, and this is also the case with all quotations from his other writings, published and unpublished. Where any of his letters is quoted from, that letter belongs, unless otherwise identified, to the National Library's collection of Cockburn manuscripts, which is arranged, for the most part, in the case of the letters, according to the identity of their recipients. The quotations from his unpublished writings preserve his punctuation and spelling as far as seemed consistent with clarity and readability—which is, in fact, very far. In the case of the texts of his poems which are published in this book, editorial action has been kept to a minimum. He was, in general, a determined user of the dash, and his dashes have sometimes been removed. One or two adjustments to modern usage have been made, such as the use of the form 'anyone' in preference to his 'any one'.

I have received a great deal of generous and invaluable help, and I would like to record my gratitude. I am indebted to the Librarian of the National Library, to the Keeper of Manuscripts there, and to their staff, for the assistance and courtesy extended to me. I have gained much from the guidance of Alan Bell, of the Department of Manuscripts, who lent me his transcriptions of many of Cockburn's letters and of large sections of the Continental journal, and who transcribed on my behalf what I have called Cockburn's 'Memorial of the Outer House'. I hope that he will go on to edit the letters: I don't think that it is the partiality of a biographer which makes me feel that they are among the best letters of their kind that I have read.

I have benefited from conversations with Christopher Ricks and Rosalind

I*

Mitchison, both of whom read drafts of the book, and I have received help
and advice from the following people: Jonathan Miller (who first told me
about the magic doctors Macnish and Wigan), Ernest Mehew and Janet
Adam Smith (who advised me on matters concerning Robert Louis Stevenson), M. I. Finley, Frank Kermode, Nicholas Phillipson, T. C. Smout,
Francis Haskell, Chalmers Davidson, Sir Robert and Lady McEwen,
Susannah Clapp, Mary-Kay Wilmers and Margaret Connor. I would like
to thank the Librarian and Curators of the Signet Library for permission
to quote from material in their possession, and Viscount Melville, the Earl
of Dalhousie and the trustees of the late Colonel Dundas of Ochtertyre for
permission to quote from muniment material now held at the Scottish
Record Office. I am indebted, for items of information, to the staff
of the Record Office and of the Edinburgh Corporation's Central
Library.

Mr J. Keenan of Edinburgh's Royal Botanic Garden went prospecting
with me for Cockburn's elm and waterfall: the Botanic Garden, transplanted
to Inverleith in 1823, was among the Edens in which Cockburn delighted.
Ross Eudall took the photograph which accompanies this book. Cockburn's
elm has been inspected by expert eyes, and spoken of as old enough for the
part: but its age has yet to be scientifically checked.

The late Frank Cockburn, a great-grandson of Cockburn's, let me have
copies of three poems by him—the first version of 'The Linn', 'Relugas' and
'On losing a staff from a gig'—and granted me permission to reproduce
them. At his death in 1974, which occurred when the chapters of the present
book had been completed, Cockburn papers which had been in his possession
—letters, drafts and other documents, including the manuscripts of these
poems—passed into the care of the National Library (MS Deposit 235).
Much of the correspondence had been published in the volume entitled *Some
Letters of Lord Cockburn*, and, having now examined the papers, I do not
think they contain any new information of importance. But they do contain
passages which deserve attention in this preface.

The originals of those letters which Cockburn's grandson Harry Cockburn
published in *Some Letters* reveal the deletion of passages and phrases which
he might have done better to retain. The original of the letter to Sir Thomas
Dick Lauder of 30 December 1830, in which Cockburn the political reformer
crows over the approaching triumph of the Whig principles of sense and
justice, and from which, in its published form, I quote at length, has him
hoping 'for a vigorous suppression of all undue encroachment by poverty
and ignorance on property and knowledge'. This Harry Cockburn omitted,
moving on to his grandfather's thoughts about a more remote but even more

apocalyptic future, when America would civilize whole continents, Britain instruct the world, and the press make 'the world one audience'. A picnic of August 1833 at Habbie's Howe in the Pentlands is described in Chapter Four with reference to a letter of Cockburn's to his daughter Jane, and I find that the manuscript of the letter has some further words about what happened in that 'pastoral, classical valley'. With the poet Allan Ramsay in mind, he informs Jane that the spot 'where the Scottish Theocritus wrote' was profaned by puns and horseplay, and confesses: 'I steal a moment (as the romantic people say) to tell all this to you.' The letter shows him for what he was: a classical person who was also a romantic person.

Cockburn's Habbie's Howe lay near another haunt of his, the kirkyard of Glencorse. A rival Habbie's Howe, a few miles to the south, was eventually judged more likely to have furnished the setting for Ramsay's play *The Gentle Shepherd*, where the name occurs. But if this was the spot celebrated by Ramsay, the other was widely believed to be, and was frequented by believers for many years.

The new letters by 'Each Sea', as he frequently signed himself, playing on his initials, are several of them in his best epistolary vein. We see him, during a storm of wind and snow, in the role of backsliding Presbyterian: 'It was very edifying to look thro' the window of a calm warm room, and observe our friends the saints struggling with broken umbrellas and flying cloaks, to church.' These are the words (to Francis Jeffrey's wife, on 2 February 1823) of a man who was to grow into a kind of Presbyterian patriot and who became, after a fashion, an elder of the Kirk. Among the papers is a document, dated 20 February 1831, on which his ordination as an elder of Calzet Church in the Tweeddale parish of Broughton, Glenholm and Kilbucho—where his detested Lord Braxfield had owned an estate in years gone by—is captured in copperplate. The ordination took place during his reign as Scottish Solicitor-General, and it seems to have been sought in order that he might have a voice in the councils of the General Assembly of the Church of Scotland. The post was probably something of a sinecure, and if he was ever the elder of any kirk less remote from either of his two houses, it can't be said to have left much of a mark on his published or unpublished writings.

Another letter to Dick Lauder, of 6 November 1820, presses the claim to a vacancy of Cockburn's friend John Richardson: the Convention of Royal Burghs required an agent (a solicitor or, in Scotland, a writer). 'Richardson and I have been so long and so intimately connected, that he used to be called my wife, and may more truly be styled (which you know is a very different thing) Myself—for indeed I am as much wrapped up in his interest as in my own.' Edwardian Edinburgh would have been struck by the frankness or extravagance of these remarks, as of the lobbying which they were intended to promote: and the day was not long in coming thereafter when to speak of being wedded to a friend would seem far from sensible, if not imprudent. The remarks also show traces of that preoccupation with doubles and second selves which meant so much to the 'Gothic' literature of the period, with its dependence on German models. On other occasions, Cockburn could regard marriage as the acquisition of a second self: a spouse was duplicated, or Siamesed, for ever. And he could behave as his own opposite or twin. He has a way of seeming to think in terms of matching or contrasting pairs: such as 'poverty and ignorance', or the two divergent meanings which he imparts, as we shall discover, to the word 'respectable'. There was a binariness in him which certain of the preoccupations of his time could hardly have failed to enhance, and which could draw him into paradox. It does so when he says here—in a letter to his daughter Elizabeth of 28 August 1844—that a taste for external nature is next only to a taste for virtue: it is the 'second one thing needful'. The paradox is beautiful. It is wise, and it is funny.

Not that he would have wanted to be thought Gothic or Germanic. Writing to Jeffrey on 26 March 1846, he tells the story of a young man who had become oppressed by the infinite promise he had displayed at the school Cockburn founded, Edinburgh Academy, and who shammed a death by drowning, disappeared for a while from the face of the earth, and then returned to the consternation of Edinburgh. This Gothic act was the product of a species of cultural conditioning which has yet to lose its power to determine conduct, and the interpretation of conduct—as the strange case of the British MP John Stonehouse, with his false drowning, his talk of having suffered the displacement of an old personality by a new, and his search for a haven in Australia and elsewhere, has lately suggested. Cockburn disapproved of the young man's trick, imagining him to have been seized by 'a sudden Germanizing of the noddle.'

Hypocrisy is a manifestation of the double life with which Cockburn may be felt to have had a somewhat specialized acquaintance, in that he was conscious of, though he did not always act upon, the need for a public repression of his belligerent wit in accordance with the hypocrisy enjoined on him by the attainment of high office. The type of joke he would have had to worry about is represented, among the new papers, by the words he inscribed on William IV's letter raising him to the Court of Session—and, as Cockburn put it on this occasion, 'making at least one worthy judge'.

Among the papers is a collection of drafts in Cockburn's handwriting—work in progress towards what became the *Memorials*. In circumstances which are explained in a footnote (page 53), the drafts were preserved from destruction at a time, many years after his death, when other papers were being thrown out. A large proportion of this material was rejected by the two trustees of the estate who were his editors, and a large proportion of the rejected material was published in *Some Letters*. Two versions of the 'character' of his enemy John Hope, which was excluded from the *Memorials* on the grounds, presumably, that Hope was still alive, are present on paper watermarked 1838 and 1849 respectively. The first version is, I believe, a transcription of what Cockburn originally wrote, in journal form, in 1822, when the youthful but very well-connected Hope was appointed Solicitor-General. The second version recasts the passages in the form of an account of the past. This is what the *Memorials* are throughout: an account of the past. They are an unbroken history, with vestiges of journal. But the *Journal*, which goes on with the story of his life, is a journal, with intervals of silence. It was published subsequently, and the same men were involved in preparing the manuscript for the press.

It would appear from the Hope versions, and from the previous evidence, that the four volumes of what Cockburn called his Red Book carried the first drafts of the material embodied in the two published volumes, including the draft which I assume to have preceded the '1838' version of the Hope passages, and that the subject-matter of the *Memorials* was first recorded in the Red Book during the 1820s. It also appears that it may have been re-corded there in a form closer to the journal form of the second published volume than Cockburn's surviving statements could be taken to imply. There was always bound to be a difference of method in view of the fact that so much of the *Memorials* is retrospect, and zealous retrospect at that. But it would seem that in the course of the later copyings-out it became more of a narrative history. It is necessary, therefore, to exercise caution in responding to the change of procedure apparent half-way through his binary autobio-graphy, in discussing changes of tone in the published work of this reviser, and in relating them to particular aspects of Cockburn's career. Nevertheless, there need be no doubt that significant changes of tone can be very firmly identified.

These manuscripts give ample evidence of the expurgation imposed by the prudent, and perhaps also prudish, editors of the *Memorials*. We learn, for instance—what can barely be glimpsed on the printed page—that the ridiculous Lord Eskgrove was ridiculously lecherous, and that Cockburn's most lavish comic set-piece was once, with its leering Esky, altogether luxuriant. I hope that it will grow again, in the setting of a comprehensive edition of his works. Among the passages cut by the editors for no obvious reason is one in which he refers to the Foxite banquet of 1821, and cites a contemporary opinion of the Whig advocates and orators who attended it. This opinion was drawn from the *Memoir and Correspondence of Mrs Grant of Laggan*, edited by her son, John Peter Grant, and published in 1844. For Mrs Grant, Cockburn and his confederates were professional talkers, and she likens them to Milton's loquacious rebel angels. Having used it myself of Cockburn, I am pleased to know of Mrs Grant's analogy. It is less damaging to the Scottish Whigs than she supposed.

A few passages of this book appear in an introduction I wrote for a reissue of the 1910 edition of the *Memorials* which was published by Chicago University Press in 1974.

April 1975                                                                K.M.

## *Abbreviations*

NLS refers to the National Library of Scotland, *M* to Cockburn's *Memorials* (to the first edition of 1856), *J* to the two volumes of his *Journal*, JLC to the four-volume manuscript collection of Francis Jeffrey's letters to Cockburn, with annotations by Cockburn, in the National Library, *ER* to the *Edinburgh Review*.

# Chapter One

## *Men of Sense*

Henry Cockburn was, among other things, a historian, a lawyer and a politician. Born in 1779, he was one of the leaders of the Scottish Whigs when, half a century later, in 1832, the Whig Government in London won the fight for a wider franchise with the passing of the Reform Bill. And, from a Northern point of view, he wrote a history of that fight. He also wrote the story of his own life, but he did so in a manner which has enabled him to remain perhaps the least accessible of Scotland's famous men: as much of a 'great unknown' as his contemporary Walter Scott was in the days when he wished to conceal his authorship of the 'Waverley' novels. Scott's anonymity was coy and yielding, moreover, whereas Cockburn, calm and stern, kept his like a vow. His treatment of the sore subjects discernible in his private life is such that he must be classed among the least effusive, the most enigmatic, of autobiographers. His several vocations did not include the confessional clean breast which came to the fore in the literature of his lifetime.

This is a book about Cockburn's public and private lives. It is also a book about fathers and sons, about obedience and disobedience, peace of mind and pugnacity, solitude and fame, pleasure and duty. And it is a book about the beautiful and mysterious Pentland Hills. These hills, with their summits of Carnethy, Castlelaw, Capelaw, Scald Law, Caerketton, Halkerside and Allermuir, rise to the south of the city of Edinburgh, and they gave comfort to Cockburn as they have given it to many others. His life might seem to show that it is difficult for a son, and still more difficult for a son who becomes a father, to be happy: yet his life was full of achievement and of honour and of humour, and he was in the habit of calling it a happy one. It was that of a son who quarrelled with a powerful father, and who himself became powerful.

The anxieties and rivalries which are apt to occur in families are, in general, no secret, though Cockburn was inclined to make a secret of his own experience of them. James Boswell, who could not be friendly with his father, was told by Johnson that 'there must always be a struggle between a father and son, while the one aims at power and the other at independency'.[1] Cockburn aimed at independency, and there is reason to suppose that a struggle took place, and that it helped to shape his subsequent life and lent impetus to his political ideas. Such struggles are apt to reappear in middle age, when the son has assumed the role of father and may be stung by his own offspring. Cockburn was so stung. In the capacity of anxious father, one of his sons having been reported wrecked at sea and then ascertained to be safe, he wrote to a friend, Andrew Rutherfurd, on 24 June 1839: 'Most filial events make the question recur to me, Why any man of sense generates sons?' His own father, a prominent Tory lawyer and laird whom he describes in the *Memorials of His Time* as 'a man of strong sense',[2] may have asked himself the same question. Cockburn may well have seemed to his father to be wrecked beyond reclaim when he chose to be a Whig.

Fathers impart to their sons the traditions of a society: these are, in a sense, a succession of filial events. Cockburn believed that the religion of his society was very much a matter of what was handed down by 'devout fathers'. He wanted to change the Scotland in which he grew up, and because of this, he disobeyed his father and resisted his authority. But it is apparent that he continued to respect the authority of fathers. Equally, it is apparent that he wanted to save, as well as to change, his father's Scotland. He was a reformer who was also a patriot, and he was a disobedient son who also became, in his own way, a patriarch.

The main preoccupations of his life were at once rebellious and respectful, and I mean to examine the writings, published and unpublished, in which these preoccupations are recorded and the activities in which they were publicly and privately expressed. He was a prisoner of the Edinburgh virtues of hard work, duty, severity—the severity which begins at home, and which punishes itself as well as the world it confronts—and respectability. During his lifetime, these virtues underwent a process of consolidation, and the word 'respectability' seems to have been used more and more in print. The aristocratic Lady Arniston was esteemed not only by her relative Henry Cockburn but by George III, who spoke of her after her death in 1798 as 'a most respectable woman'.[3] In the fifty years that followed, during which the

---

[1] *Boswell's London Journal*, edited by Frederick Pottle (1950), p. 301.

[2] *M*, p. 2. On this page, both parents are described. Thereafter, in his published works, they are rarely mentioned.

[3] In a letter of condolence published in Cyril Matheson's *Life of Henry Dundas* (1933), p. 261. The letter, dated 22 December 1798, is addressed to Dundas, who was Lady Arniston's son.

growing wealth of the country was competed for by a growing number of people, and the condition of the poor, congregating in factories and slums, became more visible and more frightening than before, respectability was widely enjoined and attempted. Later still, the term lost caste, became predominantly and irretrievably a matter of money, and tended to refer to someone who could not be reproached with poverty.

But if Cockburn was a prisoner, a patrician prisoner, of the Edinburgh virtues, he was able to escape. He retreated into play, pleasure, innocence and romance. Cut off from his father's community of Tory dynasts, he chose to be an orphan of a kind. This mutineer acquired a taste for the mutinies of others, while continuing to hold property, law and order in high regard. There have been plenty of orphans, escaped prisoners, romantic pleasure-lovers and dutiful mutineers in Scotland, and there is one in particular who may be thought to qualify in this respect as Cockburn's *revenant* or *redivivus*.

Cockburn is intensely Scottish. This is well known, and he has long been talked about, and even cherished, in his native land. But it is doubtful whether he has been properly understood. Most of his published works have been hard to obtain, and most of them have been neglected—though they have been subjected to a certain amount of quarrying by scholars. Meanwhile his manuscripts have lain unstudied in the National Library. Many of the manuscripts of his published works, and many of his other papers, were destroyed, and he himself destroyed many of the letters he received. But much has survived these successive, and sometimes secretive, incinerations.

Cockburn was himself a man of sense, but unlike most nineteenth-century Scotsmen of sense, he was extremely versatile. He was a lawyer and a writer, a politician and a poet. He was not a speculative or systematic thinker. He was, in fact, more of a statesman than a politician, and less of a statesman than a historian. It is right to think of him as primarily a historian and man of letters, a role which Gibbon, for example, would have had no trouble in recognizing. Cockburn and Scott are among the best of Scotland's historians, but neither of them is generally acknowledged to have been a historian at all. Cockburn was an annalist and an apologist, who tells of events in which he was himself an actor: but so are many other historians, including Tacitus, with whom his writings have some close affinities. Scott was an antiquarian and an artist, and most of his histories are presented as fiction: but these fictions deliver an understanding of the past to which only a historian could have attained.

Cockburn's *Memorials of His Time*, which is in narrative and retrospective form, is the story of a triumph, and ends with the arrival, in 1830, of Earl

# 4    Cockburn's Millennium

Grey's Whig Ministry, bent on an extension of the Parliamentary franchise: Cockburn himself was to draft the Scotch Reform Bill of 1832. His *Journal* then takes up the description of his times in the form of diary entries 'recording occurrences as they have arisen',[1] and goes on with it until the last month of his life. Despite this change of procedure, and despite the evidence of a darker mood, and of a measure of disenchantment, in the *Journal*, the two works were composed as a continuous account of a lifetime and of an epoch. Yet admirers of the *Memorials* are barely aware of the second half of this history, for the *Journal*, published in 1874, has never been reissued. On the basis of the *Memorials'* delightful retrospects, Cockburn is chiefly known as a specialist in nostalgia, a *laudator temporis acti*, a cosy *petit-maître* embroidering the annals of a parish. This is the Cockburn who was recently made the endearing hero of a brilliant theatrical travesty, *Cocky*, in which an actor performed colourful passages from his works. Cocky—the pawky raconteur, patriot and local worthy—contributes freely to those works. It is Cocky who remarks of a projected monument to the Radicals of the 1790s: 'Nothing that sticks up without smoking seems to me ever to look ill in Edinburgh.'[2] But there is more to Cockburn than a repertoire of fetching stories, and the *Memorials* are a far cry from Dean Ramsay's *Reminiscences*, a collection of ethnic jokes and anecdotes which they are often thought to resemble.[3]

Cockburn was born a prince of the country's *noblesse de robe*, which was recruited mainly from the landed gentry, and which constituted an estate of lawyer-lairds not unlike the scholar gentry of medieval China. His father was a Sheriff of Midlothian, a Baron of the Court of Exchequer, and a friend of the judge Lord Braxfield. Braxfield was no mandarin, but something of a war-lord temperamentally, and an aggressive defender of the landed interest: Cockburn, perhaps, was war-lord and mandarin by turns. Cockburn's aunt married a potentate, Lady Arniston's son Henry Dundas, later Lord Melville. Dundas was Pitt the Younger's able ally and much the most powerful of the Scottish managers or proconsuls of the eighteenth century. According to his nephew, Harry the Ninth, as he was known, was 'the Pharos of Scotland. Who steered upon him was safe; who disregarded his light was wrecked.'[4] Cockburn courted shipwreck by disregarding his

[1] Cockburn's words from a prefatory note to the *Journal*.
[2] Cockburn's *Examination of the Trials for Sedition which have hitherto occurred in Scotland* (2 vols), vol. II, p. 252. Russell Hunter played the part of Cocky, and remarks of this kind lost nothing on the stage.
[3] The *Reminiscences* achieved their 22nd edition in 1872, the year of Ramsay's death.
[4] Cockburn's *Life of Lord Jeffrey* (2 vols), vol. I, p. 77. All references are to the first edition of 1852.

light. But it could scarcely be ignored. Both Dundas and Braxfield were figures of the utmost consequence to him: both were lighthouses—a figure of speech which was of consequence to him too—whose beams play on many of his pages and reached into the holes and corners of his life.

His kin were Tories, and they were also, in effect, the country's ruling dynasty. During his early years, spent in the Government camp, there were blazings and bristlings at the spread of French Revolutionary principles, but the real threat to the authority of the Dundases lay in the gradual strengthening of support for political reform, which was interrupted by the Napoleonic Wars, but which assisted the eventual accession to power of the rival Whig patriciate. The sweetest revenge tasted by the Scottish Whigs came at the end of 1832, with the first General Election after Reform. The Dundases' candidate in Midlothian was Sir George Clerk, and the great houses of Melville and Arniston made every effort to secure a victory. They failed. And Cockburn had written the Bill that devised the electorate that defeated his kin.

His forebears were merchant burgesses, and before that, Border gentry, and earlier still, it would seem, Border reivers. In 1913, the genealogy was set out in *The Records of the Cockburn Family* by Sir Robert Cockburn and Harry Cockburn. Cockburn himself is silent about the antiquity of his family, but these authors manage to trace its descent back 'to the days of Flodden and before',[1] and are confident that it originated at Cockburn in the parish of Duns in Berwickshire. (Let me outdo them by hazarding the guess that, at that point inland, the earliest of the wrathful Cockburns, as they sometimes proved, may have been Norsemen.)

Cockburn is the name of a farmhouse which stands beneath the hill of Cockburn Law, near the Whiteadder, a tributary of the Tweed, and there are other Cockburn place-names not far from it. This is an austere and lonely place, suitable for a defensive stronghold, commanding as it does a good view of the southern approaches to Scotland. There is a prehistoric broch in the neighbourhood, and the mention of a Cockburn Castle by the genealogists seems confirmed by a site immediately above the farmhouse where some treated stones are scattered about. There is a smell of battle and the assaulted peel-tower. The farm people there now, who have the air of Appalachian hill-folk, appear little acquainted with the era of overpopulation and railways and other means of 'furious communication'[2] which

---

[1] *Records of the Cockburn Family*, p. 230.

[2] From a letter of Cockburn's to the Lord Provost of Edinburgh (15 January 1848): 'So many people are interested in this railway, and so many more are crazy about furious communication.'

dawned, to his dismay, in Henry Cockburn's lifetime. The Cockburns began at what remains the back of beyond.

In time, they moved down off their embattled hilltop to more grateful country west of Duns. In 1330, an Alexander Cockburn married an heiress, Mariota Vipont, which brought him the house of Langton. The clan split into separate establishments in the vicinity of Duns, and it is from the Cockburns of Choicelee, and of Caldra on the Blackadder, that those of Cockpen in Midlothian, including Henry Cockburn, are descended. A great deal has happened in these few miles of red or rufous soil, heather and woodland, where the Lammermuir Hills fall away into the rich farmland of the Merse, through which the Tweed flows out to sea. The peel-tower was succeeded by the laird's house and library, but here, too, there are traces of antiquity. The thorn tree at the once-thriving souters', or shoemakers', village of Polwarth, by Choicelee, is believed to have been the scene of pre-Christian rites and revelries, dimly commemorated in Allan Ramsay's song:

> At Polwart on the Green
> If you'll meet me the morn,
> Where lasses do convene
> To dance about the thorn.

Polwarth, with its sacred thorn, was a magic place, and a haunt of witches, and it was also a poetic place. A family of Humes settled at Polwarth Castle, now gone, not far from the farmhouse of Polwarth Rhodes, and among their descendants was the sixteenth-century poet Alexander Hume, author of the trance-like poem 'Of the Day Estivall', which may be thought to make a heaven of the pastoral summers of the Merse:

> O perfite light, quhilk schaid away,
> The darkenes from the light,
> And set a ruler ou'r the day,
> Ane uther ou'r the night . . .

Already the sons of the landowners of the area were being put to study law: Alexander Hume practised as an advocate for a while in Edinburgh, and a verse epistle of his passes judgment on the Court of Session: 'That councill house it is maist like ane hell.' For Cockburn, it was Edinburgh's adjacent Town Council Chamber that was like a hell. The same poem of Hume's says of his time as a lawyer: 'I saw sick things as pittie was to see.'[1] Such things dissuaded him from the bar, and he became a minister and a devout

---

[1] 'Ane Epistle to Maister Gilbert Mont-creif', lines 228 and 150.

Presbyterian. The law is 'a fighting life', said Cockburn,[1] and, in common with many of these Borderers, he himself was a fighter, where Hume was not. Hume's brother Patrick was one of James VI's courtiers, and one of his circle of poets: he was the author of a celebrated flyting, or *tour de force* of abuse, conducted with a fellow-poet of the court, the gifted Alexander Montgomerie.

Near Polwarth is Marchmont, designed by the Adams' father William: a grave, elegant house of blushing stone, set among rhododendrons and lush trees, where Alexander Pope's friend the third Earl of Marchmont lived. Next to it are the ruins of Redbraes Castle, where the poetess Lady Grisel Baillie performed a feat of filial piety by stealing through the woods at night to feed her Whig father, an adherent of William of Orange, who was in hiding in the crypt of Polwarth Church. The house where Henry Home, Lord Kames, the judge and polymath, passed much of his early life is a short way off. Towards Duns, Duns Scotus is reputed to have lived. Further towards the sea the philosopher David Hume grew up, in the parish of Chirnside, where the kirk session once took sceptical account of a servant girl's claim that he was the father of her child, and where his family thought that he might make a lawyer. These red braes, and certain of the callings and concerns of his ancestors and of their neighbours, may be felt to have entered the blood of the fighting, flyting, imperfectly filial, but at times, too, sublimely pacific Henry Cockburn.

By the eighteenth century, septs of Cockburns were dispersed throughout the Lothians. Adam Cockburn of Ormiston, Lord Justice-Clerk, was known for his integrity and for his ill-temper. He was also known as 'the curse of Scotland' for his devotion to the Whig cause: the nine of diamonds, which used to be called by that name, was re-christened 'the Justice-Clerk' by ladies at their cards. Another Whig curse lay in store for the country in the person of his distant relative. One of his sons was the agriculturalist and 'improver', John Cockburn of Ormiston, and another was married to the poetess Alison Cockburn.

The translation from the Borders to the Lothians of most of the now elaborate Cockburn connection was no great trek: it is a journey of some forty miles. The road runs up from the south to Soutra Hill and the Moorfoot Hills. The Lammermuirs—where Robert Louis Stevenson placed the country seat of Weir of Hermiston, his fictional version of Lord Braxfield—are on the right. To the left are the Eildons and Scott's Abbotsford. Anyone who made the journey in Cockburn's time—as Earl Grey did when he made a triumphal post-Reform Bill progress—would have been aware of the

[1] In a letter to James Grahame of 12 December 1808.

houses of Melville and Arniston, and of Gilmerton Pit, where the miners were still effectively enslaved. Suddenly, the splendours of the Pentlands would lie before him, and, over towards the Firth of Forth, the lion shape of Arthur's Seat. Soon he would be within a mile of Edinburgh town. These were the landscapes and landmarks which compelled the imagination of the autobiographical Cockburn.

His grandfather Archibald purchased the estate of Cockpen, near Edinburgh, in 1733. None of the family, unfortunately, was the original of the laird of Cockpen, wooer of the 'penniless lass wi' a lang pedigree', who forms the subject of Lady Nairne's poem (she was a contemporary of Cockburn's, and her poem was the bowdlerization of a folk-song):

> The laird o' Cockpen, he's proud an' he's great,
> His mind is ta'en up wi' things o' the State.

But it is clear that these Cockburns, with their lang pedigrees, were likewise great men: already occupied with the things of the market-place, they were shortly to be occupied also with the things of the State. Archibald Cockburn was the son of a merchant who had been a shareholder in the disastrous Darien scheme. He himself married Martha Dundas two years after going to Cockpen, and died in 1748 at the age of 45. His only surviving son, another Archibald—it was a common family name—was born in 1738. This man, Cockburn's father, became a lawyer. Martha's brother, Robert Dundas of Arniston, the first President Dundas of the Court of Session, whose second marriage was to George III's respectable Lady Arniston, was a man of sense and of the highest standing, and no lawyer would have expected to do badly with such a kinsman. The bond between the two families proved very productive, in terms of office, for Cockburn's father and indeed for Cockburn. When Archibald Cockburn—his father—married Janet Rannie (who was 15, and the daughter of a Captain Rannie of Melville) on the last day of December, 1768, the auspicious witnesses were Henry Dundas and Lord Braxfield. Henry Dundas, the President's son by his second marriage, was himself married to the bride's sister, whom he was later to divorce. He was Henry Cockburn's uncle by marriage, and his father's first cousin. The bond between the families was further fortified by the marriage of Henry Cockburn's sister—he was one of twelve children—to a member of a cadet branch of the Arnistons. Having served as Sheriff-Depute, and then as Sheriff, of Midlothian, his father became, in 1790, a Baron of the Court of Exchequer. He was also made Judge Admiral—at the nod, opponents claimed, of Henry Dundas.

This Archibald Cockburn and his friend and cousin Henry Dundas were stockholders in the Ayr Bank. The bank was operating brilliantly in the years which followed Archibald's marriage, when speculation was intense. The wives of both men had fortunes, and their capital appears to have been heavily committed. In 1772, the bank failed: a calamity for Ayrshire, most of which is reported to have changed hands, and for the cousins. No doubt almost all these Cockburns were publicly adjudged to be men of sense: but their history suggests that men of sense may become insolvent. Archibald Cockburn experienced straitened circumstances for some years to come. In 1785, he was forced to sell Cockpen, and had previously moved to Hope Park in the Meadows in Edinburgh. Around 1798, he moved to Caroline Park, near Granton, on the shore of the Firth of Forth. Caroline Park still stands, a dark, scowlingly handsome seventeenth-century house, surrounded by what looks like a wilderness of bomb-sites. From its windows can be glimpsed, like Hallowe'en lanterns, a set of gasworks the acid-green colour of detergent.

In 1784, when Henry Cockburn was 5, something happened which must have impressed him profoundly, though at no point does he write about it. A few days after Mrs Siddons—whose voice the grown Cockburn thought heavenly, and nobler than all others—had enthralled the audiences at the Edinburgh Theatre as Belvidera in *Venice Preserved*, his father, Sheriff Cockburn, seemed to the heritors or property-owners of the county to have preserved Midlothian. It was a time—not the first or the last of such times—when food was scarce, and on the evening of 4 June a crowd went to Haig's distillery at Canonmills to protest about the distribution of grain supplies. They broke open the gates, and were resisted by Haig's employees, and a man in the crowd was killed. The Sheriff was present, and according to the *Scots Magazine*, by the 'well-timed exertions' of the authorities 'the rioters were happily dispersed, without doing any further damage'. Two employees who were said to have fired at the man were taken to the Tolbooth. On the way there, they were harassed and badly wounded.

On 7 June, a large crowd assembled by beat of drum, carrying sticks and bludgeons, and went again to Canonmills. Soldiers fired at them and wounded several. The crowd burned a hay-rick and some empty barrels, and then dispersed. A general, a colonel and a considerable body of soldiers were present with Sheriff Cockburn, who informed the crowd that 'as this was a second outrage, they would meet with no mercy, if any attempt was made upon private property, or the military in the least annoyed'. Whereupon no stone was thrown, 'but bad language given'. The crowd pressed close to the soldiers, almost touching their bayonets. The soldiers made ready to fire,

whereupon the crowd fell back. A party of about seventy of them set off
and approached the Sheriff's house, but, learning that it was guarded by a
detachment of the military, they retired. The same night, a second distillery
just outside Edinburgh was burnt to the ground.

On the 19th, the heritors of the county met in Parliament House,
and Sheriff Cockburn took the chair. These were men who ran their
parishes, who were taxed or 'assessed' for parish outlays, and who saw
themselves as the state. Resolutions were agreed, among them the
following:

> That, after proper inquiries, they are convinced, that the corn of the growth of this
> country distilled within this county, is but a trifle, when compared with that distilled
> from imported grain.

> That the deluded voters are risking their lives to answer the views of self-interested
> persons, whose situation in society would render it disgraceful for them to appear
> openly as the encouragers of such insurrections.

> That the gentlemen of the county are determined, upon suspicion of any such riots
> in future, to come forth personally, and repel force by force, with their tenants, ser-
> vants, and such sober and well-disposed subjects as shall adhere to them, who are
> always ten to one in number to the unruly and disorderly.

The riots at Canonmills were not the storming of the Bastille. But the
storming of the Bastille lay only a few years ahead. And in these resolutions
can be heard the voice of an angry and affronted Scottish landed interest,
already on the *qui vive*, prepared to meet force with force, conscious of
traitors and defectors from within their own ranks, conscious, too, perhaps,
of county rather than country—whether Scotland or Great Britain. The
distiller Haig made an affidavit disabusing the public of the thought that
'all sorts of grain, wheat, oats, barley, and pease, are consumed at the distillery in great quantities', in such a way as to affect the markets. It was
explained that Haig imported substantial amounts of grain which would
never otherwise come to Scotland—perhaps the rioters had given consideration to that point—and that cattle and hogs were fattened with the refuse,
so that the public got the benefit of Haig's endeavours.

At the High Court of Justiciary one rioter was imprisoned for three
months and banished for fourteen years to His Majesty's plantations. Two
were to be publicly whipped through the streets by the common hangman
and banished for the same number of years. There were other sentences, and
two at least of the convicted were apprentices. The *Edinburgh Evening
Courant* commended the Sheriff's 'spirited conduct' at Canonmills, where
he appears to have read the Riot Act: under his direction, 'the Military

behaved with that tenderness and moderation so characteristic of true bravery'.[1]

The Sheriff was also credited with saving the life of Gladstone's grand-father.[2] The Gladstones—or Gledstanes, as they were then known—were corn merchants in Leith who were understood, again at a time of scarcity, to be hoarding grain and to be holding out for an exorbitant price. A crowd attacked Thomas Gledstanes and took him to Leith harbour, where he was saved from drowning by Sheriff Cockburn, who happened to be riding by. In a metrical and possibly more apocryphal version of the incident, Gled-stanes figures as a baker who gave poor value for the price of his rolls or baps:

> When from the pier the mob had 'Licht Baps' flung,
> Cockburn on horseback dashed into the waves.

Sheriff, later Baron, Cockburn retains a semi-legendary character as both tyrant and knight errant (though it was an alleged profiteer that he rescued, and it was the military that he protected from annoyance). He was also, unexpectedly, more unexpectedly than his son, a poet. His efforts have not been preserved, and the poetess Alison Cockburn (who wrote the polished and less familiar version of 'The Flowers of the Forest', a version based on the financial failure of seven speculating Selkirkshire lairds) seems to have felt that they did not deserve to be. She wrote to a friend:[3]

I send you a ballad composed by Sheriff Cockburn. A report went about for two days that his head was turned. No wonder! such stuff it was! However, you must send it back. He has catched the Robbers, so shall wear bays, though a worse poet I never saw!

None of his father's feats is recorded in Henry Cockburn's writings. Nor do these writings allow him to wear bays.

It is in keeping with the character of Baron Cockburn's reputation that the most vivid fact about him presents him as not unlike an ogre seen in a fairy-tale. And indeed it is a child's eye that sees him. One of his grandchildren was a Mrs Henry Dundas of Craigroyston, who died in 1905. She remembered him[4] as 'an old man—a martyr to gout'. He is known to have hirpled to Buxton—as his son might have put it—to take the waters (his cousin Henry Dundas visited the town for his rheumatism). His granddaughter went on:

[1] The account of the Canonmills riots is mainly based on the reports in the *Scots Magazine* for June 1784, from which the relevant quotations are drawn. The quotation from the *Edinburgh Evening Courant* (for 5 June) is given in *The Records of the Cockburn Family*, pp. 208, 209.
[2] *Records of the Cockburn Family*, pp. 209, 210.    [3] Ibid., p. 209.    [4] Ibid., p. 212.

'He shouted so and brandished his stick when one came near him, that we children were terrified.' The reputation of Baron Cockburn is, in part, that of a banisher and a brandisher.

The later eighteenth century was a time when Scotsmen of sense were able to prosper, through the thick and thin of scarcity and speculation, and in the midst of a population which started to rise as never before: by the time Cockburn was 44 the population of Edinburgh and Leith was almost double what it had been when he was born. The closing decades of the eighteenth century also witnessed the presence of other modes of prosperity besides the commercial, set off against a concurrent state of political and religious languor. In 1707, the Union of the Parliaments brought into being, for North and South Britain, a single legislative assembly and a common market. Scotland retained her Kirk and her courts, and these provided an arena for the energies, political and ideological, of the many who had no desire to be, or had no hope of being, drawn south to Westminster. The General Assembly of the Church of Scotland and the Faculty of Advocates served, in effect, on a series of occasions, as a Parliament. For most of the century, the Scottish representatives in London had little to say for themselves, and proved highly obedient to the series of managers who ran the North on the Government's behalf. The Scottish legal system remained distinct, as it does still.

It had been reanimated by Braxfield's beloved Stair and others, and was an amalgam of Roman (or Civilian) law, customary and common law (largely feudal), and statute law. It had gained some Dutch constituents, and in the course of the century the gentry were in the habit of sending their sons to Holland to read law and arm themselves for the forensic fight. The Scots law which Cockburn set himself to learn, with its infeftments, sasines and superiorities, its rich, grim argot of tenure and entitlement, spoke of ancient history and feudal fathers, of primogeniture and entailed estates, of counties largely owned by the one magnate. It was as if the society were held motionless in the grip of its own past, as if it were held in an unbreakable entail, sealed and sustained by the Court of Session. During his lifetime came a succession of changes in the law, changes of content and of procedure: as a result, certain of the immemorial arrangements which it had expressed and preserved, and which the purposeful had got used to circumventing or defeating, began to disappear.

The fundamental fact that the country kept her legal system while losing her own legislature was bound to give rise to difficulties, and these underlie certain of Cockburn's objections to the performance of the Scottish Judiciary, which could seem, by turns, both overbearing and inert. There was, for instance, the tendency to create new criminal offences by the exercise of its 'native vigour'. This might be thought to be the business of a legislature. But the legislature was in London. And in the years that followed the Union it was slow to concern itself with Scottish questions. As time went on, and an appetite for institutional change declared itself in British political life, the two countries were increasingly subject to the same laws and regulations. After the Union, the House of Lords assumed an appellate jurisdiction in relation to the Scottish civil courts, and this had already helped to bring the countries closer together. For all that, Scotland's legal system is still separate. It has laws of its own, and refuses some of England's. It has yet to do as England has done and allow greater individual freedom than there has traditionally been in respect of homosexuality, divorce and Sunday observance. And the phenomenon of the political judge—the judge with party ties and affiliations—is still, though considerably mitigated, an accepted feature of the Scottish scene. Cockburn himself wanted Scots law to survive, and is likely to have felt that this was essential to the country's survival as a different place from England.

Ever since the Union, the loss of Scotland's sovereignty has been deplored by some Scotsmen, who have occasionally made too much of what was lost: the feudal Parliament of the seventeenth century, for one thing, is hard to regret. They have also tended to deny that the commercial strides of the next century depended on the existence of a common market. This matter may never be determined to the satisfaction of any but the converted. There can be no doubt, however, that while English influences came into play over a wide field, Scotland was neither looted nor exploited by the South. Nor was her economic take-off impeded. Scotland's men of sense were glad to belong to the new nation, and to the Empire, and could head their letters 'North Britain'. 'Sense', originally, was an Augustan and an aristocratic Whig quality. It became a Scottish quality. It was cultivated especially by Scotsmen who knew how to take, and miss, the chances of the new age. Cockburn was something other than an opportunist, but he approved of sense and often had occasion to use the word. The subject-matter of his life and times gave ample scope for it.

English and British examples and initiatives were influential in the field of politics and government. Under the managerial system run by the Dundases and their predecessors, Scotland languished unquestionably. But then England, too, was ruled by rival patriciates, and suffered the same subjection to their interests. After the Jacobite rebellions, the British Government brought about development in the Highlands, built roads, embarked on a re-modelling of life in the Gaelic fiefs, and abolished the country's ancient feudal jurisdictions. These rebellions were important to eighteenth-century Scotland: partly as a stimulus to necessary change, and because they could be seen by men of sense as the last Highland fling of the seditions and disorders of a barbarous past. They also became a myth—precious to the literature and sentiment of later periods.

Both countries underwent a sharp rise in population and the entrench-ment of an industrial system. One element in the response to this was a zeal for political improvement and for the enfranchisement of a middle class whose interests began to impose a more vigorous claim on the landed con-federacies in, or out, of government. In the fullness of time, that claim was acknowledged. The Scotch Reform Bill was meant to be a counterpart of the English, but it was also meant to express what was due to the distinctive-ness of Scotland, and the Scotsmen who drafted it were allowed to ensure this, as best they could, in their own way. These Scottish Whigs were some-thing other than provincial—and, as has been said, incompetent—mediators of an English measure: Lord John Russell's clerks. They were far more convinced reformers than almost any of the Southern Whigs. Burgh (as opposed to Parliamentary) Reform was a cause of some antiquity in Scotland, which was not the case in the south, and no quarter of the Empire, save perhaps for Birmingham, was more avid for Parliamentary Reform than the Scottish Lowlands when the Bill was being assembled. Much of the plan-ning and delving that went into the eventual assertion of objectives, includ-ing part of the Utilitarian contribution, was carried out in the *Edinburgh Review*, which was edited by Francis Jeffrey, for which his friend Henry Cockburn wrote, and from which Earl Grey's Government obtained some of its members—above all, Henry Brougham.

The Scottish Enlightenment was in progress in Hanoverian Edinburgh and Glasgow and their surrounding lairded countrysides from the 1730s onwards. Here, too, English influences are certainly perceptible, and a self-scorning cultivation of English skills and styles is, for a number of writers, the chief attribute of the Northern literati. But the Scottish Enlighten-ment, early and late, was to a marked degree *sui generis*, while also European and ecumenical. There is a good deal about its origins which has yet to be explained, if it *can* be explained, but it is clear that the fighting vigour of contemporary Scots law, the quality of the earlier jurists and of the disciplines they laid down, and the attention given by lawyers and others to Continental learning, were significant factors, as was the solidity inherent in the existence of an estate of lawyer-lairds with the money (and the vacations) to pursue their researches, and the authority to impose a deference to their standards on a fair proportion of the polite.

During his adolescent years at Chirnside and in Edinburgh, David Hume was already preparing himself for the inquiries which resulted in the *Treatise of Human Nature*. Such precocity cannot be explained in terms of what was available to him in Edinburgh: nor can his achievements be adequately measured in terms of what they contributed to the subsequent progress of the Scottish Enlightenment. Hume seems to have impressed those who knew him as a convincing approximation to the perfect nature, but to the worthies of Edinburgh at large he was scandalous and perplexing. The historian William Robertson was neither of these things. As the leader of the Moderate Party in the Church of Scotland, the manager of the General Assembly and the Principal of the University, he was one of the town's most respected citizens. Another was Adam Smith. The middle-aged men of sense to whom Cockburn listened at his father's dinner-table as they talked of bloodshed and the French Revolution knew very little about Smith except that he 'had written a sensible book'. In fact, *The Wealth of Nations* was the charter of the country's Archibald Cockburns, whose investments had acquired new promise in recent decades—though, as we have observed, this was a promise which was not always fulfilled. But it was 'the liberal young', Cockburn writes,[1] who really *studied* the apostle of laissez-faire. 'With Hume, Robertson, Millar, Montesquieu, Ferguson, and De Lolme, he supplied them with most of their mental food.' There were those of the liberal young who, nourished on this diet, were to prove strongly averse to interfering with market forces in order to cope with emergencies occasioned by disease and distress. Cockburn was one.

Hume, Robertson and Smith were the greatest, and among the earliest, representatives of the three generations of *savants* whose achievements advanced, where they did not inaugurate, a whole set of sciences and disciplines. Two other early thinkers of consequence, as Cockburn points out, were the social historian Adam Ferguson, and John Millar at Glasgow University, a pugilist who boxed with the liberal young, and persuaded them to be Whigs, and who tutored Lord Melbourne. Lord Monboddo announced the origin of species and was derided for it by Kames, who himself attempted, in a manner typical of the time, to establish a working relationship between law and social history. The most gifted legal literatus belonged to the later Enlightenment: Cockburn's friend, George Joseph Bell. Bell was a specialist in bankruptcy—sensibly enough, for so, in their own wild way, were many of his contemporaries. Edinburgh itself went bankrupt in 1832, and its revenues and properties were sequestrated by Act of Parliament.

The Enlightenment lasted a hundred years, and whether or not its origins

[1] *M* p. 46

can be explained, Cockburn's works give a good if summary account of its development. He knew some of the élite of the first light in their old age, and his description of his mentors at Edinburgh University, such as Dugald Stewart, testifies to the way in which a body of learning, a cultural ethos and a sense of style were transmitted, in which traditions were born. The great men of the later age who sprang to mind when he undertook the invidious comparison with its predecessor were Stewart, Scott, Thomas Chalmers and Jeffrey. Burns, whom he admired, was gone. James Hogg, whom he seldom speaks of, was not thought fit to be named with these men. Unlike the 'heaven-taught' Burns, Hogg did not find it easy to be thought fit by the upper reaches of Edinburgh society: there was not nearly enough heaven about the Ettrick Shepherd.

On one occasion, however, the *Memorials*[1] make generous mention of Hogg, of *Blackwood's Magazine*, the *Edinburgh Review*'s local Tory rival, for which he wrote, and of the *Noctes Ambrosianae*, a feature containing tavern talk by (and purporting to be by) Hogg which figured in that magazine. The politics of *Blackwood's*, Cockburn felt, were erroneous, old-fashioned and nasty, but in respect of literary talent, and of energy and originality, there was no better magazine in Britain. As for the *Noctes Ambrosianae* (whose conversations were sited in Ambrose's tavern),

> it breathes the very essence of the Bacchanalian revel of clever men. And its Scotch is the best Scotch that has been written in modern times. I am really sorry for the poor one-tongued Englishman, by whom, because the Ettrick Shepherd uses the sweetest and most expressive of living languages, the homely humour, the sensibility, the descriptive power, the eloquence, and the strong joyous hilarity of that animated rustic can never be felt. The characters are all well drawn, and well sustained, except that of the Opium Eater, who is heavy and prosy: but this is perhaps natural to opium.

Opium, Cockburn suggests, makes you dull: this is not an opinion which would have endeared itself to those Romantic writers of the time who braved the dark night of this and other ambrosias, who valued the drug for the revelations it seemed to confer, as well as for its medicinal properties. Likewise, there was more to his 'animated rustic' than he realized, though he was right to praise, and in these terms, the language that flows from Hogg in the *Noctes*. Cockburn's comprehension, and incomprehension, of the talent of *Blackwood's Magazine*, in which a Romantic, and German-Gothic, literary taste was registered, is a matter of importance for the consideration of his intellectual life. In the Edinburgh he inhabited, the literatus and the illuminatus tended to be two different men.

[1] Ibid., pp. 317–19.

In time, the Enlightenment took a literary turn, which Cockburn's own bent might give the appearance of signalling. While he was a man of action, and very practical, he was a man of words, too, and his best words were those of a narrative historian. He has been blamed for being a literary lawyer. He did not speculate much, or theorize. He had no more use for the German metaphysics which became fashionable during his lifetime than he seems to have had for the fantastic German fiction commended in *Blackwood's*: no more enthusiasm for the 'abstruse profundity' of Sir William Hamilton, or indeed for that of Hamilton's master Kant, than he had for the omnivorous abstractions of the enlightened Kames.

The great men of the past had not, on the whole, been liberals or democrats. Nor were the Moderate ministers of the Church of Scotland who had sometimes encouraged them. Such ministers were not deterred by the accusations of atheism which were directed at Hume and others, and were hostile or indifferent to the fundamentalism of the time: it is unlikely that they believed, any more than Kames did, in damnation. Livings were in the gift of patrons, and during the reign of the Dundases patrons tended to favour the Government: the Moderates, who were then at the height of their success, upheld these arrangements. Patronage may be regarded as a further way—supplementary to the exiguous Parliamentary franchise—of restricting political representation to certain categories of property-owner. The local minister's activities were, in part, of a political nature: he helped to run the parish, and he contributed to what were often substantially political debates in the General Assembly. And yet he would often have been 'intruded' on his flock by a heritor patron loyal to the governing party. 'Socially speaking, they were better fellows' than their brethren, Cockburn recalls of the Moderates, but their religion could easily be represented as fushionless and lukewarm. They were opposed in the General Assembly by the Evangelicals, the party of 'the Wild': outside the Church were the Dissenting sects, together with the Episcopalians and the Catholics. In these years, Evangelicalism offered little challenge to the Moderates, and the fires of the Covenant burned low. But all this was to change.

In the 1830s, Scotland was rent by religious controversy. The outcome was the Disruption of 1843, when the Kirk split in two. The Evangelical side, led by Thomas Chalmers, proclaimed itself the Free Church. The Covenanters, the 'hill folk', appeared to walk again, and, in the fields, 'outed' ministers preached justification by faith and denied that good works could save. Then they came out of the fields and found some virtue in the creation of institutions. Evangelicalism had turned Tory—in reaction, originally, to the atheistic French Revolution—but on patronage, and on other matters too, though not on all other matters, the Wild were more aware than most Whigs of the needs and aspirations of the working class. The French Revolution reverberated for a long time in Scotland, and thereafter the two countries can give the impression of trembling together at the touch of popular discontent: the events of 1830 and 1848 in Paris were closely studied by politically-minded Scotsmen. It is doubtful whether a 'pre-revolutionary situation' existed on the eve of the Reform Bill, though revolution was feared. There was a history of suffering and of resentment, of the stacking of arms by the weavers of the West, and of limited outbreaks of violent protest. There had been agitators and arguers—and agents provocateurs. But not many wanted universal suffrage, or a republic, or a revolution.

The spasm of rioting at Canonmills was the kind of event that recurred, and such events made sense of the Whig programme of extending the vote, judiciously, and appeasing the poor. In any case, more and more people felt worthy of a vote. The country's commercial future was not to depend solely on the exertions of well-born investors who married auspiciously and maintained country seats in Midlothian: factories, and the steam-engine and other new machinery, produced, in due course, a different Scotland and a new class of merchant and manager. Increased social mobility, which turned out to be consistent with an increase in the distance between the classes, with a process of polarization, meant that men of sense very different from the Archibald Cockburns rose from the ranks, became men of substance and of standing, and asked for a say in the running of affairs. In so doing, they frequently became Whigs—who desired a wider franchise and the emancipation of Scotland which this appeared to portend, but who did not desire that all men should be equal.

Many wanted Scotland to stay Scottish. Cockburn and Scott were among them. Both disliked manufacturers, and factories, and the rascals and radicals who were to be found there. But Scott also disliked the Reform Bill. Anglophile Scottish Whigs like Cockburn wanted Scotland to share in the liberties conferred by the British Constitution, and they wanted a government which enjoyed a broader basis of consent, and which would take account of some of the problems of a country with large numbers of people, new forms of enterprise and wealth, and new forms of discontent: there were other problems, however, which they misconstrued or ignored. Cockburn was a patriot, and that meant a Scottish patriot, though not one who kept referring to Bannockburn, or who thought of Scotland's constitutional character as identified immutably and for ever in the Act of Union. He hoped that his country would survive. But he also thought of the end of the eighteenth century as 'the last purely Scotch age', recognizing that this was no longer 'a remote society, known only to itself'.[1] And some of the policies he supported were unlikely to assist his country's survival.

[1] These descriptions come respectively from *J* 11, p. 198, and from a letter to Rutherfurd of 19 November 1850.

# Chapter Two

# *The Public Cockburn*

Henry Cockburn's life could be said to have two subject-matters. In this sense, as in a related sense which I shall explore later, he led two lives. First, there is the subject-matter which he was prepared to make public. This chiefly requires an attention to the *ipse dixit* of his published works, which are copious enough. To a great extent, it has to do with the attainment of Parliamentary Reform and of other goals in the same domain, and with the attainment of happiness through a devotion to family, friends and rural leisure. The comparatively exiguous second subject-matter is not divulged, being a matter of what can be known about him that he did not choose to tell publicly, but it may be discovered or deduced. It has to do with private or secret sectors of his experience, and with the threats and impediments in relation to which his happiness may be defined. And it chiefly requires a recourse to the sizeable body of manuscript material which has survived, mostly in the form of letters by Cockburn: a very different kind of *ipse dixit*. It also requires an attention to his silences and inscrutabilities.

Outspoken though he was, and irritated by prudishness and cant, he often displays a Roman reticence and signs of a Victorian *pudeur*. It is interesting to take note of the limits he placed on what was publicly admissible. He had an eighteenth-century candour about drink, but about sexual matters, while there are occasional touches of candour and of gallantry in his correspondence, he is, in public, curt or silent. His published writings display a highly-developed, even statuesque, public manner, and a stoical composure: these, and his silences, are due to a sense of decorum which can seem like a largely guileless second nature, though he was not without guile. I hope to suggest what lay behind the Classical pose, what was contained, and constrained, in the decorum to which he adhered. But I want now to tell the story of his career with reference, principally, to his recorded achievements, to his books, and to what he was prepared to say about himself. This is the public Cockburn.

For a man who was so keen on the past, he was surprisingly unconcerned about his ancestry, and surprisingly ill-informed about the circumstances of his own birth, which took place on 26 October 1779. He says in the *Memorials* that he was born in a tenement flat in Parliament Close amidst the Old Town of Edinburgh, or at Cockpen. His earliest memory was of being terrified, when he was still in his petticoats, by the sight of a peacock in the walks of Cockpen, and the estate was not sold until around 1785. But Harry Cockburn, in the introduction to his 1910 edition of the *Memorials,* states that his grandfather was born at Hope Park, and the family certainly appear to have been living in Edinburgh when their house was threatened by the Canonmills rioters of 1784. Hope Park was in the Meadows, where the city then ceased, and the boys of the neighbourhood were able to go off and play in the Lothians, still largely unenclosed, and to wander as far as 'the deserts of Peebleshire'. From Hope Park, there would have been a clear view of the Pentland Hills, which can safely be included among his early memories.

In 1787, having previously been taught by a tutor, he was sent to the High School of Edinburgh (James VI's Schola Regia and in recent times the Royal High School), where he passed six weary years. This ancient school then stood in a street near the University: in the 1820s it was translated to a site by the Calton Hill, where it was to occupy a spectacular replica of the Temple of Theseus in Athens. The dandyish uniform, with its round black hat, was changed according to the season, and could consist of a scarlet waistcoat and a green coat. During the second half of the eighteenth century, the shops in the High Street were painted in much the same carnival colours: the greyness of its puritan resurgence had yet to descend on the town. The 'gytes', or younger boys, were introduced to a world of harshness and aggression. These pupils were as riotous as the town's apprentices, with whom they held Bannockburn-like 'bickers'. Their masters flogged them, and behaved in a manner which, according to Cockburn, would have earned them transportation in the more enlightened Edinburgh of which he was conscious in his middle age.

The headmaster Dr Adam, a Latin scholar of note, was himself a kind man, and he may be regarded as the first of Cockburn's paragons, eliciting the dry hyperboles to which his character-studies are prone: 'He was born to teach Latin, some Greek, and all virtue.' It seems that he failed to teach much virtue to the other masters, but, for his own part, he claimed to act on the principle that 'the seldomer corporal punishment is used the better'.[1] When, during Cockburn's imprisonment at the High School, the French

[1] *The History of the High School of Edinburgh* (1849) by William Steven, p. 152

Revolution broke out in Edinburgh, Adam was suspected of French sympathies, and spied on by his pupils.

Henry Brougham and the economist Francis Horner were at the school at this time, and Scott and Jeffrey went there too. It took poor boys as well as patricians, and there was a little of that 'comprehensiveness' left, along with a good deal of the old staple curriculum of Latin and Greek, when I attended it myself—in its later incarnation, now in turn abandoned, by the Calton Hill. Cockburn does not invoke this feature, and he remained inflexibly opposed to the school. He reckoned that he never read a book for pleasure there (he began to do this with the *Spectator*), but he was not prevented from acquiring a taste for Latin literature. He also acquired 'a distrust of duxes, and thought boobies rather hopeful'. Brougham, the future Lord Chancellor, was the very epitome of a dux, or prize pupil.

There is no need to think that Cockburn lacked the desire to excel, though he could hardly compare in that respect with Brougham, or even with Jeffrey, who shed tears when he lost his place in class: there were to be quite a few duxes among the Whig leadership of forty years later. But it is plain that, for Cockburn, school was somewhere to escape from. And during weekends and holidays, in pursuit of burns and glens and gardens, he escaped to the Pentlands and to the nearby country houses of Niddrie, seat of Andrew Wauchope, and Prestonfield, seat of Sir William Dick. Niddrie, he explains, was like Eden. And from these and other materials he was to devise a composite Eden, or Heaven, to which he was able to escape throughout his life.

At 14, he was enrolled at the rather more terrestrial College of Edinburgh. Here, too, the classes were in an uproar. But here, too, there was kindness. Virtue was taught at the University by that exquisite academical gentleman, Dugald Stewart, the Professor of Moral Philosophy, a follower of Hume's opponent Thomas Reid, of the school of 'common sense'. Stewart's views on 'the ethics of life', Cockburn says, changed his nature. This does not mean that he came to believe in 'common sense': it was Stewart's 'moral taste', rather than his philosophical opinions, which impressed him. Robertson, the College Principal, died in the year of his enrolment, but he was a family friend and Edinburgh neighbour, as was Adam Ferguson. Cockburn also knew Joseph Black, discoverer of latent heat, who died without spilling a drop of the bowl of milk on his knee. Here was one of the good deaths which Cockburn relished.

The *Memorials* lay stress on the violence which surrounded him in his youth: the violence of masters and boys and College students, the violence of his father's circle, frightened by the French Revolution and formidable in their fright. There was also the violence inherent in starvation: the violence of the starving, and that of those who kept them in line. In 1795, he reports, an eighth of the population of the city was being fed on charity, and he adds with regret that the countrymen of Adam Smith were willing to interfere with freedom of trade in order to ease the situation. Cockburn was to distinguish between 'sedition of the stomach' and 'sedition of opinion'.[1] The riots of the 1780s appear to have been largely innocent of opinion and to have been pre-political in character: those who could not get enough to eat became from time to time, as at Canonmills, what Cockburn's class called a mob. Starvation continued to be a factor in most subsequent upheavals, but political violence of a recognizably modern kind had to await the voicing of French Revolutionary principles in Scotland, and it was more in evidence during the years of Cockburn's middle age than it was during his adolescence.

As yet, he did not doubt his father's word on politics, and afflicted himself with the thought that the blood-bath predicted by his father's circle was bound to come. When, at the time of the sedition trials of 1793, he went to watch the French Radical Maurice Margarot being escorted through the streets by an enthusiastic crowd, he was still young enough for this to be simply one of the shows of the town, though he was scolded for giving a helping haul to the carriage—by the Lord Advocate, Henry Dundas's nephew, Robert Dundas. He also saw Margarot going to his trial, again escorted by a crowd, who carried a Tree of Liberty in the shape of the letter M. This crowd was forcibly dispersed, and the Tree smashed.

The spectacle of the French Revolution, and the levelling evangelism of men like Margarot, released in Scotland a sedition of opinion to which the courts responded—ten years after the Midlothian stomach had mutinied at Canonmills—by embarking on the banishment of Jacobins. It would be too much to say that the mob was rapidly politicized, but organized Radicalism had started to find recruits, and was already indigenous, though scarcely very robust. Among those proscribed in the 1790s were men who could be seen as spies or emissaries—from the foreign parts of England and France— but their opinions were now shared by some of the more self-confident of the poor. The United Scotsmen were leagued with the United Irishmen. Many of the opinions that were held, wild as they might appear and as they might be represented on the bench, were more or less lawful: but courses of action could also be contemplated which even the liberal Cockburn, the denouncer of Braxfield's trials, regarded as seditious.

War broke out with Revolutionary France, which made the position of

[1] *M*, p. 325.

every variety of reformer much more difficult, and the Gentlemen Volunteers were formed. Cockburn was later to command a company of the First Royal Edinburgh Volunteers, while the explosive Brougham was to man a gun. Edinburgh's Volunteers were sworn to abjure and, if need be, suppress the Society of the Friends of the People, and in general, by enlisting as Volunteers and preparing to repel invaders, the Scottish Whigs appear to have gone some way towards ridding themselves of the taint of disloyalty. Riots over food were put down with the aid of Volunteers, and in 1797, at Tranent near Edinburgh, there riots over the Militia Act when eleven people were killed by the army and Scott, another amateur soldier, took pleasure in brandishing a sabre.

Together with the example set by Stewart, who was a Whig, Cockburn's membership of two University debating societies seems to have played an important part in persuading him to renounce his father's principles. These were the Academical, which started in 1796 and lasted until 1816, and the Speculative, which he joined in 1799 and which still convenes. He remarks in the *Memorials*: 'My reason no sooner began to open, and to get some fair play, than the distressing wisdom of my ancestors began to fade, and the more attractive sense that I met with among the young men into whose company our debating societies threw me, gradually hardened me into what I became—whatever this was.'[1] Whatever this was? At no point in his published or unpublished writings is it for him to say.

The social life of upper Edinburgh had long revolved, for the males of that ilk, round clubs of all descriptions: some of them dedicated to abstruse debate, others to drink. In the Speculative and the Academical was concentrated a great part of the intellectual effort of the University, and in Cockburn's time the Speculative—with its code of hard work, duty, compulsory attendance and the exclusion of strangers—was the scene of a contest between the old, Tory members, who still attended, and his own generation, which was Whig, and which included Jeffrey, Brougham and Horner. Thomas Emmet, who was a member not only of the Speculative but of the secret directory of the United Irishmen, figured in this contest: he was in due course to be taken into custody by his Speculative opponent Charles Hope, by then a Minister of the Crown and later a judicial colleague of Cockburn's. Unsolicited testimony as to Cockburn's performance in the Academical exists in the form of some sentences from a memoir of Henry Brougham's brother Peter,[2] written by a man named J. Nairne on the flyleaves of a copy of Thomson's *Seasons*: 'Henry Cockburn was by far the most eloquent Member of the Academical, and I often still think with wonder of the beauty of

[1] Ibid., p. 47.  [2] NLS MSS.

his orations, at so early an age.' By now he had changed his mind about the politics of his country. They were no longer to be a matter of meeting force with force.

By now, too, he was clearly willing to excel. A letter of 6 December 1803 to his friend Charles Anderson discusses, with feeling, 'the wish for distinction'. It could have been written by no other person than Cockburn.

> That poor man is unquestionably undone, who, if it be not corrected by a remarkably active and strong mind, encourages the habit of pleasing his imagination with very noble prospects of possible attainments. The delight he enjoys in resolving to be great is such a liberal rapture, that he mistakes it for, and is contented with it instead of, the exulting triumph of surveying from the watch tower of his ambition—actually reached—the surrounding subject country. Don't believe that when he discovers his error he can always push forward anew. He has wasted his time, he has acquired irrecoverable habits, his character is determined. He then spurns the humble walks of ordinary men; while the very discovery of his folly, instead of making spring to recover what he has lost, gives him up to gazing, with streaming eyes and a beating breast, towards a lovely scene, endeared by the memory of early hopes—from which he is now excluded for ever. Do not call this too severe a representation. That he, for example, who writes to you has fallen from his towering imaginations is sufficiently obvious.

Cockburn had long since acquired the irrecoverable habit of journalizing: persisted with, his commonplace book was eventually to ensure his fame. He quotes passages here from that commonplace book—among them, one which refers to certain of its pages as 'so many memorials of the enthusiasm and stedfastness with which I then struggled to accomplish the most liberal purpose I ever formed. This pursuit had no vanity for its object. It arose from the unthinking impulse of literary taste; from an eager desire to examine the uttermost confines of that glorious region of science and learning which I had just begun to descry.' But the passage in question goes on: 'To fancy higher prospects than I can ever attain, and at the same time (*perhaps for this very reason that they are too highly conceived*) to dream away my time in thinking of them, without using any efforts for their realization, has ever been one of my most pernicious and lamented weaknesses.'

The letter of 1803 says that he has settled for the life of a 'tradesman lawyer', scorning 'the illiberal, the despicable celebrity of such men as John Clerk and Chas Hope'. With the word 'tradesman', Cockburn is insulting himself in order to make his point (his friend Jeffrey was to feel that, although an editor, he had never been tradesmanlike, and had dealt with gentlemen only). He no longer dreams of being as Lord Kames had been, in the great days. 'Without an ember of genius', Kames had spent forenoons and vacations away from the law, laying up literary honours, scheming for his country and for the species, beholding in his parlour Hume, Robertson, Smith and Black, behaving kindly (but the *Memorials* call him 'coarse', and charge him with 'a piece of judicial cruelty'—his proclaimed 'checkmating' of a chess-playing friend by means of a death sentence—bad enough, and funny enough, to be mistakenly attributed to Braxfield).

Kames's was 'an enlightened professional life'. Unlike Cockburn's ... And yet there is nothing in this complex letter to persuade one that his ambitions—his liberal, publicly useful ambitions—had been abandoned. It is the aspiring it disclaims that makes it live, and his imaginations continued to tower.

He remained a member of the Speculative for upwards of forty years, and was President from 1800 to 1805. In 1842, two members—Thomas Cleghorn, later his son-in-law and trustee, and William Macbean—were assigned the job of writing a history of the society.[1] They entered into correspondence with Cockburn on the subject and were told by him: 'A history of the Speculative Society is a history of the best talent that has been reared in Scotland during the most valuable 80 years the country has ever seen.' Macbean, however, died in the same year, and the annals of the society had to incorporate the erection of 'Macbean's Monument'. This was a marble slab on the wall of their lobby, for which Cockburn wrote the inscription. He was a connoisseur of lapidary inscriptions, and he seems to have been on his mettle here, reaching for the right note of chastity and discretion (there may not have been that much to say about Macbean):

To the memory
of
William Macbean
who died while Secretary of the Speculative Society
12th August 1842, aged 19.
His official services
commanded the society's gratitude
His amiableness its affection

Cleghorn went on consulting Cockburn about the history, and was informed in 1844 that 'the whole work is *very ill written*': Jeffrey's 'etherial quill' might be enlisted. Jeffrey looked at the manuscript, and mentioned to Cockburn the 'making too much of small matters'. Cockburn to Cleghorn: 'The *making much of small matters* can't be helped. On the contrary I wish we had more small matters to make more of.' The large and small matters

---

[1] See *Some Letters of Lord Cockburn* (1932), edited by Harry Cockburn, pp. 50–5.

of the society were given to the world the following year. Later in this book more will be made of the small matter of Macbean's Monument.

In 1800, Cockburn began to practise as an advocate, and to cast a sharp eye on the throngs who frequented the Outer House of the Court of Session. He had previously submitted the customary *Disputatio Juridica*: his disputation, on a theme from Justinian's *Pandects*, was dedicated as an *amicitiae testimonium* to his cousin Robert Dundas, *Regio apud Scotos Advocato*.[1] In the words of one authority, paraphrased by his friend the solicitor John Richardson, he was to make himself 'out of all sight the best *nisi prius* lawyer'—or jury lawyer—'at the Scottish bar'.[2] Soon after he began to practise, the *Edinburgh Review* did too. The '*immisericors mens* of criticism', as Cockburn called it,[3] began to bite. The *Edinburgh Review* was the forum of the eager new generation of Whig lawyers and thinkers, a generation of duxes, and Cockburn remained a contributor for the rest of his life. Among his confederates in criticism were Sydney Smith, something of a kindred spirit, and Brougham, whom he distrusted, as a fair number of other people did, and who was known to Cockburn's set, never at a loss for a nickname, as The Evil—from a joke of Smith's about his being the true old Evil Principle. Cockburn, who presided over an Edinburgh banquet for Brougham in 1825, has allowed posterity to know that he thought him 'morally, as well as intellectually, mad'. Brougham thought the *Memorials* worthless, and, in an anonymous review, sprang to the defence of Braxfield.[4]

Family connections and Henry Dundas made the renegade, in 1807, a Depute to the Lord Advocate: the latter was a political appointee with extensive governmental responsibilities and a considerable power of patronage. The recently impeached Dundas did not bother to acquaint the Lord Advocate of the day with Cockburn's appointment before it was made. It is likely that his family badly wanted him back in the fold, and judged that this might reclaim him, though he appears to have insisted that there should be no presumption of party loyalty. He accepted that the post had been offered him on terms which did not warrant a quarrel 'with my kindred'—which was as good as to say that it was a post which family considerations compelled

[1] His disputation (published in 1800) dealt with the role of coercion in contractual matters The theme—*Quod metus causa gestum erit*—may be felt to have been one that Cockburn would have found congenial: but such disputations were largely formalities, and texts were hired for the occasion.

[2] Richardson's words in a letter to Cockburn of 15 December 1826. The authority was Chief Baron Sir Samuel Shepherd. Richardson's letters to Cockburn are with the Cockburn MSS.

[3] In a letter to Grahame of 29 March 1811.

[4] Cockburn's view of Brougham was expressed in a note to a letter to himself from Jeffrey of 1 April 1838 (JLC). Brougham's view of Cockburn was expressed in the *Law Magazine and Law Review*, May to August, 1856.

2*

him to take. When he was dismissed three years later for insubordination—
having voted against the Lord Advocate at a meeting of the Faculty of
Advocates—he was pleased to go. At one point, his opinions had been
accounted by his kind 'a mere youthful fervour', mere Whiggery-pokery.
He writes revealingly in the *Memorials*: 'My fear that they might think so
had only made the fervour warmer.'

For Cockburn, as for many Whigs, Reform meant the enfranchisement of
the prosperous and intelligent, and was a means of averting revolution. More
ambitiously, he could also think of it as ushering in a Scottish millennium of
social justice. That millennium never came. But, unlike many Whigs,
especially in England, where there was a tendency to lack zeal and to see
these measures in concessive terms, Cockburn was a principled and coercive
corrector of the franchise. 'Pugnacity is the safe side for all gentlemen to err
upon,' said this Whig Reformer.[1] And in politics he acted accordingly.

Pugnacious and despotic though he often was, however, he also became a
doubter and a divided man, a man whose life may seem to modern eyes to
be composed of striking ambivalences—not least in relation to the past and
to 'the people'. He wanted to change the Scotland in which he grew up, but
he also loved it, and he poured out that love in the *Memorials*. He wanted a
wider Parliamentary representation, but he did not want democracy.

It might seem typical of the ambiguous Cockburn, but then, of course, it
was typical of others too, that his tastes were both Classical and estranged
from Classicism—both Roman and Romantic. In 1811, the year after his
liberation from the Government, he married Elizabeth Macdowall, of an old
Galloway family, and, in Horatian style, set up his rural household gods in
a farmhouse at Bonaly, which he then began to supplement with a peel-
tower, unabashedly Gothic and feudal. His town house was Classical, and
imposing: respectability gained a palace in 14 Charlotte Square. Around
him, with their so many cubic feet of property to feu and let, lay the streets,
crescent and circuses, the straight lines, squares, parallelograms and semi-
circles of the Euclidean New Town, which was still growing, and which he
tended to condemn as unromantic, mercenary and meanly mathematical.
Co-ordinate with St Andrew's Square to the east, Charlotte Square occupied
a key position in the New Town plan or grid. It is a beautiful place, which
has a kind of sober magnificence. Those who walk its public pavements
catch glimpses of the Firth of Forth and of the Highlands—of another world.

It took him most of the remainder of his life—until 1838, if not later

---

[1] To Thomas Kennedy of Dunure, whose collection of *Letters Chiefly Connected with the Affairs
of Scotland*, and chiefly from Cockburn, appeared in 1874. The letter in question is on p. 63, and
the volume is referred to hereafter as *Letters to Kennedy*.

still—to complete Bonaly Tower, which proved of vital importance to him. 'There is only one L in Bonaly,' he explains in a letter. 'It rhymes to Daily. It's only Bonally that rhymes to Dally.'[1] He means that the wrong pronunciation is the one that really suits his country retreat. At Bonaly, he dallied: in town, he led a daily life compounded of work and duty. His seasons at Bonaly alternated with his sessions in town as reformer and iconoclast, as advocate and judge and Edinburgh eminence. The two habitations fostered a double life of sorts, which might appear to complete the other dualities and contradictions of his nature—those of an Anglophile Scottish patriot, of a patrician progressive, of someone at once convivial and grave, who was blamed for his pursuit of pleasure, but who was also capable of an altogether Presbyterian severity and who had his share of sufferings, certain of which he refused to divulge to his readership. His imagination was drawn, if not to the horizontals of the New Town plan, to the perpendicularities of summits and towers and monuments and obelisks and walking-sticks, but it was also drawn to the hidden places, the secret recesses, the maternal hollows and declivities, the groves and streams and waterfalls, of his Pentland haunts: so that the accommodation he effected between town and country was also an accommodation of sorts between the true old male and female principles.

His 'Pentlandising', as he called it, his walks and wanderings in the hills, was more of a religion than a recreation. Such pleasures were sublime. He worshipped the Pentlands and hailed them as his Paradise. If you stand now, on a fine day, above Bonaly, which was further added to and embellished after his death, and which is apt to look a little bleakly and dwarfishly baronial, there is a sense, still, of Olympus, and of other heavens. There below lies Edinburgh, spread out for some god or some angel to fly down and intervene in its affairs. There below are the mortals in contention. Another windy Troy.

Elevated to Bonaly, Cockburn himself felt no wish to descend or intervene. Here was the blissful wilderness where this public man was able to lead a solitary as well as an agreeably social life, where he could forget the pugnacities of politics and the law and be, as he described the golfers of St Andrews, 'gregarious without remorse'.[2] Golf, in fact, may be regarded as a crude secular equivalent of his magic game of sticks and mountain springs.

In 1812, in his capacity as advocate, Jeffrey assisted a number of weavers from the Glasgow area, where efforts had been made to build up a trade union, or 'combination'. The weavers obtained a Court of Session ruling in

[1] To Mrs Sophia Rutherfurd, 21 June 1848.  [2] *J* II, p. 65.

favour of a legally enforceable fixed wage. There was a strike, the employers resisted the ruling, and strikers were arrested and tried. The Government repealed the Act on which the Court of Session ruling was based—an act of treachery for which the Tories were not readily forgiven. Meanwhile the strikers were defended by Jeffrey and Cockburn, who had persuaded one of their leaders, Alexander Richmond, to become an outlaw and leave Scotland. Richmond afterwards returned and was given a light sentence. In 1816, he was given money by Jeffrey and Cockburn, who were atttracted to his gentle and melancholy air, in order to set up as a fabrics manufacturer, which he did. He then visited New Lanark, Robert Owen's proto-socialist community of cotton-workers, where, in a manner reminiscent of the Speculative Society, character was formed and dancing classes were compulsory.

Richmond's *Narrative* of these events[1] shows that he was an intelligent man, and he was clearly a man who was willing to become respectable, to better himself. Respectability, however, appears to have involved him in becoming a Government spy. Cockburn was to accept, with distress, that this is what had happened. It is possible that Richmond was more of a victim than anything else, a victim of circumstances and of the contrivances of public men: in particular, Kirkman Finlay, a buccaneering business magnate with a good deal of influence at various levels and a phobia about subversion, and perhaps also Cockburn and Jeffrey themselves, who introduced Richmond to Kirkman Finlay.

Richmond undertook to report on the swearing of seditious oaths: stealth was being met with stealth. This led to another trial, at which Cockburn and Jeffrey were present for the defence, but which collapsed when the prosecution was accused of tampering with a witness by making promises to him. Richmond seems still to have been a Government agent, or at least on the payroll, when the 'Radical War' of 1820 broke out. The rather more elaborate war with Napoleon had brought good and glowing times to more than one department of Scottish life, and a building boom to the capital. It was followed by depression and deflation, and by the Corn Laws: 1817 to 1823 were bad years for Scotland, and there were further bad years after that, during which the New Town came to a halt. As a result, there was unrest and a surfacing of Radicalism. But, in fact, the 'Radical War' was the only thing resembling a Scottish uprising during decades of apprehension as to what the people might do—and that was stage-managed by the authorities through agents provocateurs. It amounted to no more than a miserable

[1] *Narrative of the Condition of the Manufacturing Population; and the Proceedings of Government which led to the State Trials in Scotland* (1824). *The Scottish Insurrection of 1820* (1970) by P. Berresford Ellis and Seumas Mac A' Ghobhainn tells—in a manner friendly to the somewhat shadowy insurgents—the story of the subsequent Bonnymuir skirmish, and of Richmond.

débâcle for a few weavers at Bonnymuir in Clydeside, where there was a brush with troops during which some of the insurgents were wounded and a horse killed. For Thomas Chalmers, Bonnymuir was a phenomenon of infidelity or irreligion: this was one respect, at any rate, in which it could have been held by some to resemble the French Revolution. Although 'Edinburgh was as quiet as the grave, or even as Peebles', the phantom operations of the 'Radical Army' briefly re-mobilized the gentlemen of that city. Lieutenant-Colonel Charles Hope, Lord President of the Court of Session, scanned the Lothians from the Castle ramparts. Cockburn donned the uniform of a Volunteer, as a member of the Armed Association, and spent an evening of alarm and hilarity in the Assembly Rooms in Edinburgh waiting for news from the West which never arrived.

After Bonnymuir, a Commission of Oyer and Terminer, with an English lawyer represented on it, tried for treason according to English law, and three men were executed. The martial Hope presided. Cockburn and Jeffrey made an objection to appearing for the defence without the aid of English lawyers, and in the end only Jeffrey, of the two, appeared. The account of Bonnymuir in the *Memorials* omits to mention Cockburn's own eventual role in relation to the trial. It might be said of these events that Cockburn and Jeffrey had encouraged a man to become a gentleman who then became a spy and betrayed people whom they later defended, and that Cockburn prepared, however sceptically and humorously, to hunt and attack people whom he was later, in principle, willing to defend. But to put the matter in this way would be tendentious. The episodes are dark and hard to read, but those he defended he considered defensible, and he never pretended to condone insurrection. And it would seem that, as a consequence of their commitments in this field, he and Jeffrey gained the trust of many of the working class: a trust which may have earned them a measure of stability and restraint in that quarter when they made their bid for Reform. His absence from the Bonnymuir trial may have been caused partly by his father's death just before it, which brought to a close a series of personal troubles.

1818 was a bad year for Cockburn. His wife was ill. His eldest daughter, aged 7, was ill, and dying. One of his friends died, the physician John Gordon. Then, two years later, his father died. It is possible to guess that there had long been a coldness between Cockburn and his father, and he apparently preferred, and indeed revered, his mother. And it is possible to guess that his father's death, together with the foregoing crises, stirred him to write the *Memorials*, which at this time he set himself to do. 'About 1821,' he explains in the preface, 'I began to recollect and to inquire.' In that work he preaches the Whig gospel, glories in the Whig momentum of the decade and in the effacements of the past that were presumed to lie ahead, and assails his father's friend, Lord Braxfield. The book performs a series of unfilial acts. But, in the tender telling of the story of his parents' Scotland and of its privileged caste, it also seems to offer, remorsefully, a kind of propitiation, and to seek, at times, a maternal comfort similar to the blessings bestowed by the Pentlands. By the time of his father's death, the time the *Memorials* began to grow, Cockburn had spent two decades at the bar. Just before this, Raeburn painted a picture of his eminence in which the pleasure-lover wears a pensive look: a look that was to pass into sombreness on the evidence of the photographs that exist of him. In a letter of 1819 to Richardson's wife, he reports his 'beautiful visage finished by Raeburn'.[1]

The 1820s were exhilarating years for the Scottish Whigs, though not for the English Whigs and still less for the Scottish poor, and Cockburn's forties were a decisive period in his development, if not the time of his life. The decade was inaugurated by the Pantheon meeting of December 1820 in Edinburgh, chaired by James Moncreiff, where the Scottish Whigs were able to stage a convincing demonstration of their gathering popularity. Cockburn regarded this as the first 'modern' political meeting, hostile to hereditary Tory rule, ever to be held in the town: since the start of the draconian 1790s, such meetings had been banned or prevented. A verse squib of the time[2] rehearsed the idea of Whigs being plucked from their families, their 'imps', to be great public figures at the Pantheon meeting:

> No tiny C-ck-n, pleased to play the groom,
> Spurs his immortal father round the room.

A few weeks later, a dinner was held in memory of their hero by Edinburgh's Foxites. 'Sad scamps,' remarked Scott of the Whigs who attended,[3] and he himself attended a dinner held, provocatively, on the same day by Edinburgh's Pittites. An anonymous pamphlet ridiculed, with jokes and shudderings, the rival feast.[4] In some hand-written notes on the flyleaf of his copy of the pamphlet, now in the National Library, Cockburn, too, deplores the feast, and remarks that the pamphlet was 'obviously got up by a latent enemy in order to expose' the Pittites. Their dinner, the pamphlet assures the world, was a shameful affair. Sir Alexander Boswell—James Boswell's manic son—behaved obscenely, and the songs of the Ettrick

---

[1] 2 April. His earlier 'journalizing' may have been largely meditative in kind.
[2] Quoted in *The Lord Advocates of Scotland* by George Omond (2 vols, 1883), vol. II, p. 267.
[3] In a letter to Lord Montagu of 17 January 1821.
[4] 'A Letter to the Vice-Presidents and Stewards of the Pitt Club' by 'a Friend to the Principles of Mr Pitt' (1821).

Shepherd did nothing to sweeten the air. Scott, 'this mighty magician', cast no healing spell on the brutish assembly: 'Even the great mind of Sir Walter, in one of its playful gambols, had shewn a little *smut*; but very little, and that little as harmless as possible: I mean in the good old joke about the kirk, and standing room.' ' "To chaunt his stupid stave" of indecency and profaneness': Boswell's stave is evoked by means of an allusion to Byron's description, in 'English Bards and Scotch Reviewers', of that of the poet James Grahame, a friend of Cockburn's.[1] The often offensively personal Cockburn was often shocked by 'the vice of offensive personality' when it was displayed by opponents. One man's wit is another man's poison. One man's latent hostility is another man's libel.

Still, the politics of the town had certainly turned reckless and ugly, and after the Pantheon meeting the Tories were minded to hit back. Outbursts of libel in the Government press—first in the *Beacon* and then in the *Sentinel*—led eventually to reverses for the Tories, including the Lord Advocate Rae, who was implicated in the libels, and to the acquittal of James Stuart of Dunearn, who had slain Boswell in a duel. Earlier, Stuart had publicly caned the *Beacon* printer. Walter Scott, too, was implicated in the *Beacon* smears, and arrangements for a duel were started, or simulated. Scott's friend (and Cockburn's), the Whig Richardson, was grieved by this news of 'Gualtero': 'It feels like parricide to think an ill thought of him.'[2] But it was explained that while Scott had been a bondsman for the paper, guaranteeing it against debt, he bore no responsibility for its contents.

When the *Beacon* collapsed, the *Sentinel* was set up in its stead, with the same covert Ministerial backing, and published some staves in which Boswell, a relative of his, anonymously aspersed Stuart's manhood, and which supplied the grounds for challenging Boswell to a duel. One of the *Sentinel*'s editors, Borthwick, passed to Stuart the originals of this and other libels, and was indicted for theft by the Lord Advocate. Having extinguished the profane and secret Boswell at Auchtertool in Fife, Stuart left for France, but returned to be defended by Cockburn, whose speech on his behalf, said Sir James Mackintosh, was not 'surpassed by any effort in the whole range of ancient or modern forensic eloquence'.[3] Cockburn was also Borthwick's counsel, but the case never came to trial. These were great days, of a kind, but it is not easy to feel as indignant as Cockburn about the offences committed by the two papers, given the nature of the Whig response: a stupid stave can rarely be considered punishable by death. As it happened, when

[1] This Scotch bard is discussed in Chapter Four.

[2] From an incomplete letter to Cockburn conjecturally dated January 1821.

[3] *M*, p. 397: a footnote by Cockburn's editors provides an extract from a speech of Mackintosh's in the House of Commons.

Boswell was in Parliament, he helped to pass an Act which laid down that, in Scotland, fighting a duel should no longer be a capital crime.

In 1823, Cockburn put these struggles with the Pittites behind him and went off with Jeffrey, Richardson and others, to gaze at the 'queer old towers' of Venice[1] in the course of a festive Continental tour. Napoleon's armies had not preserved the fascinating, dubious Venice of the Doges— which was how Cockburn saw the city—but its queer old towers were still standing. In 1828, the Burke and Hare murders came to light: Cockburn achieved another of his victories at the bar when he appeared for Burke's woman, Helen MacDougal.

At the end of the 1820s Earl Grey became Prime Minister, with 'Jeffrey and all high Whigs getting summoned into an Official career', as Carlyle puts it in an account of the Scottish scene in his *Reminiscences*.[2] Jeffrey became Scotland's Lord Advocate, and Cockburn its Solicitor-General. The *Memorials* conclude with the Whigs triumphantly in power. But Cockburn does not exult. Reform has yet to be achieved. After months of commotion and uncertainty, and anxious talk of revolution, with the Government twice brought down by the opposition of the House of Lords, the laws were passed.

The confrontations and manœuvres which preceded the passage of the third Reform Bill may be studied in four volumes of letters and notes which are now in the National Library. The lively letters are Jeffrey's (mostly copied by Cockburn's daughter Jane), and the often comical and abrasive notes ('Havers!') are Cockburn's. Cockburn assembled these volumes for his own use in the mid-1830s, and, until 1850, went on adding to them with further letters from Jeffrey when Jeffrey was in the South. He did not feel that the time was ever ripe for these secrets to be published, and his use of some of the material in his later life of Jeffrey was guarded and selective: he chose for reasons of colour and incidental human interest, rather than with a view to projecting the political substance of the correspondence. Jeffrey was based in London in order to confer with the Cabinet, to mediate the opinions of the Scottish Whigs and to speak on behalf of the Bill in the House of Commons. Cockburn, the draftsman, paid two visits to the capital during this time.

In his introduction to these volumes, dated 18 August 1835, Cockburn writes that Jeffrey's appointment as Lord Advocate in December 1830 'changed his whole habits, prospects and avocations. He had hitherto lived entirely in Edinburgh or its neighbourhood, at the head of his profession, one of the principal leaders of our popular opposition, with a great literary

---

[1] From a letter of 11 July 1823 to Richardson.    [2] *Reminiscences* (reprinted 1972), p. 330.

fame, which he enjoyed contentedly with his private friends, in the midst of such humble brilliancy as can belong to any society outside London, a splendid and happy provincial life. But he had now to quit his profession, to go into Parliament at the age of 58, with a voice lately enfeebled, and the still heavier misfortune of a great reputation, to forego the paradise of Craigcrook, and the long delicious vacations which relieve litigants, and bless the profession of the law, in Scotland, to pass many weary months, and these the summer ones, in London, to be no longer the easy critic of measures but their responsible conductor, and to be involved, thanklessly, and without official training, in all the vexatious details of official business.' In the version of this passage which reached the *Life of Jeffrey* the adjective 'provincial' is omitted, and there is an allusion to the fact that Jeffrey suffered greatly from the financial privations caused by the loss of his profession and by the expense involved in running for Parliament, as he kept having to do.[1] Cockburn was generally inclined to be defensive about his friend's record as Lord Advocate. Others have been inclined to sneer at it—at his intolerance of vexatious detail and his uncertain capacity to stay in the hunt for change. The deficiencies of reformers are rarely overlooked.

During these months in London, with his parrot and other pets, Jeffrey's sore throats exacerbated an already bad speaking manner, and he also had to have an operation. A carolling delight in the distinguished men and lovely women of the metropolis is evident in his letters. Jeffrey was a great kisser, and his kisses were told to his friend in the North, who notes on one later occasion, when the tally was transmitted: 'Idiot.' Among other women, he was friendly with Lord Melbourne's poetess, Mrs Norton. But he also longs to get 'down', as he thinks of it, to Edinburgh. He was a seasoned apprehender of the worst, and in addition to his Reform work he had to do the ordinary business of the Lord Advocate and to stoop to such small items of patronage as the assignment of a postmaster to the village of Lasswade. Meanwhile cholera creeps about the land, Jeffrey fears he has it, and Cockburn is commiserated with when the scourge arrives in Edinburgh: 'I mourn over you as the Saviour did over Jerusalem, and would gather you all as a hen gathers her chickens under her wings.'[2]

An encounter between Jeffrey and Wordsworth is recorded: 'He is not in the very least *lakeish* now, or even in any degree *poetical*, but rather a hard, and a sensible, worldly, sort of man.' The following month, Jeffrey, formerly the critic of so much in the way of lakeishness, displays a willingness to respond to one of the vistas, and to one of the words, of the poetical

---

[1] *Life of Jeffrey*, vol. I, p. 306.
[2] JLC: 3 February 1832. The cry of 'Idiot' was in response to a letter of 3 March 1840.

Wordsworth: at five in the morning, after a Commons debate, he 'took three pensive turns along the solitude of Westminster Bridge; admiring the sharp clearness of St Paul's, and all the city spires soaring up in a smokeless sky'.[1]

Few Scottish Members of Parliament favoured Reform initially, but many of their compatriots did, and the kingdom at large was alert to every development in the Parliamentary struggle. Cockburn was urged by Jeffrey for God's sake to keep Scotland quiet. A major crisis occurred when the Government was defeated in the House of Lords, in a division of 7 May 1832. Jeffrey waited on that likeable politician, Lord Althorp, in his dressing-room. Lathered, razor in hand, Althorp was half-way through shaving. Jeffrey stared at his rough hairy arms, and was given a finger to shake of the hand that held the brush. This was the hand which, more than any other, had grasped the nettle of Reform. With a twinkling smile, his mind no doubt already in the country and fixed devoutly on his fowling-pieces, Althorp announced: 'You need not be anxious about your Scotch Bill for tonight, for I have the pleasure to tell you, *we are no longer his Majesty's Ministers.*' Cockburn had always emphasized that Scotland had even less of a vote than England, which enjoyed pockets and dimensions of accountability, so to speak, and he attaches a note to the letter of 9 May in which this scene is described: 'The feeling of Scotland, whose *all*, as to representation, was at stake, was deep, intense and grave. It was a very serious matter with them. They would have shed their blood—but without noise, quietly and sternly —if nothing else could have done. It was an old covenanting business with them; who the Reform bill brought literally out of the land of Egypt, out of the house of bondage.' More figuratively, perhaps, than literally. And it is striking that he should salute his success with a Covenanting metaphor.

Throughout the struggle, the Grey Government had coerced their opponents by means of the recognition that there might be widespread disturbances if Reform were blocked, and by means of the threat to create peers in order to pass the Bill. Now, with Grey out, the Duke of Wellington failed to deliver a new government. On 27 June the Scottish Bill passed the House of Commons, and the struggle was over. Jeffrey walked home alone through St James's Square, dropping a tear or two and pondering the littleness and vanity even of such great contentions as the Reform Bill, which was certainly one of the greatest Parliamentary contentions there has ever been. In the next year the Burgh Reform measures to alter the mode of election to town councils were enacted. John Richardson seems to have helped to draft the

[1] Ibid.: 30 March and 20 April 1831.

measures whereby self-election was strangled in Scotland. Jeffrey, who bore the brunt of the measure, had previously gone down to Edinburgh for a long period of reprieve and of consultations with his Covenanting friends.

The successive excitements of Reform were deep, intense and grave, and Cockburn, for all the sober face he liked to show in public, shared in them to the full. The daughter of his friend Eliza Fletcher, who was the wife of Archibald Fletcher, an early Reformer, provides an endearing glimpse of these excitements, and of Cockburn's standing in his native city. Jeffrey was returned in December 1832 as MP for Edinburgh (along with James Abercromby) in the first Reformed Parliament. When, eighteen months before, he had been rejected by the city's unreformed electors, a tumult of 'Down with the Dundases' had broken out, and the Lord Provost had been assaulted and very nearly hurled from the North Bridge. Now the tumult took a different turn, and the call was for 'Cockburn!' Eliza and her daughter went to Jeffrey's house in Moray Place. The daughter writes that Cockburn was overwhelmed at the election 'of his friend Jeffrey, "his love for whom was passing the love of woman" ':

> He was more excited by joy on that day even than we were; and I well remember his way of rushing into the drawing-room, and looking round the crowd of Whig ladies and girls who were present, and calling out, 'Where's Mrs Fletcher? she's the woman that I want', and when my mother came from the window to meet him, they clasped each other's hands and had a good 'greet' together; and not many words were said before there was a call for 'Cockburn' from the crowd without, and he went to the balcony to respond to the call, and made a short speech of deep feeling which was cheered long and loudly.[1]

The impassive Cockburn enjoyed a good 'greet', or cry, and crowds were often in this relation to him: that of being 'without', and below.

The *Journal* discusses Reform and its sequel, and, in depth, a second triumph of a different order—namely, the Disruption, when two-fifths of the Church of Scotland's ministers broke away, because of their opposition to the preferment of ministers by local landowners, the Crown and others in possession of livings. The state in the shape of the Court of Session, of which he was by then a member, had attempted to coerce the Kirk—as he felt, unwisely and unjustly. In one way, his sympathies were with neither side: he was neither a Moderate nor an Evangelical, though it was like him to lean, as he did, in both directions. In another way, true to his rebellious form, his heart was with the mutineer ministers. They were virtuous and courageous. The sighs and supplications of their followers were the true voice of Scottish religion, and they themselves, with their battlefields of

---

[1] *The Autobiography of Mrs Fletcher* (1875), edited by her daughter Mary, p. 210.

Auchterarder and Strathbogie, were like the Covenanters of old. If only for patriotic reasons, and in spite of his distaste for 'Covenanting sublimities', he was bound to admire them. The collision between the commandments of Church and Court was perceived as a gross and horrible embarrassment, but the ministers' departure was 'the most honourable fact for Scotland that its whole history supplies'.

The *Journal*, perhaps, is drier than its more famous first instalment, the *Memorials*, but it is just as fine a work. It is less of a gallery of portraits or collection of eulogies—which is how much of the *Memorials* seems to have accumulated, the 'character' of so-and-so being an established autobiographical component. But the analyses of human behaviour are as searching as ever, and more patiently conducted; and the instances and anecdotes are as well chosen. If the pace is slower, the prose is still firm, clear and incomparably witty: as buoyant as a boat, as coercive as a Court of Session.

On their retirement from political office in 1834, those advocates and Edinburgh Reviewers, Cockburn and Jeffrey, 'benchified', joining the Court of Session—a civil court some of whose judges also tried criminal cases in the High Court of Justiciary. Cockburn was made a Lord of Justiciary in 1837. In a letter of 1830 to a political associate, Thomas Kennedy of Dunure, he had expressed a wish to be Solicitor-General, and had also said: 'I have never hypocritically affected indifference to professional preferment, but on the contrary avow that I hunger for it.' He spoke of himself as worth about £7,000, and added: 'But for my profession, I am a beggar.'[1] Towards the end of his four years as Solicitor-General, he told Kennedy of his intention to benchify: 'I am most anxious to be in harbour'—as a judge.[2] Leading advocates earned more than judges, and for Cockburn, professional preferment led to a diminished income. But it is likely that he was now less interested in money or honours than in a quieter life, and that he was content to join the bench and to leave politics.

By November 1834, the month during which he left, Grey was gone, and Melbourne, who had succeeded him as Prime Minister, was in difficulties. The London Whigs were quarrelling, and the Whig momentum, as Cockburn had known and rejoiced in it, was spent. He was exasperated with the Government's failure to grasp the thistle of patronage and help to bring peace to the Venerable—as he and Jeffrey called the General Assembly. It may be that his hunger for politics and his hunger for preferment had abated. It may be that he was satisfied, and it may also be that he was somewhat sickened. While he was, and had reason to be, proud of the Reform provisions, and of the work that he and Jeffrey had done in their four years, his

---

[1] *Letters to Kennedy*, pp. 255, 256.    [2] Ibid., p. 506.

experience of power was not without its exasperations and disappointments. Friends, he found, could be worse than enemies. 'Enemies are easily managed, but wrong-headed friends are the very devil': someone who had quarrelled with his kin might well say so.[1] Errors were made which were soon exposed, and he and Jeffrey fell foul of the odium with which Reform was regarded in many quarters in Scotland. James Hogg confided, in his shepherd's dialect, to *Fraser's Magazine*: 'We are a' goin' here to the pigs and whistles since Lord Jauphrey—Lord sauf us!—was made Lord Advocate.' Hogg then offered a burlesque of Burns:

> A king may make a man a lord,
> A belted knight and a' that;
> But he can't make Jeff. a gentleman,
> For a' that, and for a' that.

Hogg's aspersions on Jeffrey appeared in October 1831. In an anonymous Edinburgh satire published, it would seem, a few months earlier, Cockburn had been subjected to still harsher treatment.[2] He was cartooned to resemble a black dwarf with an interest in women's clothing, a vain, bad-tempered goblin, and other ugly things. The lampoon, entitled 'Little Cocky-Bendy', carries an oddly earnest-looking epigraph:

> Thou hast told me what I never dare
> to tell, even to mysel';
> Yes, thou hast told me the truth.

The scurrilities of the first half refer to his style and talents as an advocate (which were sometimes represented by political enemies as those of an accomplished liar), to his lack of inches, to the liking for fancy dress on the part of some of those who forgathered at Bonaly (of which, though it existed, he himself never speaks), and to his brisk walks in the country.

> Oh who so well could tell a lie,
> Or in a rapture'd passion fly,
> Or steal a pen when no one's by,
> Like little Cocky-Bendy.

[1] JLC: he says so in a note to a letter of Jeffrey's of 23 March 1833.
[2] The British Museum Catalogue lists as conjectural both the date of publication of the satire (1830) and the identification of Cockburn as its subject. There can be no doubt that it is Cockburn who is being attacked.

When he a pen or twa had stown,
And you accus'd him, he would frown,
As if the Deil had knock'd him down—
    Remember Cocky-Bendy.

'Twas ne'er his fault to be o'er blate,
You'd think (he tried to look so great)
You saw a Minister of State,
    In little Cocky-Bendy.

But not in stature great was he—
Stature! no, no! for trust to me,
His height was only three feet three—
    Little wee Cocky-Bendy.

The colour of his pow was jet,
His face was nearly so; and yet,
Off to a masquerade he'd set,
    To act Miss Cocky Bendy.

Who could so well his power display?
Or walk a hundred miles a-day?
And never known to go astray,
    Like little Cocky-Bendy.

    The lampoon proceeds to allege a pouring of chamber-pots over his head, and to show him as a wag who was apt to be touchy about his age. He is also shown as a man of property or pelf who was unwilling to quit his 'hovel'. The poem seems to recall certain incidents and embarrassments in Cockburn's life which are otherwise unrecorded, but this may be a reference to his rearing of Bonaly Tower—to his conversion of a humble farmhouse into an object of interest. He is shown throughout as a little wee person with the combustibility, or coerciveness, of his stature: perhaps there was a measure of truth in this. The poem talks, in a period way, about fairies and the Devil, and it makes enterprising use of the Scots language: 'singet' means shrunken or shrivelled, and 'hotty' was High School slang for someone who has a sign pinned to his back of which he is unaware. This particular game was still played in Edinburgh when I was young, and so was the game of pieries, or spinning-tops, in which, at one time, the 'hoatie' was a pierie due to be struck a special series of blows by the boys taking part. The whole poem is a hotying, or placarding, of Cockburn by a latent enemy (who may have been an old schoolfellow), but, as with so many such efforts of belittlement, the final effect is not very different from what might be that of some unsparing testimony to the power displayed—these, indeed, are the words of the poem —by the man who is belittled. Only a person of significance, one is led to think, could be felt to require quite so much disparagement. The remainder of 'Little Cocky-Bendy' reads:

> He oft was with a jordan crown'd!
> And with it's fluid almost drown'd!
> While heavenly fragrance flow'd around,
> > The head o' Cocky-Bendy.

> If you requested Cocky's age,
> He would you strike, stamp, roar, and rage;
> And act like PUNCH upon a stage—
> > Passionate Cocky-Bendy.

> Cock thought so highly of himself,
> Because he had a little pelf;
> The poor conceited silly elf,
> > Daft humphy Cocky-Bendy.

> When Cocky knew not what to do,
> And would not from his hovel go,
> He made a curious raree show,
> > Ingenious Cocky-Bendy.

> But mending sic an elf I true,
> Is not an easy job to do;
> Or any such known WAG as you,
> > Ye singet Cocky-Bendy.

> Cocky, a naughty boy I ween
> Thou art, as e'er was to be seen;
> And my most fervent wish has been,
> > To hoty Cocky-Bendy.

When Jeffrey benchified, having long been, as advocate and editor, the adversary of the bench in question, Cockburn wrote ironically to Kennedy:

Jeffrey is a Lord of Session! an actual red gowned, paper Lord. A framer and lover of acts of sederunt. An admirer of the Nobile Officium. A deviser of Interlocutors. A hater of the House of Lords. He nods over the same bench where nodded the dignified Eskgrove, and adorns the long pure cravat which typified the calm elegance of the judicial Braxfield.[1]

[1] *Letters to Kennedy*, pp. 513, 514.

Cockburn, too, was shortly to receive the same false handshakes from old enemies on the bench. The *Nobile Officium* was a discretionary power of the Court of Session which may perhaps be termed an instrument of its 'native vigour'—in effect, its legislative aspirations—and which Cockburn thought exceedingly controversial. Interlocutors were a kind of verdict or judicial opinion.

It isn't every critic who is granted the ermine of a judge, or who deserves to be: but this was the fate of these Edinburgh Reviewers. Literature had been a second string for the briefless Whig lawyer in former, Tory times, and in any case the two callings had long been rather closely linked. The Braxfieldian motto of the *Edinburgh Review*—*Judex damnatur cum nocens absolvitur*—was fair warning of the judicial temper of its literary criticism, but Cockburn was unlikely to prove a terror on the bench. Equally, Jeffrey was unlikely to prove 'the Jeffreys of Scotland', stealing from Braxfield the title conferred in the *Memorials*. To at least one poet, however—Southey —he was known as 'Judge Jeffrey'.

As a lawyer, Cockburn has been accounted, and accounted himself, a poor technician in civil matters, and the drafting of the Scotch Reform Bill has been criticized for a self-defeating ignorance of social conditions and established electoral practice in Scotland. The legal reforms for which he argued (for example, the abolition of the judge's right to pick the jury in criminal cases, and the introduction of jury trial in civil cases) tended to gain acceptance: by and large, they were the kind of things that a barrister, rather than a judge or jurist, might want accomplished. As a judge, he has had his disparagers, and in civil cases his decisions were sometimes reversed by the other Lords of Session. At the time—an important time—of the cotton-spinners' trial of 1838, he took pride in asserting, from the bench, the innocence of trade-union combinations, but he had always disapproved of the coerciveness to which they were inclined. In his youth he wrote to the poet James Grahame: 'It is *impossible* to defend a combination which is kept up by concussing me to join it.'[1]

All his books were published in Edinburgh, and all but one, the *Life of Lord Jeffrey*, were published posthumously. His experiences as an itinerant judge, and as a connoisseur of landscape and manners, are contained in the *Circuit Journeys*, a journal which appeared in 1888, as did his *Examination of the Trials for Sedition which have hitherto occurred in Scotland*. The *Sedition Trials* is a sprightly description of the brutal treatment by Braxfield and the Judiciary of various Radicals of the 1790s, and of subsequent prosecutions when he and his friends were among the defending counsel.

[1] 12 December 1808.

He looks at cases and concepts of sedition, and at the meagre precedents afforded by a society which until quite recently was too barbarous to be able to say what sedition was. 'Trials for sedition,' he says in his introduction, 'are the remedies of a somewhat orderly age.'[1] The *Sedition Trials* seems to have been put together over a period of years. He revised it in 1853, but thought it should be published at some later date.

In addition, there are two books which carry selections from his correspondence. *Letters Chiefly Connected with the Affairs of Scotland,* published in London in 1874, consists mostly of letters about politics received from Cockburn by Thomas Kennedy of Dunure. *Some Letters of Lord Cockburn,* edited by his grandson Harry and published in Edinburgh in 1932, includes material omitted from the published *Memorials.* Harry Cockburn's 1910 edition of the *Memorials* restores passages (such as those concerning Henry Dundas, Henry Erskine and the launching of the *Edinburgh Review*) which belonged, he says, to the original notebooks, but which were omitted from the first edition by those responsible for it (two of Cockburn's trustees, both of them sheriffs, his nephew Archibald Davidson and his son-in-law Thomas Cleghorn) because they had been incorporated, with little change, in the *Life of Lord Jeffrey.*

Cockburn died in 1854, and the *Memorials* came out two years later. In 1872, the *Memorials* and the *Life of Lord Jeffrey* were republished: it was hoped to build an edition of Cockburn's works, but the project was abandoned. Two years later, however, the *Journal* was issued by a different publisher in two volumes.[2] The interesting but encomiastic *Life of Jeffrey*—it is what one might expect of Jonathan, concerning David—had first appeared in 1852, just before Cockburn's death. This study of 'the greatest of British critics'[3] can only seem uncommunicative when compared with Carlyle's superb rendering of Jeffrey in his *Reminiscences,* which may be said to call attention to the defects of Cockburn's Roman reticence. 'You are so dreadfully in earnest!' the self-confident Jeffrey would exclaim to Carlyle, who, for his part, seems 'to remember that I dimly rather felt there was something trivial, doubtful, and not quite of the highest type, in our Edinburgh admiration for our great Lights and Law Sages.'[4] Elsewhere, though,

---

[1] *Sedition Trials,* p. 1.

[2] A photographic edition of the *Memorials* (the first edition text) was published in 1971 and a similar edition of the *Sedition Trials* was published in 1970. In 1948, a digest of the *Memorials* was produced by W. Forbes Gray, who decided to rewrite the text on grounds of style. In 1974, there appeared in America an edition of the same work based on the 1910 text and introduced by the present writer. This, too, was a photo-edition, but it was possible to make a limited number of changes with reference to the first edition text, in order to correct errors.

[3] *Life of Jeffrey,* vol. 1, p. 1.          [4] *Reminiscences,* pp. 327, 313.

he was warm about Cockburn, whom he felt to be the last of the old Scotch gentlemen.[1]

Cockburn was a small, wiry man—a talker, a walker, a swimmer, a skater, a bowls-player and a devotee of the open air. His step was sure but springing, he was soon bald, and he purchased his first pair of spectacles in the year the Reform Bill was passed. His amber eye, kindled by animation or wit, looked like a hawk's: the resemblance was noted by more than one observer. His wife was a stout, motherly-looking woman, with a pretty face that seems full of character: an ardent gardener. The only time when we see Mrs Cockburn plain, in the books or manuscripts, is when he tells his friend Grahame, writing from Caroline Park on 29 March 1811: 'I am writing to you with a married man's hand. I was cleeket to a decent, well-behaved, thickish woman about a fortnight ago, and as yet have no reason to repent of my choice. We are scarcely fairly settled, having never been at home, but we mean to be so in a day or two in your old house in Charlotte Street, to which, as usual, you will always be gratefully welcome; tho' man, you must really put a curb upon some of your practices if you even enter my threshold.' He may be referring here to a temporary house, lived in before he flitted nearby in 1813 to 14 Charlotte Square: at present, he says, it is 'polluted by painters'. He also says he has taken Bonaly and means to rusticate there. Grahame's practices no doubt included the 'potatorial powers' referred to in the same letter, which records that his own practice at the bar has earned him nearly £600 during the current session.

Cockburn was certainly a great light in Edinburgh, very popular, an esteemed eccentric and sage. He had a street named after him in the Old Town: suitably precipitous and tortuous, almost a tower and almost a declivity. The Cockburn Association has addressed itself, since its inception in 1875, to an object dear to his heart—the preservation of the Edinburgh environment: in his own day, his pleas on the subject were heeded, though not invariably, and in 1844 sufficient feeling was aroused to save John Knox's house in the Royal Mile. He spent a good deal of time with the artists of the city, who were not averse to schism and had a disruption of their own: a number of them walked out of the Royal Institution for the Promotion of Fine Arts and formed, in 1829, a society which became the Royal Scottish Academy, to which he was legal adviser, and which eventually swallowed the Royal Institution. Ten years later, we find him telling Fox Maule at the Home Office: 'Her Majesty, and Lord Melbourne, and you, have greatly delighted our artists. And they are excellent persons, well

---

[1] Carlyle's impressions of Cockburn are examined in Chapter Fourteen.

worth delighting.'[1] Art, felt Cockburn, had begun to flourish in Edinburgh, which would soon be accounting itself the Paradise of Calotype.

The photographer David Octavius Hill was the Secretary of the Royal Scottish Academy, and, with Cockburn, he assisted at its foundation. The two men were friends, and their friendship resulted in some remarkable early photographs—calotype pictures of the household at Bonaly (a further 'Bonaly Book' of calotypes was proposed). Hill and Robert Adamson took up the calotype method of photography, which had been invented by Fox Talbot in England, and the long exposures mounted at their studio on the Calton Hill compiled a record of Early Victorian Edinburgh which has been regarded as perhaps the finest achievement of the first photographers, and might also be regarded as a continuation, in a new medium, of Raeburn's memorials of the Scottish visage (in some of the photographs, a consciousness of Raeburn is certainly evident). These 'sun pictures'—Hill inscribed on the back of one: *Sol fecit*—were, curiously enough, a by-blow of the Disruption. The technique was developed with the guidance of Sir David Brewster, a scientist who was among the Disruption's moving spirits, and Hill made a number of calotype studies of ministers as a basis for a huge commemorative painting in which he depicted the signing of the Act of Separation at the Tanfield Hall in May 1843. Hill's painting is a kind of counterpart to Benjamin Haydon's *The Reform Banquet, 1832*, or to Sir George Hayter's *The Great Reform Bill*. It is a triumphal work. These men of God, these men of soul and sense, are shown renouncing their livings, surrendering their glebes and stipends, and among the sea of faces intent on the exodus are those of Cockburn and Jeffrey. 'There has not been such a subject since the days of Knox and not then,' said Cockburn.[2]

Hill's calotypes present, not only the serious faces of Free Church ministers, and of the Kirk Session at its momentous tasks, but also those of many other specimens of this society in their far from flashy Sunday best: gravity and sense personified in some professor or provost, shawled fisherwomen, douce ladies, braw lads, and, lending a needed touch of nonsense, the society's young men of style, in Byronic attitudes, dressed as monks, posed beside a massive bust of the Emperor, or semi-Emperor, Lucius Verus—'The Last of the Romans'. The bust was the work of an Academician whose saturnine features are to be seen beside it, set there by Edinburgh's unreliable sun. Certain of the calotypes might make one think that the last

[1] In a letter of 30 December 1839 which is among the Dalhousie MSS held at the Scottish Record Office.

[2] The words were quoted in connection with an offer for sale of certain of Hill's photographs: see *An Early Victorian Album: The Hill/Adamson Collection* (1974), edited with an introduction by Colin Ford, and with a commentary by Roy Strong, p. 36.

of the Romans was not Lucius Verus but some spriggish Scotsman whose Classical pose was also that of a Romantic poet. Fancy dress appears in several, and Cockburn's daughter Elizabeth plays the part of Miss Wardour in a version of *The Antiquary*. As we shall discover, Cockburn's Scotland was interested in disguise.

There is a ghostliness about many of the pictures, and the sense of a Northern elfhood. One consequence of Romanticism was an incidence of Byrons: another was the invasion of Edinburgh by a Gothic fairyland where men could look like goblins. Even the *Edinburgh Review* had its elves as well as its duxes, but it was among their rivals at *Blackwood's Magazine* that the Gothic influence chiefly reigned. A vying of the Gothic with the Classical was widespread and manifold, and it can be witnessed to this day in the villas built by the middle classes on the south side of the city and elsewhere. The calotype of Chalmers, with his white locks, preacher's bands and weighty Bible, makes him look both like a troll and like a wizard. At his death, says Cockburn, he received the homage of 'the hovels and the vennels'.[1] Whether he deserved their homage—or Cockburn's, for that matter, which is almost unqualified—is open to question. But this was a society whose leading lights were often wizard-like, and Chalmers's magic was the marvel of the villas and the crescents. *Pace* Cockburn, the hovels may have marvelled less, but it is right that his Bible should have the air of a book of spells. I shall be less gnomic about Chalmers in a later chapter.

In 1823, Cockburn helped to found a school in the New Town: Edinburgh Academy. 'One day on the top of one of the Pentlands—emblematic of the solidity of our foundation and of the extent of our prospects—we two resolved to set about the establishment of a new school.' The other visionary was the merchant Leonard Horner, brother of Francis Horner. In this swollen city, the High School, which was subject to Town Council control, was thought to be overcrowded, and was hard to reach from some of the new outlying districts. The Academy, to which the Town Council was initially hostile, was designed to be a public—that is to say, a private—school, with shareholders and much higher fees, and its bipartisan board of directors included, besides Cockburn and Horner, Walter Scott and a pair of Dundases. A struggle took place over the appointment of the first rector, with Scott scenting a Whig plot, and Cockburn's side was outvoted: but the 'Tory' rector who was chosen was Whig enough to proclaim a holiday when the Reform Bill was passed. The new school, which was to enable Scots boys to compete with English public-schoolboys for the more important posts in the Empire, was to have broadly the same curriculum and

[1] In a letter to Mrs Rutherfurd of 1 June 1847.

teaching arrangements as the High School, but it would teach more Greek, and the Scots tongue, still spoken by Cockburn himself, was banished.

The 'Statement by the Directors of the Edinburgh Academy', published in December 1823, explains that in this Classical school there would be 'a Master for English, who shall have a pure English accent: the mere circumstance of his being born within the boundary of England, not to be considered indispensable. The object of this appointment is to endeavour to remedy a defect in the education of boys in Edinburgh, who are suffered to neglect the cultivation of their native language and literature, during the whole time that they attend the Grammar Schools, and in most cases to a much later period.' So these Edinburgh boys were to be considered, in a sense, natives of England: the Anglophile in Cockburn—if the words are his—seems to have got the better of the Scots patriot here, and indeed the Academy was to prove, in comparison with its rival, an Anglophile school. Despite the intention to have a Master for English, the most remarkable feature of the scheme for the Academy was its strong Classical emphasis, and its lack of interest in the scientific and vocational subjects, and the living European languages, which had been taught for some while in certain schools in Scotland. The 'frequent infliction' of corporal punishment was to be 'discouraged'. This last item might suggest that the new institution, in relation to the old, incorporated some small element of revenge or reproof, but the Statement is too diplomatic to touch on a point like that, and Scott scouted any such suggestion in an inaugural speech. The High School's Temple of Theseus was shortly to go into commission—it appears to have been built as a result of the concern felt by the Town Council over the creation of the Academy, of which, for a time, they had negotiated to take charge—but the Academy, too, had a handsome building to boast of, and, after weathering a spell of financial difficulties, it went on to success in achieving the purposes for which it was called into being. Cockburn did not take lightly his connection with the college he helped to create. In 1824, he had a hand in the vetting of applicants for Academy posts, and wrote rude words of rejection—which can now be read in the British Museum—on several sets of printed testimonials. One man had the temerity to appear for interview in a white *satin* neckcloth. Ugh!

Cockburn had earlier—in 1810—helped to found a bank, the Commercial Bank, which gave credit to those denied it on political grounds. During his time as Solicitor-General, he was elected Rector of Glasgow University, defeating the Tory John Gibson Lockhart. When the Professor of Greek subsequently ran against him, Cockburn cast a vote in his own favour, deciding that the professor was ineligible. Self-election? Not exactly, one may conclude. (His rival, incidentally, was Sir Daniel Sandford—a man, he thought, who abounded in abominations.) He also spoke out against a piece of jobbery whereby one professor was preparing to retire in favour of another. In his capacity as Rector, which he was until 1834, he urged that the University Court should include at least one person directly elected by the students. He made the same point in the starkly censorious evidence which he gave as Solicitor-General to the Municipal Commission on 11 July 1834.[1] A separate Royal Commission had been looking into the affairs of the Northern universities, and had drawn up a scheme for a University Court which would be responsible for the patronage of Edinburgh University. Cockburn agreed with this approach, and stated in evidence that the Court should have no professional representatives (such as the law bodies), and that, in preference to that, while approving of neither arrangement, he would support the idea of a representative elected by the public. He also thought there might be a supervisory role here for a Minister of Education.

The Universities Commission saw itself as acting in a situation where there was a suspicion of closed corporations and a desire for the universities to submit to a greater degree of public accountability. They also saw themselves as favouring the English notion of a liberal education as against a native emphasis on vocational training, and their recommendations were, it seems, defeated by the Kirk and by Edinburgh's Town Council and professors. There had long been feuding in Edinburgh between the Town Council, which maintained an oversight of the University as of the High School, and the professoriate, or Senatus. Cockburn had a lively sense of the evils of Town Council interference and jobbing in relation to the University, though the history of this relationship seems to show that the Town Council's attentions were by no means uniformly unjustifiable, given the inertia and self-interest of the professors with regard to curricula, chairs and other matters. Cockburn remarked in evidence: 'Were it not that that I conceive it to be absolutely necessary that there should be some power of management external to the college itself, I should hold that the interference of the town council must generally be positively pernicious. It is only less pernicious than leaving everything to the professors.' A plague on both your houses: it was the kind of position that he sometimes liked to take. He also pointed out that, having been a Ministerial tool, the Town Council had now become, after Reform, 'more the creature of the people', and that 'the general body of the students are very seldom mistaken in their opinion of the academical merits of a teacher'.

[1] Parliamentary Papers, vol. 29, Municipal Corporations Report 1835, Local Reports: Edinburgh, pp. 391–3.

He interested himself at various stages of his life in the causes and concerns of teachers of another sort: Scotland's dominies, each in his small world of the parish, face to face with the kirk session and the property-owners assessed for his upkeep. An article of Cockburn's in the *Edinburgh Review* for June 1827 communicates his outlook on certain of the central issues. It calls for more schools, and for more respectable schools, in the public or parochial sector, and for regulation and improvement in respect of the educational qualifications expected of teachers. The schoolmaster should be better paid, kept from the need to take on supplementary jobs, and treated 'solely as a professional person; the friend and adviser of the better sort of people', whose children would attend his school. 'A parish school is gone, the instant it is understood that it is a place which is too low for the village aristocracy, and that it is frequented merely by those who have little to pay, and little to learn.' He wishes to increase the chalders of oatmeal statutorily accorded to teachers, and protests at the shabbiness of the treatment they have received, especially in the matter of accommodation. If the heritors or property-owners won't pay more towards their upkeep, 'the public at large' should. The character and extent of this compulsion to pay is not disclosed, and it cannot be said that his article takes proper account of the vast underprovision which existed in Scottish education at this time. Heritors should pay more, he goes on, because it would enable them to save on poor rates: education, that is to say, helped people to fend for themselves. He had strong feelings about poverty. He believed that lairds should not be compelled by the Court of Session to relieve the poor.

Cockburn's costumes are not the least of his claims to fame. Wandering in the country, he dressed accordingly—pastorally, indeed, as we shall see. His town clothes were not those of a dandy: but they were an exquisite expression of his stubborn self-sufficiency. His hat was alleged to be the worst in Edinburgh, and he designed his own very clumsy shoes. Evelyn Waugh was his great-great-grandson (another descendant, a great-grandson, is the Communist autobiographer and journalist, Claud Cockburn), and he turns his attention to Cockburn's shoes in his book of memoirs, *A Little Learning:* 'Confirmation of this peculiarity in footwear comes from his granddaughter, my maternal grandmother. At the age of eight she was staying at Bonaly when the portrait which now hangs in the National Portrait Gallery of Scotland was being painted by Watson-Gordon. When asked her opinion by the painter, she replied after long and grave scrutiny: "Well, it's *very* like his boots".'[1]

---

[1] *A Little Learning* (1964), pp. 11, 12. The story is also told in *The Records of the Cockburn Family*.

Queen Victoria, the artist's delight, visited Edinburgh with the Prince Consort in 1850, and Cockburn, in a letter,[1] feels sorry for her: 'Poor royal creature—she had never heard of the Pentland Hills!—on which she gazed with especial admiration. Think of a crowned head never having heard of the Pentland Hills! But her admiration shows that the head was not unworthy of a crown.' As for Albert, 'he particularly admired my shoes.'

[1] To Mrs Rutherfurd, 31 August 1850.

# Chapter Three

# *Filial Events*

I turn now to the hidden Cockburn, to the more or less unavowed experiences which conditioned, and contributed to, the successes and sublimities of an avowedly happy life.

He recorded in his *Journal*, in his fifties, that the thirty-four years since he became an advocate had been 'a nearly unbroken course of singular personal happiness', coincident with a splendid and solemn 'track of public improvement'. He said this the day after he benchified, in 1834. A letter of 1807 to Richardson might seem to exhibit an almost compulsive hedonism: 'It is a deep gloom indeed thro' which my eye cannot hail some scenes of serenity and bliss.'[1] In November 1856, after his death, an anonymous writer in the *North British Review*—he was, in fact, Patrick Fraser, later Lord Fraser, a lawyer—examined the *Memorials* and complained of Cockburn's 'indolent and careless love of enjoyment', adding a sardonic, epitaph-like Scottish joke: 'The great object of his horror was a lengthy bore.'

Bonaly gave access to what Cockburn called 'nature and romance': a golden age was restored to him there, he did not need to be formal or important there. He is said to have told a shepherd in the Pentlands: 'John, if I were a sheep, I would lie on the sunny side of the hill.' The shepherd replied with another Scottish joke: 'Ah, my Lord, but if ye was a sheep, ye would hae mair sense.'[2] An ominous joke, this, which its victim, at the end of his days, may well have found himself remembering.

If he was the last of the old Scotch gentlemen, there are moments when he also seems to have been the country's last entirely happy human being. His claim to that distinction, however, cannot be pressed very hard. He went in for mischief and high jinks; he was a wit; he was reckoned homely and

---

[1] June 1807.

[2] The exchange is taken from the editorial text which accompanies the illustrations in *Calotypes* by D. O. Hill and Robert Adamson, selected by Andrew Elliot with notes by John Gray (privately printed in Edinburgh in 1928). Ramsay includes it in his *Reminiscences*.

affable. But his face, in portraits and photographs, is sad and stoical, if not stricken—and some of the things that happened to him must certainly have caused him grief. He was a most emotional advocate, but for all his forensic tears, he is often very laconic in print, and tends to show a senatorial composure: he does not always specify his own role in the events he recounts. There's a good deal hidden in the folds of that toga, and on certain matters relating to 'my kindred', his reserve is absolute.

In a letter of 26 March 1852 Richardson is sure that his friend could 'make out of the red books'—the four notebooks in which the texts of the *Memorials* and the *Journal* were first recorded—'two invaluable volumes of reminiscences'. Not only would they be invaluable, they would also bring in two thousand guineas. 'If there be anything which would revolt living kindred you might to a certain degree omit or modify without creating inspidity at all.' Although, early on, he had spoken enthusiastically about 'memorabilia' that would observe a 'minute fidelity to common nature',[1] it is unlikely that Cockburn would ever have needed much coaching in the requirements of discretion. He was, as I have said, a pugnacious man, and his trustees felt they had to curb his pugnacity in preparing his autobiographical writings for the press. And if jokes could kill, and if a number of people had still been about when the *Memorials* saw the light, then some of his jokes would have done them at least a serious injury. Nevertheless, he knew very well what was expected of a man in his position, and on certain scores he was anxious to be tactful. He believed that the *Memorials* had been 'too gentle' with the worst in Edinburgh life.

A *Journal* entry of 3 February 1845 records the burning of letters received from friends:

> I have all my life had a bad habit of preserving letters, and of keeping them all arranged and docqueted; but seeing the future use that is often made of papers, especially by *friendly* biographers, who rarely hesitate to sacrifice confidence and delicacy to the promotion of sale or excitement, I have long resolved to send them all up the chimney in the form of smoke; and yesterday the sentence was executed. I have kept Richardson's and Jeffrey's, and some correspondence I had during important passages of our Scotch progress; but the rest, amounting to several thousands, can now, thank God, enable no venality to publish sacred secrets, or to stain fair reputations, by plausible mistakes. Yet old friends cannot be parted with without a pang.

'Important passages of our Scotch progress': this describes the subject-matter of his exchanges with Thomas Kennedy, his fellow Reformer. Cockburn's contribution to that correspondence was published in the

[1] *Some Letters of Lord Cockburn*, pp. 9, 10: the letter in question, probably to Richardson, is undated and in fragmentary form, and is on paper watermarked 1806.

volume of 1874: an editorial note in the *Journal*, which came out in the same year, declares that Cockburn would not have agreed to such a thing. In fact, a fair number of letters from friends remain in existence, and many of his own have been preserved from the chimney. His Red Book (or Books—it is spoken of in both ways) was soon destroyed, and his son, Francis Jeffrey Cockburn, who was of the opinion that 'the *Memorials* has had its day', destroyed many of the papers which survived his death.[1] By no means all— but the loss of letters on Reform from Cockburn to Jeffrey is regrettable.

As someone who thinks of himself as a friendly biographer of Cockburn, I do not quote his sentiments about the sacred secrets betrayed by biographers without a pang of my own. 'The promotion of sale or excitement' by making disclosures about Cockburn no longer constitutes a temptation, but the prospect of finding out more about his life does. I have yielded to the latter temptation, now that the living are less likely to be revolted, and have used the evidence of his unpublished letters and testaments.

Much of what has been written about him consists of appreciations based on his public activities, on fond memories of his personal life and on what he was willing to say about himself. One of the few pieces that goes more deeply into his career is the review of the *Memorials* which appeared in the *Edinburgh Review* of January 1857. This was written by Lord Moncreiff, a lawyer—son of the Moncreiff of the Pantheon meeting and grandson of the Evangelical minister Sir Harry Moncreiff who both figure benignly in Cockburn's memoirs: 'His natural endowments were rare in quality as well as strong and powerful, and greater than those of some who passed him in the competition for public or professional distinction. Partly from sensibilities of a finer fibre, and partly from a genuine love of the *fallentis semita vitae*, he was content to take the race for renown and the struggle for wealth easily:

[1] Francis Cockburn's opinion of the *Memorials,* and his arrangements for the disposal of his father's papers (he was a trustee), are set down by him in three memoranda dated 15 April and 19 May 1887 and 16 March 1889, and printed in *Some Letters of Lord Cockburn*, pp. 112–25. Francis Cockburn states that he destroyed a packet containing a manuscript of the *Memorials* in Cockburn's hand: this was derived, presumably, from the Red Book, which no longer existed. Passages from the manuscript, which appear to have been rejected by the two trustees who prepared the work for the press, and who were interested in cutting or toning down what might prove objectionable, escaped destruction. A great deal of this material was published by Harry Cockburn in *Some Letters*. Cockburn was given to copying out passages from the Red Book, and alternative versions of the same passage can be found among his published works. The testamentary papers drawn up at the end of his life include a formal declaration, dated 3 April 1852, which recommends that his trustees consult Andrew Rutherfurd and John Richardson about the publication of his manuscripts. Of his 'Volumes of Edinburgh Events' he says: 'If these volumes had been written by another and I had had the editing of them, I could have made a good book out of them.' Rutherfurd died not long after Cockburn, and it is not known whether he or Richardson gave advice. The declaration requires that his letters to and from his wife should be burned unread when both people were dead. A few of those to his wife have survived. In one, written before leaving for Venice, he speaks solemnly of a happy marriage.

not indeed with indifference, but with the measured exertion of a man who found his happiness in simpler things—in pleasant scenes and friendly faces. In what he wished for he succeeded.'

This passage is quoted, and badly mangled, in Harry Cockburn's introduction to his edition of the *Memorials*. Its Latin quotation is from a beautiful passage in Horace's *Epistles* (Book One, Epistle 18):

> *Quid minuat curas, quid te tibi reddat amicum?*
> *Quid pure tranquillet, honos, an dulce lucellum,*
> *An secretum iter et fallentis semita vitae?*

What is it, Horace asks, that lessens cares, that makes you at peace with yourself? What gives you untroubled calm—public office or nice little profits or a hidden passage and the path of an unnoticed life? While Cockburn himself, with his talk of 'a nearly unbroken course' of personal happiness, would probably have accepted Moncreiff's description of his life, that description may have contributed to the cosification of Cockburn which has taken place. He was not as retiring as this suggests, and his *secretum iter* was not without its cares.

In the *Memorials* he is a son of few words, and there are not many words about his parents anywhere else in his works. But those in the *Memorials* concerning his mother are loving and devoted: 'the best woman I have ever known.' She is the first of the long line of remarkable women—for the most part, strong-minded matriarchs and spinsters—who inhabit the book and who belong to his mother's generation. His portraits of these ladies are full of light and sympathy, and in their restricted sphere, his masterful women are the equals of his masterful men. His taste for dames and crones, his liking for a touch of the termagant and the Amazon—though his mother was pious and gentle—could be considered a little mutinous in a society which claimed to abide by the precepts of the misogynous Knox, though, in fact, such sympathies were not uncommon and were shared, indeed, by Henry Dundas. One way of putting the point would be to say that the book reveals a monstrous regiment of women.

Cockburn's mother was devout, but such praise is withheld from his father. His words about his father in the *Memorials* are these: 'My father was a man of strong sense, and with no aversion to a joke, whether theoretical or practical. He was one of the many good fathers, who, from mere want of consideration and method, kept his children at a distance.' Baron Cockburn's domestic rule or regiment was that of someone who was also responsible for keeping order in the country. He was a strict Tory, a catcher of robbers, a reader of the Riot Act, a banisher and brandisher, and a close friend of the ferocious Braxfield. Even though transportation would not have been seen as a very savage punishment during Cockburn's lifetime, and could even be seen as merciful, as an alternative to hanging, and even though, as a judge, he himself transported and was severe with rioters, it is possible that he felt that his *bête noire*, Braxfield the unjust judge and transporter, had a prototype or double in his own strong, sensible father. It is possible that the attack made on Braxfield in the *Memorials* served to express an attitude to his father which embodied, whatever else, a measure of hostility.

It is possible that the sense of decorum which forbade him to enlarge on such feelings in print forbade him to acknowledge them in private, or even to himself in the solitude of the Pentlands. There is a footnote in the *Memorials* which alludes to Boswell's 'Letter to Lord Braxfield'. This pamphlet, he says, 'is a declaration against the vices of the criminal judges; but as Boswell's father, to whom Braxfield succeeded, had been one of them, I doubt if he meant to attack them all.' No one attacks his father, is the thought. But it was well known that Boswell's feelings about his father were such that it was quite conceivable that he might have wished to aim a few vicarious blows at him.

A *Journal* entry for the last day of 1845 has an arresting discussion of his father's treatment of the estate of Caroline Park, where Cockburn seems to have lived with his parents at various times before his marriage:

> *Caroline Park*, where my father's family lived for about thirty-five years, must formerly have been perhaps the finest place of the kind near Edinburgh. It was the only one that, both in its building and its pleasure-grounds, and its hundred-acred park, had an obvious air of stately nobility. My father did it no good. He was agricultural, and sacrificed all he could to the farm. His friend and landlord, the Duke of Buccleuch, did not prevent him from removing several very architectural walls, a beautiful bowling-green, a great deal of good shrubbery, and an outer gravelled court at the north front, bounded by the house on the south, two low ornamented walls on the east and west, and by a tall curiously-wrought iron gate, flanked by two towers, on the north. Even when we went there it stood dark in wood, quiet, and alone. The sea and the sea-rocks were its own.

He points out that 'the abominations of Granton Pier' had not yet arrived (worse abominations were in store), and concludes: 'The very flowers knew their Goshen, and under my mother's care grew as they grew nowhere else.' This passage is quintessential Cockburn, and is charged with feeling. He was profoundly attached to trees and bushes and flowers and verdure, and loathed their destruction. He was architectural, not agricultural. He was no 'improver': at Bonaly he was made perfect, amid his dahlias and roses and beside his bowling-green. What his father did at Caroline Park, therefore, was not trivial for Cockburn. He had damaged a garden, cast a blight. By the same token, what his mother did was virtuous and affecting.

The sentence about the Goshen of her flowers is among the most significant that he ever wrote. Goshen was the place of happiness and light and plenty—not far from the first Eden—where the children of Israel took refuge during the plague of darkness. In other words, it is a paradise, like Bonaly and certain other places, and certain other objects of his contemplation, and in these paradises his mother is assigned a presence. She herself had created one of them, and his wife, also a gardener, was to create another.

It would be difficult to say anything very positive about the relationship between Cockburn and his father simply on the basis of his father's public character and of the few words that are spoken in the *Memorials*. But there is a document in the Melville Castle Muniments held at the Scottish Record Office which distinctly assists the understanding of their relationship, and which gives a valuable insight into the family life of the Cockburns, with its dependence on kinship and political jobbing. The Muniments contain a cluster of hand-written applications, submitted to Henry Dundas in 1796, for the sinecure of Presenter of Signatures, a post which involved attending the Baron of Exchequer (in this case, Cockburn's father) during term-time to help him with signatures. The cares of the world are bound up in this bundle of applications: as do the testimonials of the schoolmasters who applied for the Academy and were rebuffed by Henry Cockburn, they give a sharp sense of old and wholly unsuccessful shifts and endeavours. The demands of large families are invoked, political loyalties are confidently alleged. And one of the applications is from Baron Cockburn on behalf of his son Henry. It was written at Hope Park on 11 November 1796:

My Dear Sir,
I was glad to hear at Melville yesterday that your late attack from your old Enemy was got the better of—it has been a sad threat to you first and last.
Robert Belsches Presenter of Signatures died on Tuesday after ten minutes illness. This office is a sinecure and upon an average of seven years salary of £50 included has amounted to £400 per annum. Your namesake Henry in spite of every remonstrance and some degree of severity on my part, persists in being a limb of the Law. The chance is that my death may set him to the army—for after that, (if not admitted before) he will want the means to prosecute his studys. Could you put his name in the warrant for this office, for any share you choose—so as to enable him to go on.
I should think my son has as good a claim to part of an Exchequer office as Lord Presidents. However, do whatever you please, I have absolute confidence in your friendship for my family. I will submitt with perfect resignation and respect.
My Dear Sir,
Yours ever,
A. Cockburn

Henry Dundas suffered from rheumatism, to which Archibald Cockburn's opening courtesies seem to refer, and the autumn of 1796 was a time of setbacks for the Government. Napoleon was conquering Italy—one of his victories there, Arcola, occurred in the middle of November—and the British Navy was about to quit the Mediterranean. Even Dundas's control of Scotland was said to be failing. When wished a happy new year on 1 January, he responded: 'I hope that this year will be happier than the last, for I scarcely recollect having spent one happy day in the whole of it.'[1] And at the end of the month he collapsed from nervous exhaustion. The Presentership of Signatures would not have been high on his list of priorities.

What is new to the biography of Cockburn (as it exists in the form of memoirs and articles and of his own autobiography) is the application itself and the information that he persisted in his law studies despite his father's disapproval, and that lack of money might possibly have made a soldier of him if his father had died before Cockburn was admitted as an advocate. The talk of remonstrances and severity could quite well have come from a friendly parent. The letter does not lack 'consideration': its purpose, after all, was to secure a means whereby the son could continue with his studies. It is interesting, however, that Archibald Cockburn, who was about to take possession of the noble and substantial estate of Caroline Park, should have supposed that, if he were to die, the family would not be able to maintain his son as a law student. Perhaps there is a latent severity here. One of the applicants for the post remarks that the Lord Advocate had told him that there were many applications, and 'it would be given in a Line that would do credit to his Majesty and his ministers'. Nine years later, Dundas's namesake, then a steady Whig, was made Advocate-Depute. But he did not receive the Presentership of Signatures, and there is no sign that he received even a part of it.

We do not know that Archibald Cockburn was a bad father, or even a severe one. He can hardly have been simply a man who lacked consideration, was callous about gardens, and was an angry authoritarian in public life—though I don't doubt that his jokes (like Braxfield's, and like his own son's) were often of the injurious kind. He can hardly have been simply a frightening man with gout and a stick. At the same time, it is apparent that there were serious differences of outlook and taste between father and son, and the question arises whether Cockburn turned Whig because of an earlier estrangement from his father. His verdict on Jeffrey's opinions might appear to be equally true of his own: 'Nothing beyond his conviction of their soundness is necessary in order to account for his adoption of them.'[2] This

[1] See Matheson's *Life of Henry Dundas*, p. 231.  [2] *Life of Jeffrey*, vol. 1, p. 84.

is what many people wish to believe about their opinions, and the formulation has a pleasing elegance and succinctness. But the possibility that Cockburn's conversion was also, if not a consequence, at least an expression and confirmation of domestic tensions should not be ruled out. To this extent I am sympathetic to, and inclined to appropriate, George Saintsbury's comment on Jeffrey's conversion: 'His father was a great Tory, and, though it would be uncharitable to say that this was the reason why Jeffrey was a great Liberal, the two facts were probably not unconnected in the line of causation.'[1]

His father's death goes unmentioned in Cockburn's writings, but it is registered, I think, in a strain of liberation and aggression, tempered by one of compunction and atonement, which may be observed in his behaviour during the years that followed. Soon afterwards, he took to writing the *Memorials*, in which his father's Scotland is commemorated and his quarrel with that Scotland rehearsed, in which there is an attack on father-substitutes and a celebration of his mother and of mother-substitutes. In the *Edinburgh Review* and in political manœuvre he became very busy, lending his strength to the Whig momentum which was summoning adherents and assemblies in Scotland throughout the decade, and which was to culminate in that insult to the Braxfields and Baron Cockburns of his youth, the Reform Bill. At the same time, by virtue of the exercise of nostalgia represented by the *Memorials*, and in other ways besides, it is evident that as he grew older he grew closer to his father. For one thing, his was a pugnacity which resisted his father's, but which also came to resemble it.

Cockburn was 41 when his father died. This is the period of life when a man will often have to face his father's death, when he may make fresh efforts (Scott started writing novels in his forties) or lose heart, when his children may start to challenge him. He may catch sight of his own death in that of his father. And he may come close to the father he has fought. The recent poetry of Robert Lowell concerns itself with such matters. In 'Left out of Vacation', he makes his daughter say:

> Some fathers may have some consideration,
> but he is so wonderfully eccentric,
> drinking buttermilk and wearing red socks . . .

And in 'Middle Age' he speaks for himself:

[1] Quoted—from Saintsbury's *Essays in English Literature 1780–1860*—by James Greig in his *Francis Jeffrey of the 'Edinburgh Review'* (1948), p. 52.

At forty-five,
what next, what next?
At every corner
I meet my Father,
my age, still alive.

Fathers who lack consideration (as all fathers do) may come to receive it. Perhaps this is among the most important of all filial events. Cockburn's father, at any rate, was still alive to him after his death.

This does not mean that he was reclaimed by his kin, for although he broke with them politically, he did not sever the connection, and he always believed in kinship. He also admired the Dundases, even after he became their opponent, and something more needs to be said here about his dealings with them. The scene at the Middleton inn in the *Memorials*, with 'the aristocracy of Midlothian' at play and his uncle Henry Dundas indulging the youth, was among the first of many festivities in Cockburn's life: these scenes suggest the existence of a merry Scotland which is now barely imaginable. The inn resounds with the pride and joy of a tribe of patricians, and the *Memorials* cast no aspersions on such gatherings of the clan. They cast no aspersions on kinship and its pleasures. He was later to stigmatize Midlothian and Edinburgh, the stronghold of the Dundas interest, as 'preserves of illiberality' in those days. He was to reject his family's politics and prerogatives. His writings were to rear a monument to that rejection. He was to bite the hand that fed him. In the *Memorials*, however, the pleasures of kinship—though he is unhappy about some of its prerogatives—are felt to require no apology.

The *Memorials* make light of the admittedly not very impressive charges of corruption which led to Henry Dundas's impeachment—or Watergate. Dundas informed the Commissioners of Naval Inquiry: 'If I had materials to make up such an account as you require, I could not do it without disclosing delicate and confidential transactions of government, which my duty to the public must have restrained me from revealing.'[1] While noting that the impeachment was to aid the emancipation of Scotland, Cockburn says that Dundas deserved his acquittal.

Kinship is never without its quarrels, and some can be detected in the history of relations between the Cockburns and the Dundases. The divorce between Henry Dundas and Cockburn's aunt seems not to have caused trouble, but Henry's father, the first President Dundas of the Court of Session, wrote to a son at Utrecht in 1735 and referred to 'an intrigue that

---

[1] *Life of Henry Dundas*, p. 345.

3*

it seems hath been carried on for some time betwixt Mr Cockburn of Cockpen and my sister Martha. . . . I suppose it is to be a marriage, and so little
to my taste for many reasons, that I could as soon see her drowned. You may
judge what good blood this will make in our family, but there is no help for
it.'[1] Strong words, exuding a sour strength of mind. And the intriguer was
Henry Cockburn's grandfather. These words are not unlike those used by
Cockburn himself in a letter to his daughter Elizabeth, advising her against
a lengthy engagement to Thomas Cleghorn. This would expose Cockburn
to the longueurs of a protracted flirtation: 'I would rather have two years'
sea-sickness or jaundice than witness it.'[2] Cockburn's words are milder—
by virtue of a lesser provocation—to the extent that sea-sickness is milder
than drowning, and he does not 'feel it to be my duty to try and enforce' his
advice. But it was the advice, he felt, of a man of sense.

The editor of *The Arniston Memoirs*, George Omond, who publishes the
letter from President Dundas, has this to say about a subsequent quarrel:
'Cockburn's separation from the political party among whom he had been
brought up, at a time when party spirit ran high, could not fail to carry
with it a tinge of bitterness towards former friends. And it was no secret
that it was towards Robert Dundas that this feeling was chiefly directed.'[3]
Yet Cockburn writes warmly in the *Memorials* about Robert Dundas—
Henry Dundas's nephew, the Radical-hunting Lord Advocate. He nowhere
mentions any earlier dynastic tensions.

A letter of 1852 exists in manuscript[4] in which J. G. Lockhart, Scott's
biographer and son-in-law, discusses, with characteristic spitefulness, Cockburn's life of Jeffrey, his conversion, and his relations with the Dundases.

Cockburn is a man of great natural parts and eloquent—very—both the humorous
and the pathetic he excells in. I speak of him as barrister—as Judge I never saw him.
But he speaks broad Scotch, both the words and the accent—I think rather affectedly
broad in both—and you see he can't write *English*. In truth, of all Jeffrey's set he was
the least of a literary man—I don't believe he ever wrote in the *Ed. Rev.* except on
Scotch law matters—whence much wonder that he should have been the biographer
of one who but for his literature was really nothing. Cockburn is I believe poor—very
poor—owing to imprudence (for he had great practice) and the £1,000 offered by the
booksellers must have overtempted him. It certainly overpays.

I forgot if I told you that his mother was sister to the Lord Melville and his
father a Baron of Exchequer much esteemed. His Whiggery therefore *was* a great
sacrifice of promotional views in early life; and all considered I think his sketch of
Uncle Melville very adroitly done and in good taste. I believe it is moreover very
nearly *true*. How Scotch the clan feeling that breaks out in the picture! For I doubt
if ever as a grown man he conversed familiarly with his powerful relation. Even with

[1] *The Arniston Memoirs* by George Omond (1887), p. 88.
[2] 9 July 1848: *Some Letters of Lord Cockburn*, p. 62.      [3] *Arniston Memoirs*, p. 216.
[4] To the Rev. Whitwell Elwin, 15 April 1852: NLS MSS.

his own brothers (who were great friends of mine) I don't think he had the slightest habits of social intercourse through all the best years of life. It was indeed a terribly bigotted sphere, that old Edinburgh. What it is now I know not. My own old friends there are now mostly Judges and quite calmed down—or up rather—but very likely the heat is as before *inter juniores.*

Some of Lockhart's facts are wrong, and his perceptive letter should be taken with a grain of salt. Well on in life, Cockburn was still amicably ordering whisky from a wine-merchant brother, John. He also continued to see another brother, Robert, who was also a wine-merchant, and a Yeomanry friend of Scott's. John and Robert started in business together, with Robert then founding a firm of shippers in Oporto, but they later split up: Cockburn's port is still being drunk. Scott notes in his *Journal* that he dined on 24 November 1825 at Robert Cockburn's house together with Henry Dundas's son, the second Lord Melville, and his family. On his way home, Scott fell into a sea of mud on a building-site.

Cockburn was friendly with David and George Dundas, brothers who belonged to another family of Dundases. When the instalments of Lockhart's life of Scott were appearing he complained in a letter to George of Lockhart's 'sacrificing Scott for the pleasure of traducing Scott's best friends' —the Ballantynes, his publishing partners.[1] And to David he wrote soon after his father's death: 'Pray do remember me when you are chancellor. Cherish my old age by offices—overlook my law—and, if possible, be tender even of my whiggism. I shall rat if you desire it. But not otherwise.'[2] The preoccupations, these, of a wayward son. Offices and ratting were sore subjects with Cockburn, and so merited a self-inflicted joke. David Dundas was to become a Liberal politician, and Solicitor-General for England.

With other Dundases, however, he was on a very different footing. In a letter to Richardson of 24 December 1826, he said of the second Lord Melville: 'He and his wife have behaved very ill to me—and ten times worse to Elizabeth.' 'Ten times worse to Elizabeth', Cockburn's wife: this is the language of a man who has not been forgiven, and who may not himself forgive. The letter was in response to one of the 15th from Richardson which had talked of an approach to Melville in the hope of a jury judgeship for Cockburn, despite his 'political delinquencies' and Edinburgh Reviewing (but it could be said that he had only written there on legal subjects). Cockburn drily refers to Melville in his letter as 'the king of Scotland (my worthy cousin)', but he is handsome about him in the *Journal*, where he is reckoned to have become 'as good a Whig as a Tory can be'. As for the jury judgeship, he proposes to 'let this flea stick i' the wa' ', wanting the gown

---

[1] Melville Muniments, Scottish Record Office, 24 August 1839.  [2] Ibid., 26 October 1820.

but thinking it wrong to move in the matter himself. After all, 'I suspect that political opposition is never so offensive as when it proceeds from a relation, who was under claims of hereditary obligation and service'. Whatever the warmth that persisted in, or returned to, his dealings with the Dundases, it is certain that these must always have been problematical for him, and of burning consequence. The letters were exchanged shortly before the time when the rise of the Whigs was to threaten the extinction of the name of Melville, and when Cockburn could reflect that the citizens of Edinburgh were in ecstasies at the prospect. But Melville was the place where his mother came from, and, in a sense, Melville and Cockburn were the one name: autumns had been passed at Arniston. In a sense, he was procuring the extinction of his own flesh and blood. The ecstasies experienced by Cockburn himself at this time can only have been of a complex kind, and must have caused him to think very deeply, in private.

If Baron Cockburn went astray financially, so did his son: Lockhart was right to talk about poverty. And if Baron Cockburn had trouble with his son, Cockburn's sons gave him trouble too. It is necessary to pass now to the last years of his *secretum iter* and to some more of his sacred secrets, whose subject-matter consisted of office, the ratting or rebelliousness of kindred, and insolvency. The *Journal* entry for 14 February 1847 speaks of Scott's old house in Castle Street: ' "Dear 39", as he calls it in one of his letters, when his embarrassments compelled him to leave it'. This is the nearest Cockburn gets to referring in print to financial embarrassments of his own, which were then approaching, and which were to come to a head in the autumn of that year. These embarrassments are the subject of a collection of letters and statements in Cockburn's hand which is now in the National Library.

We have already looked at the letter to Kennedy of 1830 in which he said that he was a beggar, but for his profession. In fact, the bar brought him rich rewards, and he was not the sort of beggar in whom the assassins Burke and Hare had lately taken an interest. But he lived in some style, with a grand town house and a country house where the cultivation of a rural simplicity was perhaps more a matter of appearance than of reality. This double life, a large family, multiple hospitality—the seasonal round of dinners, picnics and 'bowlifications'—and his bibliophilia, could hardly have been cheap. And in 1847 it seemed possible that Bonaly—and, as he considered, his boys—had broken him, and that he might become a beggar, after all. 'I have been too happy,' he had written in the *Memorials* with reference to the year of his marriage, 'and often tremble in the anticipation that the cloud must come at last.' That cloud now filled the sky.

On 12 November, 'with great pain', he dismissed his agent, John Russell. He proposed, and Russell accepted, that they should nevertheless remain friends. Cockburn had taken offence at the conduct of Russell's son— perhaps in relation to business debts contracted by Cockburn's son Archibald (another son, Henry, had fallen into similar difficulties). The next day, Cockburn drew up a statement addressed to John Lindsay, a Writer to the Signet, who appears to have helped him previously when his son Laurence was in financial trouble, and who now became his agent, in Russell's place. The statement makes it clear that if a sister died before Cockburn and his brother John, Cockburn stood to receive between £2,000 and £3,000 from his father's estate: but he had already borrowed £2,000 of that money. It is accompanied by a letter which makes it clear that the man who had been happy was now no longer so. The letter speaks of 'this, at present, very unhappy family', and the statement provides the reasons for their unhappiness:

> About 36 years ago, I married, *like a wise man*, on about £250 a year. From that day till this, the growth of, and attempts to output, an enormous family, combined with the too common want of fear about futurity, has, without much positive profligacy, kept me always from making money, except by keeping up two policies of Insurance. I never had a debt, however, till within these few years; since when they have grown, and are still growing, *alarmingly*. The result is that I must now set my house in order.

'*Two things*,' he says, '*are certain—viz.*':

> 1. That there cannot be another shilling of debt.
> 2. That I can be plucked by sons no more.
>    I should like to be protected against all future plucks by some sort of a real or a quasi trust, which, without appearing, might act as a Breakwater.

The statement, which also explains that 'Bonaly, being burdened with a feu duty of about £100, I suppose is worth nothing', might remind one of the picture presented in the political squib which was aimed at the Pantheon meeting: it seems that Cockburn's imps had spurred their immortal father round the room.

Cockburn's attempt to set his house in order did not earn him a quick release from adversity. In the course of the years that followed, he was frighteningly ill—this was in 1850—and his wife was ill too, and her recovery incomplete. He tells George Dundas in 1851: 'I cannot see her, mercifully and hopefully tho' she has been dealt with, without trembling, and feeling the presence of a sad and permanent charge, were it but in diminished security.'[1] He has not lost his resilience. The letter adds: 'Set it down in

[1] Ibid., 7 November.

your convivial ledger that a festival stands in mine to your credit.' Nevertheless, the ledger of his finances still made disagreeable reading. His testament of 17 October 1852, written at Bonaly and part of the collection of testamentary papers, is very bleak. This document was 'to be given to my family, or Trustees, immediately after my death'. Those who read it then must have felt that a determined hand was being placed upon their shoulder. Its main content is this:

> My scheme for the maintenance of whoever I may leave *dependant on me* has always been that my two Insurances will be worth from £18,000 to £25,000, according to the time I may live. And so they will; and, *if left free*, this would have been ample.
>
> But my sons (except George) compelled me to contract about £12,000 of debt for their accommodation; and this at so late a period of my life that my regaining this money by saving, especially in the position of a Judge, bound to maintain a decent appearance, was impossible. In putting myself under trust, and on one half of my salary, and leaving the other half to pay Premiums and Interest, and to save the residue, I was advised by judicious friends that I had done all that was in my power. Had Mrs Cockburn continued in health I should certainly have tried to save some more by giving up Bonaly; tho' the wisdom of this would have been doubtful; because such a step would probably, after our 40 years' habits, have abridged both Mrs Cockburn's life and mine, and my best pecuniary chance is to live on and let the insurances grow. But her bad health, which absolutely requires the continuance of her old garden enjoyments, makes the scheme now impossible.
>
> My general idea has been that my Equitable Policy would pay my debt of about £15,000; and that my Scottish Widows policy, Bonaly, books etc might produce about £10,000. This is little; but if I was certain that it could be realised, I would be satisfied. But the value of the Equitable policy is very uncertain, and whatever less than £15,000 it shall be at my death, my reversion will be the smaller.
>
> *Were it not for my reliance that my sons will do their duty to their mother and unmarried sisters*, I should have very painful anticipations. But I do rely upon them, and *I beg my trustees to let them know this fact*. It is to these sons (except George, who was put out to India by a legacy from his uncle Lord Hermand) that the rest of the family has been sacrificed. And, *provided they do their duty*, the sacrifice is no tgrudged.

Cockburn says that he would like to be buried in the Dean Cemetery in the New Town, where Jeffrey lies, among other friends, such as his Pantheon confederate and the companion of his circuit journeys, Lord Moncreiff, and where Mrs Rutherfurd was to be buried the following day:

> It is my earnest request, and *indeed my positive order,* that there be no absurd and contemptible wastry at my funeral. *I forbid above £30 being laid out upon it.* There ought not to be above twelve people there. I at present can only name 9 relations who should be invited if the ceremony was to be now, to which may be added 3 or 4 friends. I would rather live for ever than have a heartless ceremonial, with Lords of Session and other show figures.
>
> I write all this in perfect apparent health; and with little reason for doing it now, except two things. Tomorrow is Mrs Rutherfurd's burial day; and this is so calm, so bright and so thoughtful a Sunday that the two together dispose one to reflect on time past, and on time to come.

May God bless the family to whom this is addressed. May they continue to live in mutual love. My confidence in the affection of my sons and brother, my sons-in-law, nephews and neaces, and other near relations, and in the advice that will ever be given to them by such old friends as Richardson, Rutherfurd, Murray, and others, is my hope and my consolation.

Strong words once more, judicial words, like those of some of his male kindred of an earlier generation—though they may inspire the thought that Baron Cockburn would not have allowed himself to be the victim of his sons. They are also moving words.

Cockburn did not go bankrupt, though there was to be a rumour to that effect. But these debts were a sore affliction for a Scots judge with a respectable appearance to maintain: the Edinburgh virtues certainly included solvency, however often men of sense went bankrupt. He was obliged to disclose his situation to friends in high places, and to enlist their help. And most of his friends were so placed: most of them were bigwigs and high Whigs. Baron Cockburn had to sell Cockpen: his son had to sell his town house in Charlotte Square in 1848 and move to Manor Place, and after his death Bonaly was sold too, along with his library.

'Most filial events make the question recur to me, Why any man of sense generates sons?' This is what he told Rutherfurd in 1839, after a newspaper report of Laurence's shipwreck had been found, in the course of the day, to be false. Just how grave a remark this was, how much it may have in it of the irony of relief, is impossible to fathom, but it does suggest that his worries concerning his sons were of fairly long standing, and there were worries concerning his daughters too. One, Margaret, died in childhood, and another, Jane, was a lifelong, though long-living invalid. In 1836, his boy Frank (Francis Jeffrey) was experimenting with gunpowder and pouring it down a horn into the kitchen furnace when his hand slipped and there was an explosion which blew off his right forearm. According to his grandson Claud Cockburn, he had received from his kin, within a week, eleven writing-desks—which were meant to encourage him to learn to write with his left hand. Frank, who was to decide that the *Memorials* had had its day, became a judge in India and a bizarrely punctilious Christian: he successfully advised the Indian Civil Service not to employ a son of his—Claud's father—who had lost his faith.[1]

Studying this bitter end to a joyful and joy-giving life, there may be those who will think that the irresponsibilities of Cockburn's sons—if that is what they were—were a nicely proportioned vengeance on his rebellious

---

[1] *I, Claud* by Claud Cockburn, the conflation of three earlier books of memoirs (Penguin edition, 1967), pp. 19–23.

youth. And they may find some further lines of Robert Lowell's, from his poem 'The Hard Way', appropriate to the case:

> Don't hate your parents, or your children will hire
> unknown men to bury you at your own cost.

Cockburn's story can no doubt be adjusted, more or less forcibly, to fit the surmises and superstitions, the sweet dreams of punishment and retribution, of a puritan society. But he himself was not superstitious, and despite his disaster his spirit soared above surmises of that kind, so far, at any rate, as one can detect from the letters to friends that are still there to be read.

Cockburn's was a temperament which persisted and persevered: his father's letter to Henry Dundas furnishes some early evidence of that. 'With temporary, exhausting diseases, Pluck is Life', said this man who was to be plucked by sons, and whose pluck was the better part of his pugnacity.[1] In 1853, he wrote to Leonard Horner's wife about the judge Lord Fullerton, a relative of his (whose death was shortly to disclose to the important people of the city another example of the financial imprudence in their midst): 'Poor old Edinburgh! Fullerton's official retirement is another sad blow to us of the past days. But why speak—or think—of the irrevocabilities of fate! Let those who are spared love, and live, the more.'[2] Cockburn died at Bonaly on 26 April 1854—and was buried in the Dean Cemetery. Three years before, in June 1851, he had written to the same woman: 'I have had a very happy life.'

Such claims are untestable. They matter to the biography of this man chiefly because he seems so strongly to have wished to make them. And yet there is a kind of confirmation of this particular claim to be found in something said about the 73-year-old Cockburn by his servant, Philip Brodie. When Leonard Horner visited 'the Baron of Bonaly and his domain', he was told by Brodie, who farmed the domain ('souple' is Scots for 'supple'): 'My Lord is as souple as an eel.'[3]

---

[1] In a letter of 30 June 1836 to an ailing Macvey Napier: British Museum MSS. Napier succeeded Jeffrey as editor of the *Edinburgh Review*.

[2] 19 November.

[3] *Memoir of Leonard Horner* by his daughter Katharine Lyell (2 vols, 1890), vol. I, p. 224, vol. II, p. 204. These quotations come from two letters from Horner to a daughter, dated 21 March 1826 and 30 September 1852.

# Chapter Four

# *Cockburn's Friends*

Harry Cockburn, as he was often called, believed in kinship, and he believed, even more, in friendship, of which he made something of a cult. He took hold of his friendships with what might seem to be the tenacity of a man who, having once broken with his kin, was twice shy of any further ruptures. His life was a tissue of conversations and expeditions, hilarious suppers and 'God-like bouzes'.[1] There were two sorts of flowing bowl at Bonaly: they bowled like devils on the green, and they drank like the Lords of Session they frequently were. How could they be so cheerful, and yet so eminent and dutiful, in such a cold and windy place, contending, as they did, with a gathering severity and with the odium of party, conscious, as they were, of the grim lives that lay beyond their charmed circle? Well, they succeeded. In Cockburn's reminiscences and letters, Edinburgh is bathed in a Mediterranean, an Attic light. It is an intellectual city, and a convivial one, where memorable and dramatic and amusing things never cease to happen. 'The day was glorious, and we sauntered in the twilight of a mild, milky evening, amid a glorious profusion of breathing roses of every description.'[2] A twice-glorious occasion, one might say. There were many such occasions at Bonaly. On 24 August 1839, he writes to George Dundas:

> I have had as yet, in spite of some ill-timed rain, a most delicious vacation; entirely at Bonaly, with some bowling, but not much, a few easy parties, one magnificent Habbies How, a little reading, prodigious reflection, endless lounging, good appetite, insatiable sleep, and a conscience of which I only know the existance because I am told that nobody can be without one, and by my modesty being often put to the blush by the conscious justice of its applauses. Rutherfurd is expected in a day or two. Ditto Richardson. Macaulay is in Edinburgh, with the hooping cough—an intervention of Providence to gag a Whig orator.[3]

[1] Cockburn's phrase, from a letter to Sir Thomas Dick Lauder of 15 February 1822: *Some Letters of Lord Cockburn*, p. 20.
[2] To Macvey Napier, 11 July 1836: British Museum MSS.     [3] Melville Muniments.

Many of these people had legal and political responsibilities, which could have the effect of turning their friendships into affairs of state. They met at a succession of festivals and ceremonies, at soirées in town and on country walks. They were poetical as well as political. Nearly all of them had their rural 'paradises': Henry Dundas's Dunira in Perthshire was his 'Paradise of the North'.[1] This was a word which could merely mean 'country house': it belonged to the pastoral vocabulary of the time, which presented the vacational upper-class male as a shepherd or swain. Scott and Cockburn's admired Lord Hermand joked about Lord Meadowbank's waterfall, but a feeling for such objects was common enough. Cockburn's use of pastoral properties, however, cannot be dismissed as mere convention: it was persistent and fervent, an organic part of his inner life.

They also met in dining-clubs and debating societies. Jeffrey said in 1803 of the very important Friday Club, founded in that year: 'It promises to unite the literature of the place more effectually and extensively than anything else.'[2] It continued to do so for almost forty years, during which time the science of the place was still, for many purposes, synonymous with the literature of the place. The Bonaly Friday Club was a playful version of this which was largely confined to Cockburn's own family. Its annals are set out in a luxurious little book which claims that its origins were ancient but that its records were destroyed in a fire which broke out in the High Street in 1824. His son Archibald is commended for reviving the club at Bonaly thereafter.[3]

Another feature of Cockburn's social life was his annual breakfasts at Habbie's Howe, a spot on the south-eastern side of the Pentlands associated with Allan Ramsay's pastoral poem, *The Gentle Shepherd*. Every year he took a company of people there for a picnic, and in August 1833 he wrote to his daughter Jane, who was in London consulting a doctor, about the latest of these occasions.[4] There was a party of twenty-three, including his friend Sir Thomas Dick Lauder and an excellent Findhorn friend of Lauder's, a Mr Smith. The handsome procession of gigs and carriage pressed on past Woodhouselee and flared up the peaceful glen. Archibald Davidson, his nephew, arrives on foot, and so does that tireless walker, James Pillans, once the tutor of Kennedy of Dunure and a Rector of the High School, and then a College professor at Edinburgh. A fire is lit, and their 'hermit fare' is devoured: cold veal pie, hot broiled salmon, tea, coffee,

---

[1] *Life of Henry Dundas*, p. 96.   [2] *Life of Jeffrey*, vol. I, p. 147.

[3] The annals of the Bonaly Friday Club were privately printed in 1842. In the *Book of the Old Edinburgh Club*, III (1910), pp. 105–25, Harry Cockburn presents memorials by his grandfather, kept up over the years, of the progress of the other, the parent Friday Club.

[4] *Some Letters of Lord Cockburn*, pp. 34, 35.

chocolate, drams of whisky, and much else. Someone is very nearly tumbled into the burn. Meanwhile the host sits on a stone apart, despising the gluttons: 'My soul was with the Gentle Shepherd.' *Et in Arcadia Cockburn:* the glen is felt to be pastoral and Classical. But this is also a Romantic occasion, with its half-in-earnest contemplative. The party then returned to Bonaly, where they 'fell to bowls', and to a 'riotous dinner', and to bowls again. Pillans rose next morning at five, walked, then fetched Cockburn and a visiting Englishman to climb the summit of Capelaw, from which they looked out on a 'glorious scene'.

Cockburn had a very wide acquaintance in Scotland, but it is worth listing some of his closer friends, together with his family and his relations by marriage. To do so is to call the roll of the élite which succeeded the old patriciate at the head of the Whig Party. His own rank was that of someone suspended below the level of the high aristocracy and above that of the professional middle class, of someone who belonged to the gentry and to the foremost political dynasty in the land. Some of his friends were from long-established landed families. Several were law lords. The lower orders were sparsely represented, even at a generation's remove.

First, his own family. There were six sons—in order of birth, Archibald, James, George (who escapes the reproofs contained in his testament), Henry, Laurence and Francis Jeffrey—and five daughters: Margaret, Jane, Graham (a female name employed in his wife's family), Elizabeth ('Wifie') and Johanna. Two of his wife's sisters were married to Lords of Session— Thomas Maitland, eventually Lord Dundrennan, and Lord Fullerton—so that there were three brothers-in-law on the bench at the same time. Mrs Cockburn's aunt was married to the judge Lord Hermand, and that worthy, who drank on principle and on a grand scale, and who sucked in the being and attributes of God at his mother's breast and felt his law in his own— '*Here,* my Laards!'—was a much-loved elder in Cockburn's circle in its earlier days. The *Memorials* cherish his idiosyncrasies wonderfully:

Neither the disclosure of the long neck by the narrow bit of muslin stock, nor the outbreak of the linen between the upper and nether garments, nor the short coat sleeves, with the consequent length of bare wrist, could hide his being one of the aristocracy. And if they had, the thin and powdered grey hair, flowing down into a long thin gentleman-like pig-tail, would have attested it. His morning raiment in the country was delightful. The articles, rough and strange, would of themselves have attracted notice in a museum. But set upon George Fergusson, at his paradise of Hermand, during vacation, on going forth for a long day's work—often manual—at his farm, with his grey felt hat and tall weeding hoe—what could be more agrestic and picturesque.[1]

[1] *M*, pp. 131, 132.

Hermand's paradise was situated in what may be thought to be the particularly blank and unappealing environs of West Calder.

Two early friends were John Gordon, a doctor, and Charles Anderson, a minister and, it would seem, a moper, to whom Cockburn delivered lectures on marriage—those of someone who had discovered that to be married was to be double the man you were before. Gordon was a man of promise who died *in flore primo*: *Quantum legit! Quantum etiam scripsit!*—the *Memorials* resort to Pliny in his praise. Andrew Rutherfurd was no less virtuous. 'Saint Andrew' was a lawyer of sterling gifts, a Lord Advocate, and the man responsible for the Entail Act, by which entails were ended and Scotland's feudal heritage further diminished. Cockburn was also friendly with his wife Sophia: he tended to be equally friendly with his friends' wives, and zestfully corresponded with them. Many of those he knew well had, of course, to do with the law, such as Thomas Thomson, the legal historian, whose last years were also clouded by money troubles, the codifier of such troubles, George Joseph Bell, Sir James Mackintosh, the penal reformer, historian and opium-eater, the judge Lord Ivory, and another judge, the metaphysical Lord Meadowbank, with his waterfall, whom Cockburn relished rather than admired and whom he numbered among the shows of the earlier bench. The neurologist Sir Charles Bell, for whom, says Cockburn, his brother George Joseph was a 'dearer self', made a welcome return to Edinburgh after winning fame in London. Then there was the Evangelical minister Sir Harry Moncreiff, and his son Lord Moncreiff ('Creeffy'), a judge. Francis Horner and his brother Leonard, a merchant and philanthropist. In Cockburn's circle, literature's sentences and those of the law could often be uttered in the same breath: but the *immisericors mens* of criticism and of the bench co-existed with the high humanitarianism of the Horners and others. As Cockburn saw it, Francis was a man without family or fortune whose merits were such that the House of Commons, irrespective of party, united to mourn his death.

The prominent Whig politicians whom he knew well included Kennedy of Dunure, Sir John Murray, James Abercromby (Sydney Smith's 'Abercrusty', who became a Speaker of the House of Commons and Lord Dunfermline), and Sir James Gibson-Craig, a tall and imperious party boss, who went about in riding-boots. Then there was James Pillans, Sheriffs Cleghorn and Davidson, and Eliza Fletcher. Other early friends included Sydney Smith, the novelist Henry Mackenzie, author of *The Man of Feeling*, and the various Miss Hills of Woodhall, out towards the Pentlands. Octavius Hill was, I think, no relation to these women, but was as well named: his engravings for an edition of the works of Hogg have all of the period's fondness for heights and waterfalls. James Ballantine began as a house-painter and became a poet, artist and self-professed 'gaberlunzie' or pastoral vagrant. His calotype—a proud profile fit for some coin—depicts him as very much the bays-wearing Roman who is also a Romantic bard. Another artist is depicted elsewhere in the calotypes as the Gaberlunzie in *The Antiquary*. Fancy dress was among the entertainments of these thousand and one Midlothian nights: but their true theatre, in the case of most of the adults, was the theatre royal, the serious charades, of the Court of Session and the Venerable, and indeed of the House of Commons. Oratory was certainly among their dearest arts. Ballantine worked in stained glass, reviving the technique, and designed windows for the new House of Lords. The mathe-matician John Playfair was a friend of Cockburn's youth, and his nephew, the architect William Playfair, had a hand in the building of Bonaly. He also designed the thrillingly sombre edifice of St Stephen's Church in the New Town, whose cavernous entrance smacks as much of pharaohs as it does of pharisees or elders. Such was Cockburn's circle—together with the Edin-burgh Reviewer John Allen, lost to London, George and David Dundas, and four other men who were, with Rutherfurd, his chief intimates.

The being and attributes of Francis Jeffrey are not, perhaps, very well known: but his failings are notorious. He can seem very pleased with himself, and he has traditionally been condemned as a dour spokesman for the lite-rary taste of the Northern bourgeoisie who missed the point of the Lake poets: but this, I would say, is to miss the point of Jeffrey. While his achieve-ments were substantial—in the line of bringing fluent and expansive argument to the consideration of literature and politics—Cockburn overstates these achievements in his biography. In print, the wish to make his friend seem virtuous can succeed in making him seem stiff and statuesque: Craig-crook, his house at Corstorphine to the west of the city, is saluted in the *Journal* as 'morally the Paradise of Edinburgh villas'. In fact, he was gay and mercurial and rather French (Scotch wit, as practised by both, can look very like a form of *esprit*). And these qualities, neglected in Cockburn's public testimonies, are captured in the letters that refer to his friend. For the corresponding Cockburn, Jeffrey is like a lovely little bird, full of flight and song. This little bird was sufficiently highly strung, however, to fill his own letters with bulletins about the state of his throat. In a letter of 1837, 'the Elf of Craigcrook' is said by the Gnome of Bonaly to be 'delightfully well. No owl more wise; no lark more aerial.' Cockburn's own finest epistolary flights tend to be on the soaring subject of this friend. Rutherfurd is told that Macaulay is 'like a heavy strong Flanders draught-horse, beside the light fiery Arabianism of Jeffrey'. Cockburn had his doubts on the subject of

Macaulay's prose: his 'brilliancy'—it seems that draught-horses can sometimes be brilliant—was 'the worst thing about him'.[1]

Byron's 'English Bards and Scotch Reviewers' is rude about Jeffrey, whom
a postscript to the second edition calls 'the great literary anthropophagus' of
the North, and about his contributors: 'A turn for punning, call it Attic
salt.' It sneers at 'paltry Pillans'—so much for a virtuous pedestrian—and at
a certain Scotch bard, 'sepulchral Grahame': 'And godly Grahame chant a
stupid stave.' We have seen how this sneer was used to beat a Pittite.

James Grahame was born in 1765 and died at 46. 'Tall, solemn, large-
featured, and very dark, he was not unlike one of the independent preachers
of the Commonwealth,' says the *Life of Jeffrey*.[2] After trying the bar and,
like Alexander Hume, sickening of it, he became an Anglican priest. Cockburn threatens that he and Richardson will come to him at Bath, when he is
in his pulpit, 'like thieves in the night. You are not to know of our approach
till you descry us in a remote pew quizzing you, when you are demonstrating
the propriety of supporting a rich church establishment and praying the
Lord to save the land from the abominations of Presbyterianism.'[3] Grahame
was a Scottish patriot, and his Whig principles were those of a soft heart
which ached for birds, beasts, the countryside and the poor, and which
loathed the slave trade and the sportsman's murderous tube. *The Sabbath*
is an example of the humanitarian vein found in later eighteenth-century
poetry: a set of carefully worked meditations which offer an idealized picture
of country life—Crabbe might never have written—and which are not at all
remote from the Augustan norms and from Thomson's *Seasons*. In this
poem, Sabbath Grahame, as he was called, hopes 'that Heaven may be one
Sabbath without end.'[4] Cockburn's vacations were an attempt to reach an
everlasting sabbath by way of Bonaly, but his was much less godly and
sepulchral than the one laid up in Heaven for Grahame.

*The Sabbath* proved very popular, and later works included *British
Georgics*, from which Cockburn and Richardson obtained a prescription,
which was then executed, for smoking out a beehive for the honey, and *The
Birds of Scotland*, in which Grahame claims 'the title of the poor man's bard'.[5]
Cockburn suggested to the poor man's bard an autumnal theme: the annual
examination of a country school before it breaks up for the harvest, with the
minister asking questions, and the laird too, if he has the sense to join in,

---

[1] The letter of 1837 (15 March) is to James Rutherfurd, Major RE, Andrew's young brother.
The description of Macaulay is from a letter to Andrew of 31 May 1839, and the reference to his
'brilliancy' is from a letter to Napier of 9 October 1844 (British Museum MSS).
[2] *Life of Jeffrey*, vol. I, p. 111.     [3] To Grahame, 18 September 1809.
[4] *The Sabbath* (third edition, 1805), p. 14, line 50.
[5] *The Birds of Scotland, with Other Poems* (1806), Part First, p. 26.

and with ABCs, pasted on boards, as prizes. After that, the school is to make its way, led by their teacher and by a bagpipe and fiddle, to the curds and cream-grozzets of a *fête champêtre*[1] .... When winter came Edinburgh skated, not least the literati, but Grahame does not forget those who could not afford to glide across Duddingston Loch:

> Now to the icy plain the city swarms.
> In giddy circles, whirling variously,
> The skater fleetly thrids the mazy throng,
> While smaller wights the sliding pastime ply.
> Unhappy he, of poverty the child!
> Who, barefoot, standing, eyes his merry mates,
> And, shivering, weeps, not for the biting cold,
> But that he cannot join the slippery sport.[2]

The preface to the third edition of *The Sabbath* (1805) indicates that he was not as green as these cabbage-looking lines, or as old-fashioned as his diction. It reads:

He who has seen threescore and ten years, has lived *ten years of Sabbaths*. The appropriation of so considerable a portion of human life to religious duties, to domestic enjoyment, and to meditative leisure, is a most merciful branch of the divine dispensation. It is the grand bulwark of *poverty* against the encroachments of *capital*. The labouring classes *sell* their time. The rich are the buyers, at least they are the *chief* buyers; for it is obvious, that more than the half of the waking hours of those who earn their bread by the sweat of their brow, is consumed in the manufacture of articles, that cannot be deemed either necessaries or comforts. Six days of the week are thus *disposed of* already. If Sunday were in the market, it would find purchasers too. The abolition of the Sabbath would, in truth, be equivalent to a sentence, adjudging to the rich the services of the poor *for life*.

The preface has insights to which Jeffrey did not attain. The Elf of Craigcrook did not dream of a socialist sabbath. Like Cockburn, who was prescient about pollution, communications and leisure, Grahame seems to have had the ability to reach towards the outlook and vocabulary of a time to come.

Sir Thomas Dick Lauder (1784–1848) was as playful and convivial as Cockburn, and had a touch of Jeffrey's aerial nature. This Scottish bird made its nest at Relugas in Morayshire, which Cockburn numbered among his Edens. Cockburn first went there, with John Gordon, some time before

[1] To Grahame, 18 September 1809. This letter shows a sparkling responsiveness to Grahame and his subject-matter. Cockburn tells him that his *Georgics* are being taken as complimentary to the Royal Family.
[2] From 'February': *The Birds of Scotland*, p. 128.

1818. They were met by Dick Lauder at the Bridge of Carr. 'After an alarming breakfast—alarming both from its magnitude and its mirth, we rolled along in two gigs, on a splendid autumnal day, till we annihilated the twenty-two miles between us and Eden.'[1] The paradise of Relugas was to suffer a deluge, chronicled in Dick Lauder's book, *The Great Floods of August, 1829, in the Province of Moray and Adjoining Districts*, which is dedicated to Cockburn.[2] The Biblical analogy was not missed. A minister remarked to the author: 'Before these floods was the Garden of Eden, and behind them a desolate wilderness.' An ancient prophecy concerning two local rivers was repeated at dinner by a woman in Moy just before these rivers surged through the village:

> Says Divie to Dorback whar shall we sweep,
> Through the middle o' Moy when a' men sleep.

No one in Cockburn's circle could write poetry like that.

Relugas, having survived its Flood, was given up in 1831, and Dick Lauder moved to the house of Grange in Edinburgh: it is as if he came to town to help sustain the Whig *dominium*. Elizabeth Grant of Rothiemurchus offers a graphic description of the pleasures of Relugas:

It had been a common small Scotch house, but an Italian front had been thrown before the old building, an Italian tower had been raised above the offices, and with neatly kept grounds it was about the prettiest place ever lived in. The situation was beautiful, on a high tongue of land between the Divie and the Findhorn—the wild, leaping, rocky-bedded Divie and the broader and rapid Findhorn. All along the banks of both were well-directed paths among the wooding, a group of children flitting about the heathery braes, and the heartiest, merriest welcome within. Mr and Mrs Lauder were little more than children themselves, in manner at least; really young in years and gifted with almost bewildering animal spirits, they did keep up a racket at Relugas! It was one eternal carnival: up late, a plentiful Scotch breakfast, out all day, a dinner of many courses, mumming all the evening, and a supper at the end to please the old lady. A Colonel Somebody had a story—ages after this, however—that having received an appointment to India, he went to take leave of his kind friends at Relugas. It was in the evening, and instead of finding a quiet party at tea, he got into a crowd of popes, cardinals, jugglers, gipsies, minstrels, flower-girls, etc, the usual amusements of the family. He spent half a lifetime in the East, and returning to his native place thought he would not pass that same hospitable door. He felt as in a dream, or as if his years of military service had been a dream—there was all the crowd of mountebanks again! The only difference was in the actors; children had grown up to take the places of the elders, some children, for all the elders were not gone. Sir Thomas Dick Lauder wore as full a turban, made as much noise, and was just as thin as the Tom Lauder of twenty years before.[3]

[1] *Circuit Journeys*, p. 13.    [2] Third edition (Elgin, 1873), pp. 57, 83.
[3] *Memoirs of a Highland Lady*, edited by Lady Strachey (1928 edition), pp. 105, 106.

In Edinburgh, turbanned Tom Lauder, a scion of the Fountainhall family, was a canvasser for the Whigs, and on 25 August 1835 Cockburn wrote in his *Journal*:

> He is the greatest favourite with the mob that the Whigs have. The very sight of his blue carriage makes their soles itch to become the horses. He is one of the persons whose Whiggism is so liberal that it enables him to keep the Radicals in some order. The chief part of his influence, indeed, is owing to his being very much one of themselves; but besides there is something even in the outward air of this representative of old Fountainhall very captivating to any populace. A flow of rambling natural talk; ready jokes; the twinkle of a mild laughing eye; a profusion of grey grizzly hair tossed over head, face, and throat; a bludgeon ludicrously huge for civil life, especially in his powerful though gentle hand; raiment half fashionable, half agrestic; a tall, gentleman-like, Quixotic figure; and a general picturesqueness of appearance.

Like Cockburn himself, he was a type of the Augustan virtuoso, and could have made his way as a fiddler, a ballad-singer, a geologist, an engineer, an artist or a landscape gardener. He wrote historical novels—such as *The Wolf of Badenoch*. He cared about suffering, as Sabbath Grahame did, and he was admired for that, and for his sense of humour and of the picturesque, as well as for his blue carriage. He was ill for his last 18 months, but his song was not extinguished: he gave himself to articles in praise of Scottish rivers, and Jeffrey called to take lessons in the art of holy dying.

When Cockburn and his contemporaries were young, long before they were Lords of Session or anthropophagous British critics, lowly suppers were held at which Jeffrey was present, and Grahame, with his Jacobite ballads, and John Richardson, who played the flute. Richardson—a small man, like Cockburn and Jeffrey—was born in 1780 on his family's acres at Gilmerton, a mining village near Edinburgh. He was soon to lose both his parents. In an appreciation which appeared in the *North British Review* of November 1864, and which was written by the same Lord Moncreiff who wrote about the *Memorials* in the *Edinburgh Review*, he is credited with 'the impressible temperament of an orphan lad': his mother's plaintive songs sounded in his head for the rest of his life. For all his reveries and fancies, however, for all his worship of the ideal, he was led to the practical, and did not flinch: he became a successful solicitor. In this respect, he was like Cockburn and others of the set: practical dreamers and languishing landed orphans, men of standing with the capacity to feel sorry for Scotland's ragamuffins in their hovels and vennels, for those whose homelessness was less symbolic than their own. Moncreiff found it a pleasure to work with him: 'The hard dry thing was to be done, and done it was.' Scott felt that his friend Richardson was right to keep his taste for writing verse in check (he was roused by the example of Burns, but did not resemble him) and concentrate on his conveyances.

Richardson owned a Whig pedigree of purest ray serene. Moncreiff quotes from his annotations on the subject, which were committed to the flyleaf of a family Bible. A Covenanter by the name of Roland Richardson, also a Gilmerton feuar, married Euphane or Effie Elphinstone, and in 1679, after he had taken up arms for the Covenant, Effie and their infant child went in search of him. Claverhouse's men are said to have caught these searchers, and to have set them up as a target: her son was to be fired at till he was wounded—no doubt in order to extract information. The son, however, survived. At the time of Bothwell Bridge, a quarrel broke out between Roland and Balfour of Burley (John Richardson supplied Scott with material for *Old Mortality*), and a jeering rhyme had been handed down:

> Rin, Burley, rin,
> Or Roland Richardson
> Will flype your skin.

Moncreiff observes of John's Whiggery: 'Roland Richardson would not have gone more cheerfully to the question before Lauderdale, than would his descendant have suffered martyrdom for his belief in Fox.' John Richardson was also related to the historian Robertson and to Henry Brougham, and Brougham's younger brother Peter was a college friend. In relation to his accomplished brother, Peter gloomily cast himself in the role of changeling, and he was killed before long in a duel. Richardson and Cockburn were changelings of a kind, too: successful changelings, who survived.

Cockburn and Richardson were like the kind of brothers who do not disturb each other's peace of mind, and their lifelong friendship was never darkened by a single shadow. Cockburn's firm footstep up Ben Ledi in the early days was to run in Richardson's mind, with his mother's songs, and a child was christened Henry Cockburn Richardson. Under the stimulus of the French Revolution, Richardson's Whiggification seems to have proceeded along similar lines to Cockburn's, except that he was drawn, more than his friend was, to Continental thinkers. He paid a visit to Germany: playing his flute in the Hartz Mountains, he was transported in spirit to the Pentlands. Moncreiff also quotes from an autobiographical memorandum in which he makes it clear that his first political sentiments were quite fierce and flyping: 'From the time I was 17 I supposed myself a decided democrat and philanthropist of the new school. I read Condorcet, Volney, Southey, and Hugh Trevor, and occasionally associated with Irishmen under the ban of the law. I wrote some democratic songs (sad trash).' This did not stop him from becoming a Volunteer in London, where his musket was to singe Grahame's jacket. Grahame, it appears, was willing to turn a murderous tube on the enemies of his country.

In 1806, Richardson was seen off sorrowfully at Leith, by Cockburn, Jeffrey and Grahame, on the boat to London. Another interesting man had gone south. 'A Provincial should not talk' of some matter to 'one of the Wen': this was Cockburn thirty years later, to Macvey Napier,[1] who took Jeffrey's place as editor of the *Edinburgh Review* and was then in the South. Cockburn is making a joke on what had turned into a sore subject: it was now apparent that the emancipation of Scotland could coincide with its becoming, through the loss of its Richardsons, in some ways provincial. As we have seen, Cockburn could even joke deprecatingly about his Pentland Hills, looked at by Queen Victoria, though he also refused to quit them, one fine summer, to wait upon her at Dalkeith. In time, the *Edinburgh Review* itself became somewhat Anglicised, was bought by Longmans, and eventually, after Napier's death, was edited in London.

Richardson set himself to corner the lion's share of the Scots law work in London, and this, after the conventional long travail of the ambitious Scotsman, he did. A firm of Parliamentary solicitors and draftsmen was founded, which acted as Crown Agent for Scotland, and he specialized in peerage business. He went to live in Hampstead, and spent his leisure with writers such as the poets Thomas Campbell, Joanna Baillie and Crabbe. He was married to a cousin of Campbell's—who may have been one of the Miss Hills of Woodhall—in the year that Cockburn, too, got married. On 29 March 1811, Cockburn sprang one of his epistolary tricks or tropes on Grahame: 'You have heard, no doubt, of Richardson's intention to avail himself of my divorce and to marry again. Betsey is very well, an excellent girl, tapering away like the new-bursting poplar.'

Walter Scott recommended to Richardson an estate in Roxburghshire, where he later pursued his agrestic pleasures, and he was privy to the secret of the *Waverley* authorship, as he was to the contents of Cockburn's Red Book. His memorandum supplements a story told in Lockhart's life of Scott about a fishing expedition during which Richardson hooked some huge thing. This was landed, after a struggle. Scott's servant Tom Purdie said: 'It will be some sea-brute.' But no, it was a river trout. Richardson then moved away, and Scott noticed Purdie giving the trout a kick on the head, with the words: 'To be ta'en by the like o' him, frae Lunnon!'

[1] 30 June 1836: British Museum MSS.

Moncreiff has an account by Richardson of a visit to Abbotsford when Scott's bankruptcy was approaching, though his embarrassments had not yet been divulged. The two men stood in moonlight on the terrace, and Richardson spoke of his 'admiration at Sir Walter's efforts and success, and merited station and happiness'. Scott sighed, and, referring to his daughter, 'said, "I wish to God I had the means of providing adequately for poor Annie." Knowing that his life was insured, I observed that that fund was ample. He made no explanation, and was silent, but I could not but feel, when his misfortunes were soon after disclosed, what a pang I must have inflicted; the fund I had alluded to, and all he had, being absorbed in so overwhelming a pecuniary ruin.'

Moncreiff's *North British Review* memoir ends with a piece by Cockburn ('a hand that our readers cannot fail to recognize'), dated 11 April 1845. The piece represents a cut version of some cancelled pages in the *Circuit Journeys* manuscript which were written on that day at Bridge of Tilt: these appear to have been omitted from the book because they were the sort of thing that belonged to the *Memorials*. The *North British Review* removed, in turn, certain of the more monstrous, and interesting, of Cockburn's sallies, together with the sexual references. The cancelled *Circuit Journeys* version is printed in full later in this book.

It is a lively memorial to the legal Edinburgh of Cockburn's youth, and may be said to supply a commentary on some passages of *Guy Mannering*. Hermand loved that novel, and the legal Edinburgh of its time was fond of the poem by Richardson which Cockburn is concerned with here. Scott, who might not have been, was also amused. In 1805, Scott scaled Helvellyn with Wordsworth and Sir Humphry Davy, and both Scott and Wordsworth wrote poems about a recent disaster on the mountain: a young fisherman, a connoisseur of the picturesque, Charles Gough, had fallen to his death and been watched over by his dog. Wordsworth's poem, 'Fidelity', commends the dog, and Scott's 'Helvellyn' does so too, but Scott is mainly drawn to the forlornness of his master. 'Helvellyn's opening stanza reads:

> I climb'd the dark brow of the mighty Helvellyn,
>   Lakes and mountains beneath me gleam'd misty and wide;
> All was still, save by fits, when the eagle was yelling,
>   And starting around me the echoes replied.
> On the right, Striden-edge round the Red-tarn was bending,
> And Catchedicam its left verge was defending,
> One huge nameless rock in the front was ascending,
>   When I mark'd the sad spot where the wanderer had died.

Richardson promptly wrote a parody of this poem—as well he might have done. He transfers Scott's dactyls to the contemplation of Parliament House, where the law courts were divided into the Inner House and the Outer: the parody deals with the second. In those days, the Inner House was a slum in which sat the judges of the Court of Session, attended by the ghosts of their predecessors. 'Very little fancy was necessary,' say the *Memorials* in perhaps their most brilliant sentence, 'to make one see the ancient legal sages hirpling through its dim litigious light.' The Outer House, where the Lord Ordinary sat, drawing up his interlocutors, as the representative of 'the haill fifteen'—the judges of the Court of Session— was crowded with starving, drunken or bogus lawyers, and with the sensible kind too, and with litigants and spectators and hangers-on: there walked the ghosts of men like *Redgauntlet*'s harrowing, law-crazed Peter Peebles. Cockburn, Jeffrey and their friends took pleasure in the sights of both Houses. To the Inner House and their *sederunts* returned the Lords of Justiciary from their circuit journeys, crimsoned with the blood of Highland felons. In the Outer House, saffroned with study and penury, on fire with chicanery and whisky, lingered the inhabitants of that still dimmer twilight where the Law and the Underworld met. The creatures described by Cockburn are like the hacks in Pope's 'Epistle to Arbuthnot', and their postures and plights can also call to mind Swift and Samuel Beckett: the Outer House was certainly a place where there was waiting for Godot. His creatures seem to pass, in their crepuscular way, from the barely human to the animal to the inanimate, John Wright being successively mistaken for a seal and for luggage. Perhaps there is some pity in the portraits, though there is much else besides. Richardson's parody begins:

> I climbed the High Street as the ninth bell was ringing;
>   The Macer to three of his roll had got on;
> And eager each clerk to his counsel was springing;
>   Save on thee, luckless lawyer, who fee had got none!
> On the right Nicodemus his leg was extending;
> O'er the stove Johny Wright his brown visage was bending,
> And a huge brainless judge the Fore-Bar was ascending,
>   When I marked thee, Poor Otho! stand briefless alone!

The parody is dense with parochial ironies and nuances, and Cockburn's notes identify the people in a series of portraits similar to those published in his books. Poor Otho was Otho Herman Wemyss, who had studied civil law at Leyden, whose name was translated by Grahame as

*O quamvis parvula puella*, who made a nuisance of himself with washer-women (not that the readers of the Free Kirk's *North British Review* were allowed to know that), and so on. When Otho had shrunk away almost to nothing—then it was that 'Whiggery marked him for its own', and made him a Sheriff Substitute. Cockburn relates, in the manner of the Gothic fiction of his time, that Otho had a 'second self' in another unfortunate. And his notes identify the 'Corsican faery' as someone other than Napoleon and no approximation to the Emperor's second self.

*The Court of Session Garland*, a collection of transcripts and tattle which appeared in various editions during the nineteenth century, and which tartly mentions Cockburn's shortcomings as a lawyer and his 'stale jokes', prints a text of the parody and makes a few comments on it, which are corrected in Cockburn's notes. The edition of 1871[1] states that 'the sobriquet of Nicodemus' was awarded to the man in question by the advocate John Clerk. But a letter of 1849 from Richardson to Cockburn[2] remarks that the parody 'owed the felicitous "*Nicodemus*" to you'. All or most of the second stanza seems to have been by Jeffrey. Some of the best legal minds of the period were applied to this lampoon.

The line about the brainless judge is really very menacing: not every Parliamentary Solicitor has been responsible for so much in the way of *lèse-majesté* or contempt. And it is a little disappointing when Cockburn's notes explain that the reference is not meant to be generic—to the kind of blind justice with which no one is unfamiliar—and simply points to one particular 'good man, but huge and brainless, certainly. In voice, stare, manner and intellect, not much above an idiot; but respectable from bulk, good-nature, broad Scotch, and slow, gracious stupidity'. The readers of the *North British Review* were left unaware that this was poor Lord Pol-kemmet.

The story of the response to Scott's 'Helvellyn' was to take another turn in the course of the high days of holiday and parody enjoyed by Cockburn and Richardson in their youth—a less irreverent turn, to which I shall come later.

---

[1] *The Court of Session Garland* by James Maidment, pp. 22, 125, 126. This edition seems to have taken into account Cockburn's notes, as published in the *North British Review*. Review.
[2] 6 July 1849.

# Chapter Five

# *I Peregrini Scozzesi*

In 1823, Cockburn and a party of friends performed their grand tour of Europe. A tour had been pondered for some time: a letter of Richardson's of 1819,[1] conscious of the *mezzo del camin* of a man's life, urges one for the following year. Their dilatoriness was taken by Cockburn to be a proof of their ordinary happiness, but he was longing to go abroad, and on 11 July 1823 he wrote to Richardson: 'Lord! to have seen Venice before October!!!' 'Yon Antique Towers' had cast a spell, it seems, on this appraiser of antique towers, and he says elsewhere: 'Venice was our main object.'[2] They set off through Flanders and Germany, crossed the Alps, descended into Italy—the old goal of the grand tours performed by the British gentlemen of the eighteenth century—and returned home rapidly by way of Paris. They travelled mostly in a char-à-banc drawn by a pair of horses, but in Italy they hired carriages from the Post for each stage of the journey.

Cockburn kept a journal of their experiences, and there is a transcription of this journal in the National Library: 'carefully and faithfully made by me, Charlotte Jeffrey, one of the companions of his tour.' Charlotte was Jeffrey's daughter by his first marriage, and the other companions of the tour were Richardson, Jeffrey himself, Jeffrey's American second wife and his father-in-law—the admirable Mr Charles Wilkes of New York. Three Scotch gentlemen and an American one, all virtuous and vivacious—excellence on wheels, encountering the wonders and squalors of Europe in a great gaudeamus of wit and glee, accompanied by Jeffrey's womenfolk and by a maid-servant and a German manservant. Wilkes, a banker and a nephew of the well-known John Wilkes, had been intent on a tour of his own, and this had induced the Scots to forsake their ordinary happiness. According to Jeffrey,

---

[1] To Cockburn, 15 September.
[2] *Life of Jeffrey*, vol. I, p. 272. The *Memorials* do not mention the tour.
[3] In a letter from Basle of 13 August to a niece: *Life of Jeffrey*, vol. II, p. 215.

the party 'agreed very well—Cockburn being despotic, and the rest of us dutifully obedient'. They were a little discommoded by Jeffrey's late rising and 'aversion to the dawn',[1] which obliged them to travel in the heat of the day. As far as possible, the journey will be recounted in the words of the journal, which is different from his other narratives in that it reveals a more casual, a relatively dishevelled Cockburn: it was rather at the mercy of their always having to drive on to the next wonder. It also reveals a disposition— somewhat shared by Jeffrey and Richardson—to read Europe in terms of Scotland, in terms of an indefatigable series of homely comparisons, invidious and otherwise.[2]

Cockburn did not think highly of the sea. It was something you took haddocks out of. But on 26 July he condescended to sail across it—from London to Ostend. He lay down on the boat to sleep, but 'was very restless for a sight of our first continental town'. The entry for the 27th proceeds: 'Nothing can exceed the meanness of Ostend; yet nothing can exceed my pleasure in being in it. It is the first place I ever saw on the continent, and everything in it except the dress of the people is as unlike what I have been accustomed to as if it were in another planet. We ran all over the streets and went into the Cathedral, which is large but unadorned. The people were praying with expanded arms this morning at five o'clock. It is the first Catholic place of worship I ever saw.' Glimpsing 'Scotch-like' people and cottages, 'but both neater', they moved on to Bruges, 'the perfect model of a picturesque town'. Their palates were startled by their first Continental dinner: Jeffrey and Wilkes grumbled, Cockburn approved. But his Caledonian eye was caught by 'a Catholic procession in honor of St Jacob—a contemptible and debasing exhibition of poor ceremonies, brutish priests, and ignorant people. Every house was wreathed with flowers and the street was strewn with sedges. The whole front windows of one dwelling house were entirely shaded by geraniums.' Scotland was rich in ceremonies, and Cockburn could be considered an expert on the subject.

On the road to Brussels the party quarrelled with a drunken coachman (in general, Europe proved no match for Scotland when it came to this sort of thing). The coachman threatened to unyoke: 'this made us sing low'— and capitulate. There were no houses worth seeing:

---

[1] *Life of Jeffrey*, vol. I, p. 273.
[2] The rest of the material quoted in this chapter is taken from Charlotte Jeffrey's transcription of Cockburn's journal. Jeffrey, too, kept a journal of the tour—in handwriting bad enough to ward off the impious pryings of most biographers. In the *Life of Jeffrey* (vol. I, pp. 272, 273), Cockburn remarks: 'Jeffrey's journal is full of dates, places, and striking observations and descriptions, but contains nothing worth making public.'

They don't seem to know what a gentleman's place is. They have no flowers—at least about their perceptible premises. We watched (our heads being full of Dutch flowers) but could only detect two rose bushes between Ostend and Brussels. The horses are admirable—far better than the English ones of the same class—having a far better union of bulk with activity. They are splendid creatures; every one as if it thought itself a gentleman. They are indebted for a part of this to their all having fine, gay old harnessing, studded with brass nails and twisted ribbons. Their carts are low, strong, narrow and very long and the labour of the horses gets fair play by their being generally driven three abreast. The people are very handsome, but not so clean in their persons as in their utensils.

In the library of the old palace at Brussels, 'my fingers itched for thousands of handsome folios which were laying on the floors, with a view to be catalogued and sold—being all duplicates'. The old houses of the city inspired ungrateful feelings about Classical Edinburgh: 'I can scarcely conceive anything more striking than the long lines of irregularly ridged roofs which everywhere break the top edges of the narrow streets. Would that the planner of the new town of Edinburgh had seen them! How they would have changed the characters of our heavy, dull, lengthy uniform fronts!'

The Church of St Paul at Antwerp was 'full of saints and sinners of all ages and sexes, trades and appearances, at their mummeries and in all attitudes and recesses. To me these Catholic ceremonies, performed by ladies and by beggars, by fine gentlemen and by common soldiers, by crutched old men and women and laughing boys and girls, in quiet niches and under the great domes, kneeling on rushy chairs or on the hard pavement, with their eyes cast up to heaven or their brows prostrate in the dust, and all telling beads or muttering words or performing gesticulations why or wherefore they know not—these curious, but debasing sights form the most interesting spectacle I have seen.' In Antwerp, too, they found 'a model of Mount Calvary, representing in pictures, models and statues all the scenes that took place there and ending with hell, where certain people are burning with great effect. A most contemptible piece of foolery. Yet it is one of the Antwerp sights, and this hell was the great place where the devotees knelt and muttered.'

'Bruges and Ghent were like moss roses, Antwerp only like a full cabbage.' The party decided, incidentally, not to waste a day on Waterloo, which was now only a field of corn. Mrs Jeffrey bought lace, with a view to some light, ladylike smuggling. At places where they spent the night, they were being pestered to show their passports and describe themselves to the police. One official was told by Mr Wilkes: 'And you may add—who always wears spectacles.' 'No, sir,' replied the official, 'for if you commit a crime you can easily take them off.' From a requiem mass at Breda wafted a 'horrid stink'.

4

It is by now crystal-clear that Cockburn was not going to return from his tour a Papist.

Impressed, in Rotterdam, by the statue of Erasmus and by some 'interesting tombs', he was also struck by the fact that, 'in the way of public decoration', nothing had been done by this commercial city 'for literature, for the arts, for religion or even for war; or indeed for anything at all'. Yet 'its streets and endless canals exhibit a most extraordinary appearance and render it without any intended public ornament a singular and beautiful town'. The man who hankered after the Old Town of Edinburgh while inhabiting the New pronounces romantically on Rotterdam: 'These houses are invariably full of projections and irregularities which make them very picturesque—in so much so that they are not anxious even to make the front walls stand straight up. They have often and thro'out whole streets a fearful projection forward, so that the result is that the whole town is roughened into beauty by mere independant individual caprice.' As his tour proceeds, there will be further reason to conclude that Cockburn was very interested in the roughness of the picturesque.

Holland was a wilderness of canals and stagnancy, of still waters running deep and smelling bad. Cockburn, who swore by streams, was shocked by the sight of fine villas standing in 'ugly and eternal troughs of dead green water'. There were 'coffee and smoking parties in hundreds of summer houses; which houses are generally very costly, if one may judge from their painting, their gilding, their furniture and their size. Yet we could not see one that had not a putrid ditch close round it. The "Lust hous's" as they are called in Dutch (Lust being pleasure) are generally advanced a little in front of the villa.' Perhaps the damp and the smell gave 'a zest to the tobacco and the coffee'. One evening, such an exhalation arose from the fields 'that we seemed to be in the midst of a sea of cold white fleece—yet the children were playing and the village lovers flirting very naturally in the heart of it'. Amphibious Holland was a 'composition of liquid land and of solid water'.

The Hague had 'large, plain, nobleman-looking houses': 'not unlike the second order of large houses in Piccadilly'. The town was 'quiet, genteel and clean', but 'blighted with the Dutch curse' of standing water. At Scheveling, the fishing people 'differ as much from other persons here as our New Haven fishwomen do from their neighbours'. Jeffrey 'flirted' with one of the women, 'tho' as ugly as fishing, old age and Dutch weather could make them'. At Leyden, a court was sitting: 'Wilkes thought them more decorous than the Court of Session, we thought them as intelligible.' 'Not intelligibill!' as Lord Eskgrove is heard to cry in the *Memorials*. The women who ran the Golden Lion in Haarlem were so 'cheerful and kind' that Jeffrey 'at first doubted the reputation of the house'. This is a comment which may be felt to rebound on Scotland: there was no doubting the reputation of many of Edinburgh's inns.

In Amsterdam they witnessed some scourgings, but one of his old High School masters, Christison, would have put this 'easy executioner' to the blush. The criminals, two nice girls among them, were then roped together and led through the town: everyone, including the criminals, was much diverted. 'Scarcely ever are the female breasts seen in a divided state—what it is that swells them below I cannot say, but it surely cannot be pregnancy in the whole sex at once.' Let leafy Amsterdam, he thought, be a lesson to Edinburgh, where they imagine that George Street is too narrow for trees. Cockburn records that

> there are four things good in Flanders. 1. the towns, 2. Cathedrals, 3. the pictures, 4. Animal and Vegetable productions. Of these there are only two good in Holland, and these inferior. Viz. the towns and the pictures. Their churches are poor, and smell of Presbitery; their crops, people, cattle and horses are not to be compared to those of Belgium. The people want the cross with the French which makes so good a mixture with the Flemish temperament. Even in their amusements they seemed to us to be dull and cold—more gregarious than social. They smoked under their arbours, but never talked. Their whole country too, or at least the greater part of it, is made loathsome by these universal and disgusting plains and lines of green, black and yellow puddle.

While Catholicism stank in the nostrils of the touring Cockburn, Presbytery, too, was not without its smell. Smells and puddles apart, however, he and Richardson appear to have felt that the Low Countries were ridiculously clean. Some travellers are never pleased.

The Rhine, when he washed his face in it, proved 'wider than the Tay at Perth'. He spied hills that put him in mind of Corstorphine, and near Cologne, where they arrived on 5 August, a 'curious ridge' with the same profile as 'the Southern aspect of the Pentlands'. There was nothing native to compare with the unfinished tower of Cologne Cathedral, which was grand and noble. But he soon reverts to his Scotching of the Rhine: 'Except in size, it is just the Tweed below Melrose, or the Tay below Perth.' He goes on: 'Let anyone therefore enlarge the Tay and its valley, fix the temperature at 70, line its course with calm smokeless villages bosomed in orchards, top many pinacles or projecting points with tall or huge architectural ruins, give all these a local history, and breathe over the whole an air which will cover the summits of the hills with ripe grasses, and he will have an adequate conception of the Rhine.' There are moments when he can almost seem to invite comparison with the eighteenth-century Scotsman who is said to have

called out at a performance of John Home's tragedy *Douglas*: 'Whaur's
your Wullie Shakespeare now?'

By now he had seen his first vine, and the journal has a judicious and
characteristic discussion of whether trees or vines look better in a landscape:
'My conclusion is that both are best.' At this stage of the journey they came
upon a great rock with an echo, climbed it and, in the euphoria of travel,
'ventured to shout Napoleon and other doubtful sentiments'.

The Rheingau was not unlike the carse of Falkirk, and near Heidelberg,
which was about the size of Dalkeith, Corstorphine Hill loomed up again.
There, too, he saw hills that were extremely like the Ochils. Somewhere else
was extremely like Dunkeld. And in these pages of the journal, if nowhere
else in his writings, Cockburn is extremely like Polonius, when questioned
by Hamlet about the cloud in the shape of a camel. The red sandstone or
freestone of Strasbourg Cathedral—the high point, this, of his patriot's
responses—was 'the colour of Arbroath'.

At Heidelberg, he took against the students,

> who seem a most offensive race. We have seen very few of them anywhere, not
> apparently lunatic. Their fashionable dress consists of a small green or black velvet
> skull cap, or else a large white straw hat, stiffened by wire, upon their heads, their hair
> combed downwards, and upwards, and outwards, so as to be as wild as possible;
> their necks quite bare; a long wide green frock; wide pantaloons and an enormously
> long pipe. Their object is to look swaggering and quarrelsome, or wrapt in thought
> and sentiment—very few of those we have seen would be allowed to go at large in
> Britain. They were smoking and drinking beer in the walks at the castle by a little
> after seven in the morning.

The party reached Radstadt on 10 August, and at the Golden Cross ate
a golden dinner: soup, pike, 'bouille' (beef soup, I think), omelette, cold
ham, sauerkraut, kidney beans, boiled potatoes, beetroot, stewed cucumber,
beef and potatoes, roast boar, soufflé, turkey poults (young turkey), salmon,
stewed plums, veal, salad. At the frontier, crossing to Strasbourg, they were
ruffled by some military fuss over their passports—enough to try the temper
even of 'the philosophical traveller'. So, in their philosophical way, they
'cursed the Holy Alliance again and all military governments and all laws
in general'. The Holy Alliance—the Christian brotherhood formed by
Russia, Austria and Prussia—was virtually defunct by now, but the thought
of it was to intrude on their travels, and they were also to pour libations to
Spain, where the monarchy had been under pressure from reformers. They
looked at the view from the tower of Strasbourg Cathedral: 'All such perpendicular prospects, however, tho' curious, are painful. Indeed it is the
strange pain that constitutes their pleasure.' This is the kind of sentiment

that men of taste had long entertained. According to the aesthetics of Burke and others, and to the practice of certain Gothic and Romantic writers, the notion of pain was inseparable from the sublime.

Beyond Colmar, in the distance, the Swiss mountains: 'We hailed them as the land of promise and never ceased to gaze on them all the rest of the day.' At Basle, the grave of Erasmus, and the Protestant church of St George: 'Thro'out the whole structure and all its accompaniments there is an air of rude provincial simplicity, and of reverential attachment to the good cause, which makes this ancient edifice far more interesting than those noble cathedrals which have to boast only of their wealth and their art.' He clearly felt closer to Scotland here: Presbytery, perhaps, began to smell sweeter. It was hot that day, and Jeffrey vanished into the church to write letters. A gang of convicts in chains was weeding the pavement. 'It is perhaps not inappropriate for a certain class of the guilty, but it is degrading and painful to the innocent spectator.'

He marvelled at the famous Falls of Schaffhausen, painted by Turner a a number of years before, but their grandeur was marred by an encroaching manufactory. The town exhibited 'all the symptoms of ancient provincial distinction'. In Zurich, where the inn, like all Swiss inns, smelt of dung, he was pleased to see a first edition of Quintilian, and displeased to be beset by well-dressed and healthy beggars—though it would have been worse had these been known to be well-dressed and healthy beggars supported by the state on the proceeds from a property tax. Near the lake the ground sloped gently 'as at Barnbougle, or rather at Donibristle'.

Quitting Zurich, he saw some genuine Alps and 'panted to be on the tops of them'. The party's four gentlemen duly climbed Rhigi, an ascent 'not nearly so difficult as that of Ben Nevis'. They supped at an inn on the summit—on a huge eel, three roast hens and much else. In the kitchen two old witches cooked with clumsy utensils, and the mixed company of tourists eyed one another as the rain pattered on their Alp. 'There was a man there who has made maps and panoramas of Switzerland and some coarse German woman who wrote perpetually in books and no doubt had us down.' And Cockburn had *her* down too. The following morning he rose early, ran to a knoll and 'never beheld a more magnificent spectacle'. From the summit they were able to see the Jungfrau, 'bright with unapproached snow'. Around this time Wilkes and the womenfolk broke off and proceeded on their own to Geneva.

Cockburn liked Switzerland: the Swiss knew as much about William Tell as the Scots did about Wallace and Bruce. And his eye was caught, not only by the streams and waterfalls that hung from the hillsides, but by the fountains that flowed even in the poorest villages, one of which was set in a valley something like Habbie's Howe. These fountains prompted the reflection that 'there is scarcely a town containing 1,000 people on the continent in which more has not been done for the recreation of the inhabitants than in the largest British cities'. He was cast down, however, by the female costume: 'Their breasts and their bottoms are invariably as flat as flounders.'

The ascent of the St Gotthard Pass was 'one long scene of utter desolation': 'Anybody may have a tolerable idea of it who will think of Glenco—or even Glencroe—only making every object tenfold greater and crowning the hills with snow.' And so over and down into Italy—amid 'the same sublime and savage rock work'—and the Leventino valley. 'I counted the waterfalls till I was wearied.' The crossing of the Alps was felt to be sufficient reward for the entire expedition.

Poor grapes at Bellenzone on 20 August, noise, filth, no attendance and inferior local wine at the Corona at Lugano, a 'jingling din' of morning bells at Lake Maggiore—Italy did not look promising. Things began to improve, though: 'The people were coming from the fields as brown as copper and with wains so rudely yoked to mild-looking cattle that I must examine the *Georgics* to see if it be not done in the very way it was in the days of Virgil.' Labouring men's skins were a wonder: 'literally as brown as mahogany,' he exclaims elsewhere. Como by moonlight was 'liker a fairy scene than any I ever beheld'. Passports were still demanded, but in Italy a small bribe would do instead. The agrestic Cockburn could hardly object to the fact that so much business was done in the open air or under arches and awnings. At Brescia, 'tailors work there, girls sew, men read, soldiers sleep, and we even saw a school assembled of about twenty very nice young children with an old withered duenna at their head'.

Of the 'Palazzos' of North Italy, by which he means country houses or gentlemen's houses, he has this to say:

There is nothing rough or picturesque in them, nothing whatever. There is more roughness in one Flemish house than in all the Italian ones we have seen—when they do ornament, it is by correct cornices, or friezes, or pediments or the like. The result of all this is, that their buildings are plain, angular and simple, and have generally a very architectural air. There are two things to which much of this is owing. One is, that their roofs are almost always set at a very pleasing angle. They are not flat, but they are not much raised. They are broad and low; in which I wish our Scotch raisers of precipices of slate would imitate them. The other is, their addiction to strait horizontal lines. Their windows, roofs, doors, and every eminent object about the buildings, carry the eye along thro'out the whole range of the same house, and often of all the houses on the same level, without shifting. In so much so that even when a town stands on a steep so that the horizontal line cannot be preserved entirely thro'out, it is preserved as far as possible in stages. All this gives their buildings a severe, but correct air. There is nothing picturesque, but there is much that is pleasing. Everything is in the style of calm elegant regularity.

These palaces are being judged according to the criteria of the Picturesque. Men of taste had long been in the habit of searching for, and creating, landscapes which corresponded to the landscapes painted by their favourite artists: when he was found dead on Helvellyn, Charles Gough was carrying a 'Claude Glass'—an aesthete's mirror for securing suitable views. 'Picturesque' was a word for what might be trapped, or snapped, in such a glass, and could simply mean pictorial or worth painting. In the closing years of the eighteenth century, however, the word was made to mean rather more by, among others, Sir Uvedale Price, a Whig squire who taught that the picturesque was different from the beautiful and the sublime, and that roughness and irregularity were its attributes. Whatever was rugged and ragged and shaggy—rocks, waterfalls, Gothic buildings, gypsies' hovels, Highland cattle, scenes like those of Salvator Rosa—was picturesque, and Price's Picturesque, so to speak, grew into a dominant taste of the time which was presently embodied in Romanticism.

It was a taste to which Cockburn responded—in his capacity as traveller and Pentlandiser. His friend Dick Lauder took an interest in Price, and edited writings by Price on the picturesque.[1] Cockburn's set gave a good deal of guidance on aesthetic matters, and Richardson's friend, the poet Campbell, was responsible for what may be regarded as a leading precept of Romanticism: ' 'Tis Distance lends enchantment to the view.'[2] With its balanced assessment of Italian palaces, this particular passage from Cockburn's Continental journal makes it possible to suppose that, over the years, he had been host to an inner dialogue in which were asserted the rival claims of the rough and the correct, the picturesque and the regular, the fantastic and the convenient, the romantic and the classical. But roughness could exercise a powerful magnetism—luring him from that significant proportion of the architecture of Italy which was undeniably architectural. In all this, he is like Scott, who was devoted to Price's ideas.

Meanwhile Italy's roads remained 'equal to the very best Macadam', and took them to Verona, where it was very hot: 'Tho' it looks and sounds well to see or to say that an Italian ditcher rests on his long spade to eat a bunch of grapes, let no one who ever tasted a good potatoe with moderate heat envy him.' The inns and houses were built round an inner court, which made the good inns noisy since it led ostlers, waiters 'and every creature to hold their

---

[1] *Sir Uvedale Price on the Picturesque* (1842). The Price texts are based on an edition of 1810. Dick Lauder prints an essay of his own on taste, and there are numerous editorial interpolations.
[2] *The Pleasures of Hope* (1799), Part One, line 7.

conventicles within hearing', and 'it makes the bad ones stink by presenting a convenient place for dunghills'. In general, however, the Continent proved cleaner than Scotland. Vicenza had what purported to be Livy's house, and it also had learned commissionaries or guides: 'I pity a poor foreigner with one of our Edinburgh chairmen. Which of them could talk in French and German and Italian about Burntsfield house and Napier, the old owner's logarithms, and then go home and clean the stranger's shoes, and in the evening introduce him to all public places, and all this for a shilling or two per day?'

About five on Sunday, 24 August, 'Venice unexpectedly stood before us,' looking flat and mean: but for its size and its spires and cupolas, it was like any fishing town. They got out of their carriage, and met, it would seem by prearrangement, two Dundases—possibly his friends the brothers George and David. Venice was the main object of the tour, and his description of Venice is the most interesting section of the journal: I therefore propose to give it very nearly in full.

For Cockburn, Venice was more than a matter of architecture, more than a collection of queer old towers. It is likely that he already had strong political feelings about the city, as will become clear in due course when his politics are examined in detail, and such feelings are certainly evident in the *Memorials*. The Venice he was approaching was the Venice that came after the deluge represented by the arrival of the conquering Napoleon. In its earlier days, the days of its glory, it had been admired by many, and for many reasons. But in recent years there had been a tendency to see the city, in the light cast by the French Revolution, as the seat of a corrupt despotism —the Venetian oligarchy—whose evil ways had led to its climacteric and destruction. Cockburn's entry into Venice was that of a patrician progressive who may well have been expecting the worst, politically—fascinating though the city was bound to be. The few words about politics in the following account, however, indicate that these suspicions were, to some degree, allayed. In terms of 'public decoration' and public institutions, the Venice he encountered was scarcely oligarchic.

> Our feelings in entering the internal canal of this strange and famous place were enviable. We were soon rowed up to the door of the Leone Bianco where the landlords and waiters were standing. . . . We were ushered into a room with large mirrors, silk flock paper, brown velvet and gilded sofas and chairs, a composition floor, which, as usual, was not discernible from marble, two beds, as is also usual, in the room but divided from it by a tall white curtain. We soon got into a boat (I believe I should call it a gondola) and in half an hour were under the Rialto, and over the place de S. Mark, and into the Doge's Palace, and opposite the bridge of Sighs, and in short, in the heart of all the scenes of which the names and stories have been long familiar to our ears. After Dinner, we went to the Theatre. The house was very handsome and not

ill filled, and everybody remarkably decorous. We then sailed about again in moon-light, and walked, and eat ice, in the place of St Marc, and at last went to bed with the stars glittering in the water under our windows, and nothing heard but the splashing of a few oars, and the voices of their Gondolieri. This morning we were thro' other parts of the town in a boat, before breakfast, and we are just cooling our-selves in a darkened room for a little before we set out again.

It is not so difficult as is commonly supposed to imagine Venice. Anybody will have gone far to form a good notion of it, who will just conceive a town standing in the sea, with from 100,000 to 130,000 people, and that above one half of the whole streets and lanes were suddenly to disappear and their places to be supplied by water. There is not an absolute extinction of the land. Narrow, short streets constantly oc-cur and a still greater number of bits of pavement like ours for foot passengers. So I am told that it is quite possible to go over all the town on foot, tho' certainly this could only be done by skillful steering and by endless turnings. But there is such an extinction of land that it may practically be said that the houses all stand in the water and that the streets are canals. The consequence of this may easily be figured. If a lady wants to go to church—instead of going from the steps of her door into a carriage, she goes from the same steps into a boat. If an old woman wants 1,000 melons put down at her stand in the market, she empties them into a boat. If a quantity of neatly cut wood is required for the kitchen fire of a house, it is brought to the door and sold out of a boat. If a boy wants to cross to the opposite house and does not chuse to go round by some bridge, or lives in a house round which there is no walking path, he gets into a boat, and gives it a push.

In a word, they do in boats, what we do in carriages or on foot. And the canals pierce into the most remote recesses of almost every street and corner. The boatman takes you to the front of a house or to the back of it, as easily and naturally as if there could be no other way of going. Most respectable families have boats of their own, which are rowed by their own servants and stand undisturbed hooked to posts stuck in the water at their own doors. But every boat without exception is black. Those not meant for goods have all a place near one end covered in by very awkward con-fined sides and roof, which both, however, can be taken off, but seldom are. These coverings are half cloth and half wood with small openings for windows at the sides. Now the whole even of this apparatus is black—jet black—and looks horrible. It is painfully funereal. Nothing can be liker the conveyance of a dead body. There is not an ounce of coloured paint on all the boats of Venice. It is their fashion to be univer-sally black.

Having thus supposed the water and the boats, it must be observed that the town *in general* is not handsome; that is, when the Great Canal and the chief lines of the principal houses are gone out of. There are always striking pieces of old building occurring everywhere, but in general, the inferior parts of the town are not nearly equal to those of Rotterdam or of many other places. The canals are salt water, and seem to receive most of the filth of the town, and when the tide is out, they have a slight smell. But it is a marine odour and not offensive, and is not the least like the Dutch putridity. When the tide is in, there is not the least smell. But tho' the ordinary parts of the city be mean, the whole tract of the Great Canal, at least from the Rialto to the palace of the Doge, which I should suppose was somewhat above half a mile and the canal 200 feet broad, is one continued series of magnificent Façades on both sides. Detached striking buildings are sprinkled over all the city; but this is the scene of its chief architectural glory—and nothing can possibly be finer. There must of course be considerable sameness in the buildings of the same people, nearly in similar situations, and erected either in the same age or after the national taste was fixed—when they are viewed in the gross. But when examined in detail by one who

4*

has knowledge and leisure for such a task, I am satisfied that there is architecture enough to adorn a whole nation and to furnish inexhaustible materials to a genius of the richest order.

The general style and air of these Palazzos is this. They have all a row of long, flat steps in front from the water to the door. The door is the centre, with two or three or four windows on each side. Along the lower floor of some of them, there is a range of columns, with the windows between them, and the entablature (if this be the right word—I mean the tip) of these columns serves as the base of a smaller range of pillars in the second story, and the top of these again for a still slenderer range above. But this columned front is not common. It is more usual for them to have only one row of pillars in the second or third tier, or to have almost none at all. In this case, the building is ornamented by pilasters, placed equally and gracefully between the windows and the different parts of the edifice, or else the wall is without even pilasters, but then it is fretted with decorations about the door and windows; particularly with a long handsome stone gallery above the door, extending the whole length of the house, and with smaller, but beautiful, balustrades of carved stone projecting from each, even the highest windows—in which it was very striking to see the people of the house sitting, with the boats and the canal right beneath them. They are admirably made for the enjoyment of aquatic shows. Very often the whole of these styles seem to be mingled, and almost invariably the junction of the wall and the roof is concealed by a noble balustrade of columns, or by a row of handsome statues or urns, with which two last indeed their whole houses are apt to be profusely covered.

All this seems at first to present the image of something very splendid. But splendour is not its character; and some deductions must be made before its exact impression can be caught. The word palace has a tendency to mislead. They are not architecturally ornamented or composed *all round*, nor is there in general a great mass, or a long range, of front exhibited. The space seems to have been so valuable next the water, that the great bulk of the houses is behind, and the sides are closely pressed upon by other buildings, so that it is only a single and not a very large façade of each house that is to be admired. And the line of these houses along each side of the Great Canal is not so continuous as to form actually one unbroken front of building. They are separated from each other by groups of dirty boats; by the ends of small canals; by mean tenements, and by many such things which would shock the eye of a person who went there expecting to see bright marble and great combined plans. There is nothing like marble, or cleanness, or care, or anything showy about them. They are of a whitish colour, or rather of a decaying grey, not unlike Burlington House, or the gate of Northumberland House. The windows of their lower story are generally crossed with iron bars, like those of a prison, while their upper ones are boarded up. In short, these Venetian noblemen's palaces are like beggarly gentlemen's houses—richly ornamented and finely imagined, at first, but mouldering now into ruin.

Still, however, enough remains to show distinctly the original conception, and all the details. Not one of them is roofless, or has any appearance of falling down, in any part, so that if a person will rid his mind of the idea of bright marble, and living domestic purity, and will think of the carving, and the columns, the pilasters and the balustrades, the statues and the urns, of some centuries ago, and recollect that he is taking his last gaze of a city in its death-bed, he will overlook all these mean obtrusions on the scene, and will *in effect* behold nothing but a noble range of superb edifices— over which time has breathed only to give the character of venerableness to their original splendour.

The Place of St Mark, including its accompaniments, the Doge's palace, the four horses, the square, the coffee houses, the minareted church, the detached square tower, the three tall red wooden poles, and everything about it, is perfect.

It is a glorious collection of what is interesting in history and what is profuse in architecture. There are many things fantastic in it, many that are mean, and many that are only strange from their Turkish oddity. But so much the better. These only improve the delightful mixture. Such a place! Its curious projecting lines and points, its rows of windows, of roofs and of friezes, its arcades, its shops, its carved doors, its broad awnings, its public edifices, its hoarse bell, its smooth tessellated pavement, its crowds of lounging people, its antiquity, the events it has been the scene of, its statues, its unlikeness to everything else, the noble approach to it by a canal 200 feet broad and lined by palaces! When I sailed down there and stood in the middle of that singular quadrangle, my longing for novelty and for old architecture was for once completely satiated.

The appearance of all this in moonlight may easily be conceived. When we sailed last night there were few boats on the water, and everything was strikingly silent. As we glided past the old columns and balustrades, sometimes in the faint light and sometimes in the dark shade, and heard the distant foreign voices and saw the Gondolieri dash the watery stars with his oar, I could have fancied myself in another world. But as soon as we left the boat, landed on the broad stairs and entered the *place*, all was life and stir. The people, mostly all well dressed and all well behaved, were strolling or sitting on small rushy chairs in the open air or under awnings, eating ice or fruit or doing nothing—in great numbers. I don't suppose there could be fewer than a thousand lolling under the awnings in front of the coffee houses alone. Yet even here, there was a prevailing impression of silence and repose. It was life—but still life. They seemed exhausted by the heat of the day, or it is not the fashion to be active, but the fact is that I never saw so many people, socially employed too, so quiet. It seemed to be all sipping iced water, or eating ice, and looking at each other, or conversing in a low, comfortable, composed voice. It seemed as if they wished to be in harmony with the moon and the old buildings.

Indeed, the silence of the whole town is very remarkable, and no wonder. We have gone thro' most of it, yet *literally* we have not detected one single horse or one single carriage of any kind, whatever. All burdens are carried by water, men and women included. Then there is almost no trade. The vessels and boats that are seen are for internal accommodation solely—so that not only is everything done by water, but there is not much to do. The chief noise that is heard is the bawling of the Gondolieri to each other, which is done in a curious high key, and is unceasing. The owners of the stalls too, and the hawkers on the shore, seem to have no other way of announcing the excellencies of their wares but by competition of the same sort of cry. But these inland cries are not heard on the water, as they generally issue from small, back, narrow, crowded lanes, where the shops stand like those in Cranbourn Alley. These shops are small and very open to the street, and from generally having a large black iron chest in them for holding valuables have an old and Jewish air.

The whole city is in a state of miserable decay. It is full of poor bricks disclosed by the falling off of the outer plaster, of rotten boat posts, broken stairs, boarded-up windows, dirty balustrades, and every symptom of an incapacity to maintain things in the state they were originally meant for. The Palazzos in particular are in a melancholy plight—not a fourth of them are inhabited by landlord or tenant, and not a third of them even furnished or cared for. They are not taken down, merely because, for fear of injuring the canal, the law does not allow it. So the poor nobles go elsewhere and let the palaces of their fathers settle it with nature any way that they may.

Yet even this adds to the peculiar interest of the place, and I am not sure but what the silence and the mort-cloth boats do so too. There is enough left to remind one at every step of the former glory of the rich and independant individual Aristocrats by whom these noble edifices were erected; while the universal decay makes us sympathise the more with the faded and still fading splendour of an old and fallen republic.

This forenoon we went into the interior of several buildings. We saw two collections of pictures and statues, one public, belonging to the Academy, and one private, belonging to Manfrini. Of these I say nothing. Jeffrey and Richardson thought them both admirable; as they must have been since they contained many works of Titian, Raphael, Guido, Correggio, Angelo, Canova and other eminent masters. But the Doge's palace!! It is in vain to attempt to describe it; or the church of St Mark. They are full of everything that Genius, conquest, pride, time and wealth could bring together to adorn the national edifice of a powerful people, ambitious of signalizing themselves by art, as well as by arms. There are pictures, and statues, and books, and halls, and marble, and carving, in profusion, and all admirable, probably not to be exceeded out of Rome. These, this place shares with other places. But there are some things in which, so far as we have yet seen, Venice stands alone.

These are 1st Her *roofs*—I mean the inside ones. I had no notion what could be made of a flat roof, by gilding and painting, till today. The prodigious mass of gorgeous and unsparing ornament in the ceilings of the palace gives an impression of magnificence greater than far finer arts could bestow. 2ndly Her *mosaic*—almost the whole inside of the church of St Mark, from the floor, up the walls, to the top of the dome, is composed of it. And it is laid out on excellent subjects, excellently done. 3rdly Her *floors*. They are made of variegated marble, richly and beautifully figured. 4th Her peculiar air of *Antiquity*. It is not *mere* antiquity. Many things are much older. But it is the antiquity of the Modern world. Everything is stamped with the impression of the oldest republic in Europe, as we have known Europe. 5th The *public purposes* for which everything was plainly intended. This palace is not the least like the palace of a common King. One apartment of it is a long grand hall, made of mahogany, very much ornamented, but very simple, with mahogany benches standing all round, which are divided by little arms for each person. This was where the Senate of Venice met. These mark public institutions and principles, and accordingly there is no place where things give one less the idea of having been made merely for the personal accommodation of one man, or for the idle ceremonies of the Catholic religion. And tho' the Venetian government, no doubt, was very bad in reality, still it was received by the people in their public works as free and as theirs.

We ascended the great tower of St Mark. It is the only tower I ever saw which it is easy to ascend on horseback. There are almost no steps. The way up is by an inclined plane, by which, in point of fact, the materials for building it were carried up on mules. Seen from the height, the city looks very mean, a mere confused collection of red-tiled houses. But its situation and bearing is brought well under the eye. It is in the sea; but is surrounded by lines and dots of buildings which stand on low bits or streaks of sand, not visible except from the houses that are upon them. There is an almost total want of wood. It puzzled us to find out a single green tree or green leaf, tho' at last we did find out a few. The want of verdure in Venice, a spot built in the ocean, is not wonderful. But thro'out all that part of Italy which we have seen, the same defect is conspicuous. There is never a tree in their towns, and tho' they seem to wither from heat, and to court every artificial shade, there is never a branch extended over their villas. There are more trees in Rotterdam than in all Lombardy, so far as we have seen it.

We also saw a church of which I forgot the name a little above the Rialto, said to have been built by seven private families. Even without this last circumstance it is a splendid collection of marble, statues and pictures. But it is not safe to see these things anywhere else, after being in Flanders.

Cockburn, we discover, had seen with his own eyes the hall in which had sat the Senate of Venice, whose dark designs are compared in the *Memorials* to those of the Edinburgh Town Council. The fascinating strangeness of the sights of Europe—encountered at a time when the British could still bring to their travels an astonished insularity—was never more astonishing than at Venice. It is very like Cockburn to detect a want of wood, and very like him, having noticed how Rotterdam had been 'roughened into beauty by mere independant individual caprice', to be delighted, too, that Venice should prove so public a place, where things had not been made 'merely for the personal accommodation of one man'.

These passages of the journal seem to have been written, hot foot, on 24 and 25 August. The following entry was written at 'eight o'clock p.m.'— presumably on the 25th:

A warm, warm, pure, serene night. We are just going forth again. The boat is laying just under the window and the old white-haired, red-faced, blue-breeched, white-stockined boatman is profoundly asleep upon it. The voices on the water are loud, incessant and to a native I should think rather annoying. But to us they are only strange, and like the sound of people in the fields in harvest, only deepen the general silence. The number of persons sleeping in the streets is very odd. They lay in boats, on barrows, or under the arcades and along the tall thin shadow of solitary columns, profound and undisturbed. We have been in many booksellers' shops enquiring for Dempster's *Historia ecclesiastica gentis Scotiae* for Maitland; but here, as everywhere else, in vain, tho' we found it in one Catalogue here—but gone. All the booksellers' shops on the continent have disappointed me. They are in general mere stationary shops, or their books are all about the Catholic service. The china shops in Holland were equally unsatisfactory. There is plenty of old china there, but it is only to be found in use as jars in ordinary shops. There are no places, at least that I could find, professedly for the sale of old china.

At ten o'clock he resumed:

We have been again in the place, and on the water. Both beautiful. The former not nearly so crowded as last night, tho' there were more itinerant singers. It is curious to hear the people talking Italian. French and other tongues strike us at first as odd from their novelty, and difficulty, but the Italian sounds like its parent the Roman language, and one starts to hear them discoursing familiarly in an ancient and learned tongue. I heard the Ostler at Ecclo talk of us as the '*Perigrini*'.

*Peregrino* meant foreigner, wanderer, pilgrim, falcon: it seems a good word for at least one member of the party.

The next entry is dated Tuesday, 26 August:

We were out this morning in the boat for two hours before breakfast. The heat still great, but when properly managed I don't think necessarily oppressive. We went into the church de la Salute, which is rich in the usual ornaments of such places. Then we sailed to what is called the Garden, being the only thing of the kind they have. It was made lately by the French, to whom they seem to be indebted for the very few patches of living vegetable matter (for it cannot be called verdure) they have. It is a poor affair, only an acre or two in size; laid out in regular oblongs, lined with young acacias and altogether contemptible; tho' it be now one of the Venetian shows. We then sailed round a great part of the outside of the city, by the sea. It is all in a most wretched state of depopulation and disrepair. We terminated the tour by visiting the church of St John and St Paul, an interesting and splendid edifice. It is the burial place of the Doges and Venetian great men, and both outside and inside is composed chiefly of marble. Its mere architecture is immaterial but the tombs and reposing statues of these old Doges make it very striking. It is on this account better worth seeing than any other church in the place, except that of St Mark, of which the mosaic and the Antiquity throws everything else into the shade. It has some good stained glass, and is the only one in Venice that has.

Every time that we have been in the Place de St Mark we have been struck with its exact resemblance, not only in its general outline but in its smallest details, to the Panorama of it by Barker. Those who have seen that Panorama may not have *felt* Venice, but they have seen this, the most interesting, part of it.

Richardson and Jeffrey (I have no doubt) have been greatly disappointed in one thing. Courtezans are associated in one's imagination with the idea of Gondolas and Venice. Yet a more decorous city in its lanes, its boats, its place and its Theatre I never saw and can't conceive. I cannot suppose that the decay of the town is already so complete as to have extinguished these functionaries, or that these two inquisitive travellers have been negligent in their search. But they report that they have found none, and I have seen none, so far as I know. Such is the effect of travelling in company with one virtuous man. Fleas abound. The state of science here may be judged by the fact that on going into one of the best-looking optical shops in St Mark, and asking for a thermometer, the owner said he knew what it was, but had none and did not believe that there was one to be bought in Venice. Except on (or rather in) the hands of one gentleman who was plainly a German, I have not been able to discover one single person with gloves. The people here, especially the men, are remarkably handsome. The practice of rowing standing and pushing, instead of sitting and pulling, seems to save them from the stoop of the shoulders which is so common with our sailors, and gives them rather a graceful air. The dress of the men is *precisely* our own. The women's only differs in this (if it be a difference), that they generally go bare-headed, except that they put a thin muslin or linen shawl, not over their shoulders alone, as is usual with us, but over their heads too.

Their main object was now accomplished, and Venice lived up to its reputation. Simultaneously, and as nothing else had ever done, the city satisfied Cockburn's deep desire for new things and old things, for novelty and antiquity. These were the last days of an 'old and fallen republic': he felt himself to be gazing at its death-bed. And it seems to have mattered to him that this *was* a republic, and not a monarchy. Indeed, a state whose people could think that so much of it was 'free and theirs' was bound to have appeared to him to be less of a despotism that had been rumoured. Part of the appeal of his description is that this sophisticated man can look at times like a country cousin. Courtesans! It is quaint that they should have exhausted themselves so with inquiries about a copy of Dempster's *Historia Ecclesiastica Gentis Scotiae*. Quaint that Cockburn, in his lust for verdure, should seem to leave out of account the influence of climate on vegetation. He also finds it rather hard to get over the fact that Venice, like Holland, is amphibious.

Before leaving, the party took a last look at the Doges' Palace and St Mark's, and a last ice in the square. 'It was right in them to get four beautiful horses put up,' he reflected, 'in order to let the people know what these creatures were like.' At the church, 'on asking whence several parts of the building came we were told—"These porphyry columns were brought from Constantinople. These twisted alabaster pillars were found buried in the plains of Troy!!" And thus, without any deception, the imagination is carried back, beyond even this edifice, to still earlier places, from which its ornaments were taken as spoils.' Antiquity!!! The church was darker than most, 'and this, combining with the dimmed glory of the decorations, gives the scene the last charm of which it is susceptible, that of wonder at the power that made it, and of awe that that power is gone.'

*I peregrini Scozzesi* then made their way to Padua, and to Mantua, where a new bishop was being installed: 'We met his carcase making four poor horses sweat, this morning on its way to glory.' They saw, in Milan, 'the place where the original, or the pretended original, of Da Vinci's last supper stands painted on the wall', and in his response to Milan Cathedral, that Gothic miracle which had long been sought out by foreign travellers, the voice of Edinburgh is heard: 'It wants simplicity and calmness if it be to be considered as of a grave cast, and if it be to be viewed as of the florid order, then its floridity is not good.' The voice of the *Edinburgh Review*, for whom Wordsworth's *Excursion* would never do, is also heard: 'White marble is too sparkling and showy for a great building. It may do in the Parthenon, where it is sobered down by remarkable solidity of design and appropriate chasteness of ornament, but I can hardly conceive its not not making a large florid gothic church look ridiculously gay.'

By Lake Maggiore he welcomed the imminent return of the Alps. He also welcomed the presence of the works of man amid the wildernesses they were re-entering—'tho' it be usual to prefer solitude and what is called nature'. Villas and villages were 'great ornaments to the scenery'. At other times, of course, he could prefer solitude. And indeed he remarked of the 'pure Italian or picturesque Swiss' buildings on the islands of Lake Maggiore that 'umbrageous trees and untouched nature might often be better'. Not that he minded these buildings. But the famous artificially-wrought Isola Bella, with its 'pagoda-looking temple', would not do: 'The whole thing is contemptible and reminds one of Squire Pocklington's operations on Keswick.' Domo D'Ossola wasn't half the size of Dalkeith.

Napoleon's Simplon Pass was ascended, and at a couple of places they came across 'a public officer who reminded us of one at home. He was called "the President of the Mules".' Cockburn was glad to be back in Switzerland: 'The Italians, except the postilions, were perfectly civil and respectable people: but they want the homely, honest, provincial air of these hat-doffing Switzers, whose very wooden cottages, standing aloft on high hillsides, upon bits of green sward, seem innocent and wild. We have ever since we were in Italy had our beds made by men, but here the repulsive custom is given up.' At Chamonix the guide 'called out *Voilà Mont Blanc!* I shut my eyes for a few moments longer and pushed on, and then looked up and saw this monarch of European hills, standing, in a cloudless sky, apparently beside me.' He presently went part of the way up, side-saddle—to the Mer de Glace: 'Like other seas, by far the finest thing about it is the shore.'

Coming over the Simplon, Cockburn caught a cold, and began to suffer from headaches and exhaustion. The journal entries begin to suffer too, and become less responsive: the final pages were written in London on 23 September. They arrived in Geneva on the fourth of the month (perpendicularities on the way there put him in mind of Salisbury Crags), and were reunited with the rest of the party. Cockburn saw a doctor, leeches were applied, and he felt better. He watched the sun setting on the Alpine peaks—even on the seemingly 'unsubduable' summit of Mont Blanc. Where was Scott's Helvellyn now?

> Nothing could be a more striking or sublime index of the height of this mountain than the great length of time during which it remained radiant, after every other object, even mountains which had appeared not much inferior to it, were left in almost nocturnal darkness. At last the sun sank too low even for the loftiest peak of Mont Blanc; but then before yielding to temporary obscurity, a most extraordinary change took place. Its colour became precisely that of a dead body. The great object in the scene is to catch this particular moment. We did catch it. It lasted several minutes, and certainly between the going away of the sunshine, and the falling down of such darkness as made the mountain invisible, the cadaverousness of the snow was complete and fearful.

Cockburn and Richardson left Geneva and covered the 300 miles from the Jura to Paris in six days. Uninteresting country is reported. Where was *La Belle France*? Where were its 'gay, lilied fields', 'France's bright domain'? Dijon, however, was 'old and respectable'. In Paris he was joined by his wife and his daughter Jane, and his son Henry, who was touring independently, lay ill in that city. No doubt his son's illness, and his own, contributed to the jaundiced view of the city which is set down in the journal. 'It is impossible not to lament that Napoleon did not get time to finish his designs for improving it. I was much struck with the miserable poverty of the river, and with the total absence of all that blackguardism of air and manner which the revolution has taught us to associate with the populace of Paris.' Their Champs Elysées are 'contemptible; poor regularly-cut trees, no grass and little space'. And 'Bonaparte's bronze pillar in the Place Vendôme is not equal to ours, taken from the same model, in St Andrew Square.' On the pillar in St Andrew's Square stands the statue of Henry Dundas, and as it happened, they sailed home on a steamboat called the *Lord Melville*. Cockburn's namesake was not only the first of the two kings of Scotland among his kin: he was also, for many years, Treasurer of the Navy.

Cockburn's journal closes with a rendering of accounts—literally, to begin with: he counts the cost and decides that 'if I had not had to pay for three in Paris and to Calais, but only for myself, my whole travelling expences would have been under £90'. The 'principal objects' seen were the Flemish and Dutch towns, 'including pictures and cathedrals', the 'Castled scenery of the Rhine', 'the Berg-strasse, from Darmstadt to Heidelberg, both inclusive', 'the whole of Switzerland', Venice and Paris. He is against the use of public transport for such a journey: 'The only rational way of proceeding is, to have a good small party of one's own, a carriage, a servant who has a smattering of the languages and understands how to manage the posts and passports, and then to seek for foreign society, or to enjoy one's own independent party, as one likes.' He remarks that 'the ordinary statement that there is nothing worth seeing or worth enjoying out of Britain is an absurd British boast. On the continent they put us to shame *1st* in their towns, *2nd* in a great part of their scenery, *3rd* in the spaciousness of their inns, and the handsomeness of their furniture, *4th* in the profusion and variety of their viands, *5th* in their free, public exhibitions, *6th* in their uniform liberality and preference to strangers, *7th* in the singular and undeviating politeness of all classes of people.' On the debit side: 'the great defects abroad' are 'the want of bells and of attendance at inns', 'the horrid and perpetual annoyance about passports', and 'the miserable condition of all the water-closets. If the Holy Alliance would let the second of these alone, and turn its attention to the last, how much more gloriously would its memory descend to posterity!!' The presence of a valet helped them to put up with some of these defects. When it came to confronting Europe's contemptible water-closets, however, they were left to their own resources.

While Cockburn's journal is a little travel-stained, and indeed touristic, and while it suffers from a certain lack of incident, and, specifically, from an

absence of explored encounters with other human beings, it provides a
clear and welcome sight of his zeals and prejudices—on the wing, as it were.
Hills and running water were hunted high and low across Europe. So were
perpendicularities: the dizzy heights and distant prospects afforded by a
succession of queer old towers and glorious mountain peaks. Tips and
tops and drops imparted their strange painful pleasure. Regularities were
reprehended and praised, and roughness was often preferred. Novelty and
antiquity were found, on occasion, to coincide. Beggars were disapproved of,
and so was the bossiness of soldiers or policemen. The countries they passed
through were often found to take better care than Britain of the comfort and
recreation of their citizens, and were found to contain many happy people.
One of the most agreeable features of the journal is the persistence of Scottish comparisons. There in the midst of these foreign parts were Arbroaths
and Dalkeiths. All Europe's roads may be said to have led back to Scotland
and to Bonaly, where, after his jaunt, there can be no doubt that he was
delighted to re-racinate himself—to use one of his own words—among the
roses.

# Chapter Six

# *A Scottish Whig*

Cockburn had mixed feelings, not only about those benevolent despots, the Dundases, but about several of the undertakings to which he put his hand. He responded to the conflicting attractions of a romantic past and a rational and stirring, but inherently problematical future. If the old Scotland was so merry and delightful, why should it be changed? There was a dilemma here—for him and for many of his contemporaries, such as Scott. Scott's attachment to the notion of a rosy national heritage had to contend with his approval of the Hanoverian succession and of the commercial advances that followed the Union of 1707. 'The practical Walter Scott', as he is called in the *Memorials*, was sometimes, like the practical Harry Cockburn, a little lachrymose, and the dilemma represented by his compromised patriotism could bring tears to his eyes.

Such tears were to flow when the short-lived Whig Administration of 1806 proposed measures to reorganize the Court of Session, in the hope of reducing the congestion and confusion pictured in Richardson's parody of this very time, to institute a court of review, in the hope of reducing the heavy volume of Scottish appeals to the House of Lords, and to bring about the employment of juries in civil cases. Two years later Melville's son created an Inner House of two divisions for the Court of Session, and jury trial was eventually to be established, though the court of review was not. Scott had previously been in favour of reforming the Court of Session, but he was greatly upset by the Whig proposals. They were the first attempt for many years to effect judicial improvements, and Scott felt they were a threat to Scotland, civil juries being an English phenomenon. Lockhart's *Life of Scott* tells how, after a debate on the subject by the Faculty of Advocates, Scott walked away with Jeffrey 'and another of his reforming friends', who were inclined to be playful about what had taken place. Scott 'exclaimed, "No, no—'tis no laughing matter; little by little, whatever your wishes may be, you will destroy and undermine, until nothing of what makes Scotland Scotland shall remain." And so saying, he turned round to conceal his agitation—but not until Mr Jeffrey saw tears gushing down his cheek— resting his head until he recovered himself on the wall of the Mound.'[1]

The disparity between the proposals themselves and Scott's response may partly be accounted for in terms of an awareness of his own complicity, as a Hanoverian or North British man of sense, in this process of destruction, though it is also true that he was inventing a separate Scotland of his own— which is sometimes thought to have been the only Scotland to survive his death. Cockburn comments in the *Memorials* on the incident—on Scott's sorrow at 'the probable decline of Scotch character and habits': 'Properly applied, this was a sentiment with which I cordially sympathised. But it was misapplied by Scott, who was thinking of feudal poetry, not of modern business.' Scott's dilemma in these matters was related to other dilemmas in his life. On matters of class, for example, his rancorous private politics were at odds with his politic fictions. Cockburn was the more rational and prac- tical of these two divided men, and the more conscious of their shared predicament. A sense of that predicament went to the making of the Whig- gism of his youth and prime, which I am concerned with here, and it was not absent from the Whiggism of his old age.

In 1824, the year before Scott fell in the mud on the way home from his dinner with Robert Cockburn, a different kind of fall occurred—caused by an act of demolition which supplied the *Memorials* with a striking image.[2] After a fire in the medieval High Street—the fire in which the records of the Bonaly Friday Club were supposedly consumed—a wall has become dangerous, and is blown up. A fog of lime dust descends, powdering the coats of the onlookers. 'The shout of the people was heard through the white gloom,' says Cockburn, who was looking down on the scene. He intends no pun or playfulness when he adds: 'It was sublime.'

With the passing of the Reform Bill, Edinburgh would prove a Jericho, and some old walls would come tumbling down. It wasn't the people, in the sense intended here, that brought this about, but the burrowings of their betters—the intermittent efforts of Whig politicians, and the steady in- terest taken by members of the middle classes in search of representation and influence—though the various agitations by and on behalf of the poor, and the skirmishes, such as Bonnymuir, to which these gave rise, contri- buted warnings of what might come if nothing was done. In describing his tumbling wall, Cockburn puts a pause between the crash and the shout—the sort of pause that falls proverbially 'twixt cup and lip. And the effect of

---

[1] *Life of Scott* (second edition, 1839, 10 vols), vol. II, p. 328.    [2] *M*, pp. 424, 425.

dreamy disconnectedness is apt. In his writings, the shout of the people is often heard as through a white gloom, and as from an adjoining height. And yet, in another sense, Cockburn and the people were one. He can seem in two minds about the people, as about the Dundases.

In his *Journal*[1] he compares the institutions of his country to an old house: 'It is dangerous to touch an old house; but the danger of letting it alone is sometimes greater. I am for preserving nothing that is inconvenient merely because it is feudal. Some people think that feudality itself has a charm.' Here, too, there might appear to be a significant pause—between the second last of these sentences and the last, which completes the entry. He himself thought that feudality as such had a charm. He was a defender of old houses, which were for ever being knocked down, and a disparager of the New Town (which now needs to be defended in its turn). In his 'Letter to the Lord Provost on the Best Ways of Spoiling the Beauty of Edinburgh',[2] written in his last years, when he had come to care about conservation rather as he had cared in his youth about emancipation, he says that, in respect of plans like the one to drain the North Loch and drive a railway through the valley between the Castle and Princes Street, 'I listen to the plea of convenience nearly as if it were urged in recommendation of a crime.' That particular crime had by then been committed, and entitling the station Waverley has not atoned for it.

There was a great deal that he was willing to 'let alone'. An unsigned article in the *Scotsman* for 22 January 1874 contains an amusing illustration of this proposition. He is quoted as having complained: 'I was invaded the other day by an old ruffian, who came with some barbarian proposals about knocking down old houses.' And the old ruffian, Admiral Sir Charles Napier, is quoted as complaining: 'That Lord Cockburn of yours is a downright fool. He seems to think that everything that is old should be let alone.' (Napier was an opponent of the Corn Laws, and the *Journal* smiles on his 'rambling off-hand spirit and jocularity'.)

Letting alone was a part, too, of what Cockburn understood by political reform. In his article on the 'Parliamentary Representation of Scotland' in the *Edinburgh Review* for October 1830, he argues, with reference to those currently in possession of the county franchise, that 'every existing right ought to be left untouched,' and goes on: 'Everything that is being let alone, the first thing to be introduced is a proper qualification.' The tactics of conciliation are evident here: the county voter was being wooed with the thought that he would retain his vote for the rest of his life, despite the projected changes. At the same time, the expression 'everything-that-is to

[1] *J*, vol. I, p. 105.  [2] It is printed as an appendix to vol. II of the *Journal*, pp. 315–38.

be let alone' is one that closely corresponds to the way in which many of its enemies and many of its friends were to speak of the fundamental strategy of the Reform Bill: abuses were to be eliminated, the vote was to go where the money was and not to impostors and interlopers—so that the country could continue with the same system as before. Here, in such a letting alone, was a further meaning for laissez-faire—which could also mean, as could the Whigs' 'civil liberty', a free hand for private profit.

'Convenience'—spoken of to the Lord Provost—figures in the *Journal*[1] as a kind of Corryvreckan, the name of a whirlpool off the coast of Argyll:

> All things now are melted in one sea—with a strong Corryvreckan in it, sweeping everything towards the metropolis. This has been the process in all provincial capitals. Improved harbours, railroad stations, better trade, and larger masses of migratory people have succeeded; and those who prefer this to the recollections of the olden time will be pleased. My *reason* is with the modern world, my *dreams* with the old one. And I feel, as to the ancient days, that much of their enchantment arises from distance.

This passage suggests that while his loyalties were staunch and vivid, they were not free from uncertainty. Dreams and reason, the old and the new, custom and convenience, tradition and reform: such opposites ruled his life, and are visible in the form of tensions and dilemmas. Having hesitated, paused, the passage ends on a practical note—but it does so by invoking Campbell's 'romantic', if also equivocal, precept-proverb about distance and the view!

It is necessary to add that his dreams, however much he might doubt them, inspired objections to convenience or progress which were to a large extent reasonable and responsible. Were this not so, he would not have earned the right, as I think he has, to be considered an early, and cogent, environmentalist. His was an eye which caught sight of 'polluting smoke'.[2] His emphasis is ecological in that he wished to preserve the environment as it had been shaped to meet the needs and pleasures of human beings: this, of course, meant saving old houses and trees. In the 'Letter to the Lord Provost' of 1849, he is interested in what Edinburgh will look like in 1949 or 2049, and he is also interested in 'public control' of the environment. But public control was something that public bodies exercised in relation to their own concerns, and private property had to remain more or less immune. Landowners might be chided and adjured: it took many years for them to allow an adequate water supply for Glasgow to be fetched from Loch Katrine. But environmental considerations could not be legislated for at the expense

[1] *J*, vol. II, p. 91.    [2] *Circuit Journeys*, p. 25.

of the 'individual caprice' of landowners—to lift a phrase from the Continental journal—or in defiance of the regrettable demands of the economy. It is as if all that could be done was to plead.

His position is in keeping with his position on the poor. This was another matter on which he wanted things to be let alone: as against the taxing, or assessment, of property in order to relieve destitution, he favoured the traditional, charitable arrangements. His attitude lacks the insouciance of that prince of Whig letters-alone, Lord Melbourne, who remarked: 'Walter Scott was quite right when he said "Why bother the poor? Leave them alone." '[1] But it may be thought to have placed a further constraint on his commitments as a reformer, which have already been shown to be less than exhaustive, and it will be investigated in detail in the course of a later chapter.

When, with Reform in the air, his friend James Moncreiff, chairman of the Pantheon meeting, became a judge, and Jeffrey became Dean of the Faculty of Advocates, Cockburn was very elated. On 1 June 1829, he wrote to his political associate Kennedy of Dunure, the MP for Ayr Burghs who was to be a Treasury Lord in Grey's government: 'The Scotch Millennium seems to me to have arrived.' In the same way, in March 1831, Jeffrey felt that 'the Millennium' was at hand.[2] The collection of letters to Kennedy is a valuable source for the study of Cockburn's energies and ambitions. 'If the thing is to be carried, or well fought, it would make me eat my heart, that we had not the doing of it,' he writes in the months that followed his announcement of the Millennium.[3] The hedonistic Cockburn is rarely seen in these letters: here he is diligent and unrelenting. During the years covered by the Kennedy letters—the years of the run-up to Reform and of its realization—he acted in the spirit of his advice to a later reformer, Rutherfurd, in a letter of 1839: 'Persevere. A Lord Advocate's history is best attested by improvements in the law.'[4]

The Kennedy letters also make clear what the Scottish Whigs wanted from Parliamentary Reform. The volume contains a Memorandum[5] addressed to Lord John Russell in November 1830 which states that the franchise should be extended to include those in possession of 'property and intelligence'—the words form part of the Preamble to the Reform Act, and Cockburn's words for the same thing in the *Journal* are 'wealth and sense'— and that the great object of Reform was to allay discontent by 'uniting the middle to the upper ranks' of society, and by 'giving assurance to the lower orders that their interests would be protected'. This, in fact, was what most of their Southern counterparts wanted too. In his *Edinburgh Review* article

[1] See *Lord M* by David Cecil (1954), pp. 194, 195.　　[2] JLC, 7 March.
[3] *Letters to Kennedy*, p. 245.　　[4] 23 October.　　[5] *Letters to Kennedy*, pp. 258–66.

of October 1830, however, Cockburn stressed that Scotland was worse-off
than England politically, more at the mercy of the town councils and of the
great proprietors: this was true, and it is also a reason for thinking that the
Scottish Bill was more revolutionary than the English. For Cockburn, the
people of Scotland were beyond the pale of the Constitution: and 'by the
word people, we mean that great central mass of property and knowledge
which everywhere else is admitted to form the only good body of electors'.
When the people, so defined, were given the vote, Scotland, hitherto virtually unenfranchised, would become 'respectable'. This was what should
be striven for. This was 'the popular side' in politics. There would be no
peace until the tiresome 'visionaries' who advocated a universal or a wider
franchise were silenced, and moderate change was a way of silencing them.

Cockburn was able to believe, with what might seem like a whole heart,
that the attainment of Reform would mean the attainment of a Millennium.
Before the Bill was passed, he believed that Scotland was about to come in
from beyond the pale of the Constitution, and would share to the full in the
freedoms of the South: in effect, it would *gain* a Constitution. Nevertheless,
even at the moment of triumph, with the Whigs in office and the emancipation of Scotland looming, he is capable of mixed feelings. The *Memorials*
end on the eve of the Millennium, and in that same year, on 30 December
1830, he sent a euphoric yet anxious letter to Dick Lauder.[1] Jeffrey, who had
once been denied the little law post of Collector of Decisions and had edited
the *Edinburgh Review* instead, was now

> Lord Advocate of Scotland! Brougham, long the horror of the respectable, Chancellor
> of England! both by their genius and principles alone! Grey permitted to close the
> end of his days by realising, in power, all the splendid visions of his youth! Toryism,
> with its narrownesses and abuses, prostrate. Whigism no longer the watchword of a
> faction but expanded into the public creed! Government by patronage superseded
> by the necessity of governing by right measures. The last links of the Scotch feudal
> chain dropping off under the hammers that one may distinctly hear erecting the first
> Hustings our country ever saw!
>
> The majesty of public opinion—that true representative on earth of Omnipotence—
> omnificent, just, instinctive, resistless, the Asylum of all right, the exposer of all
> wrong—established not in newspapers and pamphlets but on the very seat of govern-
> ment.
>
> These are the scenes that we have lived to see, and been allowed to assist in pro-
> moting. On the other hand, black specks there are, which tho' at present no bigger
> than a man's hand, may finally darken the prospect. Ireland—Poor rates—over
> population—the national debt—the rise of manufactures abroad, and the consequent
> decline of our commercial monopoly; above all, the fearful and as yet unknown
> dangers which may be doomed to accompany that extraordinary rise of popular
> influence—each of these is well calculated to make the most sanguine ponder.

[1] *Some Letters of Lord Cockburn*, p. 29.

For Cockburn, by and large, 'the people' were those people who deserved the vote. As Brougham put it, a year later, in the House of Lords, 'if there is the mob, there is the people also.'[1] But there was, besides, that other 'people', in whom the populace or mob was comprehended, and *their* influence, too, was likely to increase as a result of the changes meditated by the Whigs. It is worth noticing that the coming of a respectable Scotland could involve the installing of a Chancellor who had long been the horror of the respectable; and that Grey's visions were obviously very different from those of the visionaries Cockburn disliked. Such are the semantics of his internal contradictions, some of which were also those of the party and the politics he supported.

A year later, in the *Journal*,[2] he describes a people's procession held in Glasgow to celebrate the Coronation of William IV—'the reforming king', as he fulsomely calls him. Such processions could be seen—as could Earl Grey's visit to Scotland in 1834—as competition for the famous festivities of 1822 when George IV came to Edinburgh and climbed into a kilt to receive the homage of the lairds in their borrowed tartans. The festivities had been supervised by Scott and had enacted his fantasy of a Celtic survival: a dimension of his profoundly influential imaginary Scotland. Cockburn's workmen were no less of a spectacle—a 'gratifying yet fearful spectacle'. This passage was written at the time when the Reform Bill, having weathered a Commons vote, had been taken to avizandum—in the Court of Session phrase for judicial consultation, or for procrastination and obstruction—by the House of Lords. The Government was defeated at a second-reading division in the Lords, and riots broke out, a week after this procession, at Nottingham and Derby.

It is one of the pleasing or (as it may happen) alarming features of these modern movements, that the people completely understand how much their force is increased by being orderly. All their plans were previously explained to the authorities, and whatever was objected to was changed. The procession took above two hours to pass, walking four abreast. Those engaged were about 12,000. They were divided into crafts, parishes, towns, mills, or otherwise, variously and irregularly, each portion bearing its emblems and music. The carters to the number of nearly 500 went first, mounted, their steeds decorated with ribbons. They were arranged according to the colour of their horses, and in honour of the administration the greys led. Then followed a long and imposing host in the most perfect order, all cheering the Provost as they passed, and all splendid with music and decorations. The banners were mostly of silk, and every trade carried specimens of its art, many of which were singularly beautiful, consisting of printing-presses, harpsichords, steam-engines, steam-vessels, looms and all sorts of machinery, all working, and generally with glass sides so that the working might be seen. The interest of these really exquisite models

[1] 7 October 1831.  [2] *J*, vol. I, pp. 18–21.

was not diminished by the countless efforts of grotesque wit with which each craft
endeavoured to make its calling emblematic of the times and of the cause. Nothing
surprised me so much as the music, even though I had been previously told that there
was scarcely a mill or a village without its band. There could not be under fifty really
good bands, generally consisting of about fifteen performers. King Crispin was to the
eye fully as glorious as George IV when he entered Edinburgh. His retinue consisted
of about 500 persons arrayed and arranged in mimic royalty, and all really splendid.
No description of workmen was too high or too low for the occasion. The chimney-
sweeps walked, and so did the opticians. Though there were groves of banners, we
could only detect two tricolours, and these from their accompaniments were plainly
not French in their principles.

Nothing very fearful here, one might suppose. Yet this is an apprehensive
account as well as a relieved and enthusiastic one, with a strain of nostalgia
for a well-behaved and picturesque medieval past. The houses these people
came from were picturesque in the sense of insanitary, and Glasgow was
on its way to becoming one of the world's worst slums. By no means all of
them would be getting the vote, and many of them could have been
forgiven for thinking that the 'cause' in question was someone else's. Cockburn was afraid of what these orderly people might eventually be organized
to do.

As if to comfort himself, he seems to want to bring out the resemblance
between the procession and some submissive medieval pageant—not a very
difficult task, admittedly. The procession is made to appear at once utopian,
or ideal, and utterly traditional. In this and other respects, his description
is like a page from the Babar books, in which kindly King Babar rules over
his socialistic, Owenite community of obedient elephants. Babar holds his
own 'memorable pageant', during which, seated on a kind of dais, and on a
kind of charger, and having shed his apple-green suit for an ermine robe,
he watches his subjects march past, the arts and crafts guilds distinguishing
themselves. Babar's bowls-playing élite—General Cornelius, Fandango the
scholar, Podula the sculptor, Capoulosse the doctor—is certainly reminiscent
of Cockburn's literati (among the worthies calotyped by Hill is Dr Capadose,
a Dutch Calvinist physician). And Babar also has his Bonaly in the Celesteville Garden of Pleasure. I believe that these resemblances can be explained
in terms of the notion that, well before the triumph of Reform, the past
became, for Cockburn, more utopian than the future. It could even be said
that it became divine, and that nostalgia grew to be his religion. The political
millennium which he predicted did not arrive. But another millennium had
already happened, and was there to be remembered and revered. He never
wanted a new world based on fearful and fundamental social change. And he
did not want to lose the old world of feudal Scotland.

The description also hints, incidentally, that the country-loving Cockburn was fairly unfamiliar ('I had been previously told . . . ') with the more specifically human aspects of the remoter Scottish countryside. Up to this point in his life, he had been a barrister whose activities did not often sever him from Edinburgh, and his circuit journeys had not yet started. Not only that, his rural paradise was within walking distance of Parliament House, and is now within range of Edinburgh Corporation transport.

The Glasgow procession was one of several occasions on which the people of Scotland, at various levels, gave evidence of their support for Reform, of their fears for its attainment and of their satisfaction at the outcome. Ten days before the procession, a meeting in Edinburgh was addressed by that imperious equestrian, James Gibson-Craig: 'The people can do without the peers, but not the peers without the people.'[1] Spoken, one might say, like a peer. Possibly the most remarkable of these occasions came during Grey's visit to the North, after his retirement and with Peel impending at the head of a new government, in September 1834, and it is worth glancing ahead at what happened.

The country now paid homage, Cockburn's *Journal* reports, to its 'greatest public friend', and the 'popular joy' which greeted Grey's entrance into Edinburgh surpassed that accorded to George IV. When he crossed the stream at Coldstream, the bridge was turned into a triumphal arch of flowers and shrubs, and the journey to Edinburgh 'has rivalled a royal progress'. Over the hills he came, and he was received with demonstrations at Pathhead and Dalkeith. Fifty horsemen rode out from the city to meet him, representatives of the trades forgathered with him in the Lord Provost's house at Newington. He was awarded the freedom of the city in a gold box, and a banquest, supervized by Gibson-Craig, was held in the evening.

Pavilioned in gaslight in a structure of canvas and wood erected in the High School Yards, where Cockburn had suffered his concussive education, nearly 2,800 persons feasted their greatest public friend: there were 249 women, but few males, no doubt, of the pedestrian order. The scene, enthused Cockburn, might have come from the Arabian Nights. 'All the ordinary Edinburgh talkers drew back, in order to make way for better men.' These better men included the dangerous Earl of Durham, 'Radical Jack', who talked in character at the dinner—foolishly, says Cockburn, who was due to speak but left early, tucked up in bed the more soundly for the knowledge that his turn was being called. His days in government were numbered. Jeffrey, who had already retired and was ill, absented himself with a sigh. There were fears about the behaviour of Brougham, who was reputed to have plotted against Grey, but, in the event, the Evil did not

[1] See *Church and Reform in Scotland, 1797–1843*, by W. L. Mathieson (1916), p. 217.

explode. The Radicals, who had gained in respectability since the 1790s, had tried to curtail the celebrations, but in vain. Cockburn was always conscious of the difference in station between his own kin and kind and the high aristocracy, and he mentions the abstention of 'our deluded nobles' from the banquet. Eleven of these, in fact, attended.[1]

Why did the changes made by the Whigs give so much pleasure, and what was it that needed changing? There are no grounds for doubting that Scotland's situation was quite as unsatisfactory as Cockburn, even at his most polemical, was given to claiming. The faults of the unregenerate feudal Scotland in which he grew up have often been rehearsed, and in a manner which owes much to his own testimony. The essence of the Scottish situation was that a tired social system was forced to cope with Cockburn's Corry-vreckan of industrialization, expanding trade and a steeply rising population: the urban centres of the Lowlands were flooded with newcomers from the north, Ireland and elsewhere, and were ill-equipped to attend to the mounting problems of discontent and destitution produced by trade recessions and insanitary living conditions. Edinburgh was still governed with reference to a statute dating back to 1469. Those who hoped for solutions to these problems were inclined to place their faith in a wider franchise which would combat the domination of Scottish politics by a narrowly based self-interest.

Political representation was conducted in two ways: through the burghs and through the counties. Town councils were self-electing oligarchies, who elected delegates who chose a Member of Parliament. Cockburn pointed out in his article of 1830 that the Edinburgh Town Council was then 33 strong, a higher number than usual, and, having estimated the value of the town property held by the 33, he concluded that 'the right of voting is engrossed by less than the three-thousandth part of the population, and by about the one hundred and fiftieth part of the real property'. The burghs sent south a third of the country's Members of Parliament, and many of these burghs were or had been bankrupt, were ridden with graft, and were remote from the areas of economic growth. The Whigs, who wanted political change, also tended to favour a laissez-faire expansionism: the burghs, therefore, were doubly obnoxious: idle as well as tyrannical. Cockburn himself was at best a reluctant expansionist, and was never fond of manufacturers.

The counties operated differently, but, for Cockburn, no less abominably, though it could be said that they constituted the 'open' part of the system, since the burghs were all closed corporations. By the end of the

[1] Ibid., p. 227.

eighteenth century the population had risen to one and a half million, and was on the brink of a further take-off: in 1788, the nominal voting power for the counties was 2,662, and because of the devising of notional vote-carrying freeholds, and for other reasons, the actual voting power was well below that. A vote was an item of property and could be sold, so that votes were bought as an investment: this was true of both countries, and compensation for their prospective loss was demanded in Parliament during the debates on Reform. In both the towns and the shires, according to Cockburn, votes were 'steeped in temptation': with arrangements like these, electors could not have 'a public heart'.[1] They were arrangements, however, which could help a government to govern, in view of the patronage at its disposal. Patronage was exchanged for the support of MPs and of electors. During the 1790s, Henry Dundas, a past master at availing himself of the opportunities furnished by such arrangements, could reckon on the loyalty of three-quarters of the forty-five MPs.

In England, and particularly in the counties, with their forty-shilling freehold and other entitlements, there was a degree of representation, and of political expression, that far exceeded what was known in Scotland: there was more of a public heart. Scotsmen had few rotten boroughs, or Old Sarums, to complain of, but then, as Norman Gash has written, 'from 1707 to 1832 Scotland resembled one vast, rotten borough'.[2]

Scottish seats were rarely nomination seats, rarely in the hands of a single patron, but they were, instead, at the mercy of the burgh oligarchies and of the processes of influence, and of purchase and reward, that obtained in the counties. A key factor was that of those feudal superiorities which, while divorced from the ownership of land, continued to attract a vote: in 1831, half the county voters were 'parchment barons', as their owners were called. Ancient rights, and the land valuations of Charles II's reign, determined the county vote, in that superiorities were based on these, and not only attracted a vote but could be split up in order to attract more. The distinction in Scots law between *dominium utile* and *dominium directum*—between the beneficial interest and, in effect, the superiority—meant that the first

---

[1] *ER*, October 1830.

[2] *Politics in the Age of Peel* (1953), p. 36. In offering this account, and subsequent accounts, of the Scottish politics of the time, I acknowledge my indebtedness to Norman Gash's distinguished book and to a number of others: in particular, to three recent histories of Scotland, William Ferguson's *Scotland 1689 to the Present* (1968), T. C. Smout's *A History of the Scottish People, 1560–1830* (1969), and Rosalind Mitchison's *A History of Scotland* (1970), and to L. J. Saunders's very enterprising earlier study of the social background, *Scottish Democracy 1815–1840* (1950). Among other works consulted were *Scotland and the French Revolution* by H. W. Meikle (1912), *The Making of Classical Edinburgh* by A. J. Youngson (1966), *The Democratic Intellect* by George Davie (1961), *The Passing of the Whigs* by Donald Southgate (1962) and *The Great Reform Act* by Michael Brock (1973).

could be relinquished by someone who retained the second, and with it the associated franchise. Meanwhile, unlike the English, the Scottish voting qualification in terms of land had not been devalued, which made the county electorates small and easy to manipulate.

A trade was done in these superiorities. Attorneys acquired them for the purpose of speculation; the younger sons of middle-class families also acquired them, as did the nominees of major landowners. They were used as a means of gaining patronage—for applicants who exercised patience as well as influence and could overcome snubs, postponements and competing claims—in the form of appointments, emoluments, sinecures, colonial posts, military commissions, Presenterships of Signatures, the Postmastership of Lasswade, and so on ad infinitum and avizandum. Required to deliver patronage to those who had elected them, Scottish MPs were closely tied, down the years, to the patronage-dispensing government of the day. As a result, India and other outposts of the Empire were tied to the Scottish shires, where jobs and openings abroad were so often secured. The fact that many of the parchment voters were landless and of no social consequence supplied Jeffrey with an appeal to the wealthier proprietors, who could feel aggrieved on their own account at the state of the representation. Not only were there few county voters, but the few there were were poorly representative of the realities of ownership and interest in the counties. It was the realities of ownership and interest in the nation at large—among them, the wealth and power of the manufacturing districts—to which the Reform Whigs wanted to do justice: to these, rather than the realities of population growth and change. The Scottish Reform Act accordingly stated that the principle of 'bare superiority', as a franchise condition, should be deserted, and in this as in other ways it was hoped that the Augean stables of the North could be cleaned out. At the same time, they were to be let alone, and it was not the case that government by patronage ceased with the Act. We have already seen Jeffrey, as Lord Advocate, in the act of managing, or perhaps of having to manage, the flow of Scottish patronage. There seems to have been some attempt to mitigate it, and to enforce considerations of merit, but there were plenty of Whigs about who felt that Whig nepotism, or a Whig job, was relatively virtuous.

Black as its politics were, Cockburn was always sure that the society of that time had great merits, though I shall argue later that he did not fully appreciate these merits. It was a time of wigged and brocaded formality, but a time, too, of learning and elegance, a time which shone all the more brightly in contrast with 'the very recently softened barbarism of the country'. He grew up among people who had experienced the 'Forty-Five rebellion, and who had seen the Young Pretender at Holyrood with his savage host. The seventeenth century, he declares in the *Sedition Trials,*[1] had been 'one long rebellion': except in the context of family life, where sound opinions might lead to a rupture, rebellions were something from which you escaped or evolved. And the wits of the *Edinburgh Review* were persuaded that in the course of the eighteenth century an evolutionary step had been taken: civilization had come to Scotland. Nevertheless, at the end of that century the country had yet to be emancipated politically. As yet, Cockburn says in the *Journal,* 'the people had not arisen. There was no Public.' By 'people' and 'public' he means, once more, the mean of 'wealth and sense' who were due to be enfranchised. He means the evolving middle class. If, as Jeffrey supposed, a struggle between the aristocracy and the democracy of Scotland was enacted in the earlier part of the nineteenth century, then it was the respectability of Scotland which emerged victorious.

Cockburn could also talk about what had happened in a way that does not bring to mind a process of evolution. The *Memorials* refer to the 'regeneration of Scotland' as a result of the political improvements he worked for: in common with other reformers of the period, and of other periods, he could envisage a reversion to an imaginary early state—to an antique purity if not a paradise lost.

In what is far and away the *Memorials'* best-known passage,[2] he evokes the temptation-steeped Edinburgh Council Chamber—'a low-roofed room, very dark, and very dirty, with some small dens off it for clerks'—in the days when the people were excluded from its transactions:

> Within this Pandemonium sat the town-council, omnipotent, corrupt, impenetrable. Nothing was beyond its grasp; no variety of opinion disturbed its unanimity, for the pleasure of Dundas was the sole rule for every one of them. Reporters, the fruit of free discussion, did not exist; and though they had existed, would not have dared to disclose the proceedings. Silent, powerful, submissive, mysterious, and irresponsible, they might have been sitting in Venice.

If there was a note of apprehension in his words about the Glasgow procession, there is a certain enviousness here. It would be wrong to attach great significance to this: he is clear, after all, that the Town Council was servile as well as strong. But the exaggerations, exoticism and flamboyance of the account indicate that he is savouring and celebrating, as well as blaming, the behaviour of those worthies whose authority he helped to supplant.

The government headed—or figureheaded—by the Doges was less despotic than he assumes, and he writes as if Venice were an object of special horror.

---

[1] *Sedition Trials,* vol. II, p. 110.   [2] *M,* pp. 95, 96.

Hostility to Venice was widespread then in Western Europe, and a book arrived in Scotland at the time when he was beginning the *Memorials* which could well have assisted in the promotion of a superstitious dread of that city. In a letter of 1821,[1] his friend Sir James Mackintosh discusses the *Histoire de la République de Venise* by Pierre, Comte Daru, which had lately been published in Paris: the letter is addressed to another friend of Cockburn's Thomas Thomson. Mackintosh, whose *Vindiciae Gallicae*, many years previously, had argued against Burke on behalf of the French Revolution, remarks that the opening-up of the Venetian archives had given historians 'access to the most secret recesses of that tyrannical policy which was so long thought the model of wisdom'. Wordsworth for one had thought well of Venice. His sonnet 'On the Extinction of the Venetian Republic, 1802' proclaims her as formerly 'the safeguard of the West': she was 'the eldest Child of Liberty' who had held 'the gorgeous East in fee'. Now the truth would be known. In the same year, 1821, Daru's book was said by Lady Morgan to be 'in the hands of every liberal reader'.[2]

Daru was Stendhal's cousin and one of Napoleon's staff officers: he appears to have been respected by Napoleon, and was awarded the thankless task of planning the food supplies for the Russian campaign. The first volume of his history says that Napoleon's arrival in Venice was necessary *pour que ce gouvernment impénétrable n'eût plus de mystères*,[3] and it is likely that this is where Cockburn got his 'impenetrable' and 'mysterious' from. Daru frequently alludes to *les vices intérieurs de cet état inquisitorial*. This was the common coin of anti-Venetian invective in Europe, but there is a Gallic glitter here which should also be taken into account. The inquisitorial character imparted by Cockburn to the proceedings of the Edinburgh Town Council can fairly be called exotic in that it seems to have been partly derived from Napoleonic France's verdict on the Venetian oligarchy.

Renaissance Venice, the Venice antecedent to its eighteenth-century decline, whose system lasted until the intervention of Napoleon, is thought once again, by some modern historians, to have been, if not the model of wisdom, at any rate a well-conducted and responsible society by the standards of its time: as far as representation is concerned, it can probably bear comparison with the Scotland which succeeded the passing of the Reform Bill. But Cockburn was shocked—politically shocked, though in other ways allured—by the very idea of Venice, and, for polemical purposes, turned

---

[1] The letter is printed (p. 173) in the *Memoir of Thomas Thomson, Advocate,* compiled by Cosmo Innes (who is shown calotyping in the country in a *Circuit Journeys* entry of 15 September 1849) and published by the Bannatyne Club (1854).

[2] She says this in a new edition (3 vols) of her *Italy*, vol. III, p. 367.

[3] *Histoire de Venise* (second edition, 8 vols, Paris, 1821), vol. I, p. 7.

its secret recesses into the dark and dirty dens of the Edinburgh Town Council. This passage in the *Memorials* was written, I think, after he had read Daru and before he embarked on his Continental tour of 1823, during which he discovered that the government of the Doges, though no doubt 'very bad', had had its redeeming features. Daru's book could hardly have failed to sharpen his desire to see Venice and die.

It appears that Venice was pondered by Scotsmen at various times in the course of the 1820s, and there can indeed be no certainty that Cockburn drew on Daru for this passage of the *Memorials*. One later event would certainly have served to stimulate his curiosity. The *Edinburgh Review* for June 1827 carried an article on the 'Democratical Constitution of Venice', an article which Cockburn is known to have been aware of, and which acknowledges the importance of Daru's researches. It was the work of the Italian writer Ugo Foscolo—loathed by Scott, who saw this liberal as a conceited haunter of literary parties and 'ugly as a baboon'.[1] Foscolo stresses that Venice, originally democratical, was soon subverted by the rudiments of the State Inquisition and eventually by the Oligarchy: 'Democracy gradually dwindled into hereditary Aristocracy; and that, in its turn, into a mysterious and unrelenting Oligarchy.' Venice was subsequently the victim of a Constitution which veiled its operations in 'impenetrable secrecy'. Here again is the language employed by Cockburn.

Scott's *Journal* tells of a meeting in Paris in 1826 with a friend of his, Jean-Antoine-Gauvain Gallois: the author, according to Scott, of 'the *History of Venice*', which he also describes, shortly afterwards, as *The Decay and Fall of Venice*.[2] Another friend of Gallois, Sir James Mackintosh, was in Paris two years earlier, and the *Memoirs* of his life[3] tell how Gallois informed him that 'M. Daru, the historian of Venice, is out of town, to whom I was anxious to be introduced'. Here we have further evidence of the Scottish interest in Venice, together with some incitement to suppose that Scott confused the writings of Daru with those of Gallois. There is no record of Gallois's having written a history of Venice.

It will be recalled that by 1830—in his euphoric letter to Dick Lauder— 'the majesty of public opinion' had become, for Cockburn, 'omnificent, just, instinctive, resistless, the Asylum of all right . . . ' There is, I would say, a significant similarity between this passage and the description of the Council Chamber. A Pandemonium is usually somewhat different from an asylum, yet Milton's rebel angels found asylum in their Pandemonium, and it turns

---

[1] *The Journal of Sir Walter Scott*, edited by W. E. K. Anderson (1972), p. 10.
[2] Ibid., pp. 224, 226.
[3] *Memoirs of the Life of Sir James Mackintosh*, edited by his son Robert (2 vols, 1835), vol. II, p. 413.

5

out, on this occasion, that the two establishments have certain characteristics in common, and that the power Cockburn deplores in the Town Council is rather like the power he applauds in public opinion: omnipotence is much the same as omnificence. The people of wealth and sense have arisen in their might, deposing the old town-council oligarchs, and it is plain from a comparison of the two passages that might appealed to Cockburn. He was not unmoved by the blacksmith's power he saw in Braxfield, however much he deplored the blackguard's use he made of it.

Before the Reform Bill was passed, of course, he already had his doubts about the majesty of public opinion, and about the rise of popular influence. He was convinced that the growing might of 'the people' could be abused, as the old power had been abused. The term could hardly be indefinitely employed in such a way as to exclude those people—many of whom had neither the wealth nor the sense to qualify them for consideration—whom Cockburn called the populace and who were subsequently called the proletariat. And that, indeed, was the trouble. He had doubts about the willingness of such people to keep the peace. These and other doubts of the kind increased, it would appear, as he grew older, and as the political challenge to the left of the Whigs increased in vigour: more might! He came to be quite severely sceptical about the improvement of Scotland and the educability of human nature. At the age of 68, he told Rutherfurd: 'Amidst the wreck of Ireland, and the coming storms in our manufacturing districts, I hope that the Whig Flag of sense and justice is in no present danger of being struck.' At the age of 71, discussing 'sectarian hatreds' and the progress of 'general education', he told Eliza Fletcher: 'On these matters the human mind has not advanced one inch during the last five hundred years, and considering the nature of that mind it may be doubted if it will advance one inch in the next five hundred years.' At the age of 72, discussing Parliament, he told Richardson: 'I have not become a Tory; but no Whigism I have had required me to make members slaves of the low multitude any more than of the high aristocracy.'[1]

A few months later, in a *Journal* entry dated 30 January 1852, he struck a similar note: 'Age has not made me a Tory, but distaste of the monarchy, or of any of its props, was never a part of the Whiggism of my youth.' Lord John Russell's Government had been stirring 'the Reform mud' in urban areas by promising to introduce a successor Bill. But the Government fell shortly afterwards. The glory of the first Bill, Cockburn says, was 'that it not

---

[1] These quotations are drawn from a letter to Rutherfurd of 22 January 1847, from the *Autobiography of Mrs Fletcher*, p. 289, and from a letter to Richardson of 17 October 1851 (*Some Letters of Lord Cockburn*, p. 69).

only avoided a revolutionary triumph of just discontent, but by giving its due influence to property, steadied the whole political system.' He writes of the electorate and of the House of Commons: 'If the elective qualification shall ever be reduced so low that the property element is made merely nominal, and a greatly increased portion of that House shall be returned by mere population, I fear that our boasted constitution must soon sink into that democracy which seems to be the natural result of every government where the people have become politically free. I wish I could believe that any people who have obtained the means of engrossing supreme power can be induced by education to refrain from grasping it.' He shrank from a future which would bring Reform Bills 'every twenty years or less'. The glory of Reform was in the past, and for Cockburn, in certain moods and at certain moments, its name was now mud.

All this, of course, was towards the end of his life, long after his own years in the mire. By then, he was prone to such reflections as those of 1841 when he learnt from the census that Edinburgh and Perth had increased their populations very little in the previous decade: 'It is comfortable to have a few Goshens, a few spots where taste, and intellect, and peace can enjoy themselves in their old way, undisturbed by steam-engines, mobs, and upstart temporary wealth.'[1] The present chapter has dealt with a different Cockburn: with his feelings about the politically benighted state of the Scotland of his youth and early middle age. It is time to say what the Whigs did to improve it. It is also time to set out in greater detail the limitations of their outlook, and of his account of it, and to say what became of the Scotch Millennium.

[1] *Circuit Journeys*, p. 146.

# Chapter Seven

# *The Scotch Millennium*

The announced millennium never came. But then it was only in moments of euphoria that it had been felt to be impending. Reform was more often seen, by those anxious for it, as a perfection of the status quo, as a gloriously sound arrangement, as a step away from revolution, rather than towards it. The French principles of liberty, equality and fraternity were abhorrent even, or especially, to those Scottish Whigs whose early lives had been fired by the French Revolution.

Much has been said about the limitations of the Reform Act, and about the poverty of motive among certain Whigs, both in Scotland and England, for whom the courting of the democracy of the nation was chiefly a matter of opportunity or advantage. Carlyle[1] spoke of the Whig Ministry's programmes in the 1830s as a Barmecide feast—altogether less filling than the one consumed in the High School Yards. It is certainly true that Parliamentary Reform was the work of men who wanted to let things alone as well as to change them, and that it made less of a difference in the short term than its enemies feared it would, or than Cockburn sometimes predicted. Nevertheless, what the Whigs did in 1832 was very important. It opened the way to government by consent, or to as much of that as we have now got. It started the rot which it was meant to stop.

The Scottish Reform Bill was drafted by Cockburn, with Kennedy's co-operation. In order to confer with the Committee of Four (Russell, Durham, Duncannon, Sir James Graham) to whom the Cabinet had assigned the task of working out a scheme for Reform, Cockburn spent a week in London in December 1830: thereafter Jeffrey shared increasingly in the preparation of the Scottish Bill. The three Scotsmen were expected to produce a version of the English Bill which was designed to meet Scottish requirements. In a letter of 13 February 1831, one of the letters from his friend which Cockburn collected and glossed, Jeffrey points out that their

[1] See Chapter Nine of Carlyle's *Chartism* (1839).

English colleagues were 'very desirous to have the scheme as much the same in the two countries as possible'. A letter of 10 February, together with Cockburn's note, throws light on the relationship of the Scots to their English colleagues and on the circumstances in which the Bill was devised and debated: the atmosphere of haste, hostility, strain and stratagem ought not to be forgotten by anyone attempting to form an estimate of the measures that resulted. The Reform project has been brewing for long enough, but in the course of the English (as opposed to the Scottish) 1820s it had been neglected by Whig politicians: now it was to be brought abruptly to the boil. In Parliamentary terms, moreover, it was a project of unprecedented scale and difficulty.

In the letter in question, Jeffrey blames his friend for dilatoriness, and Cockburn rejoins in the note: 'His impatience, since his masters hurried him, was excuseable enough; but theirs was ridiculous. Their very first hint of their views was given to me personally on the 21st of December 1830, in London; and without communicating the English draft, knowing Scotland's utter inexperience of everything connected with popular election, and gagging us from speaking a word, they wonder how our draft is not ready in about five weeks!! As many *months* could not have produced a well-prepared bill, by Scotchmen, in these circumstances.'

While the Scottish Whigs' Memorandum of November of that year was broadly consonant with the intentions of the Southern Whigs as they made ready to face the Parliamentary challenge, a distinction favourable to the possession of land, as opposed to property held in towns and villages, was mooted there in respect of the county vote. But this was not persevered with. In the course of the debates there was a move, which Jeffrey did not repudiate, to accept a Scottish franchise qualification that was higher than the English by five or ten pounds, but it was successfully resisted—by Cockburn, among others.

In a House of Commons speech of 9 March 1831, Jeffrey explained that the Ministry's aims with regard to Scotland were to increase the representation of the towns, particularly the large towns; to see to it that the representation was based, in a realistic fashion, on a property qualification; to adapt the system whereby burghs were grouped into districts for the purposes of returning MPs—a system that was due to be retained, as were, in essentials, the existing arrangements for dividing up the counties—in order to curtail or abolish the influence of the small burghs. A central feature of the Scottish Act's attempt to correct specifically Scottish abuses may be expressed in the words of the time—those of an expert on franchise questions, Sheriff John Cay of Linlithgowshire. The Act sought to attach the county franchise 'to *actual property*, to the *dominium utile* of the subjects affording the qualification, dispensing with the ancient requisite, viz. that the lands must be held of the Crown, and abolishing (prospectively) all qualifications depending on *bare* superiority'.[1] In all time coming the vote was to be withheld from feudal lordship as such. From now on, the superior must receive from his vassal at least £10 in feu-duties in respect of the property on which the vote was claimed. Existing rights were, however, to be respected: the parchment baron would retain his vote for the rest of his life.

While the total number of seats in the House of Commons remained the same, Scotland gained eight more, and now had 53 MPs. This figure was, in fact, disproportionately low in relation to her population, which was about a sixth of that of England and Wales. Town councils forfeited their responsibility for the election of MPs. The Parliamentary monopoly of the royal burghs was at an end, and a new category of burgh, the Parliamentary burgh, was devised: in response to the process of urbanization that had taken place, large non-royal burghs (Paisley, Greenock) became constituencies. Glasgow, Aberdeen, Dundee and Perth were drawn out of the districts of burghs to which they had hitherto belonged. Glasgow now had two Members and Edinburgh gained a second Member. The number of burgh constituencies was thereby substantially increased. Cockburn afterwards remarked that 'the burgh representation should all have been for single towns, and the rest should have been thrown into the shires'.[2] As it was, the royal burghs of Peebles, Selkirk and Rothesay were thrown into their respective shires. The number of county constituencies remained the same: the old system of pairs, whereby two areas took turns to be represented, was abandoned, and certain counties were joined for election purposes. In the burghs, adult male householders (landlords or tenants) whose property had an annual rentable value of £10 and above were awarded the vote. In the counties, owners of property—land, houses and other heritable subjects—worth £10 or more were awarded the vote, as were tenants if they had a life lease, or a lease of 57 years or more, on property rated at £10, if they had a shorter lease on property rated at £50, or if they were *bona fide* tenants of property worth the same amount.

In other words, the vote still did not extend, in the country, beyond well-to-do farmers and the like, who remained under their landlord's eye and largely submissive, nor, in the towns, beyond the middle class. There was, as yet, no secret ballot—which did much to strengthen the long arm of the

---

[1] *An Analysis of the Scottish Reform Act with the Decisions of the Courts of Appeal*, Part One (1837), p. 3.

[2] JLC: in a note to a letter of Jeffrey's of 3 February 1831.

landlord. The police burghs—a system which ran parallel to the town council jurisdictions in certain areas, and which had already introduced voting on a wider basis of participation than the existing Parliamentary franchise— continued to deal with public health and related matters. As a result, it could be claimed that the town council doges were simply adjured to be solvent and acquitted of crucial obligations. But their Parliamentary power was broken, and in 1833 Burgh Reform introduced town-council election by £10 householders and above. Sped by the greater uniformity of the 'setts' or constitutions of Scottish towns, Burgh Reform preceded Municipal Reform in the South by some two years. The third of the three statutes authorized the £10 householder in certain towns to opt for a 'police system'. This confirmed what was already in train. By maintaining two separate burghs, some towns could lead a double life.[1]

Many abuses, in various quarters, were put right in 1832. But the country gentlemen held their own, and new abuses began in the shires. William Ferguson, an authority on the electoral history of the period, has observed that 'a measure designed to abolish fictitious votes merely served to bring their price down'.[2] And, with a new electorate of 65,000 at the end of 1832 (the old electorate stood at around 4,500), it could scarcely be claimed that the people—in any sense other than the narrow one espoused by the Whigs— had arisen. Consent, or something like it, had yet to come. Perhaps it has still to come. Consent, perhaps, is strictly millennial.

In 1966, Ferguson argued that the Scottish Bill was incompetently drafted. Bad drafting produced results which are characterized as 'vicious'. It left loopholes which were attacked by the surviving Melville connection by means of expedients—such as the buying up of properties for bestowal on supporters —which are described as worthy of 'the great Henry Dundas himself'. Cockburn is said to have taken too little trouble to adjust to their Scottish setting the 'English things', like the £10 qualification, which he was delighted to be importing. And he and Jeffrey—men of letters that they were— are charged with a contempt for Scottish feudal law and for the facts of Scottish agrarian life. Some people may feel that on occasion, like William Macbean, Ferguson makes too much of small matters: his case is that it was feelings of this kind which damaged the Bill.[3]

---

[1] In 1822, Cockburn published 'A Letter to the Inhabitants of Edinburgh on the New Police Bill' from 'a Fellow-Citizen'. The Letter deals with the implications of a quarrel that had broken out between the elected Commissioners of Police and the Superintendant. In a Reform spirit, Cockburn resists a move to raise the qualification to vote for the Commissioners, while granting that persons 'of doubtful intelligence or independence' should be excluded from voting.

[2] *Scotland 1689 to the Present*, p. 289.

[3] *Scottish Historical Review*, April 1966. Cockburn refers to his 'English things' in the *Letters to Kennedy*, p. 400.

The worst consequences ascribed here to the Act were the new ways of coercing tenants that were made available to landowners, who manipulated leases and took advantage of another English thing, open nominations and polls. The same bullying and trickery went on in England, though it was less of a novelty there. Ferguson talks of 'a new era of faggot votes' in the Scottish counties, and notes that Gladstone was able to win his Midlothian campaign of 1879 by resorting to such contrivances. It has been alleged of the Scottish Whigs that technicalities tended to elude them: according to this indictment, Cockburn and Jeffrey ran true to type.

Among the technical questions said to have been mishandled were the position of existing freeholders, which, Ferguson insists, could often be understood only with reference to the old electoral law, and the position of the eldest sons of Scottish peers, who were to be enfranchised. Cockburn and Jeffrey are blamed for not seeing to it that the position of these eldest sons was made clear by stating that they had to be otherwise qualified for the vote: apart, that is, from being the eldest sons of Scottish peers. The clause was intended to remove a disqualification, but was then treated by some as a qualifying clause. Cockburn later granted that a 'clerical blunder' was made here,[1] but Ferguson says that the point was not put right when an amending act was passed after Cockburn's day. I am inclined to think that this *is* a fairly small matter—smaller, at any rate, than the muddle attributed to Cockburn over the way in which the concept of 'possession' which figured in the English Bill was translated to the Scottish one. From such muddles further feudalities of various kinds, and a new oppression, are said to have emerged.

Ferguson cites Sheriff Cay as a critic of the Scottish Act, and Cay was also one of those who advised at Westminster when the Bill was being prepared. This may serve as a reminder of the many interested parties who advised, decided and coerced in relation to the Bill, and of the efforts that were made to prevent and weaken it. Nor was there much in the way of official or 'clerical' support. It would be wrong to lay the blame for the vulnerable product of these labours and contentions entirely at the door of Cockburn and Jeffrey, and their literary foolishness.

Certain of the constraints which were imposed by drafting defects on the operation of the Act were akin to others which were introduced expressly, and at its very conception—in the egg, so to speak. Given the inferior state of the old Scottish representation, the Scottish Act could be thought, and has been thought, more revolutionary than the English. But this is a word which it is perhaps better not to use of either of them. The suggestion that

[1] JLC: in a note to a letter of Jeffrey's of 24 February 1833.

the Scottish franchise be hoisted to a level higher than the English was dropped: but as it turned out, property values being what they were in the Northern burghs, the eventual burgh franchise was too high to yield constituencies large enough for there to be the prospect of eliminating influence and graft. Equally, the county constituencies tended to be small by Southern standards, and they were undoubtedly too small to escape magnate dictation, as Cockburn was to recognize, though the main objection to the county franchise appears to have been that it would give too much of a say to the small-town voter armed with a county vote. So Scotland was still rotten.

Both Bills were founded on property—at a time when even many Radicals could conceive of no other foundation for a measure of this kind. The powers and possessions of the aristocracies of both countries were such that no Bill which set the franchise qualifications at these levels could have ensured the early collapse of the aristocratic supremacy in British politics. But then the Bill was never meant to accomplish this. The brief given by the Cabinet in 1830 to the Committee of Four was of an uncompromisingly conservative cast: property and the status quo were to be protected, the Bill was to be a fortress for resisting further innovation. And the ensuing contentions did not democratize the measure. During that same year, while the Tories were fearing a *facilis descensus Averno*, 'finality' was the watchword of the less militant Whig Ministers. In the heat of the battle, Macaulay told the House of Commons: 'Reform that you may preserve.'[1] None of the chieftains of the Northern Whigs would have disagreed with that, and the Scottish Revolution was very much a conservative and comparative affair.

This is not to deny that the Act made a huge difference: along the lines of ensuring, while also postponing, a comprehensive suffrage, and because it improved, while also at times impairing, the political practice of both countries. And it is not to deny that the sensations of certain Scots Reformers were those of a kind of revolutionary. Reform was glorious as the Revolution of 1688 had been glorious. Down the years, moreover, to preach and teach and scheme on its behalf had been an activity that smelt of cells and clandestinity, and of ostracism: part of Cockburn's circle had once had the character of such a cell. At the Pantheon meeting of 1820, a Whig leader, John Clerk, was gleefully accosted by a small elderly man, a veteran of the plots of the 1790s: 'Weel Sir! ou're at the auld wark again.' These words about their old work could well have brought to mind not only the Covenanters—for Cockburn, as we have seen, Reform was 'an old Covenanting business' in Scotland—but the Jacobites. They recall, too, the sort of thing that used to be said of the Devil and of his missionary activities on earth—

[1] 2 March 1831.

5*

of the conversions to his party effected among the sons of men. Reform could
be seen as glorious and virtuous, and it could be seen, however fleetingly, as
conspiratorial and infernal: both as a bulwark against change and as a subversion of the status quo. The Act itself was intensely equivocal, and productive of ironies. Both ultra-Tories and Radicals could favour it—and it
was also possible for the liberal-minded to reject it, on the grounds that it
was an invitation to demagoguery and mob rule.

Conspiratorial and euphoric as the history of Scottish Reform can sometimes seem, however, there is no question but that Cockburn was, for the
most part, one of the Whig letters-alone, who believed that Reform should
go so far and no further. 'The great thing,' he wrote to Kennedy at the time
of the Bill, 'is to avoid Radicalism.'[1] He did avoid it, as he avoided democracy. And some of his readers now will decide that he was a patrician
people's friend who remained faithful to the interests of the rival factions
which composed the ruling class: a true blue-blooded Whig oligarch.
Early in the nineteenth century, Cobbett, whom Cockburn thought an
impudent fool, was asserting that the people would only be exchanging one
set of masters for another when the high Whigs came into their own. But one
set of masters may be preferred to another, and Cockburn, though a high
Whig, seems to have been popular, in the ordinary sense, with the lower
orders. The notion of the people's friend, and of paternalism, has long
appealed to the Scots. One of the country's biggest popular newspapers is
still called the *People's Friend*: it has never been at all subversive. The
Anglo-Scottish Society of the Friends of the Pople, whose activities came
under scrutiny during the sedition trials, was run to a marked degree by
gentlemen: Grey himself had had to do with it, in his early days. It did not
avoid Radicalism, though, and Cockburn did not belong. Still less would he
have wished to join a body like the United Scotsmen: he was never enough
of a conspirator for that.

His maturing opinion of the people, including those people who could be
inflamed by agitators and who did not deserve the vote, is clearly perceptible
in his writings, and could well be made by some the principal grounds for
a disapproval of his history of the age. Here was a man who could refer,
eventually, to 'the low multitude'. In the earlier part of his life, however,
he was unequivocally friendly towards the claims of the people, so far as
these kept clear of anything that could properly be termed sedition; he
defended his weavers and upheld the right to strike; and before that, he was
nerved to defend the cause of Reform at a time when to do so was reckoned
not so much heretical as criminal. During the 'Scottish Reign of Terror', as

---

[1] *Letters to Kennedy*, 23 November 1830.

it was called—the obverse repressions and severities that followed the events of 1789 in France—those who feared what the people might do were appalled when Jacobinical propagandists appeared on the scene. 'We were a' mad, sir,' said Francis Horner's father, one of Braxfield's jurors for the sedition trials. The upper classes were internally divided, but the weight of feeling seems to have been on the side of severity, and for some years respectable persons of liberal leanings, like Dr Adam of the High School, were spied upon and intimidated. Around 1794 it was whispered in Edinburgh that Eliza Fletcher had obtained a small guillotine and was practising on her hens, against the day when French principles would stalk the land. Here, according to rumour, was one aspect of 'the old work'.

A book of memoirs by William Chambers, which appeared in the 1870s, looks back at these 'deplorable' rancours, invoking Cockburn's testimony. 'My father's views of public policy,' Chambers writes, 'were not calculated to make friends in an age of political sycophancy. In 1807, on the occasion of a contested election for a member of parliament for the group of burghs of which Peebles was a member, he was threatened with oppressive measures for simply refusing to advise his brother to vote in a particular manner.' He was faced, in fact, with commercial ruin: yet the oppressive landowner is judged to have been 'undoubtedly a man of amiable character'.[1]

Of the jokes made on and off the bench by Braxfield at the expense of the Radicals tried and transported in the 1790s, one at least—as retailed by Cockburn, possibly—has passed into the folk memory. The prisoner Gerald ventured to say that Christ, too, had been a reformer. 'Muckle he made o' that,' replied Braxfield: 'he was hanget!' The Dundas despotism was a mild one compared with what went on in other countries at the time, and with what has gone on in the world since. And the Dundases saw to it that Braxfield was removed from control of such trials. But the Lord Justice-Clerk was a tremendous force for order and orthodoxy. Braxfield held, and held judicially—at the trial of Thomas Muir, the central figure in these prosecutions—that reform was intrinsically unconstitutional, and that the landed interest 'alone has a right to be represented' in any government. Only those with a stake in the country—in both senses—should have a share in ruling it. 'As for the rabble, who have nothing but personal property, what hold has the nation on them? What security for the payment of their taxes? They may pack up all their property on their backs, and leave the country in the twinkling of an eye. But landed property cannot be removed.' As for the French, they are 'monsters of human nature'.[2]

[1] *Memoir of Robert Chambers* (second edition, 1872), pp. 46, 47.
[2] *Sedition Trials*, vol. I, pp. 176, 177.

Naturally, in the light of Cockburn's bravura condemnations and of the self-praise engendered by the Whig triumph, Braxfield has had his defenders. This underdog has been commended, bark and bite, by William Roughead:[1] and his anthologized growls certainly have their charm. William Ferguson says of the Muir trial: 'Not only the prosecution but also the defence can be seriously criticized.'[2] He means that Henry Erskine, Muir's counsel, withdrew, having been denied full control of the defence by Muir, who then made a mess of defending himself. Ferguson also says that Cockburn exaggerates Braxfield's misdemeanours on this occasion. It is true that other courts acted similarly to Braxfield's on such occasions, both in Scotland and England, and that Scottish juries were always picked by the judge, with greater or less impartiality: but in the Muir trial Braxfield picked men who were all known to be active Government supporters. Braxfield has always been very popular in Scotland, and he also seems to have been learned and able, as well as funny. Stevenson's tender fictional account of the Braxfield curmudgeon in *Weir of Hermiston* makes the most of his charm, though little of his jokes—jokes which were not exclusively to the effect that such-and-such a prisoner would be 'nane the waur o' a hanging'—and the novel may be thought to emerge unscathed from a recourse to the records of these trials. *Weir of Hermiston* can be regarded as a classic defence of that monster of human nature, the bad father.

Scotland's early Radicals are commemorated in the Radical Road which runs round the base of Arthur's Seat: a public work performed by destitute Western weavers in the year of Bonnymuir, under the supervision of a committee of gentlemen. They are also commemorated within the city itself. Towards the end of Cockburn's life the foundation stone was laid for a 'Martyrs' Monument' to the men transported in the 1790s. But Cockburn thought they were not worth an obelisk. They had made rash, excessive and unseasonable demands: universal suffrage would never do. They had obstructed the course of moderate reform and public improvement. As such, says the *Sedition Trials*, which devotes most of its space to the enormities committed by the men who tried them, they were 'the enemies of liberty'. The same book says of three Chartists, lightly punished in 1848, at the time when Cockburn hoped that the Whig flag of sense and justice was still flying: 'The prisoners were all respectable men, and, except as politicians, sensible.'[3]

The people themselves, he came to think, might one day prove to be the

---

[1] In an essay, 'The Real Braxfield', included in a collection entitled *The Riddle of the Ruthvens* (1919).

[2] *Scotland 1689 to the Present*, p. 256.     [3] *Sedition Trials*, vol. II, pp. 250, 242.

enemies of liberty too. His reflections on this subject are very valuable:
to turn them simply into the material for a poor view of his politics would
need a considerable effort of will. It may be said of him, for example, that he
could foretell the future. There's a prophecy in the *Journal*[1] in which the
paternalist and the environmentalist and the Malthusian mingle their
misgivings. These are not the sighs of an expiring *ancien régime*:

> That man must be very blind who does not see the shadow of the popular tree is
> enlarging and darkening; and he must see well who can tell us what its fruit will be.
> Chartism has superseded Radicalism, and draws the whole starving discontent of the
> country in its train. It is far more a matter of food than of principle. Extension of the
> franchise is the phrase, but division of property is the object or the expected result;
> and with a manufacturing population, that is a population of which about a half is
> always hungry, and the passions of this hunger always excited by political delusion,
> it is not easy to see how wealth and sense are to keep their feet. The next century will
> solve this problem, and a few more. Will experience and education change human
> nature, and men become wise and good? Or shall we go on in this perpetual swelter?
> Or will manufactures be given up, and the pastoral-poetry state be recurred to? Or
> will they retire from our blighted fields and ruined cities? Or will slavery, with the
> master's right of the domestic sword, be restored? Or will life, without a capacity to
> maintain itself, be made a capital offence? Or human productiveness be controlled
> by physical checks on fecundity? Or population be fitted to the means of subsistence
> by a regulated system of infanticide, to be executed as a piece of sanitary police by
> public officers, under the direction of the Registrar of Births and Deaths? Meanwhile,
> as many passengers as choose are allowed to crowd the vessel, and to eat each other.

This passage belongs to the same year of 1848—a revolutionary year for
Europe. In Scotland, the people had arisen, according to the Whig prescription, and it could also be supposed that, despite a good deal of official
discouragement, the Tree of Liberty had grown taller since the time of
Margarot. Just before this in the *Journal*, Cockburn has observed that democracy 'is the doom of the most tyrannic systems first. It will be in Russia
before it is in Britain.' But risings can lead to revolutions, and he himself
had helped the people to arise, and the *ancien régime* to expire. He cannot
have been unable to imagine that he had helped to bring nearer the doom
represented by democracy.

By 1848, Chartism was finished, and Europe's revolutions did not come
to Britain. But between 1832 and 1848 the Whigs were harassed by pressure
from political movements of the 'visionary' sort—Radicalism, Chartism
and others—which made converts even among the respectable, and in 1834,
when Jeffrey vacated his Edinburgh seat in order to become a judge, there
was an election at which their encroachments were plainly in evidence. Its
atmosphere is caught in 'The Book of the Chronicles of the City', which

---

[1] *J*, vol. II, pp. 215, 216.

appeared soon afterwards. The British Museum copy is annotated by Cockburn, who explains that 'this Scriptural account' of the election 'is by several hands, but chiefly by Douglas Cheape Esq Advocate'. The account is modelled on the earlier *Blackwood's Magazine* 'Chaldee Manuscript', which had been exclaimed over (by Whigs especially, no doubt) as rather blasphemous. Gibson-Craig plays the part of a Chief Scribe, imperiously changing his mind ('hold thy peace') over the choice of the Whig candidate. But the really arresting verses concern the Radical candidate, James Aytoun, and are found in Chapter Two:

21. Now James was a strong man, skilful in speech from his youth up, a despiser of Princes, and of their servants;

22. Whose voice was as the voice of the bulls of Bashan.

23. And he gathered unto him as many as were in debt, as many as had fled to the place of refuge, which is the Sanctuary; as many as were of evil report; as many as were given to sudden change;

24. Also many from Miletus, which is the green island of the sea, whose hats and hosen were as the hats and hosen of the likenesses of the living things whereat the ravens are affrighted and flee away.

25. With sticks and with staves did they come.

A seeker of refuge himself, in a manner of speaking, and latterly, in point of fact, a debtor, Cockburn nevertheless shared the opinion expressed here of Radicalism and of Miletus: he was never nice about the Irish, who had shown themselves, over the years, to be far more seditious than the Scots. Early in 1833, when the Whig Government was being rocked by the Irish coercion question and Whigs were ratting to the Radicals, he felt that the Irish were savages who deserved to be punished.[1] Some seven thousand of them were now in Edinburgh and Midlothian, adding their scarecrow presence to the bristling Radical ranks. And yet only a year before the election Jeffrey had ventured to say that Edinburgh was 'an aristocratic and un-mobbish place.'[2]

1834 saw the Whig surge exhaust itself, and this election, which took place in June, was a pointer to the way the times were going. The Whig candidate got in, but the Scottish party had been experiencing serious difficulties. Patronage and the ecclesiastical Veto Act, which permitted the refusal of a minister by the parish, were a political issue, and it was not one

[1] JLC: see his note to Jeffrey's letter of 26 February 1833.

[2] JLC: 12 March 1833. Edinburgh had had its share of election disturbances a short while before, at the time of the Bill. But these may have been thought less 'mobbish', since the disturbances were in support of the Whig candidate—namely, Jeffrey. Cockburn and Jeffrey believed that Edinburgh's lack of industry had meant a merciful freedom from mob action. Figures for the incoming Irish are given in Saunders's *Scottish Democracy*, p. 389.

which helped the Whigs. The Radicals, who had strong Dissenter support, were for the end of patronage, and it was felt that they would rather let a Tory in than side with the Whigs. Voluntaries, as they were called, felt that they could use the franchise to bring about the disestablishment of the Kirk. The dinner given to Grey in Edinburgh in September, soon after which Cockburn was to say goodbye to office, must have come uncomfortably close, for all those brave faces, to resembling the kind of feast that follows a funeral.

For all the distinction of his utterances on the subject, Cockburn's objections to democracy can also be made an objection to Cockburn. They rested on the conviction that democracy was unacceptable to the public, and that the demands for it were hopelessly premature. But they rested no less on the conviction that wealth was sense, that sense could be assessed in terms of rateable value—or, at least, that it was safe (in more ways than one) to assess it in such terms. He denied Braxfield's proposition that the landed interest alone had a right to be represented. But he would not have been eager to deny that property alone had a right to be represented. The new thing was that property was to be re-defined. Those vassals—in the shape of liferenters, wadsetters and the rest—whose property could not be packed up and carried on their backs were to be admitted to the electoral elect. In March 1852, when, as he recognized, the *Journal* was presenting a still darker view of politics than that expressed in 1848 when he was writing about the democratic and Muscovite doom, he was still clinging to property: it should, he felt, be a more than nominal element in the elective qualification. The Reform Act has been regarded as the thin edge of the wedge for democracy. It cannot be regarded as a clean break with the past.

Cockburn was a friend of the people, but his touch sometimes deserts him when he writes about the poor, who are apt to seem, in his own words, like 'the low multitude'. And a low multitude is very like a rabble, which was Braxfield's word. From this point of view, even one of his best anecdotes may be thought problematical.[1] Henry Mackenzie used to visit Kilravock Castle, at whose festivals the drunken lairds would slip down from their chairs and lie slumped, and in danger of choking to death, under the table. On one occasion at which the Man of Feeling was present,

> those who were too far gone to rise lay still there from necessity; while those who, like the *Man of Feeling*, were glad of a pretence for escaping fell into a dose from policy. While Mackenzie was in this state he was alarmed by feeling a hand working about his throat, and called out. A voice answered, 'Dinna be feared, Sir; it's me.' 'And who are you?' 'A'm the lad that louses the craavats.'

[1] *J*, vol. II, p. 67.

This is meant to be, and is, a funny story. But it is also a depressing and poignant story: that 'Dinna be feared' addressed to the lords of the earth! It all happened in the unregenerate olden time, but such 'household officers' went on discharging similar duties for a long time to come: and other lads, and lasses, were crawling about below the earth for fourteen hours a day. The lad that louses the cravats can appear to haunt the writings of Cockburn every bit as much as the growling ghost of Lord Braxfield, if only because, as one might think, the imagination of hands working at the throats of himself and his friends has made him, at a number of points, irascible and unfeeling. In certain respects, Cockburn was his father's son.

To turn now to a very different aspect of his treatment of Reform, it is possible to argue that it undervalued what was reformed. But it is only possible to argue this with discretion, for the point is not a simple one. He loved his parents' Scotland, for its friendships and festivals and for much else, and he sought refuge in its contemplation. At the same time, he abominated its politics. The abomination of its politics, however, caused him to be unfair to its public virtues, which cannot be successfully separated from its political arrangements. I don't mean by this that Henry Dundas and some other Scotsmen were among those responsible for the government of Britain during these years, though that is not irrelevant. I mean rather that important things were done at home in Scotland, which Cockburn scants. In particular, the New Town was built.

At one level, his disregard for the importance of the New Town, like other disregards of his, is no more than a matter of partisanship or propaganda. At another, it represents the defeat of his 'rational' prejudices—involving a qualified approval of commerce and convenience—by his aesthetic prejudices, which were full of paradox. This exponent of the Roman virtues, and of a Classical prose, was not drawn to the Classicism of the New Town. This Augustan felt romantic about old buildings, preferring the patina, the 'grave grey hue', of age, and could not recognize that what Augustus had done for Rome the Venetian oligarchs of the Town Council had done for Edinburgh. His progressive politics, compounded by his romantic medievalism, induced him to resist this part of his parents' Scotland. On other parts his nostalgia fed to repletion.

Out of Edinburgh's Pandemonium came the desire for a second city, which would make money, and would commemorate the nation's new-found wealth and efficiency, and which was presently designed in accordance with high notions, Classical and cosmopolitan notions, of reason and proportion. There really was a kind of omnipotence at work: town-councillors and their cronies had achieved a triumph of their own. It was the bad old feudal

Scotland, abject and insolvent, which fashioned the beatific New Town. Such a triumph is not dreamt of by Cockburn, who is left, as the buildings go up around him in the *Memorials*, cherishing memories of 'lost verdure', of still summer nights when he stood in Queen Street or Charlotte Square with Richardson and Rutherfurd and Jeffrey and 'listened to the ceaseless rural corn-craiks, nestling happily in the dewy grass'. Now, he reflects, alien corn-craiks: and 'everything is sacrificed to the multiplication of feuing feet'—to the rapacity, as it were, of property development.

The gaiety and energy and amenity and learning of the Edinburgh of his youth Cockburn admired: but he also felt that in some respects, and not only politically, it had been superseded and surpassed. This was the society which had housed, however uncomprehendingly, the Scottish Enlightenment in its pristine years. Hume and Scott had lived in the Old Town when they were young, together with many other superlatively gifted men—by no means all of them liberals. The Enlightenment, in fact, associated as it was with privilege and capable as it was of the defence of privilege, can almost seem, at moments, like one of the casualties of the Whig Millennium—to the extent that this was inimical to privilege. But it would be more accurate to say that the ethos of the *Edinburgh Review*, along with the countervailing Tory creativity of the time, chiefly vested in Hogg and Scott, was the Enlightenment's completion. Associated as it was with economic growth and a concern for intellectual standards, the earlier Enlightenment was far from obnoxious to that later generation of Whigs who projected a millennium. Yet the earlier Enlightenment can also seem like the truer millennium of the two—so that Scotland's good time or golden age had come and gone before Cockburn reached manhood.

The Old Town not only created the New: moribund and deeply compromised, it was in its own right a great creation. It was, as the *Journal* concedes, 'excellent in itself', just as Henry Dundas was excellent in himself, for all his manipulation of servility. The excellence of the Old Town was no dream, he says in the *Journal* entry in question, which was written on 27 October 1847. As we have already seen, this was a period of his life when he could feel very pessimistic about the political future. Moreover, in a few weeks, as he must by then have known or suspected, his financial troubles were due to reach a crisis. In the circumstances, the entry shows an exemplary calm, supplying a measured appreciation of the old Edinburgh and the new, and an evocation of the former which rivals anything of the kind in the *Memorials*, where such evocations occur with, as I think, significant frequency. The Old Town lacked royalty and much of the apparatus of government, but it thrived on the presence of a resident nobility, pigging it mirthfully in their commune-like tenements: 'One good effect of rank or high family is that it confers respectability on its remoter members without wealth, and enables them to be poor, or to follow humble avocations, without degradation; and this feeling brought some even of our deserving shopkeepers within the privileged class, which thus formed a little world of itself.' But that resident nobility has now departed—to London.

This, he believes, was

> the last purely Scotch age. Most of what had gone before had been turbulent and political. All that has come after has been English. The 18th was the final Scotch century. We, whose youth tasted the close of that century, and who have lived far into the Southern influence, feel proud of a purely Edinburgh society which raised the reputation of our discrowned capital, and graced the deathbed of the national manners. No wonder that we linger with affectionate respect over the deserted or degraded haunts of our distinguished people, and that we feel as if we could despise ourselves if we did not prefer the memory of those scenes to all that is to be found in the commonplace characters of modern men, and in the insignificance of modern refinement.

On the other hand—Cockburn is usually ambidextrous—he considers the change inevitable. A man, he feels, 'must be a mere fossil of those days if he does not acknowledge that a greater variety of eminence and agreeableness is to be found in the system that is. A wise man would like to have seen the past age, but to live in this one.' 'Agreeableness' is vague (the Old Town, after all, was very agreeable), but perhaps it can be taken to include convenience and political progress. Talent and knowledge are now more widely diffused, which enables him to ask: 'Could the force and the variety of the native talent that created the *Edinburgh Review* have been collected out of all Scotland in the last age?' He makes his own lifetime seem strangely free from turbulence, and there are pianissimo passages which are strikingly at odds with the predictions offered elsewhere in his writings of the period. There is a sense that he has decided to keep calm. He writes of the inhabitants of Edinburgh in 1847: 'We remain a quiet and intelligent native population, relieved by strangers and by families from the country, full of liberal institutions and beautiful scenery.'

Come to Scotland, he seems to be suggesting. And he very nearly adds: but stay away from its industrial cities. This is virtually a rural Edinburgh, and one that hardly seems capable of housing the better world he speaks of. Some people might prefer to say that this is a city on its death-bed, like Cockburn's Venice, though the point here is rather that Cockburn himself is now approaching his own death-bed. And yet there was indeed something rural about the new Edinburgh, for all his former fears about the loss of verdure at the centre. Small country houses, Classical and Gothic, were growing up around its verges: paradises, rows of Bonalies, surrounded by token swards and clumps of boscage, brought a foretaste of the modern suburb. For the first time in the history of Scotland's double life of burghs and shires, the country entered the town, and Auld Reekie became semi-agrestic.

His description of the Old Town, though generous, is even more diminishing. It becomes a charming little world in which it is hard to conceive that anything of importance could happen. But the Old Town was a serious place, a place which did not lack authority. For all his relish of power, Cockburn was unaware of certain of the powers that lay in the putrescence of the old system. Had he been more of a Calvinist, he might have guessed that grace can come to those who lack merit. The justified sinners in their Pandemonium could do things which the Whigs, with their asylum of social justice, could not do and could not imagine: so that the Whig version of justification by works was in some ways inferior to Walter Scott's justification by fief—with all its unhealthy respect for what Cockburn called 'Dundasship'.

The objections I have expressed to Cockburn's treatment of the politically unregenerate Edinburgh of his youth may be thought to have been partly anticipated by one of the opponents of his middle age. On 8 March 1823, not long before he left for Venice, a further Pantheon meeting protested about the way in which the city's MP was elected, and he published a pamphlet in support of this meeting: 'Considerations submitted to the Householders of Edinburgh, on the state of their representation in Parliament'. The pamphlet takes for granted two things: 'that what is constitutionally called *popular election, is in itself expedient*'; and 'that no system of election can be said to be *too* popular, which excludes the whole of what are properly termed the lower orders, and merely comprehends a fair average of intelligent and substantial householders'. The Edinburgh system, of course, did not comprehend this fair average. Cockburn always believed in the existence of a Scotch progress, a moral progress, a track of enlightenment and improvement which his countrymen had begun to follow in the eighteenth century, but whose greatest glories were reserved for the age of Parliamentary Reform. It seemed right, in 1823, that the improvements in the institutions of Edinburgh which had already been secured should be succeeded by a reform of the representation. The attention given in the pamphlet to the procedures of the Town Council, and the language used to characterize it ('respectably mysterious' in its 'inner chamber'), suggest, incidentally, that the *Memorials*' Pandemonium passage may well have been written about the same time, predating his departure to inspect the death-bed of the Venetian oligarchy.

The following year, James Simpson—advocate, devotee of the cause of non-sectarian education, author of 'Lectures to the Working Classes', phrenologist and friend of Scott—took Cockburn's 'Considerations' to task in a pamphlet of his own. '*Whether it be now fit that the electors of this member should consist of thirty-three persons out of above a hundred thousand?*' This had been Cockburn's grand and simple question—propounded in the italics to which he was often drawn. Of these thirty-three electors, nineteen were self-elected: that is to say, elected annually by their predecessors in office. The rest were deacons of the crafts, of the incorporated tradesmen— elected by their corporations, but in a manner that permitted Town Council manipulation. Simpson noted that the figure of a hundred thousand, re- presenting the multitude that was to be fed by the Whigs with the loaves and fishes of a selective suffrage, was an inflated one, since it included those such as women and minors who were not entitled to vote. Hardly a disastrous mistake, one might think. In relation to the question of Edinburgh's moral progress, however, as treated in Cockburn's 'Considerations', Simpson had what may appear to be a more telling point to make: 'It is not a little extraordinary to find all this fair description of the improvement of Edin- burgh, coupled with an unqualified attack upon those very establishments, which have been the sources, and the guardians of our prosperity.'

Cockburn answered this point in a pamphlet of 1826: 'An Explanation of the State of the Case of the Edinburgh Representation in Parliament'. ''The greatness of the improvements supposed to be referred to is not questioned,' he wrote: 'but no one acquainted with the facts can doubt, that they have all succeeded *exactly in proportion as they have been removed* from the influence of that maternal council, which is supposed to brood over the city, and to hatch all the beneficial changes that have arisen.' The justice of Cockburn's rejoinder may be felt to be doubtful even by those who would readily accept that the system needed changing. And perhaps it is sufficient to say here that good grounds for doubting it are provided by the record of George Drum- mond, Lord Provost at the time of the 'Forty-Five and later: besides help- ing to launch the New Town, Drummond did valuable work in the field of medical provision. This pamphlet of Cockburn's introduced excerpts from a House of Commons debate of February 1824, which dealt with a petition from the Pantheon meeting of the previous year. In the course of the debate, the description of an *aristocratie roturière* was sarcastically invoked for the petitioners. On behalf of the bourgeois patriciate in question, Cockburn speaks in the pamphlet of 'the weight that is due to property, to intelligence, and to numbers', and it is interesting that the notion of numbers is absent from the Whig franchise formulae which were current later, at the time of the Reform Bill, whose Preamble speaks, as we have seen, of the weight that is due to 'property and intelligence'. Numbers were among the few prerogatives of 'the lower orders'.

Despite his rejoinder of 1826, it seems evident that Cockburn made too much of the difference between the old Edinburgh and the new, and that he sometimes underrated the former. It is also the case, I think, that the two simultaneous Edinburghs of his own lifetime, that of the Whigs and that of the Tories, co-existed and sympathized with one another more than Cockburn divulges—more than his militant moods, which were far from rare, allowed him to recognize. In the life of Jeffrey, he mentions that Scott 'observes in his *Journal*, "I do not know how it is, but when I am with a party of my opposition friends, the day is often merrier than with our own set"; and he accounts for this, by saying, that "both parties meet with the feeling *of something like novelty*". The fact that even to a person of Scott's joviality and frankness, a dinner together was a novelty, shews that their friendship, though solid, was not embodied in habitual intercourse.'[1] Cockburn modestly misses out another reason touched on by Scott in this passage for his merrier meetings with his Whig friends: 'Is it because they are cleverer? —Jeffrey and Harry Cockburn are to be sure very extraordinary men.'[2] And Cockburn is keen to stress how few these meetings were. 'Something like novelty' is placed in italics, and is then turned into 'a novelty', and a rather fine distinction is drawn between solid friendship and habitual intercourse. For Scott, the Pantheon Foxites of 1820 were 'sad scamps'. For the repentant Richardson in after-life, his own democratic songs were 'sad trash'. The two descriptions seem to echo one another, and to attest to a coincidence of feeling. It may be said that for Scott, Cockburn and Richardson were sad scamps who were also his friends.

Late in the *Journal*,[3] Cockburn imagines all the Edinburghs—old and new, Whig and Tory—united in Elysium and closeted in talk as if round some celestial fireside. It is possible, I find, to be visited by the wild thought that this scene is perhaps closer to the realities of the place during his lifetime than eloquent histories of conflict, or the best-laid theories of change and division, may lead one to guess. For his 'good Scotch dialogue' he chooses a party of gentlemen: that is one kind of division which can seldom be left out of the reckoning. And it is as if they have been chosen to represent this group or district of imaginary burghs. Representation, however, is on the

---

[1] *Life of Jeffrey*, vol. I, p. 144.  [2] *Journal of Sir Walter Scott*, p. 251, 9 December 1826.
[3] *J* II, pp. 164, 165: the entry is dated 17 October 1846.

basis less of wealth than of sense, and of character and conversability. He has
been saluting the death of John Thomson, once a weaver and then a renowned physician. Baron Hume, a gentleman by adoption, was the philosopher's nephew, and a Tory jurist whom Cockburn did not care for.
With Thomson in mind, he writes:

> I have the idea of a good Scotch dialogue between him and his great friend John Allen
> in Elysium, joined by Baron Hume, the first Lord Melville, Braxfield, Sir Harry
> Moncreiff, and Sir James Gibson-Craig who must die by anticipation. Braxfield, who
> was called to the bar in 1744, and probably never saw a good Scotch change except his
> own promotion, should represent the coarseness and political prostration of that last
> of our barbarous ages; Hume should be the type of our respectable narrow-minded
> bigotry; Sir Harry, of the best of our old Church, and he would certainly lament that
> he did not live to avert or to join the Free; Sir James, of that resolute band who stood
> in the dark period and actively forwarded the brighter day that he survived to see.
> Thomson would be his companion in this, and he and Allen should be the chief, and
> the best, provokers of the talk. Both medical; both risen from a humble origin to great
> eminence; intelligent believers, free thinkers, and fearless talkers, but in different
> styles—Allen gentle, Thomson dogmatical. Melville should represent all sides; de-
> fending the old system as natural for Scotland in the last age, and the new in this.
> Except Hume, they would all end in jolly good humour, and with a strong bias towards
> the prevailing tendency of what cannot be helped; but Hume would retire in horror,
> and pass his eternity in solitude or with Glenlee.

So much for all the bitter contentions which he has been writing about.
There had indeed been such contentions, and he does not forget about them
even here. But he also contrives to lend countenance to the view that
Reform was something that could not be helped, and that all these contending Edinburghs were simply aspects of a unanimous upper crust which had
remained securely in authority for a hundred years. Cockburn did not think
this, and it cannot, in fact, be thought. But the jolly good humour of these
merry meetings of gentlemen, which he here translates to eternity, no doubt
contributed to that softening of the blow, that sweetening of the inevitable,
whereby, when the time came to make changes, many things were let alone.

None of this alters the fact that for Cockburn, as for the majority of those
in Britain, the Reform Act was a momentous event. For some, it was a
triumph. For others, a disaster. Cockburn strove for it for the best part of
thirty years in the knowledge that his efforts were profoundly resented. He
was its Covenanter. He did not feel that he was letting things alone, and he
was never to disavow what he and his fellow Reformers had done. His
millennium was no millennium. The Reform Act was in the nature of a
provisional reshaping of the electorate, and it contained flaws which were
seized upon in order to subdue its intended consequences. But it has also
to be seen as a great and necessary change.

# Chapter Eight

# *Cockburn in Paradise*

Cockburn's Millennium never came, but he did enjoy a golden age of a kind. And there is a great deal in his writings, both published and unpublished, which might seem to entitle one to say that his true millennium consisted of the past, as reconstructed in the *Memorials*, and of his explorations of the Pentland Hills. It is his dreams which make him a romantic, and for him, the past and the Pentlands often appear to have the character of a dream.

His attitude to the past, by which I chiefly mean the Scotland of his childhood, and to the Pentlands, can be explained in terms of the set of opposites by which he lived. First of all, there were two contrasting types of virtue: there were the virtues of duty and of public service, and there were those of solitude and seclusion. Then there was reason, on the one hand, and dreams, on the other. There was work, and there was pleasure. There was practicality and convenience, and there was nature and romance. There was the new and the old, the present and the past. There was his Anglophilia, and there was his patriotic love of Scotland. There was the town, and there was the country. There was Reform (or, for that matter, his professional activities as an advocate and judge), and there was the Pentlands. There was the 'parricide' represented by the rejection of his father's politics, a rejection which culminated in Reform, and there were the paradises represented by the country estates—chiefly Bonaly, but also Niddrie, Caroline Park and Relugas—to which he went for comfort throughout his life, as to a mother. At Bonaly he was reborn, and indeed pre-born. Eden and Elysium were on earth and at hand in these various places, which provided him with a variety of regressive and restorative roles and pleasures. Some of his letters are headed 'Bonaly Castle': one at least, from the same place, is headed 'Eden'. At Bonaly, he thought, he and Mrs Cockburn were as Adam and Eve, and only the strongest obligations or temptations, such as Macready's Macbeth, could expel him from Eden to Edinburgh.

All these pairs of opposites may in some degree have been determined by the last pair of all. In the succession of choices and contradictions which he experienced can be seen the contours of a quarrel with his father, which may or may not have come at the start of his life. I am suggesting that this quarrel was renewed in his work as a Reformer, and that his recourse to the past and to the Pentlands renewed his first response to the pain of such a quarrel. To say this is to say that the Pentlands and the past inhabit the same dream and are part of the same paradise—a paradise whose many mansions may even be said to have found room, at certain times and for certain purposes, for the otherwise alien Millennium of his earlier political predictions: at certain times and for certain purposes, the Whig Asylum was paradise enough, comprising as it did the harrowing of the Tory Pandemonium and the coming of an emancipated, constitutional Scotland and of a better world. In his original capacity of renegade (or rival), Cockburn was expelled from Eden, and in his capacity of rememberer and recluse he was able to regain that paradise.

On one occasion in 1827 when duty called him to the work of Reform, he remarked to Kennedy: 'Deracination from Bonaly during the honeymoon of our vacation is too much virtue for man—unless perhaps for Abercromby.'[1] On another occasion, he urged that Rutherfurd be persuaded to go to the country and 'enjoy a week of virtue and cream'.[2] These things give an inkling of his two types of virtue. Another inkling may be gained from the letter of August 1839 to George Dundas from which I have already quoted, where Cockburn speaks in a contradictory way of 'a conscience of which I only know the existence because I am told that nobody can be without one, and by my modesty being often put to the blush by the conscious justice of its applauses': one of his consciences slept at Bonaly, that is to say, while the other approved of his being there.

It becomes apparent, particularly in his manuscript letters, that while the virtues of hard work and public service—the Edinburgh virtues, as I have called them elsewhere—could uproot him from Bonaly, the Bonaly virtues were probably superior. In his youth, he once used these words in praise of Richardson: 'Tell me a single defect but what flowed from a source purer than the noblest virtues, the influence of his affections in blinding his judgement.'[3] The noblest virtues—that is to say, the noblest *public* virtues—cannot, in the last analysis, compete with those that are grounded in the affections—and which flourished among his roses at Bonaly. The history of Cockburn's rebellion against his kin may possibly be detected in some of his

[1] *Letters to Kennedy*, p. 176.     [2] Writing to Mrs Rutherfurd on 17 April 1840.
[3] To Charles Anderson, 24 January 1806.

statements on the subject of virtue. That rebellion made him a leader in his own right: together with his talents, and indeed the standing supplied by his kin, it took him to a position of power and consequence. And it may be that power and consequence remained unbreakably associated in his mind with his own original offence against the affections. It may be that they carried a Satanic taint—that of the archetypal rebel.

'Unless some avenging angel shall expel me, I shall never leave that paradise.' He is referring to Bonaly, and to the recesses and eminences of the Pentlands. 'Human nature is incapable of enjoying more happiness than has been my lot here.' In this passage from the *Memorials*,[1] one of the most meaningful that he ever wrote, he compares himself implicitly to the disobedient Adam and Eve (Cockburn may be said to have eaten of the Tree of Liberty), but perhaps also to Satan, who revolted and was banished from Heaven. Why might Cockburn be banished from Bonaly? What was his offence? Pleasure, happiness—the pursuit of these in a disapproving land? I am certain that he also had somewhere in mind his offence against his kin. And it was the sword of kinship which took revenge, effecting a posthumous expulsion from his paradise.

Cockburn was a rebel angel to whom the poetry of Milton seems to have mattered. Milton sent his rebel angels to Pandemonium—a word which he invented and which was still indelibly Miltonic. Cockburn's Pandemonium housed the servile, but also the powerful: there were those of his town-councillors who would have been quite at home with Beelzebub and the rest, mighty in defeat, burning with eloquence in the Council Chamber of Hell. And Cockburn's rebelliousness sent him to the Whig Asylum which supplanted this Pandemonium. An asylum is a place of safety, but both these places were seats of power—as emerged in the course of an earlier discussion which tried to show that there could be a measure of fellow-feeling on the part of this critic of the Town Council. I think what this means is that while his rebellion took him to the Whig Asylum, it also threw him simultaneously into the Pandemonium of public life, which produced, in its turn, the necessity for a true asylum, for a paradise of the affections to which he could retreat, for a place of safety where the responsibilities of Satanic power, and the pugnacities of public life, could be shed. That is why this rebel angel went to Heaven, or returned there.

Rebellion is power and responsibility, and can be very ambiguous. Cockburn's enabled him to assist in a virtuous act of corporate will: Reform. In his country havens, however, he created a sphere in which, if only briefly or seasonally, Reform, among other things, was renounced. The quarrel with

[1] *M*, pp. 254, 255.

his father was perpetuated in his political activities, and these activities were fled from as the pain of the quarrel itself was presumably fled from and as if they were part of that quarrel, which in a sense they were. Milton's rebelliousness was that of a regicide who stood for order and government, of a puritan who was awake to pagan pleasures. Cockburn's was no less ambiguous, and not, perhaps, very different.

A glance at Classical China may serve to bring out the character and flavour of Cockburn's distinction between his two types of virtue. The contrast between the Confucian and Taoist philosophies, which could co-exist within the one individual, appears to have embodied a similar distinction. Confucianism, a social code rather than a religion, encouraged conformity, practicality, discipline. Taoism encouraged individualism, and a devotion to solitude, contemplation and the worship of nature. It prescribed periodic retreats to a mountain hermitage where the man of affairs, the official, could exercise such tastes and admire his waterfall. Taoism enjoined the rejection of power—the essence of Cockburn's retreat to Bonaly. In 1837, he thanked Mrs Leonard Horner for a present of china plate, and said mock-patriarchally: 'In my own house I am Emperor of China.'[1] He was certainly a mandarin—of the kind who embraced the rigours and remorse of public life while abandoning them at weekends and holidays in favour of a mountain hermitage. He was both a busy Whig and a nature-worshipping Augustan virtuoso, whose double life may be thought to affirm the principle —typical perhaps of high civilizations—that human needs are complex, and should be met, where possible, in terms of habits and habitations that are complex too.

If such conjectures can reasonably be made in respect of his attitude towards the Pentlands, they can also be made in respect of his attitude towards the past. He dreamt of a feudal and purely Scottish past, and assigned virtues to it in the *Memorials*. But the past had virtues of which he did not dream. In however restricted a fashion, it was more dynamic, and more civic, than he admitted. More often than not, the ruling class of his youth is given the air of a timeless and delightful enclave, which was all holiday and hilarity, which could not invent or achieve. In fact, the little world of Lady Arniston and her like—with its close ties of affection, its assemblies, its punctilio and decorum—was doomed. And he himself had pronounced that doom. Yet he often chose to celebrate, as well as to blame, the hereditary might and judicial intolerance which he imagined he was about to annul, sweetening it with a stress on its attendant quirks and cordialities. It may be that what drew him to the past was its demise, and his own responsibility for

[1] 2 November 1837.

that demise. It may be that his most taxing dilemma was to love what he had killed.

'Old Edinburgh was no more,' the *Memorials* say, in assessing the implications of the Pantheon meeting of 1820, when the Scottish Whigs felt themselves to be gathering resolute support, and to have reached an understanding with middle-class democrats. It is easy to love what is lost or forfeited: but Cockburn's 'regrets' are of a rare order, belonging as they do to a masterpiece of mixed feelings which also declares itself the record of a seasoned intent to change the face of the country. In the *Memorials*, he repents the destructions which are also his pride and prime subject, and that 'repentance' is expressed in a passionate nostalgia. His nostalgia became operational, so to speak, as the governing outlook of a protracted literary enterprise, at the start of the 1820s—the very years during which the annulments contained in the Whig programme of reform began to seem attainable, and formidable, and were eventually completed.

Throughout the 1820s, according to Nicholas Phillipson in a thesis on 'The Scottish Whigs and the Reform of the Court of Session',[1] Edinburgh was 'a whig city'. The great Henry Dundas had been dead for ten years, Scott was dying, and bankrupt, Toryism was despondent. This was the environment in which the *Memorials* were composed, and to which they were addressed. Thereafter, in the *Journal*, Cockburn gave up looking back in so rapt a manner, and concerned himself mostly with contemporary topics. He explains in a letter to Richardson of 17 October 1851 that in 1830 his Red Book—from which the *Memorials* and the *Journal* were taken—'ceases to be narrative and becomes entries of things as they arose: a far more valuable form both for the truth of facts and of impressions, but less agreeable to a person reading straight through'.[2] The *Journal* also has a prefatory note which quotes him as saying: 'This habit of making a note of things worth observing at the time coincided with the change of life implied in my becoming Solicitor-General.' So his writings, too, suffered a change of life. The arrival, or dispersal, of the Millennium put an abrupt stop to the exercise of nostalgia. It is as if his experiences as Solicitor-General taught him something he did not know about millennia, as well as a new attitude, less confident and less embattled, towards 'the truth of facts and of impressions'. At the same time, his Whig work was done, or largely done: his 'parricide' was completed, and there was less need to make up for it, to make amends,

---

[1] 'The Scottish Whigs and the Reform of the Court of Session, 1785–1830', p. 61. Phillipson's PhD thesis (Cambridge University, 1967) breaks a considerable amount of new ground with its account of the legal and political manœuvres of the time.
[2] *Some Letters of Lord Cockburn*, p. 68.

in terms of indulgent evocations of the past. So there was bound to be a change of tone, and perhaps of procedure.

By the mid-1830s, after decades of contention and frustration, of fighting and faltering and Edinburgh Reviewing, directed at a number of objectives, the Scottish Whigs had had their way. The franchise had been broadened, burgh administration had been corrected, civil-jury trial had been let into the Court of Session, the criminal jury system had been revised, and only the feudal law of entail remained to be put right. As 'Scottish nationalist Anglophiles', in Phillipson's phrase,[1] Cockburn and his friends had wanted the Scots to enjoy—in forms distinctively Scottish—the liberties and opportunities available to Englishmen: Cockburn describes their intention, in the *Life of Jeffrey*,[2] as that of bringing Scotland 'within the action of the constitution'. This involved the introduction into Scotland of distinctively 'English' things, as in the case of juries, where the move was towards English, and away from French, practice. And now that Scotland had been brought within the action of the Constitution, its distinctiveness, and the importance of its capital city and Court of Session, seemed certain to diminish. With the attainment of their reforms, the Scottish Whigs found themselves faced with the possibility that they had had their day, as well as their way. They had lost their established political role, and they were afraid that Scotland, too, might be lost. Phillipson speaks[3] of the 'lassitude' that descended on them as a result: the new Edinburgh was 'demoralised and fatalistic'—a mood which may be felt to be communicated in Cockburn's notion of a rural Edinburgh full of scenery and visitors. His *Journal* was composed in the new Edinburgh, and the tension which marks the *Memorials* —composed at a time when the past was being abolished, yet poignantly aware of its virtues—is absent from the sequel. It is an altogether less hedonistic work, and it has its moods of fatalism. Some of this may be due to the sad state of the new Edinburgh. But some of it may be due to the fact that he is becoming an old man, and to his private worries.

As we have seen, there were private worries in the 1820s too, and as I have just been suggesting, some of these worries went to the making of the *Memorials*. His nostalgia, his passion for what was old and gone, could scarcely have avoided an element of self-incrimination or remorse. In certain lights, the *Memorials* can be seen as Cockburn's cross or Canossa—as an expiation of the very depredations which are triumphantly chronicled there. 'To keep a diary in order to understand': these are the words of Antoine

[1] 'The Scottish Whigs and the Reform of the Court of Session', p. 171.　　[2] vol. I, p. 82.
[3] 'The Scottish Whigs and the Reform of the Court of Session', p. 345.

Roquentin in Sartre's novel, *La Nausée*.[1] Cockburn kept his diary in order to proclaim—to state the achievements of his party and the changes they had made: but he also did so in order to preserve, and perhaps to atone.

Cockburn, of course, was very much more than merely regretful or remorseful in this somewhat specialized or figurative sense. He was a politician and public figure who meant what he said, and he was often carefree and gregarious. And there is more to be surmised, not about his regrets, but about the behaviour which caused them, and of which he could also be proud. Not that it is easy to make surmises: he was too reserved for that. And besides, while the remorse which might seem implicit in some of his writings is likely to be less easy even for an 'enlightened' modern reader to understand than the aggressions which seem to have caused it, these aggressions are themselves open to doubt, and are in part of a kind that was unrecognized or inadmissible in his own time.

Cockburn's imagination, buoyant and brisk with filial intransigence, has an oedipal cast, and his life was not only paradisal but parricidal. His society was one which worshipped the stern father, and God ruled Scotland in the manner, and in the interests, of such fathers. 'Our God is in the heavens,' said the Psalms: 'he hath done whatsoever he hath pleased.' Baron Cockburn's stick was brandished in a great tradition. In a filial and respectful Scotland— a Scotland evolved and civilized, moreover, a Scotland which had renounced its old habits of treason and civil war—his son's rebelliousness would not have been overlooked. The love of pleasure for which Cockburn was blamed after his death may have been perceived as that of a man who had gone against his father's pleasure, and God's, and this may help to account for the hints of irresponsibility which are dropped about him in the gossip and memoirs of the time.

His first recorded disobedience was the rejection of his father's political principles. From this flowed a career in opposition to his father's party. Insult was added to injury—and Cockburn could be very insulting—by, among other things, the slow assembling of a book containing much hostility towards his father's friends—the generation of law lords which included Braxfield and Eskgrove. Not many barristers openly attack the bench, and while these writings seem to have been shown to very few of his friends, their existence may well have been known to a large number of people, including his kin: it was widely known, anyway, that he held the views expressed there. His father no doubt turned in his grave, as Scottish fathers have often been reckoned to do, and was little mollified by the years of compunction that had gone into the *Memorials*, along with the irreverence.

---

[1] *La Nausée*, translated by Robert Baldick (Penguin edition, 1965), p. 9.

But the supreme assault on authority was the Reform Bill itself. At long last, the Reform Bill brought, or appeared to bring, the bitter end of the world of Lady Arniston, which was also his father's world, and that of his own childhood. The mirth and ceremony of the past were silenced, or appeared to be. On 18 May 1831, with Reform looming and after trouble with the populace at Jedburgh, Walter Scott recorded the end of this world in his *Journal* with the words: *Troja fuit.*[1]

Scott began his *Journal* in 1825 and went on with it until a few months before his death in the year the Reform Bill was passed: it ran parallel, therefore, with Cockburn's compiling of the *Memorials*. This is one of several coincidences and accords which bind together the lives of these friendly enemies. 1832, Cockburn's *Annus Mirabilis*, was Scott's Armageddon. And the two men wrote very different diaries of the end of the era. Cockburn, victorious, is stoical and self-effacing. Scott is at times distressed and confiding: bound by the same code, the same imperatives, of courage and self-control in relation to distress, but less tightly bound, and with a great deal to be stoical about. Cockburn's backward-looking stance, remarkable in a reformer, though not unique, contrasts sharply with Scott's concentration on the minutiae of his daily struggle for solvency and survival, interspersed with angry glances at the state of the country. Scott's powers and possessions start to take flight, as in a fairy-tale. All the circumstances of his life rebel and conspire against him, supplying a domestic version of the political cataclysm: he keeps mislaying things. Scotland, too, was being mislaid.

His efforts to restore respectability are the main subject-matter of the *Journal*, but there are times, towards the end, when Reform can appear to matter just as much. James Hogg held that the coming of Reform and the threat of democracy were the death of Scott. A wooden horse was being wheeled inside the Tory Troy, and very soon Scott himself, together with his Troy, was no more. His cry of *Troja fuit* belongs to a *Journal* entry which describes how he went to Jedburgh for the election of May 1831 to be greeted by cries of 'Burke Sir Walter'—'burke' being the new word for 'stifle' or suffocate'. His carriage was stoned and he was in some danger. He must have felt that he was not simply imagining his disaster. Hogg says in his *Familiar Anecdotes of Scott*: 'From the moment he perceived the veto of a democracy prevailing he lost all hope of the prosperity and ascendancy of the British empire.' Hogg goes further: 'The Whig ascendancy in the British cabinet killed Sir Walter.'[2] This is not the kind of opinion that would

---

[1] *Journal of Sir Walter Scott*, p. 656.
[2] *Memoir of the Author's Life* and *Familiar Anecdotes of Sir Walter Scott,* edited by Douglas Mack (1972), p. 132.

look very impressive on a death certificate, but Scott's *Journal* is not without supporting evidence. All his days he had been a hearty yet sensible Melvillite. In 1831 and 1832, however, when illness was destroying him, his politics became a symptom of that illness. Resentful and obsessive, they became a reason to die and a way of dying. He keeps insisting that he is 'heart whole as a biscuit': but 'I am determined to write a political pamphlet *coute que coute*. Aye should it cost my life.'[1]

His courage can't be questioned, and his mind fought on. This can be seen in the sparkling joke he makes about the unpunctuality of his amanuensis Laidlaw and his own problems in dictation: 'I am like the poor wizzard who is first puzzled how to raise the Devil and then how to employ him.'[2] His stoicism was as much a style as it was a reality, and the *Journal* does not lack self-pity and bravado. But even in his terminal state there was nothing poor about the Wizard of the North. The *Journal* is more concerned with the preservation of a style (the style to which he was accustomed, in a sense), and with the preservation of face, and is rather less confessional, than is usually supposed. Nevertheless, it is remarkable for its readiness to speak more candidly about private matters than the autobiographical genres of the time generally permitted. It is very different, in this respect, from the *Memorials*. Much of the drama of Scott's life was to do with money, and he is candid about that, while also affecting, here and there, to be an innocent: after attending a meeting of the Edinburgh Assurance Company, of which he was a Director Extraordinary, 'off I came my ears still ringing with the sounds of thousands and tens of thousands and my eyes dazzled with the golden gleam effused by so many capitalists.'[3] Scott wanted posterity to think that he wasn't a businessman. Cockburn, by contrast, seldom mentions money, and posterity was not meant to know about his struggle for solvency.

Scott felt no need to restrain his candour on the subject of Reform. For him, as for many more, it was deathly. It was an act of destruction. It was a series of 'awful gashes into the vitals of the idol that our grandfathers worshipped'. These last words are, in fact, from a *Journal* joke of Cockburn's concerning some legal changes of an anti-feudal character introduced in 1847 (and relating to such matters as 'the transference of heritages not held burgage'). The violence of the humour is revealing, and he writes to Rutherfurd in a similar vein in 1831: 'I saw a note from a Peer today, who shall be nameless, but who lives at Yester, in which he says that if the bill passes, he has not long to enjoy his title, nor, if it fails, his head.'[4] The gallows humour of a Scottish Whig, in which heads roll and grandfathers are gashed.

---

[1] *Journal of Sir Walter Scott*, pp. 650, 653.   [2] Ibid., p. 635.
[3] Ibid., p. 36.   [4] 8 March.

In his strange, spiteful, dandyish book, *The Castes of Edinburgh* of 1859,[1] John Heiton relates that Cockburn declined to visit the site of Jeffrey's grandfather's barber's shop in the romantic Old Town. He 'bolted, with his finger on his nose, declaring—for Harry would not have given a pun for a page of romance any day—that the place was *barbarous*.' Heiton remarks: 'Harry had not much of the romantic in him; though fond of flowers, he had no relish for "the flowers of Edinburgh" '—its stinks, that's to say. The hint of truth in that story, which gets Cockburn badly wrong, is likely to lie in Cockburn's capacity to think (as well as not to think) that *grandfathers* were barbarous, rather than Bell's Wynd and its barber's shop, and deserved to have the vitals of their idol gashed. His romanticism about the past did not preclude such jokes. Nor did it prevent him from destroying the past.

This believer in order was a confirmed rebel, and it is not surprising that he should have supported the mutineer ministers of the Disruption. These were rebel angels driven from Paradise by the flaming sword of the state— a sword which, as a Lord of Session, he himself helped to wield. These ministers combined a zeal for the traditional Presbyterian pieties with a dislike of the Erastian recent past, and this appealed to a man who loved the past he had abolished, whose burning concern with 'the olden time' was the conscience of his iconoclasm. It is as if a first reluctant disobedience—which may have come very early—led to a life of aggressions and amends, and to mixed feelings concerning certain of his most important undertakings. It is as if some primal reluctance or constraint were repeated in a succession of difficulties which came to him in adult life, and of which one can construct a paradigm in the question: why, if the old Scotland was so delightful, should it be changed?

This interpretation of his 'two minds' cannot be made to yield a comprehensive account of his emotional development, but it is clear that the drama associated with these two minds was lifelong. Even the destruction of his papers by his son Francis, whose explanation[2] is like a deed of self-administered manumission and who thought the *Memorials* had had its day, may be read by some as an episode in this drama, which is a drama of family life. And as we have seen, the last difficulties in his life were of the same kind as the first. The biter was badly bitten. The paradise of nature, romance and the affections to which he escaped from his indefinitely renewed resistance to his father betrayed him to the extent of contributing to an impending bankruptcy. Kin, as a source of anxiety, came cruelly full-circle for him. Bonaly and his boys threatened to break this unruly son, and his tower was not long done before it had to be sold. A bleak view of Cockburn's life might

---

[1] *The Castes of Edinburgh* (third edition, 1861), p. 324.     [2] See page 53.

resort to a play on words (as Byron alleges that the Edinburgh Reviewers used to do and as Heiton alleges that Cockburn used to do, though the writings cannot be said to be rich in puns) and insist that parricide led to the Harricide of irrecoverable disgrace. But this would be to exaggerate. Financial troubles were virtually the daily news of Cockburn's Edinburgh, and he was far too firm and shining a presence in the world to be extinguished by debt, far too much of a pharos for that.

Such is the story of the pugnacious Cockburn—which was rarely experienced as bleak by its principal actor, though it became so for a while towards the end. In any case, there is always the other, the paradisal Cockburn, whose bliss may have enabled him to deal with those quandaries which re-enacted the consequences of a defiance of his father's authority. His bliss may be felt to cast doubt on the interpretation I have been offering. If it is right to infer the possibility of an early transgression or original sin, or of one which occurred in adolescence, and if this transgression was extensively repented and repeated in adult life, why do his recollections of the past have so little of the *appearance* of guilt? Why has his guilt been spoken of here as if it were figurative or metaphorical? Why does he seem so happy?

There is, I believe, an answer. If he experienced feelings of guilt or contrition, these would probably not have been considered fit to be divulged: yet there is no reason to think that such feelings were disguised or dissembled or disowned. There is some reason to think, though, from what we know of his imaginative life as it is divulged in his writings and in his habits and preoccupations, that such feelings were repressed: that they were embodied, and at the level of consciousness eluded, in his work as a historian—that outpouring of 'penitential' memories which converted the past into a paradise —and in his other paradise of Bonaly. This may be why he proclaims his bliss with such consistency and with such intensity. His happiness may in part have been a refuge from his guilt. In a more or less literal sense, which lends a new and badly needed lustre to the word, he sublimated the recognition of his own destructiveness, elevating it to that realm of the geographical sublime, the Pentlands.

The past which he describes contains within it both transgression and regression. It can seem like the mother who is anxiously sought in infancy and cherished long after, and it can even seem womb-like. There are times in the *Memorials* when the *ancien régime* appears eternal, for ever welcoming and safe, even though it is known to be doomed, and doomed by his own hand. The Pentlands can appear eternal too. 'Cockburn is immovable on the Pentlands,' Jeffrey once reported in a letter,[1] and it was in order to be

[1] *Letters to Kennedy*, p. 1

immovable, and immortal, that Cockburn went there. He laboured to reproduce at Bonaly the Edens or Goshens to which he retreated in his childhood and youth, and the Pentlands may be thought to have commemorated, and incorporated, 'the best woman I have ever known'. In the same way, his remembrance of things past includes, like Proust's, a search for the mother, and one might well appropriate for the study of Cockburn the title of a story by Proust: 'Filial Sentiments of a Parricide'. There may be as much of Proust in Cockburn as there is of Tacitus, and there could be no more evocative comment on Cockburn's sense of the past than Proust's well-known claim that the only true paradise is the paradise lost.

Cockburn's pugnacity was tempered or corrected by a cultivation of filial sentiments and heavenly dreams. Like the British Constitution which he wanted Scotland to enjoy, his life depended on checks and balances. Historians of Romanticism (and students of human nature) should pay attention to the case of Cockburn, which seems to show that romanticism, with its regressions and irrationalities, can be publicly useful and privately benign, and that fantasies, forlorn hopes and vain regrets can bear a great deal of weight, and create a balance, within the individual personality. His dreams were, in that sense, structural and salutary. They led him to concern himself with projects no less important than some of those dictated by his 'reason', though such projects tended to make less of an immediate impact, and indeed, in a worldly way, to be comparatively unsuccessful. It was his dreams which led him to challenge convenience and progress, to be the landscape's friend. And they may also have enabled him to live with the anxieties and aggressions which must have accompanied those of his 'fits of public virtue', as he called them,[1] which were approved by his reason rather than his dreams. To talk as I have done here of 'repressions' and 'regressions', and to talk, as I have also felt bound to do, of 'contradictions' and 'dilemmas', may be taken as an attempt to devise a pathology for his experiences. But I don't think there could be such a thing: if only because the decorum he observed goes quite a long way to ruling it out. And, in any case, the attempt, the emphasis, would be misplaced. Cockburn is pugnacious and paradisal. He is not pathological. Whether or not he was as happy as he asserted, his Edens ensured a marvellous composure.

---

[1] Ibid., p. 22.

# Chapter Nine

# *'The Linn', and Other Poems*

Cockburn, who was many things, was also a poet—a Sunday or Bonaly poet. This was known at the time to friends, but has since attracted no attention. I have located five poems, one of which, 'The Linn', exists in two versions.[1] The six manuscripts are held in two places. The National Library of Scotland has 'Geraldine', 'How solemn the close' and one version of 'The Linn'. The Cockburn family has the other version of that poem, together with 'Relugas' and 'On losing a staff from a gig'. These poems, none of which has hitherto seen the light of day, belong to two separate periods of his life. The last two belong to the mid-1820s, and the others to the first decade of the century, when he seems to have started to write verse again after a silence of some ten years. The poems are vividly imprinted with his habits and predilections: that walking-stick 'by me as foreign prized the more' reminds one that he was an Anglophile, as well as the patriot who could utter the indefatigable Scottish comparisons of his Continental tour. And they are also of interest in relation to the conception of his psychological development which I have been trying to express.

His fits of verse are likely to bring a better understanding of his pastoral or paradisal bent. In the hills, he wore a Pentland uniform of white hat and grey jacket, and carried what he called 'a long pole' (another name for his sticks or staffs, one of which he lost). And in the hills he thought of himself as 'Cocky'. Thus the Solicitor-General longs to throw off his duties and be Cocky once again: 'The Scotch Bill is in an excellent condition. Oh! for my grey jacket and the sound of the burn!'[2] In a letter to his to Dick Lauder, written around 1833,[3] the pole-bearing Cocky is memorably identified. A

---

[1] The poems are printed and annotated later in this book. The order in which they appear is that in which they are discussed in the present chapter. The order of composition cannot be fully determined.

[2] From a letter published in the *Memoir of Thomas Thomson, Advocate*, p. 207.

[3] *Some Letters of Lord Cockburn*, p. 33. The letter is on paper watermarked 18

visitor from Findhorn is due at Bonaly: this is the Mr Smith who was present at the Habbie's Howe of that year.

> I hope that Mr Smith is aware that whatever Mr Cockburn was, His Majesty's Solicitor General is a decorous person—arrayed in solemn black—with a demure visage—an official ear—an evasive voice—suspicious palate—ascetic blood—and flinty heart. There is a fellow very like him, who traverses the Pentlands in a dirty grey jacket, white hat, with a long pole. That's not the Sol. Gen. that's Cocky—a frivolous dog; Mr Smith may use all freedom with him.

It can be said that Cockburn was two fellows, one frivolous and the other demure, and that this man of sense led a double life.

The Cocky persona may be regarded as a way of simultaneously dissembling and proclaiming Cockburn's commitment to public affairs. A 'suspicious palate' is what a Venetian Doge or oriental despot might have, rather than a Solicitor-General (as his Continental journal makes clear, he thought of Venice as somewhat Turkish and Eastern), and he is dressing himself here in the majesty of the law and the mystery of office in the very act of disowning them: a posture reminiscent of his 'envy' of the power enjoyed so distressingly by the Town Council in their Venetian Pandemonium. On the other hand, part of his life consisted of a deliberate retreat from his oppressive public responsibilities, a retreat which created a second self and a separate geography, and he wanted this alternative life to be proclaimed too. Cocky was a no less authentic presence than that of His Majesty's Solicitor-General, and, in his own eyes, perhaps a more virtuous one.

What's in a name? In Cockburn's case, a good deal. Even his Christian name counts for something, savouring as it does of Dundas-ship, and in his poems he lives up to his surname. Cocky's long pole and Pentland walks are in evidence, the sound of the burn is heard, and the burn itself—the burn of burns, that is to say—is given a local habitation: and in a preamble to one of the poems it is also given a name. If it can be said of him that he had two selves—one which was animated by his Whig principles and professional ambitions, and a second self which rejected reason and iconoclasm, which dreamt of birth and Bonaly, and of the past, and which was the more receptive to subconscious promptings—then it is the second self which is mainly disclosed in the poems. This is Cockburn in retreat, recurring to the pastoral-poetry state, partaking, as one poem puts it, of 'Bonaly's constant holiday'.

The poems suggest a grounding in the Augustans which was not forgotten, and a backward-looking literary taste which was unequal to the themes of nature and romance into which he was adventuring. As late as 1850 he was urging James Ballantine to '*Be select*. Don't, as is so common, let your Life

Boats, your imperishables, be sunk by heavier matter, of which most poets have an overstore. See what Collins, Gray, Goldsmith, and even Campbell, have gained by mere select paucity.'[1] The poet Cockburn certainly made a virtue of paucity, rather than pugnacity, and he made another of the avoidance of vulgarity. To James Grahame, on 28 December 1808, he wrote: 'As to our "first principles", I don't believe you and I differ much, if at all. We are both satisfied that the worst fault that Poetry (the essence of purity) can have is Vulgarity, and differ only as to the application of this rule—i.e. what is vulgar.' Neither the tact nor the trenchancy of his prose is to be found in his verse, and his regressive Pentland pleasures may be thought diminished by a further regression to the styles and stateliness of an urban past, to a time of wigs and brocades. Previous arguments have tended to indicate that the two regressions were ultimately the same: nevertheless, it has to be said— so to speak, provisionally—that his more promising themes do not always go well with a poetic diction which takes 'umbrage' to mean shade. It is a word of Milton's: Eden is 'umbrageous'.[2] But in Cockburn's Scotland 'umbrage' meant umbrage, and in that sense it may seem to be, still, something of a Scottish word. The *Scots Magazine* for August 1784 (at the time of the Canonmills riots) reported that an insane youth had taken 'umbrage' at his grandmother and put arsenic in her porridge. Cockburn would perhaps have been intrigued by that report had it come at a later date. But it would not have stopped him from putting Miltonisms in his lifeboats.

In most matters of literary judgment, he delighted to concur with Jeffrey, who is famous for objecting to Wordsworth's 'childishness' while shedding tears over his poems. Childishness was for private consumption: it was unfit to be offered to society at large, or to the unsophisticated. Yet the subject-matter of Cockburn's version of pastoral has much that is private and childish. There, perhaps, he was at his least old-fashioned. But the literary taste which he and Jeffrey shared could not deal with such subjects.

Jeffrey's comments in the *Edinburgh Review* on Wordsworth's *Excursion* ('This will never do') refer to this question of childishness, and show that Jeffrey had a rather restrictive attitude to the quality of tact in literary contexts: tact meant not divulging what is intimately important to you, unless you could be sure that it would meet with the approval, as much of it would not, of most of the people about you. And the people he often had in mind on such occasions were those of wealth and sense. Such attitudes were supported by philosophical argument, some of it drawn from Associationist aesthetics and concerned to stress the importance, for the consideration of

[1] 9 September 1850.
[2] *Paradise Lost*, Book Four, line 257. It is also, admittedly, a word of Wordsworth's.

objects and images, of associations that were of universal or wide appeal. What Jeffrey says here may be found objectionable, though it is also, I would say, challenging and instructive: 'An habitual and general knowledge of the few settled and permanent maxims, which form the canon of general taste in all large and polished societies, a certain tact, which informs us at once that many things, which we still love and are moved by in secret, must necessarily be despised as childish, or derided as absurd, in all such societies —though it will not stand in the place of genius, seems necessary to the success of its exertions.'[1]

Jeffrey's comments have an Augustan ring, just as Cockburn's poems carry the remnants of an Augustan decorum. But it is also the case that these poems have an element that is childish and absurd and secret. I do not think they are altogether polished and polite, or merely deficient in trying to appear so, however much they may allude to an old civility. And it may be that Cockburn and Jeffrey concurred in thinking that in a civilized Scotland such poems were unpublishable, that they were privately amiable but publicly vicious. But I doubt whether this would really have been the view. It is more likely that they were left unpublished because Cockburn lacked confidence in them, or felt that they belonged to the Pentlands.

Despite their at times 'Wordsworthian' subject-matter, Cockburn's poems are, in respect of form, more strongly marked by the example of Scott than by that of any other poet. It turns out that the two men also coincided in matters of verse and versification, and that Scott's romantic floridity and afflatus, and his galloping dactyls and four-stress iambic lines ('Lives there a man . . . '), were emulated in Bonaly Tower. But there is more to it than that. It also turns out that 'The Linn' has a prototype in Scott's 'Helvellyn'. It can't exactly be considered a seond parody of that poem, but it does allow one to say that 'Helvellyn' was made both a target and an object of admiration among Scott's merry Whig friends.

The preamble to the first version of 'The Linn', the version which is in the possession of the Cockburn family, reads as follows:

The Linn, a little to the west of Bonaly, is nearly the first distinct beginning of what afterwards becomes Braid burn, on the banks of which almost all the summer Saturdays of my boyhood were passed. I never discovered the Linn till about 1803. The Miss Hills lived then, and for several years afterwards, at Bonaly and Woodhall, when they and Richardson and Sabbath Grahame and I were constantly exploring the Pentlands. This little retired cascade became our favourite retreat, and was almost worshipped by us. We took it into our heads that the old solitary Elm that hangs over it was going to die, and therefore that the Dryads might have leaves, we

[1] John Clive writes interestingly about this passage (*ER*, November 1814) in his book about Jeffrey and his circle, *Scotch Reviewers* (1957), pp. 160-5.

planted the hollow. Not having also fenced, the sheep of course nibbled our grove away; but not anticipating this, I was ordained to celebrate the planting in verse, and I see from the tattered, and nearly illegible, original, that the 18th day of July AD 1809 produced the following moving, *and not obscure*, lines.

He clearly set the utmost store by the Linn and the elm, and his manuscript letters reveal that he continued to do so for the rest of his life. Much later, the Linn was threatened when reservoirs were proposed near Bonaly. Writing to Mrs Leonard Horner on 25 November 1846, he refers to 'the glen west of Bonaly ending at *The* Linn', and says: 'Well, that's to be made into a lake—90 feet deep!!!' There were to be two further lakes—and 'all that the people of Edin. may get their faces better washed.' Public virtues could prove privately vicious.

A year later, on 1 October, he returns to the subject, in a letter to a neighbouring landowner, Sir William Liston-Foulis:

I beg you to excuse me for meddling with what you may think I have nothing to do with. My apology is that it is well meant and concerns you also.

You know *the Linn*, on your property, a little to the west of this. Much of our happiness here depends on it; and its beauty depends much on the solitary elm that hangs over the cascade.

The Water Company have begun their operations close beside it, not under their new, but their old, act, and are soon to have a great number of Paddies and other devils, who will be working there till the end of the year.

You are aware of an Irishman's love of Shillela's. This love is so strong that nothing except warning and threatening can save a leaf of that tree.

I have spoken to the foreman, who *professes* fairly enough. But as he knows that the tree is not mine, of course he estimates all my threats at very little.

Now I take the liberty of submitting to you whether you should not write to the Manager of the Water Coy, admonishing him, at his peril, to touch that tree—or anything about the Linn. No part of it is *on their line*, and except from carelessness or mischief, none of their people have any occasion to touch it.

Again, begging you to forgive this officiousness, believe me

Yours Faithfully

H. Cockburn

Knowing that these reservoirs had come to pass and might have swallowed both linn and elm, I decided to follow the directions in the preamble and find out whether his shrine had in fact been deluged and destroyed. I ascended from Bonaly and skirted Torduff Reservoir. The path rose towards the higher ground occupied by Clubbiedean Reservoir. And there before me, in a cleft at the head of the glen, was a waterfall, and an elm. I walked on, thinking of Auden's lines in his poem 'Now the leaves are falling fast':

Cold, impossible, ahead
Lifts the mountain's lovely head
Whose white waterfall could bless
Travellers in their last distress.

'Out of a sullen hollow in a livid hillside her mind could make an Eden,'
wrote Charlotte Brontë of her sister Emily.[1] Cockburn's mind had done the
same, and here was his Eden—the heart or penetralia of his Pentlands paradise—preserved, the road curling round to the left of it like a protective arm.

Cockburn disclaimed all responsibility for the Richardson parody of
'Helvellyn' of around 1805. But he responded to it four years later in 'The
Linn', paying it a kind of homage. The dactyllic metre scheme is much the
same, and some of the properties of Scott's poem about the dead mountaineer
and his dog are present in 'The Linn'. Both poems are about a lover of nature,
a pilgrim. Scott writes: 'Where the Pilgrim of Nature lay stretch'd in decay'.
Cockburn's first version has: 'The wonder-struck Pilgrim stood still at
thy view.' Scott has: 'Unhonour'd the Pilgrim from life should depart?'
Cockburn's second version has: 'Not unhonoured hereafter thy fountain
shall flow.' The details of Cockburn's poem can be difficult to take in: this
is due to its rhetorical blandness, but also, I think, to its dependence on an
unspecified original. The effect, at moments, is like that of a smudged copy
of this original. Scott's pilgrim is dead: 'No mother to weep, and no friend
to deplore him'. Cockburn's pilgrim is alive, but the second version intro-
duces a corpse, a 'desolate stranger' with an absent mother and no friend to
deplore him.

The mention of Charles Cotier of Dunkirk, the desolate stranger, while
serving to assimilate the poem still closer to Scott's, was, for a while, a
puzzle. I could find no grave near the Linn, and no Charles Cotier was
registered among the deaths for the period in question. It seemed worth
inquiring into this, in that the additional stanzas of the second version which
form a requiem for Cotier ('no requiem read o'er him,' says Scott of his
mountaineer), and which are preceded by the text of a tombstone inscription with the dates omitted, were, coming from Cockburn, rather arresting.
The first of the stanzas is this:

And here hast thou perished, oh! Desolate stranger,
Nor given thy dust to thy own garden grave!
But sunk amidst objects thy memory knew not,
And struck by the hand that had promised to save!

[1] In a memoir of her sister quoted in *Emily Brontë* by Winifred Gerin (1971), p. 55.

There was an access of feeling in these stanzas, and a suggestion of the orphaned or the oedipal, which seemed to me to be the voice of certain of Cockburn's unmemorialized inner concerns. I felt, too, that the Cockburn who wrote the *Memorials* was plainly visible in the lines:

> And the scene of thy infancy kept all unchanged,
> By a mother beholding an Image of thee!

Who was this Cotier, and who had struck him? I discovered that someone else had gone, in his own words, *à la recherche de Cotier*: a Frenchman with the exotic name of A. W. Stewart produced a monograph in 1936 which tells the man's story.[1] He claims, unconvincingly, that he was really Charles Marant, a *pilote côtier* (coastal pilot). Cotier was captured during the Napoleonic Wars and held at Greenlaw House in Midlothian (where the barracks of Glencorse now stands). Early in 1807, Ensign Hugh Maxwell of the Lanarkshire Militia, possibly drunk, one night ordered a soldier to fire at random into a barrack-room where a light had been seen, and Cotier was killed. The case occasioned an outcry—both against Maxwell (a remarkable thing for a time of war, which was also a time when the Whigs were briefly in power) and in his favour. He was tried and sentenced to nine months' imprisonment in the Tolbooth. Cotier was buried nearby at the parish church of Glencorse, a few miles away, across the hills, from Cockburn's Linn, and a headstone was set up. Stewart says the grave—that of a prisoner shot by his captor in a strange land—has always excited interest. An approximation to the words on the headstone is given by Cockburn before he embarks on his requiem. The words on the headstone read in full:

ICI REPOSE CHARLES
COTIER DE DUNKERQUE
MORT LE 8 JANVIER 1807

Cockburn's Linn is a 'little retired cascade', a 'secret rill', round which he hopefully plants his grove, and this 'favourite retreat' seems to have figured as the centre of the earth for the agrestic, unaggressive part of his nature, and as a place where it was natural to pay tribute to a stranger, a prisoner, the victim of a transgression against a code of protection and hospitality—a transgression which may be thought to resemble an offence against kinship.

---

[1] Stewart's privately printed monograph was filed with the Historical Society of Dunkirk and its Administration de la Marine.

6*

How purely thy rill from its old rocks descends,
Amusing the ear by its breeze-varied sound!
And fixing the eye on the arches it bends
Unheeding the Wildness that watches around!

How long have these mosses gleamed rich in thy dew!
This Elm, thy companion, thrown o'er thee its shade!
The wonder-struck Pilgrim stood still at thy view!
And the Sun shone in peace on thy lonely cascade!

With his Satanic pugnacity and his saintly or heavenly peace, Cockburn is sometimes, as I've said, reminiscent of Milton. For a hundred and fifty years, Milton's epic had proved doctrinal to the nation: admired and meditated, it had imposed styles of life as well as of verse. At various points, the works of Cockburn's imagination can bring to mind the drama, and the psychology, and the geography, which appear in *Paradise Lost*. In particular, Milton's Eden, that 'happy rural seat' with its 'umbrageous grots', helped to supply the landscape for other Edens that followed, among which Cockburn's can be included. It has a subterranean river, to which 'nether flood', from a 'shaggy hill', descend the rills of a fountain: the scene is made to seem like a body—and, for the most part, a female body.[1] Another of the later Edens which seem to have drawn on Milton's is that described in 'Kubla Khan'. Coleridge's potentate decrees his pleasure-dome on a site similar to Milton's Eden and Cockburn's Linn:

But O, that deep romantic chasm which slanted
Down the green hill athwart a cedern cover!

Out of this chasm flows a fountain, which becomes a 'sacred river'. The scene, however, is invested with a feeling of 'holy dread' from which the Milton and Cockburn landscapes are quite free.

The resemblance between Coleridge's poem and Cockburn's is likely, I believe, to be more than a matter of a common awareness of Milton, and the question might be thought to arise whether Cockburn was also aware of the Coleridge: whether, beneath his Whig Reformer's pleasure-dome of Bonaly, he was essaying a Scottish 'Kubla Khan', less childish than the original, *and not obscure*. Coleridge dreamt the dream after which he wrote his poem— and which may have been an opium dream—in 1797, but it was not published until 1816, when it came out together with 'Christabel'. Scott knew 'Christa-

---

[1] *Paradise Lost*, Book Four, lines 247, 257, 231, 224.

bel' long before that, and it is possible that Cockburn knew both of these poems before he wrote 'The Linn'. But there is no evidence of this. There are hints, though, that throughout his career as a Bonaly poet he was aware of Coleridge. I doubt whether his title 'Geraldine' is an allusion to 'Christabel' but I don't doubt myself that the 'sunless' dell in 'Relugas' was produced by the 'sunless sea' of 'Kubla Khan'. And it is probable that the remark about obscurity in the preamble to 'The Linn' was directed at the kind of poetry written by Coleridge and the Lake school, given the attitude towards that poetry of the *Edinburgh Review*, and the canons of taste that prevailed there.

Both Coleridge's site and Cockburn's have a sexual significance, though Cockburn's is a douce, dulcimerless Edinburgh damsel by comparison, and no object of holy dread. The meaning of 'Kubla Khan' has been argued over a great deal. It is only necessary to say here that, in my opinion, those who have seen in it an oedipal content, arguing that the taboo which seems to be referred to is that of incest, are right. I also believe that the Cockburn has an oedipal content, though there is no sense of taboo, or of Coleridge's punitive or prohibitive 'war'. The union with the mother which is celebrated in the poem is serene, though the womanly presence is not only life-giving but death-dealing: the grove that he planted by his waterfall was meant as a 'Porch that conducts to the Mansion of Rest'.

'The Linn' suggests that for Cockburn, the Pentlands were home and play and pleasure; they were femininity and fecundity; they were death and eternity. They were holy ground: and the use of the word 'holiday' for his sojourns there is like a reversion to its original or literal meaning. It should be acknowledged that the Pentlands were, and are, well worth his worship. They are a good place to consecrate a shrine to a mother goddess.

Scott shared something of Cockburn's feeling for these hills. The *Journal* entry for 11 November 1827 tells of a drive to Melville Castle: 'I think I never saw any thing more beautiful than the ridge of Carnethy (Pentland) against a clear frosty sky with its peaks and varied slopes. The hills glowd like purple amethysts, the sky glowd topaz and vermilion colours. I never saw a finer screen than Pentland considering that it is neither rocky nor highly elevated.' These ecstatic words are like a glimpse of Paradise. They are also like a glimpse of Milton's Paradise, where the firmament 'glows' with 'living sapphires'.[1]

*Weir of Hermiston*, some of the landscape for which was taken from the Pentlands around Glencorse, has a passage which deserves to be compared with this. Stevenson is writing about Mrs Weir—'Braxfield's' wife—and her relationship with her son, later to rebel against his father: 'There is a

[1] Ibid., lines 604, 605.

corner of the policy of Hermiston, where you come suddenly in view of the summit of Black Fell, sometimes like the mere grass top of a hill, sometimes (and this is her own expression) like a precious jewel in the heavens. On such days, upon the sudden view of it, her hand would tighten on the child's fingers, her voice rise like a song. "*I to the hills!*" she would repeat. "And O, Erchie, are nae these like the hills of Naphtali?" and her tears would flow.'[1] Naphtali is one of the sons of Jacob, who says of him in Genesis: 'Naphtali is a hind let loose: he giveth goodly words.'[2] This is the best of all descriptions of Cockburn, whose hills were certainly like those of Naphtali. *Naphtali* is also the title of a work, once famous, which celebrates the sufferings of the Covenanters: among their other attributes (which include the place-name Hermiston), the hills have Covenanting associations.

There are telling words about the Pentlands in the *Memoir of Robert Chambers* by his brother William, which was discussed previously. In Peebles, a zealot or 'Covenanter' came up to their mother, who was holding her first-born, William, in her arms: 'Ye're mickle pleased wi' that bairn, woman. If the French come, what will ye do wi' him? I trow ye'll be fleeing wi' him to the tap o' the Pentland Hills. But ye should rather pray that they *may* come. Ye should pray for judgments, woman—judgments on a sinfu' land.'[3] Here, too, the heights of the Pentlands are associated with maternal comfort. They are a place where you can be safe: safe from the French— and safe from the virtues, and judgments, of Edinburgh.

I was born in a mining village just beneath the Pentlands, and I, too, found them numinous and comforting. All these words of praise, had I known them during my childhood, would have made sense, though for me the hills were always blue, and not, as for Scott on this occasion, purple. I remember my grandmother telling me of the deer that used to come down to the door in winter, their eyes glazed with ice. The Pentlands, lifting their thrilling heads so near the city, are, to this day, an authentic wilderness: yet they are also a human haunt, a place of public resort, practically a park. Cockburn once pronounced Bonaly's 'apparent wildness interesting and its cheapness very refreshing'.[4] A less romantic view than the one he generally took.

To this day, for all that, the Pentlands have remained holy ground—a solemn and mysterious region to which his awe and transports seem altogether appropriate, a region which might exact a shrine, and which now wears its touristic ski-lift like a scar. For all their tourists, they are inviolable. When I visited my mother not long ago in a hospital whose windows look out on

[1] *Weir of Hermiston* (1920 edition), p. 13.      [2] Genesis 49, v. 21.
[3] *Memoir of Robert Chambers*, p. 13.
[4] In a letter to Dick Lauder of 16 October 1815: *Some Letters of Lord Cockburn*, p. 14.

this wilderness, their moving presence, kind and admonishing, filled the ward of old women. I felt that these hills could attract, or supplant, a filial devotion; that these were hills to which orphans might lift their eyes; that these were slopes on which you could be exposed and left to die, but where you could also expect aid and comfort. They were like a heaven on earth.

I want now to examine the rest of his poems. One of the two earliest seems to be 'Geraldine', of which the first seven stanzas exist in what seems to be a calligraphic version of his ordinary hand: the other poems are entirely in his ordinary hand. The paper on which the first seven stanzas are written is watermarked 1805, and paper by the same maker, watermarked the same year, is used for a letter to Grahame of 12 December 1808 in which, while conferring a title on the poem, 'The Holy Grove, or, Geraldine', he disclaims authorship:

> If Geraldine had been written by me, I should have held your opinions respecting it to be well founded, and been indifferent, as I could truly say it was almost the only verse I had written since I was 15. But the joke has taken. You have been censuring one of Shakespeare's best little pieces—modernised by Warton. This is the poem of which Shakespeare says in a letter to a cousin of Spencer's, a relation of Sir Henry Wotton's—"Well beloved Sire, I send you on off my best litt. pieces ycleped The Holy Grove, or Geraldine, composed upon the sadde goinge awaye of yr nieece. Methinkes it bee on of the verry best of yr kinde greetinge friende W.S." You will see this letter in the 3d vol. p. 201 of the last edition of Spencer's works. So you may criticise Geraldine as you please or dare—being Dick's own.

This letter harks back to two separate Shakespeare vogues: the vogue for modernizing and improving him, and the vogue for drafting letters by him, in fantastical antique spellings, which was touched off by the Ireland forgeries of a dozen years before. Neither Shakespeare nor, as far as I can discover, any modernizer wrote 'Geraldine', and I have soberly decided that Cockburn is indeed joking here, and that the joke is that the poem is Harry's own. The reference to the 'last edition' of Spenser, which I take to be Todd's Variorum of 1805, turns out to be a false trail. The name 'Geraldine'—despite the poisonous nature of Coleridge's lofty lady—could conceivably have come from 'Christabel': equally, it could have come from the poems by the Earl of Surrey which invoke a woman of that name. These are discussed by Thomas Warton in his *History of English Poetry*, and are at least in accord with the sixteenth-century references provided by Cockburn. But who is Dick?

The diction of the poem is certainly Cockburn's. 'Peace', 'the past', 'pleasures', 'transports', 'lovely scenes', 'solemn', 'heaven'—these are the bricks (and straw) with which he made his other poems and with which he made some of the lovely scenes and set-pieces of his memorabilia. In a letter of 1803,[1] as in this poem, 'serene' is used as a verb. But the most Cockburn-like feature of the poem is its title, 'The Holy Grove', and its worship of that 'Hallowed Spot'. It is true that on this occasion the recollection of 'favrite days' can't console as it does elsewhere. But the comforts afforded by the hallowed spot are still accessible, though at times they appear not to be, and it is with these, rather than with Geraldine or her absence, that the poem is really concerned, I think. It is hard to imagine Cockburn in the posture of a love poet, and 'Geraldine' does not make it necessary to try.

The lines which begin 'How solemn the close . . . ' are far more attractive. The paper on which they were written is matched by that of the letter of 28 December 1808 in which he conveys to Grahame his opinions about Vulgarity. It seems likely that 'Geraldine' and 'How solemn the close' belong to 1808 or a little before, and that both versions of 'The Linn', to which the present lines are very similar both in metre and matter, belong to 1809, though Cockburn is not always sound on dates. It might appear that this vale is the same as the one which contains his Linn, but, as has become evident, it is not easy to find your way about his poetic landscapes, and in any case, the nuclear geography of waterfall and tree and hollow was bound to be fairly widely reproduced throughout his hillside haunts. In fact, the geography and time-scale of the poem argue for its being a different vale. The preamble to 'The Linn' states that he did not discover the place till he was about 24: but in these lines he is haunting the vale in question in childhood. The 'Blessed Relic' does not seem to resemble the grove he planted, and 'the feet of th'unhallowed', though they could well suggest those of the Irish navvies who might have cut shillelaghs from his sacred elm, do not suggest those of the sheep who nibbled his grove away. Nor are there any woods near the Linn.

This is a different vale, and I believe I know the one he is referring to. It is some distance further down the Braid Burn towards the city. The *Memorials*[2] tell of a broomy glen between the Braid and Blackford Hills where he and his school friends used to forgather and play. Scott played there, too, in his time. To commemorate their departure from school, Cockburn and others built a pillar of stones in the stream, which was washed away. They then 'deposited' (as the poem says, 'placed') a tin box full of precious coins, including a new Glasgow halfpenny, in the cleft of a rock. It lay there unmolested for more than twenty years. Learning that the road trustees and their workmen were about to wreck their valley, he rescued the box, and he has 'the relic at this hour'. This, I reckon, is the blessed relic

---

[1] To Anderson, 6 December.     [2] *M*, p. 12.

mentioned in the poem. The landscape, with its rock, is right, and the time is right.

The endeavour to trap the past in a shrine or memorial is of the essence of Cockburn, and the last two stanzas, in particular, of the poem in which he salutes this endeavour are among the most illuminating of all his auto-biographical deposits or depositions:

> Thou Hope of the future and Pledge of the past!
> Revered be the hour, tho' in childhood forgot,
> When something foreboding that Youth would not last,
> I vowed to revive it in this lovely spot!
>
> For the vows of our childhood in Heaven are sealed!
> And lest ever the virtue they sprung from expire,
> In our favourite haunt to our bosoms revealed,
> The Spirit that breathed them rekindles their fire.

These lines addressed to his tin box, 'Hope of the future and Pledge of the past', say a good deal about his Janus-faced politics, as they also do about his conception of virtue. And the poem as a whole makes it clear that, for him, landscape and the past were elements of the one religion, that his hikes and his histories were the one worship. This brooding on the favourite days of his childhood, counted like coins, told over in an avaricious ecstasy of Proustian recall, brought him satisfactions which a letter to Anderson of 18 February 1808, the year in which these lines were probably written, helps to explain. He writes of a happy early time:

> Surely nothing is so delightful as the remembrance of hours so passed. The scenes and the days steal sometimes unexpectedly upon our memories, and let us feel how good it is to treasure what the world so early bestows. When I want to be sated with delight, I lye on the top of the Braid Hills in a warm, rich, silent autumnal day, and survey all the places I can recollect ever to have liked. The sight of them brings back the circumstances, the hours, the seasons, the period of life, the friends, the hopes they used to be connected with. A crowd of emotions, so confused, but so exquisite, comes over the heart that the thought of their ever being obliterated is less tolerable than that of personal annihilation.

Two years later, in a letter to Grahame of 29 March 1811, he returns to the subject—if he can ever, in adult life, be said to have left it:

> Have you such a thing as a Burn near you? Lord pity you if you have not! But to a true Scotsman, the burns of his native land are ever tinkling in his ears and trickling over his heart, and the breezes which he recollects to have felt come over his imagination, softened and endeared by the distance from which they have blown. These

remembrances, if abused, may easily be converted into so many sources of wretched-
ness. But when thought of as the poetry of life, as pleasures long enjoyed actually,
and more intensely enjoyed in memory, when connected with changes which suggest
the idea of increased usefulness elsewhere, and used as evidences of the power of man
to be delighted with whatever he accustoms his heart to love, they become, like past
duties and future hopes, treasures of felicity which distance can only endear and time
can only perfect.

There is more than soulful patriotism here: there is doctrine too.

With their common emphasis on 'connection', both passages represent, I
think, what Cockburn made of the doctrine of Associationism, developed by
Hartley in England, taken up by the Reverend Archibald Alison, an Episco-
palian clergyman in Edinburgh, and of interest not only to Jeffrey, as we
have seen, but also to Wordsworth and many others. 'Connect' was a
favourite word of Alison's. Dealing with the period around 1816, the
*Memorials* record that Alison's sermons were 'the poetry of preaching',
and it was no doubt Alison's influence which induced Cockburn, in his letter
to Grahame, to speak in this manner about 'the poetry of life'. The *Memorials*
go on to say: 'He was almost the only preacher I have ever known who habi-
tually made the appearances of external nature, and the kindred associations,
subservient to the uses of the pulpit. This copious and skilful application of
the finest, and most generally understood, elements of taste was one great
cause of his peculiar success.' And much later in life he says: 'The first thing
that made me truly see what was before me in Nature was Alison's *Essays
on Taste*.'[1] The reference in this passage of the *Memorials* to 'the most
generally understood' elements of taste may appear to point to one aspect
of the use that was made of Alison's ideas by Jeffrey—the aspect discussed
in relation to Jeffrey's notion of universality of appeal.

In his elegant *Essays on the Nature and Principles of Taste*, Alison writes:
'There is no man, who has not some interesting associations with particular
scenes, or airs, or books, and who does not feel their beauty or sublimity
enhanced to him by such connections. The view of the house where one was
born, of the school where one was educated, and where the gay years of
infancy were passed, is indifferent to no man. They recall so many images of
past happiness and past affections, they are connected with so many strong
or valued emotions, and lead altogether to so long a train of feelings and
recollections, that there is hardly any scene which one ever beholds with so
much rapture.'[2] It is easy to see why Alison appealed to Cockburn, though

---

[1] *M*, pp. 305, 306. His later words are from a letter to his daughter Elizabeth of 11 May 1841:
*Some Letters of Lord Cockburn*, pp. 43, 44.

[2] *Essays on the Nature and Principles of Taste* (2 vols, 1811), vol. I, pp. 23, 24. This is a second
edition of the *Essays*, which has additional material, and which was reviewed by Jeffrey (*ER*, May
1811). The first edition was published in 1790.

1.  Lord Braxfield: one of the two Raeburn portraits, engraved by G. Dawe

2. Cockburn, from Benjamin Crombie's series of etchings 'Modern Athenians',
executed between 1837 and 1847

3. Cockburn's waterfall and elm

4. A Hill/Adamson calotype of the Bonaly household, with Cockburn standing at the extreme right and his wife seated at the foot of the stairs

the school where he was educated did not take pride of place among his pleasant memories. For Alison, beauty and sublimity existed in the eye of the beholder, and depended on trains of thought occasioned by objects that were connected with the 'simple' emotions. Such connections were often established early in life. The experience of beauty or sublimity could be heightened by associations attributable to the further presence of the picturesque. Associationists disagreed with Uvedale Price about the picturesque, but it was possible to admire both Price and Alison, and Dick Lauder was still doing this in the 1840s. Elms were especially picturesque.

Some of Cockburn's letters are Alisonian in outlook, and so is much of his verse. He was, in general, resistant to intellectual theories, but he would have been vulnerable to one which permitted him to contemplate the significance of associations acquired in childhood, and to ask why landscape mattered to him, why burns were beautiful. Less doctrinally, but no less decisively, his feeling for burns, with their power to renew in him a child's sense of safety and well-being, breaks out in an earlier letter to Grahame,[1] written after a supper of macaroni when he was staying with the Miss Hills at Woodhall: 'The uniform sound of the river below, that lulls every chamber at this still and solemn hour, imparts a character of sequestered peacefulness, which is invaluable.' There is a suggestion here of childhood's safest place of all.

'For the vows of our childhood in Heaven are sealed': this, and 'Struck by the hand that had promised to save', are the most personally revealing lines in his poetry. The intensity of his concentration on early happiness, and of his imaginative search for security and perpetuity, may be felt to have been a way of extinguishing a consciousness of dark and precarious days suffered when he was a child: such things are virtually absent from his recollections of the past. They may also have helped him to live with the aims, ambitions and responsibilities which characterized his adult life. At the same time, he seems to be moving, in this poem and elsewhere, towards a cult of childhood as such which owes a certain amount to other childhoods and other poetries of the period.

Wordsworth's Ode on the 'Intimations of Immortality from Recollections of Early Childhood' was published at this time, in 1807. In October, in the *Edinburgh Review*, Jeffrey called it 'illegible and unintelligible', but Cockburn could not have been unimpressed by its assurance that 'Heaven lies about us in our infancy!' Whatever the impediments may have been to a full acknowledgement on Cockburn's part of the power of this poetry—so far as his own was concerned, at any rate—these were Cockburn's sentiments,

[1] 18 September 1809.

and these were to be some of his very words. I am inclined to think that what we are witnessing here is a debt to Wordsworth: a secret debt, so to speak, which mattered more than all the overt resemblances to Scott, and which may, in fact, help to account for this crop of poems, after a long silence, at this stage of Cockburn's life. At all events, these two lines of his may be regarded as leading texts for the views advanced in this book concerning his emotional development. What happened to him in childhood would never cease to happen. It is as if his fate, like his vows, were sealed.

Cockburn's 'Relugas', though dated 1828, is quite close, in terms of sub-ject-matter, to the earlier crop of poems, but the shorter line seems to have released in him a lighter and defter touch, and a welcome lucidity. Here are the landscape and attributes of another Eden—the Dick Lauder family's Morayshire estate. This, too, is holy ground. The first verse combines a distinctly ante-natal feeling—akin to that expressed at Woodhall—with the sense of a child in bed, hoping for his mother. Relugas is that mother.

> When wakeful in the night profound,
> The fearful pulses of my heart I hear,
> And long for some external sound,
> Relugas! be thy whispers near!

The pith of 'Relugas' lies in its address to the sacred herons. In the *Circuit Journeys*,[1] he refers to the heronry as 'a royal burgh, and a very ancient one, of these civic birds, nobly placed'. And the address breathes the atmosphere of his Scotch Millennium:

> Ye winged sages! Feathered Gods!
> How calm your social city rests;
> While ye, within your old abodes,
> Sagacious watch your solid nests.

Old abodes were no less dear to him than a social city, where those of all stations could agree together. Let there be property and sagacity, wealth and sense. No feathering of nests in that social city. But let there be solid nests.

A cancelled version of the last line read: 'Like burghers watch your solid nests'. Milton's Satan leaps over the wall into Paradise like a burglar intent on

> the cash
> Of some rich burgher, whose substantial doors . . . [2]

---

[1] *Circuit Journeys*, p. 263.   [2] *Paradise Lost*, Book Four, lines 188, 189.

If there is any echo of this in Cockburn's line, it cannot be called a distraction, since Cockburn is engaged here in making property seem paradisal. His change involved the substitution of one Milton word for another. 'Sagacious', too, has a certain prominence in *Paradise Lost*, and this, too, was a word to please a Scottish Whig. Burns's 'Address to the Deil' gives a suitably agrestic, a far from burghal, picture of the Fall of Man and of Satan's burglary of Eden:

> Lang syne, in Eden's bonnie yard,
> When youthfu' lovers first were pair'd ...

Burns was a warm admirer of Milton's Satan, that 'very respectable Personage'.[1] Here, however, he addresses him more fondly than respectfully:

> Then you, ye auld snick-drawing dog!
> Ye cam to Paradise incog.

Cockburn's occasional poem 'On losing a staff from a gig' was written some two years earlier: his manuscript dates it, with a question-mark, 'before 1826'. This is a very different piece of work, or play. Cockburn's literary tastes were both pre-Romantic and Romantic. Neither description is to be preferred: as he said himself when faced with a dilemma on his Continental tour, both are best. But his tastes did not remain stable, and it seems clear that this poem is more 'Augustan' than those written in his twenties. In the course of his life, Romanticism 'came in', but there are signs that, with Cockburn, as he grew older, it went out, and was shown to have been, in some degree, the stuff of his youth. This poem is such a sign, and so is the list of poets whose example he was pressing on Ballantine in 1850. Cockburn was a partial, a part-time Romantic, and the preoccupations of his solitude, early and late, should not be mistaken for the whole man, or for a complete conversion. The sympathies stirred by the French Revolution made him, as it made Richardson, a philanthropist and comparatively democratical, one of the new school, and they also helped to make him an impressible orphan lad who was attached to victims and to burns. The bliss of that dawn did not and could not last, though I doubt if he ever entirely outgrew his early fervours.

This poem could be thought to desert the maternal hollow for the emblems of the male. Nevertheless, the sound of the burn, of his secret rill, is still heard, and it is apparent here, as in his writings at large, that the Bonaly ambience was bisexual. His imagination was a harmony of solids and liquids, verticals and recesses, ups and downs, trees and clefts, towers and declivities.

---

[1] From a letter to Mrs Dunlop of 30 April 1787.

It reveals no war between the male and female principles: each was granted its territories, and there was plenty of common ground.

The dilemmas, the stark opposites, the reversions to childhood, and the flagrancy of 'Freudian' symbols, which appear in his writings, and especially in his verse, might be taken as reasons for assuming that there was some sort of civil war in Cockburn, or for trying to diagnose an overriding problem of a kind known to psychiatry. One way and another, his was a double life: was there, then, a 'divided self' in the modern clinical sense? It seems very unlikely. While some of the problems that troubled him may well have been shaped by a single early crisis, there is no reason to believe that they ever became a 'problem' in that sense. He dreamt his dreams in innocence of the interpretations which have since been fashioned for dreams of all descriptions. It may be that, in many parts of the world, this innocence has now gone. And it does not seem too much to say about a paradise such as Cockburn's, which required a faculty for dreaming innocently and elaborately about the individual's hopes and fears, and which may now be a paradise lost, that it may sometimes have ensured that a problematic life never became a problem.

Cocky's long pole or stick was that of a prototypical or antediluvian hiker and seeker of the open air. As such, his pole may be thought to have been bequeathed, figuratively speaking, to the Boy Scout Movement, which has long been attracted to the region of Bonaly. The particular stick lamented in his poem, having hiked with him across the hills, was lost in the course of a journey in his gig between the New Town and the Pentlands: *hinc illae lacrimae.*

The logistics of these journeys, these commutings between heaven and earth, were a matter of concern to Cockburn, to judge by two unpublished letters in the Signet Library. In 1829, he asks a friend:

> Is there such a thing as an excellent Droskie horse in Edin.? My vehicle has a double seat, and four wheels. It scarcely ever goes except from Edin. to Bonaly, and is crammed each time with children, processes, lamb legs, women—and all sorts of domestic accommodation or incumbrance. And occasionally the steed must be degraded by bringing vegetables into town in a light cart.

He wants 'a strong, broad, sensible, punchy beast—like Lord Craigie; but somewhat more active'. He got what he wanted (a 'Droskie' is a four-wheeled gig, a 'punch' is a short-legged, round-bodied horse), and sixteen years later he applies for a replacement to the same man: 'One good turn, they say, deserves another. And this too often means that when a man has done you one favour, you may ask him to do you a second.' He praises the previous horse: 'Good sense, good manners, good temper, and good principles—a moderate whig attached to the Free church (tho' this last I have sometimes suspected was owing to the superiority of the Free to the Established stable'). Once again he wants 'a strong, practical punch—with legs something like Lord Craigie's, and an understanding like Sir Harry Moncreiff's'. The very beasts of these stick-bearing lawyer-lairds were what Harry Dundas is said to be in the *Memorials*: sagacious.[1]

The stick as a symbol of both pleasure and punishment, of both serenity and supremacy, could hardly have failed to mean much to a man who had gone against his father's pleasure in seeking his own, and so it proves in this poem. It is mock-elegiac in character, and the sarcasm to which fatherhood is subjected attests to his pugnacity, a pugnacity which is partly turned on himself, since, by now, *he* is a father too. But the poem has more to offer than that. Written during the years when he was writing the *Memorials*, it is also the work of the compunctious Cockburn. He jokes about the loss of a father's authority, but he also enjoins his 'imps' to respect that authority. For all his recollections of early childhood, one might say, they were not to spur their immortal father round the room. There can be no doubt that, by middle age, he would have taken such an injunction seriously, and there's a real earnestness in the poem, only faintly dissembled by the wit.

If the poem is about the loss of a stick, it is also, at one remove, about the destruction of the father which is implied in filial disobedience. Cockburn, figuratively speaking, had stolen his father's stick, and these lines—with their attention to the paternal, the patriarchal significance of his own stick, which was to have been handed on to his children—are a sign that the thought still mattered to him (or mattered afresh) in his forties. The man who had stolen his father's stick had lost his own: he was hoist on his own pole. Later, as we know, he was to be hoist again—near-Harricidally. But I don't think it is an exercise of hindsight to perceive, hidden in his merry words about the reverence expected from his boys, an emphasis not altogether remote from that expressed in his final testament. His stick was more than patriarchal, and this passage would be more than comical even if it hadn't proved prophetic.

This rather bizarre piece of light verse can look dense enough when the circumstances of the life that uttered it are borne in mind. Here are the later stages of the poem: he is addressing his sportive and supportive stick.

[1] The letters were addressed to William Sharpe, Writer to the Signet. The second is dated 10 October 1845.

And oft I thought, when coming age
Should bid these sports no more engage,
I still might find thy faithful stem
(Respectable, with mounted gem)
Reposing in thy untouched nook
And blest with thee, and thoughtful book,
Might still step forth on level walk
By beechen hedge to read or talk.
And when at last that prop shall fail
And time o'er my frail leaf prevail,
I still had hopes these playful boys
Might share with thee their mountain joys,
And tenderly for many a year,
The old paternal staff revere.
But oh that Gig! and him who drove
Through Morton's mean and rutted grove!
They gave to some unconscious hand
A more than patriarchal wand,
And left these arms without a friend
In danger's hour who could not bend.

The playfulness of the Pentlands, the needs it served, and its conditioning regrets and difficulties, are fused in this *jeu d'esprit*. Why so many comic tears about a lost stick? Because it was, in part, Baron Cockburn's—transferred by his unconscionable son, one might almost add, to the unconscious hand of the risen people. This, in part, is a plea for faithfulness from one of the unfaithful. Henry Cockburn figures in his poem as father and son, and the poem ends in fatherlessness, with the richly ambiguous and disconcerting spectacle of an orphaned patriarch.

In wanting his children to be both playful and deferential, he was effecting, as so often, a reconciliation of opposites. His own protacted disobedience, which may have driven him to explore the past and the Pentlands, to seek comfort in various motherly havens, had in time to be reconciled with the obedience that was owed to him as a father and as a public man: he himself became a leader like Baron Cockburn, and a transporter and a queller of riots. It is likely that this reconciliation, too, was effected, though I should imagine there were difficulties. Cockburn's was a household which had to deal with a commitment to pleasure and freedom on the part of a paterfamilias who firmly expected to be obeyed. His was not the sort of stick which one can readily imagine being brandished, but I am sure that he expected to be obeyed. His later political opinions suggest as much, and in particular his attitude towards the risen people, whom he had helped to rise. So does the tough line he took—in common with many other public men—on poor relief. So does the tone of his acquiescence in his daughter's long engagement. So, faintly, does his sally about 'children, processes, lamb legs, women', So do his testamentary papers. And so does one part of the imagery associated with his Eden and with its Edinburgh environs.

Kubla Cockburn decreed a pleasure-dome at Bonaly, where the landscape was female and where the Edinburgh virtues could not claim him. To the end of his days he roamed the Pentlands, worshipping the secret rills and retired cascades of his parricide's paradise. But there were other commitments too, other propitiations, and these, too, were commemorated, and strongly symbolized, in his writings. For all his jokes about the virtues of hard work and public service, and for all his sarcasms about respectability, he was also thoroughly virtuous and respectable. For all his belief in leisure and indolence, he was also pugnacious and diligent in pursuit of Reform and of his career. He became the ruler of eleven children. He became an eminent Scotsman—and eventually an eminent Victorian Scotsman—honoured and enfiefed. Up went the patriarchal wand, up went Bonaly Tower, up went the obelisks and towers he applauded in his native city. 'Nothing that sticks up without smoking seems to me ever to look ill in Edinburgh': it takes the voice of the patriarch to deliver a sentiment like that. Even his roses stood up straight. He remarked of a squad of these roses: 'They have been for some time in a perpendicular posture at Bonaly, much struck with the Pentland Hills.'[1] His own posture was to stand up straight while worshipping the supine, and remaining much struck with the Pentland Hills: to be at once intensely public and intensely secret. A happy marriage of male and female, of perpendicularities and penetralia, was duly solemnized in his writings.

Eminent friends of his were particularly perpendicular. Henry Dundas was a pharos. Thomas Thomson—by virtue of his hospitality rather than the soundness of his finances—was another. Of Gibson-Craig, he said: 'Long may that pillar, with all its defects, stand' (Gibson-Craig had gone too pugnaciously about his Whig work). Sir Harry Moncreiff was a 'column' of the Church of Scotland, and of Thomas Chalmers, who broke that Church in half, he said: 'His name was a tower.' In this respect, the rebellious but right-reverend leader of the Free Kirk resembled Milton's Satan, who was also 'like a tower'—and who, like Cockburn, wielded a wand. In Cockburn's imagination, it was public worth, and the authority of leaders and fathers, which assumed a perpendicular posture: these and rebelliousness. Chalmers

[1] *Letters to Kennedy*, p. 215.

was a Satan, and a Samson, a man who pulled down pillars. And he was himself a pillar, just as the Free Kirk was a 'pillar' to Government folly.[1]

I to the hills will lift mine eyes. . . . I to the rills will lift my stick. To interpret Cockburn's imaginative life in terms of a kind of spiritual or sexual golf, as I have done, may seem absurd, or may give offence. I see nothing offensive or absurd about it myself. Of the golfers of St Andrews he said: 'Their talk is of *holes*.' And so, in point of ascertainable fact, was his—of holes and corners, and of heights and sticks. It may be that in this sort of thing (which was not, of course, peculiar to Cockburn, though he made more of it than most) can be glimpsed the origins of golf itself and of other sports; and few will doubt that the stick has been a mighty instrument and a mighty symbol, though it is fading now, and has been replaced, for certain purposes and in both capacities, by the gun. The interpretation of poetic symbolism with reference to the poet's unconscious desires is widely regarded as offensive too. But it is questionable whether it could have been avoided in Cockburn's case. The life of these poems, if it is anywhere, is in their symbols, in their encoding of an inner life, and in their inadvertencies. That is why they are Romantic poems, despite the laggard literary taste of which they also give evidence.

Drawn by Wordsworth's poem, or at any rate by intimations of immortality derived from recollections of early childhood, an amateur poet came under the compulsion of an exacting subject-matter. This subject-matter was prohibited, or at least discouraged, by the taste he approved of, and it lay beyond the type of nature poetry, the versions of pastoral, with which he grew up, and which was essentially urban in character. Cockburn's interest in the country was itself urban in character, but the old city styles were bound to prove confining when he made his attempt on these new subjects. His poems are, in their small way, adventurous and even evolutionary. They are a discovery, a reluctant or compunctious discovery, of the romantic. Despite the *Edinburgh Review*, which awarned that childishness should be kept secret, Cockburn capitulated to the doctrine that 'Heaven lies about us in our infancy.'

Though Jeffrey has long been considered incapable of understanding the Romantic poets, it is also recognized that he was eager to read them, and that he was accessible to romantic dreams and desires. We can now see more

---

[1] The reference to Gibson-Craig is in a letter to Napier of 30 June 1836, that to Sir Harry Moncreiff in a letter to Anderson of 1 October 1825, and that to Chalmers in a letter to Mrs Rutherfurd of 1 June 1847. The reference to Satan is in *Paradise Lost*, Book One, line 591, and that to the Free Kirk in the *Circuit Journeys*, p. 251.

clearly that, in relation to literature as well as to architecture, his friend was accessible too. A Lakeish Cockburn is revealed in his poems. The notion of the *Edinburgh Review* as a bulwark of old-world conventionality will never do: it is wrong as far as their private reading went, and it is not right for Jeffrey's public pronouncements either. Nor is this merely a matter of their loving the adventurous Scott. Jeffrey took a lively interest in the Elizabethans at a time when many took none at all, and he could write discerningly about Keats.

I have said that Cockburn concurred with Jeffrey in most matters of taste, but they had their differences, and these differences may be seen to confirm what I have said about Cockburn's tendency, as he grew older, to be less Lakeish and to revert to the old decorum. His manuscripts[1] contain an episode in the running dialogue between the friends which indicates the extent, and limits, of Jeffrey's romanticism, and the narrower limits of his own. The writers under discussion here were considered by some to be as babyish and obscure and vulgar than as many of the Lake school. Jeffrey was not put off: at the same time, this is an occasion when both men may be thought to figure as armchair or drawing-room Romantics. During the summer of 1835, recovering from his Reform labours, he took his ease on the West coast of Scotland. A letter to Cockburn tells how he has been watching the peaks of Arran, the seals and porpoises, the yachts and steam vessels— and reading Keats and Shelley. Cockburn points out in a note: 'He had always a foolish passion for these two.' And in another letter from the same paradise Jeffrey threatens the recalcitrant Cockburn with a holiday task: 'You shall read Shelley, and allow a tame ferret called Susan to bite your fingers.' Whatever their differences, Cockburn and Jeffrey appear to have agreed that Shelley was like a tame ferret for whom the supercultivated might have a foolish passion.

I believe myself that Freud's arguments concerning incestuous wishes, and the need for the individual to reach an accommodation with these, may have a bearing on those of Cockburn's experiences which inclined him to- wards Romanticism. Such wishes were whispered in the Romantic literature of his lifetime and later, and it may be that certain of his imaginative com- mitments took him, highly inadvertently, a little way towards the periphery of that field of force. But Freud's arguments refer to normative experiences, to those that many may have, and Cockburn's were largely of this order too, no doubt, and a long way from the dooms and fatal passions of Romanticism. I also believe that his feelings as a son were communicated to his work as a reformer, and that some early experiences were re-enacted there. A hostility

[1] JLC: Jeffrey's letters of 25 July and 4 August 1835.

to his father may have caused him to seek shelter in his love for his mother. Later, in seeking shelter in the paradise which perpetuated that love, he was seeking shelter from the hostility to his father which was perpetuated in his work as a reformer, and which was crowned by a supposed destruction of the past. In the *Memorials*, the past was turned into a paradise: if it was guilt and anxiety which drew him to the world of his childhood, what he found there was pleasure.

He feared the destruction of the past, just as he feared deracination from the Pentlands. He produced a euphemistic version of the dynastic past in his histories, whereby it became uterine, timelessly serene and secure, a variant of Bonaly's constant holiday. The past was redeemed for him in the image of his mother's body, which was also the image of his favourite hills. If there was death in that double Eden—intimations of Thanatos as well as of Eros—then it was a happy, balmy death: the Pentland Hills adjoined the Elysian Fields, affording a blissful passage to the constant holiday of eternal life. Cockburn's Arcadia was compact of pleasure and desire. His Pentland idylls, and the idyllic past, laid up for him 'treasures of felicity'. Not for the first time, his mother had taken his pain away.

In his poem 'Adolescence', Auden writes:

> By landscape reminded once of his mother's figure
> The mountain heights he remembers get bigger and bigger:
> With the finest of mapping pens he fondly traces
> All the family names on the familiar places.

This is the voice of a poetry which has lost its innocence, which is acquainted with Freud. And it provides a kind of hindsight in relation to Cockburn and to the two dimensions of his paradise—the geographical and the historical. Auden is quite right (and so was Scott): the Pentland Hills are not, indeed, very high.

It is difficult to attempt such conjectures without being conscious, over one's shoulder, of the sneer of the man of sense, of some growling new Braxfieldian disparager of Cockburn and his affectations. It seems to me, however, that the conventional view of Cockburn as a political partisan whose zeal was tempered—or, for some observers, effaced—by sociability and gossip ignores the importance of solitude for him and the extent to which his life was organized to procure it, even though it was also possible to be gregarious on the Pentlands: up came the cognoscenti to dine and to bowl like devils on his green—Cockburn's holy place was as jolly as the Celesteville Garden of Pleasure. And it seems to me that any attempt to improve on the conventional view is bound to set out in the general direction of the hypothesis I have been arguing for, however much it may adventure into imprecision on the way. No account of his mental life will do which overlooks its divisions and enclaves. They appear to constitute its fundamental structure.

# Chapter Ten

# *Cockburn and Stevenson*

It was far from unusual in Cockburn's day for a successful lawyer to 'double' as a country gentleman, complete with waterfall: it was probably easier for him to be a Confucian Taoist than it was for him to be a classical romantic, or a patrician progressive, or an orphaned patriarch. It is far from unusual now, for that matter, to make much of the rival claims of business and pleasure, the office and the golf-course. In fact, Cockburn's heartfelt insistence on distinguishing in principle between business and pleasure, between his two types of virtue, may look reassuringly familiar to a society in which work has remained important, but in which there is also a belief that it should be segregated, minimized and escaped from. In Cockburn's life, that of a hard-working man, can be seen the phenomenon of an early or prototypical abhorrence of work and esteem for leisure. 'Off goes the grey jacket and on the black coat': to his daughter Elizabeth, in 1841,[1] he utters what was to be the complaint of the suburbs. In this grey jacket we seem to see an early approximation to the magically-transforming sports jacket of later times. If he was one of the first tourists, he was also one of the first suburbanites.

Cockburn's secret life, by which I mean his reclusiveness, his retreats, was neither dark nor shameful: indeed, he thought of it as the very opposite, and was fully prepared to avow it, or a version of it, publicly. It was secret by virtue of the fact that it was the obverse and denial of his public commitments, and not because it resembled the sinister secret lives led by those Victorian gentlemen who went in for a species of sexual slumming in the Babylon of urban Britain. And yet it has, I think, to be understood in relation to the social conditions which produced such clandestinities. Cockburn's

---

[1] *Some Letters of Lord Cockburn*, p. 44. This is the letter in which he explains how much Alison's essays have meant to him.

secret life was improvised from Classical and Romantic materials in a situation where institutionalized religion was no longer wholly credible to such a man, and where sexuality was, to a considerable extent, publicly inadmissible. For those of his class, sexual experience was engulfed in the silence of the marriage bed, or it was a matter of platonic flirtations such as those which gave pleasure to Jeffrey, or it was unpublishably childish, or it was debauchery —something to be bought and enjoyed and condoned, or to be fled from, in the underworld of Burke and Hare.

Nineteenth-century Scotland was not the paradise of sexual abstinence that the Kirk or Kirks would have liked. Sexual morality seems to have varied rather sharply in accordance with locality and social standing, and the constraints laid on men were very different from those laid on women. T. C. Smout has suggested[1] that if it can be assumed that a polarization took place in the course of the century whereby the classes stood off from one another more and more as the population rose, then this might account for the increased anxiety and guilt which have been observed to characterize inter-class sexual relationships. Whether or not the assumption is correct—and I would say that it was—these relationships were a significant feature of the scene. The upper-class male was comparatively licentious, and so was the working-class male. The upper-class and middle-class male could often act in conformity with a double standard, enjoining chastity on his women outside marriage, while taking, or excusing, an interest in women of a lower class. The fate of women of rank was involved with the movement and management of property: for this reason among others, respectability entailed the avoidance of sexual reproach. All these things tended to favour the seduction of servants and a thriving prostitution, which does not seem to have reached a down-turn until well on in the century.

In *Magdalenism*, a study of prostitution which was published in 1840, a doctor named William Tait estimated that there were 200 brothels in Edinburgh, and that, not counting 'sly' or part-time performers, there was one prostitute for every 80 adult males (the ratios for London, Paris and New York are given as one for every 60, one for every 15 and one for every six or seven respectively).[2] Tait took a more anxious view of sexual delinquency than that to be found in many parts of the Scottish countryside (for example, the rural hinterland of Edinburgh), where pre-marital pregnancy could sometimes be thought more excusable than stealing, and where the Ball of Kirriemuir appears to have been held quite often in quite a few

---

[1] In an essay due for publication entitled 'Aspects of Sexual Behaviour in 19th-Century Scotland', from which some of the information in the early part of this chapter has been taken.

[2] *Magdalenism*, p. 5.

communities over the years. When figures became available later in the century, however, it was apparent that Scotland's illegitimacy rate was no more flagrant than those of many other European countries, though the contribution made by the country districts was higher than certain moralists had insisted.

Tait was very censorious about most manifestations of his subject, though that did not prevent him from trying to deal with it accurately, or from furnishing a great deal of interesting detail, some of it of an exotic and indeed 'Gothic' kind: their visitors were known to prostitutes as 'cowlies'—the reference being to a monk's hood—because they were accustomed to paying their calls in disguise. It is characteristic of him to write: 'Having spent a great proportion of their days in scenes of the utmost wickedness, and seen all the ups and downs attendant on their profession . . . '[1] He thought that swearing was perhaps the least excusable of faults, and was distressed by the knowledge that loose women could pass without detection in public—as at the ceremony in 1840 for the foundation-stone of the Scott Monument: 'There is something disagreeable in the thought that a lady of respectability has to sit or walk beside a woman of the town. Nothing, however, is more common. There is no possibility of distinguishing them from ladies of quality.'[2] The year before, Lord Eglinton staged a medieval pageant, of which Cockburn writes in the *Journal*: 'There was a splendid gathering of gentles, native and foreign, and a vast collection of commonalty.' There was also a vast collection of whores, who had flocked to avail themselves of the assembled chivalry and commonalty. These gay deceivers are ignored by Cockburn, who was not there, and had he gone, he might even, it seems, have failed to detect them. Such 'feudal revivals', he reflects, 'are fully as interesting and respectable as most other costly amusements'.

Neither what is known about the habits of the upper class, nor what was rumoured about some of the men of his acquaintance, such as Brougham, allows one to be expansive about the sexual lives of Cockburn's circle. But it does allow one to guess that, while scarcely resembling that of the old Whig grandees in the South, their sexual experience was probably more resourceful than they would have divulged, and that there were those who did not consider themselves bound by the more repressive pronouncements of the Kirk (any more than some ministers allegedly did). There are times when they can appear broad-minded and relaxed on the subject. A woman who could say what Mrs Cockburn said to her husband when he became a judge is unlikely to have belonged to a set that was strait-laced in anything

[1] Ibid., p. 75.    [2] Ibid., p. 195.

resembling the style of the Edwardian Edinburgh bourgeoisie: 'Preserve me this! I never slept wi' a Lord o' Session i' my life?'[1]

Jeffrey may have belonged to that company of upper-class males who were willing to do more than flirt with the women of the poor, but the nearest we come to supposing so in Cockburn's unpublished correspondence is hardly near enough to secure a conviction—ours or Jeffrey's. The context is one of Cockburn's shortest stories, and one of his most exquisite. He writes to Rutherfurd on 14 February 1847:

> We had a large convocation at Jeffrey's on Friday. He is delightfully well. His shrill sweet voice was heard over the general buz, like a lark's in the blue sky, above a rookery. And he is concupiscent anent a handmaid brought to town by the Browns.

Here is the miniature portrait of a Scottish Whig: charming, clever, important—and intent, who knows, on that *de haut en bas* which took so many of his peers into the arms of the people. 'Concupiscent' is unusually strong for Cockburn, but, of course, it proves nothing, and Jeffrey was certainly prepared to speak sternly about openly scandalous behaviour by members of his own class.

On 24 June of the same year, Cockburn wrote to Rutherfurd's wife Sophia, giving news of his son George, who had been sent out to India and was home at the time, and his merry little wife:

> George's lady has presented him with a fourth daughter. Don't say anything about it; but (*entre nous*) there is Hindoo blood in the babe. It is exactly the colour of dark gingerbread. But George, good-natured fellow, is quite at ease.

This is a joke. The miscegenation was imaginary. It is the kind of joke that might have occurred to Evelyn Waugh, who was descended from George, though perhaps it is not a joke that he would have liked to find laid on his own doorstep. Perhaps the joke suggests a patrician calm—suggests that Cockburn was quite at ease—in relation to the subject of sexual irregularity. It is more likely to have been a way of showing his affection for George, who appears to have been cherished as one son who had no hand in the financial troubles which in a matter of weeks were to break over his head.

These, at any rate, were among the social conditions which affected his life, and which affected the construction of his paradise. Sex, overwhelmingly, was marriage—and, in some cases, a recourse to handmaids and the underworld. In Cockburn's overworld, there could be no cult of the sexual life or of romantic love or of adultery. It can't be imagined that he aspired to

---

[1] Cockburn confided the remark to Mrs Rutherfurd in a letter of 29 April 1837, and he confided it to many others.

any such thing. But it can be said that the Edinburgh cult of drink and male companionship, which, then and later, has sometimes seemed to operate as a substitute for this, was evidently insufficient even for the clubbable Cockburn, who went to the Pentlands for meditation as well as for conversation, for solitude and child's play and transports and vertigos as well as for the rites of male friendship. There is a sense that he went to the Pentlands for what religion could not provide and for what the sexuality of his time and place could not adequately encompass. *O Altitudo!* He might have said, had he been ready to divulge it, what I once heard the modern Scottish poet Norman MacCaig say: 'Landscape is my religion.' And it also became an aspect of his sexuality. The aspect in question may be called Cockburn's 'family romance'. This is the name which Freud gave to the fantasies employed at a certain stage of development in order to enact a defiance of the father.[1]

As we have seen, Cockburn's life was arranged in accordance with the requirements of his family romance. It was also arranged in accordance with pastoral and Romantic preconceptions, but the conventions to which he adhered cannot account, unaided, for what he did. His life had to accommodate that paradise of the affections in which he placed his trust. He built a house for it, paced out a park for it, established a parish for it, and a shrine— the penetralia of his secret rill. The infinitely penetrable Pentlands became his true asylum,where he could dream that he was an orphan, and be comforted, where he could retreat from his pugnacious public duties, where his fighting will could unclench in the performance of his idylls. His two selves demanded their respective seasons, duty and deracination alternating with bliss, and these seasons are dwelt on continually in his notebooks and letters in a manner that transcends convenience and the customs of his time and class. At the appointed hour, His Majesty's Solicitor-General obeyed the call of the burn. And when the railways spread out through Scotland, his rustications were assisted by a consultation of time-tables. While suspecting that 'too much *railery* is an unbecoming thing for an aged judge',[2] the aged judge was plucked from the circuit, and the new routes quickly re-rooted him at Bonaly. Bonaly was timeless, trance-like and erotic, all idylls and altitudes: but it was also, of course, domestic and routine, all time-tables and bills. What is clear is that he was something of a separate person there. And it may be thought that the one Cockburn was as different from the other as Dr Jekyll was from Mr Hyde.

---

[1] See, for example, the short essay, 'Family Romances': *The Complete Psychological Works of Sigmund Freud*, edited by James Strachey and others, vol. IX (1959), p. 237.
[2] *Circuit Journeys*, p. 373.

The Pentlands were his *alma mater*, and the High School of Edinburgh certainly was not. He hated his schooldays: according to his autobiography, they were almost the only odious part of his childhood. A haunting passage in the *Memorials*[1] recounts how he awoke in the middle of the night and left the house, thinking he was late for his lessons:

> On reaching the High School gate, I found it locked, and saw the yards, through the bars, silent and motionless. I withdrew alarmed, and went near the Tron Church to see the clock. It was only about two or three. Not a creature was on the street; not even watchmen, who were of much later introduction. I came home awed, as if I had seen a dead city, and the impression of that hour has never been effaced.

Above him, as he stared through the bars of the gate, was the summit of Arthur's Seat, where the justified sinner—in Hogg's novel of 1824— attempted, amid the confusions of an early-morning mist, to murder his genial stepbrother and was threatened by him in return: a strange, vertiginous episode in the conflict between virtue and pleasure—which may also be a conflict between the two sides of a divided nature—that has long been known in Scotland. It is not hard to picture Cockburn turning away from his dead city, walking back towards the Meadows, and looking in the direction of the Pentland Hills. There lay his future paradise. It may already have been the place where the brutalities of his school could not reach him, the place to which he could escape from his cage. One day, he, or his step-self, would live there.

One day, another man would live there too, and think it a paradise, a man who, in his youth, would wish for 'consideration', and would resist the authority of a stern father, as Cockburn had done, and would be reconciled with his father, in some measure, and would celebrate the relationship in a work of fiction, for which he prepared himself by requesting a copy of the *Memorials*. That work is *Weir of Hermiston*, written in 1893.[2] If Cockburn's life resembles Scott's in some respects, it equally resembles Stevenson's, and, if anything, the coincidence are more engrossing. On a symbolic level— the plane of the Pentlands, as it were—both men were Braxfield's bairns. Cockburn blamed in Braxfield traits he might have found in his own father, Braxfield's friend. In writing about Braxfield, on whom Lord Hermiston was modelled, Stevenson, in part, was writing about his father and about the contest of wills between father and son which occurred during his adolescence. In projecting a fiction (the novel was never completed) in which his judge

---

[1] *M*, p. 8.

[2] Stevenson talks of his 'feverish desire for consideration' when he was young in the *Memoirs of Himself* which he started to write in 1880. The expression is quoted in the opening paragraph of the latest of the Stevenson biographies: *Robert Louis Stevenson* by James Pope Hennessy (1974).

had a son whom he condemned to death, who was due to be 'struck by the hand that had promised to save', he was addressing himself to the subject-matter of Cockburn's family romance. There are intimations of Baron Cockburn, I feel, in these words about Weir of Hermiston: 'If he failed to gain his son's friendship, or even his son's toleration, on he went up the great, bare staircase of his duty, uncheered and undepressed. There might have been more pleasure in his relations with Archie, so much he may have recognized at moments; but pleasure was a by-product of the singular chemistry of life, which only fools expected.' Weir of Hermiston is said at one point to be 'an Alp'. He is certainly a tower.[1]

But so is his son Archie, who is shown to be 'pugnacious' as well as 'impressionable' and vulnerable. When his father sentences Duncan Jopp to the gallows, Archie's heart goes out to the prisoner, and he notices his pathetic sore throat. The treatment Jopp receives leads Archie to challenge his father's authority. Soon afterwards, he is 'brandishing' his staff, and behaving, in the Speculative, in a manner reminiscent of his father, whose 'hanging face' he has inherited. (Stevenson, like Cockburn, was a member of the Speculative Society.) He becomes a Byronic recluse who writes 'loose, galloping octosyllabics in the vein of Scott'. Before that, his father had ordered him to give up the law, and Archie had spoken of becoming a soldier. Shades upon shades of Cockburn. . . . There is a sweet, wistful portrait, by Romney, of Cockburn's mother: Weir's wife must surely have looked like this.[2]

As if to advertise the affinity between the two writers, Stevenson even lived for a few months in a house called Bonallie Towers, Branksome Park: despite its reminders of Cockburn and Scott, however, it was situated near Bournemouth, and had neither tower nor turret. He read law at Edinburgh University, and was admitted as an advocate, remarking of his circumstances at the time: 'Meanwhile, I must whistle in my cage. My cage is better by one thing; I am an Advocate now . . . I walk about the Parliament House five forenoons a week, in wig and gown.'[3] There's a verse epistle of his, to Charles Baxter, which gives a description of Parliament House in winter and brings to mind the Richardson skit:

> And at the Court, tae, aft I saw
> Whaur Advocates by twa an' twa
> Gang gesterin' end to end the ha'

---

[1] *Weir of Hermiston*, pp. 28, 58.    [2] Ibid., pp. 13, 35, 95.
[3] *The Letters of Robert Louis Stevenson*, edited by Sir Sidney Colvin (Tusitala edition, 5 vols, 1924), vol. II, p. 12. The letter (1875) is to Colvin himself.

In weeg an' goon,
To crack o' what ye wull but Law
The hale forenoon.

Stevenson's kin were the builders of Scotland's lighthouses: practical obelisks which marked a new kind of male supremacy. 'Sea-towers', Stevenson called them.[1] His family were consultants to the Commissioners of Northern Lights, and his father was himself a Northern light, a pharos fit to stand beside those of Cockburn. Stevenson's quarrels with this patriarchal engineer, High Tory and Calvinist left a lasting impression on him: an impression which some of those close to him are reckoned to have tried to obscure—in the interests of respectability. He ended his short and courageous life memorializing Scotland and his kindred, and living in a style both respectable and patriarchal—with an entourage of native servants in the South Seas. The estate at Vailima had two waterfalls, and he sometimes referred to the house as Abbotsford.

'You may look into the queer face of that portrait for as long as you will, but you will not see any hole or corner for timidity to enter in, 'wrote Stevenson once of Raeburn's Braxfield.[2] And, in their different ways, both he and Cockburn can be considered to have found a hole or corner for timidity, and to have embarked on a career of compunction as well as revolt. At 22, he told his friend Mrs Sitwell: 'I am killing my father. . . . If only I could cease to like him, I could pull through with a good heart.' And in the same letter he said of a bitter dispute: 'There is a jolly scene for you— there is the staff I have been to his declining years.'[3] Stevenson, that's to say, had stolen his father's stick: a predicament similar to Cockburn's. Part of the difficulty for Stevenson was that his father was in many ways an amiable man: but then those who resist their fathers often think of them as amiable men, and this is what their fathers often are. Like Cockburn, Stevenson made amends: in *Weir of Hermiston*, written at the age when the *Memorials* were begun, and elsewhere. There's a poem of his in *Underwoods* which shows him obedient and faithful to the Stevensons:

Say not of me that weakly I declined
The labours of my sires, and fled the sea,

[1] In a letter to Harriet Monroe of June 1886: *The Collected Poems of Robert Louis Stevenson*, edited by Janet Adam Smith (second edition, 1971), p. 485.

[2] 'Some Portraits by Raeburn', in *Virginibus Puerisque* (edition of 1897), p. 216. An engraving of the portrait in question is reproduced in the present book.

[3] From a letter of 22 September 1873, quoted in *The Strange Case of Robert Louis Stevenson* by Malcolm Elwin (1950), p. 70.

The towers we founded and the lamps we lit,
To play at home with paper like a child.
But rather say: *In the afternoon of time*
*A strenuous family dusted from its hands*
*The sand of granite, and beholding far*
*Along the sounding coast its pyramids*
*And tall memorials catch the dying sun,*
*Smiled well content, and to this childish task*
*Around the fire addressed its evening hours.*

In one sense, both men were like children, playing with paper—and like Naphtali, giving goodly words.

Cockburn's arcadian behaviour corresponds to Stevenson's bohemian behaviour and gypsy leanings: both dreamt of themselves as vagabonds or vagrants. Stevenson went about with Edinburgh prostitutes in his youth, and some researchers used to fancy that he proposed marriage to one—a 'Highland Mary' by the name of Kate Drummond. The Edinburgh virtues induced him to be wild, just as they induced him to worship the Pentlands. He felt that he had repudiated these virtues, which is why his Pentlands may be said to have pastured a herd of scarlet women. By Edinburgh standards, the opinions of the youthful Stevenson were less those of an advocate than of a devil's advocate, and he acquired notions of sexuality which were very different from those of Cockburn's time and which were also in advance of his own. In 1894, he wrote to his cousin, the art critic R. A. M. Stevenson: 'If I had to begin again . . . I believe I should try to honour Sex more religiously. The worst of our education is that Christianity does not recognize and hallow Sex.'[1] There is a bohemian poem of his in which he explains how he loves 'night in the city', and in which

I walk the streets smoking my pipe
And I love the dallying shop-girl
That leans with rounded stern to look at the fashions;
And I hate the bustling citizen,
The eager and hurrying man of affairs I hate,
Because he bears his intolerance writ on his face
And every movement and word of him tells me how much he hates me.

Sexuality, and dallying in general, were the enemy of respectability, and a

[1] September 1894, *Letters*, vol. v, p. 168.

possible rival to religion. But these subversive attitudes did not lead to an irrevocable break with his kindred. His fictional Braxfield, at the end of his life, does not express a repudiation of the Edinburgh virtues: he had never ceased, after a fashion, to respect them.

As for Cockburn, he did not repudiate these virtues so much as retreat from them. His primal repudiation of his family's politics, and of men like Braxfield, was itself virtuous, though perhaps not altogether respectable at first: translated into the possession of power and responsibility, however, it was presently included among the virtues from which he wanted to retreat. His overworld demanded an underworld of a sort, and this is what he devised in the Pentlands, where his dreams took charge and where duty and responsibility were forbidden. This is why it may be proper to refer to his 'secret life', though his was a secret life which belonged to an earlier Scotland than Stevenson's, and which was beyond reproach and without recourse to brothels or to the rounded sterns of handmaids. Scotland's insistence on duty and respectability has produced many a divided nature, many a secret life, and many varieties of Jekyll-and-Hyde.

In the ordinary way, the behaviour of a Jekyll-and-Hyde is thought to be that of a hypocrite, and Scottish rectitude has often been thought to promote hypocrisy. But neither Cockburn, with his pole, nor Stevenson, with his donkey and his doxy, were hypocrites. The public and political Cockburn has been accused of hypocrisy in a book about Bonnymuir and the Radicalism of the time, which asserts that he was 'inclined to run with the hare and hunt with the hounds'.[1] And it is true that both lives display elements of equivocation. But if both men were, in a manner of speaking, poseurs, they were also justified poseurs. Cockburn's poses, poles and polarities were, by most standards, a virtuous response to the Edinburgh virtues. He could be 'sensible' and calculating, and could think like a politician (though there was no deceit in his attitude to Radicalism). But his underworld or Arcadia—his belief in the importance of what was restored to him through the practice of a cult of leisure—was largely innocent and sincere.

Swanston Cottage was Stevenson's Bonaly. This was his family's retreat in the Pentlands, which began life, as if in Celesteville, as a municipal Pleasure House—except that it was built by the magistrates for their own use. Its praises are sung in his poem 'Ille Terrarum':

> Frae nirly, nippin', Eas'lan' breeze,
> Frae Norlan' snaw, an' haar o' seas,

[1] *The Scottish Insurrection of 1820*, p. 33.

Weel happit in your gairden trees,
A bonny bit,
Atween the muckle Pentland's knees,
Secure ye sit.

It seems that Stevenson's Pentlands were female too, and the blessings of Swanston, with its gillyflowers and roses, were clearly very like those of Bonaly. In the same poem:

Here aft hae I, wi' sober heart,
For meditation sat apairt,
When orra loves or kittle art
Perplexed my mind;
Here socht a balm for ilka smart
O' humankind.

Cockburn took Tacitus with him to the hills: Stevenson says here that he took Horace and Montaigne, and, 'weel neukit by my lane', fell into a dream and left them unread. 'Neukit' is by way of being a Scotch Miltonism: Milton more than once uses the word 'nook' with reference to Eden—so that Cockburn's reference to the 'untouched nook' where his stick reposed, in the poem about its loss, is Miltonic too, perhaps. All Edens, and most varieties of heavenliness, are likely to be well-nooked, but *Paradise Lost* may have helped to confer a few such holes and corners, or bonny bits, on Milton's successors in the field.

In the same way, the reveries in Stevenson's *A Child's Garden of Verses* can recall the first, 'nursery' stanza of 'Relugas', and in the Land of Nod— in the poem of that name, a name Cockburn might have wanted to bestow on the old Court of Session—the child is

All alone beside the streams
And up the mountain-sides of dreams.

When he went abroad, Stevenson, in dreams, beheld 'the hills of home', as Cockburn might have done, and as Richardson did in the Hartz Mountains. From their crests the glorious scene was disclosed:

The tropics vanish, and meseems that I,
From Halkerside, from topmost Allermuir,
Or steep Caerketton, dreaming gaze again.

Far set in fields and woods, the town I see
Spring gallant from the shallows of her smoke,
Cragged, spired, and turreted. . . . [1]

Cockburn was startled that Queen Victoria had never heard of the Pentlands:
but then, rejoins Stevenson, 'crowned heads have no great business in the
Pentland Hills'.[2] Both men were wounded in the wars of Scottish family
life, but neither of them renounced it. Both wished to escape the Edinburgh
virtues, which they nevertheless relished and admired. In these uncertainties,
the Pentland Hills were their refuge and their strength.

I have left till last the most curious corner of the common ground shared
by Cockburn and Stevenson. It appears that Stevenson, too, took an interest
in Charles Cotier of Dunkirk, and worshipped at the shrine of the desolate
stranger. In a letter to Mrs Sitwell of June 1875,[3] there is a passage that
might almost have made a page in the *Memorials*:

> I've been to church, and am not depressed—a great step. I was at that beautiful
> church my *petit poème en prose* was about. It is a little cruciform place, with heavy
> cornices and string course to match, and a steep slate roof. The small kirkyard is full
> of old gravestones. One of a Frenchman from Dunkerque—I suppose he died
> prisoner in the military prison hard by—and one, the most pathetic memorial I ever
> saw, a poor school-slate, in a wooden frame, with the inscription cut into it evidently
> by the father's own hand. In church, old Mr Torrance preached—over eighty, and a
> relic of times forgotten, with his black thread gloves and mild old foolish face. One
> of the nicest parts of it was to see John Inglis, the greatest man in Scotland, our
> Justice-General, and the only born lawyer I ever heard, listening to the piping old
> body, as though it had all been a revelation, grave and respectful.

The *poème en prose* which he mentions, 'Sunday Thoughts', was written
early in June, and was eventually published in the *San Francisco Call* of
14 April 1895.[4] It is an exercise in nostalgia in which he dreams about
Glencorse Church, 'the small kirk whelmed in leaves', with its flowering
rhododendrons, and, as Cockburn had once done, fancies himself a sheep:
'if I were a sheep and lay on the field there under my comely fleece. . . .'
He also sighs: 'Oh, to have wings like a dove. . . .'

The novelist S. R. Crockett was a minister of this kirk, and Stevenson, a
friend, wrote to him from the South Seas on 17 May 1893: 'Do you know
where the road crosses the burn under Glencorse Church? Go there, and
say a prayer for me: *moriturus salutat*. See that it's a sunny day; I would like
it to be a Sunday, but that's not possible in the premises; and stand on the

---

[1] From his collection, *Songs of Travel* (1896).
[2] *Edinburgh: Picturesque Notes* (1889), p. 167.    [3] *Letters*, vol. I, p. 238.
[4] I am indebted to Ernest Mehew for the first-publication text of 'Sunday Thoughts'.

right-hand bank just where the road goes down into the water, and shut your eyes, and if I don't appear to you! well, it can't be helped, and will be extremely funny.'[1] Both Stevenson and Cockburn had a taste for sunny days, and for the sunny side of the hill.

The Lammermuir kirk in *Weir of Hermiston* is based on the old kirk at Glencorse, and Stevenson retains the minister's name, Torrance. The kirk is deserted now, whelmed more than ever in leaves. When I went in search of it, it seemed to have disappeared. But then the road crossed a certain burn, and I knew I was near. A willowy ghost was signalling, accompanied by a wiry one, with spectral boots of a peculiar make. . . . I climbed a path from the road, and soon, Old Mortality, I stood before the grave of Charles Cotier. Like the linn and the elm, it was still there.

There are motorways only a mile off, but they have not killed the charm of Glencorse. I was evacuated just beyond it during the Second World War, when one of Midlothian's few bombs fell on the place where Cotier had been imprisoned. As I looked at the lettering on the gravestone, I remembered running away from my place of refuge and fleeing past Glencorse on the road to Edinburgh. On arriving home, I was immediately re-rusticated by the Edinburgh virtues, and became an orphan again.

Cockburn and Stevenson both felt themselves to be orphans, and were likely to pity a desolate stranger. Cotier was what they were. Their lives seem to show that family tensions may inspire not only a special devotion to the mother but an imagined solitariness and bereavement. Stevenson's work is full of orphans, and here at Glencorse was the epitome of orphans, the opposite of all duxes and men of affairs: a captive in exile struck down by those responsible for him. There is a little-known and unfinished Stevenson novel, *St Ives*, laid aside so that he could get on with *Weir of Hermiston*, and set in the same period, which suggests that the Frenchman's grave may have stayed in his mind for some twenty years. In these two novels, and in the disparity between them, Stevenson, *moriturus*, conveys the filial sentiments of a parricide. *Weir of Hermiston* pities a resisted father: *St Ives*, a slighter book, pities an alienated son. Like Cotier, St Ives is a French prisoner-of-war: desolate in Edinburgh Castle, and, to Edinburgh eyes, scandalously, dandyishly foreign, he is plainly to some extent a type of the writer himself, in his bohemian posture. Prisoners are like children, the novel says: prison is 'the next thing to being in the nursery'.[2] At the same time, they are like orphans. When St Ives escapes, as he was bound to do, where should he go but the Pentland Hills, where his love lives, and then south in secret with shepherds over the old drove roads, where he meets the

---

[1] *Letters*, vol. v, pp. 29, 30.     [2] *St Ives* (Everyman Edition, 1934), p. 5.

good Sir Walter Scott? As if by a mother, the orphan is comforted. The runaway is taken up to heaven, wrapped in the stealth that his heart desires.

So Cockburn wrote a poem, and Stevenson a novel, about the forlorn figure of Charles Cotier. And the two men also took an interest in the forlorn figure of William Macbean of the Speculative Society, for whose memorial Cockburn composed the inscription. The dedication at the start of *Kidnapped* speaks of 'the beloved and inglorious Macbean', and in *Memories and Portraits* Stevenson remembers sitting in the library of the Speculative, proud of his proximity to three 'very distinguished students' who were gathered round the fire in the corridor, 'under the mural tablet that records the virtues of Macbean, the former secretary'. Stevenson says that 'we would often smile at that ineloquent memorial, and thought it a poor thing to come into the world at all and have no more behind one than Macbean. And yet of these three, two are gone and have left less.'[1] Cockburn's Classical inscription did not appeal to him, but Macbean himself did. Like Cotier, Macbean was a victim, and therefore pleasing in the sight of both Cockburn and Stevenson.

A *Journal* entry by Cockburn for 18 April 1847 contains a by no means ineloquent memorial to Thomas Guthrie, the Free Church clergyman who worked on behalf of 'Ragged Schools'—schools for destitute children. I used to wonder, when I was a boy, about Dr Guthrie's School for Girls at Gilmerton, thinking it a mansion full of lovely delinquents. These dangerous girls were seldom seen, and the place had the air of some nunnery on the outskirts of Salamanca. It still exists in all its seclusion, and not far away (but far enough—I expect the matter was carefully planned) is a Dr Guthrie's School for Boys: both now appear to be, largely or entirely, state reformatories. In the generation before Guthrie, public opinion began to respond to the pathos of orphans. During the cholera epidemic of 1832, a House of Refuge was opened in Edinburgh, and many of its inmates were raggit laddies, who were taught, apprenticed, trained to be servants. The concern with homelessness survived into later times, and Cockburn shared in this concern: but he did so in a manner which, though common enough among his contemporaries, we may be entitled to think equivocal.

His attitude to Ragged Schools can be contrasted with Jeffrey's. Cockburn had worked hard to found and assist a school for laddies that were far from ragged, and around 1849 Edinburgh Academy ran into financial difficulties. He seems to have wanted Jeffrey to be publicly associated with the Academy, and he consulted him on this occasion. But Jeffrey took the line that 'schools for the wealthy classes' should go to the wall—rather than be

---

[1] *Memories and Portraits* (11th edition, 1903), pp. 66, 70, 71.

rescued by means of special subscriptions—if they proved unable to support themselves. And he felt that Ragged Schools deserved more encouragement than schools devoted, like the Academy, to Classical learning. He appears to have cared more about Ragged Schools than his friend did, though he declined to make representations, when asked to do so by Cockburn, against the policy which restricted them to Presbyterians. It is not altogether easy, now, to imagine a Presbyterian orphan, but these alone were to be admitted.[1]

In the *Journal* entry of 1847, Cockburn worries about the consequences of 'making the destitute child more comfortable than the child of the ordinary poor working-man', and goes on to say: 'This last is the canker that lies at the heart of every British scheme for reforming the poor or the guilty. The problem to be solved is to keep paupers and criminals in a worse condition than the honest poor man, and yet to avoid the imputation of cruelty; or to raise them to a better condition without giving the honest poor an interest to become one of these classes.' Let them louse cravats. Cockburn speaks here of avoiding, not cruelty, but the imputation of cruelty, and he places the poor and the guilty in the same boat. He was willing to weep for orphans, being one himself, though not the kind that needed to be saved from starvation. But he was also willing to dry his tears and find them—by association—guilty. These are the actions, not of a hypocrite, but of a sentimentalist.

Cockburn and Stevenson were scarcely, in the colloquial sense, very like one another, but there are important resemblances between the lives they led—resemblances which might seem to be attested by the interest they shared in Cotier and Macbean. For the Cockburn who believed in political perfectibility, 'the public' was composed of the good and the clever and the financially secure: those whom he wished to receive the vote. By the time of Stevenson's adolescence, 'the public' had acquired the capacity to obsess and sour the minds of such amiable people as his parents. The power of the people had not produced a social revolution, as Cockburn had feared: but 'what people might think' represented a new terror. The moral sanctions that were brought to bear, among the higher castes of Edinburgh especially, were now intense, the people had arisen with a vengeance, and had shown themselves tyrannical. As a result, the Stevensons' changeling son turned away and joined the outcasts of Edinburgh. No Scotsman was ever more of an outlandish stepchild: he was a waif who became a wraith, a 'scarecrow of a man',[2] and who was also a tower. The Sargent portrait painted at Bournemouth in 1885 wonderfully states what he became: a leaning tower,

[1] JLC: 25 January 1849.    [2] *Robert Louis Stevenson* by James Pope Hennessy, p. 13.

about to fade or flit, but one which took quite a long time to do so, and which gave a steady and loving light.

Cockburn, if only seasonally, was sufficiently estranged from the public he approved of, sufficient of a changeling, to take to the hills and to make a virtue of solitude: a virtue derived from the traditional esteem for the country as opposed to the town, from landed desires, from eighteenth-century pastoral play, and from Romantic sentiment and doctrine. His vagabondage was a game, though a holy game. By virtue, perhaps, of the need to escape from a bondage that was worse than anything of the kind known to Cockburn, Stevenson's was not. He lived by it, and died for it, risking his life on the road—while also growing up to be a Savile Club lion. Both in the Edinburgh of 1807 and in that of 1870 there could be literary orphans, with or without the goodly or glamorous words of a Naphtali. At neither time was it always possible for a sensitive son of the higher castes to bear the public. But the public became harder to bear, and altogether more oppressive. None of the devout women recalled in the *Memorials* can readily be imagined as the servant of the public that Mrs Stevenson was. These were mostly of the aristocracy of Midlothian, and are possibly to be reckoned above such states of mind. By the 1870s, however, the devout women of the aristocracy of Midlothian, departed and depleted as much of it was, would no doubt have agreed with Mrs Stevenson of the high bourgeoisie of Heriot Row about the delinquencies of her son.

# Chapter Eleven

# *Double Lives*

Cockburn led a double life of sorts. Many other Scotsmen have done the same, and the double life has sometimes been taken to be a distinguishing feature of Scottish experience, and of the literature which has proclaimed that experience. 'Causeway saint, house devil' is a proverb of the country which is quoted with feeling to this day. Double lives of one sort or another are, of course, an ancient and probably universal thing: Ovid's *deteriora sequor*, his disapproval of his own irresistible delinquencies, has been held to be an early instance, and St Paul's distinction between the spirit and the flesh expressed a divided condition which has proved highly contagious. Who shall deliver me, both men asked, from myself? In the later eighteenth century, the theme of the double life was revived and elaborated by various Romantic writers, and broadcast through Europe. It was taken up in several countries, and a proliferation of all manner of twos and twins ensued in the course of what has been termed 'a century of dualistic thought'.[1] Nevertheless, Scotland in particular has been felt to specialize in double lives and second selves.

There as elsewhere, duality has assumed several guises, but those most often discussed have depended on the simultaneous presence within the individual of two selves, one bright and one dark. The second self resists or corrects the first. It tends to embody the wilder or worse proclivities, or the animal appetites, of a given nature, and duality also tends to involve duplicity. A simple form of the double life is, indeed, hypocrisy or deceit. And among the sophisticated forms can be included the possession of a dual nationality by the post-Union Scotsman who was also a North Briton, who spoke two languages and was therefore in two minds.

Cockburn's double life can be seen straight away to be very different from those with which the literature and hearsay of the country have been

[1] *Robert Louis Stevenson and Romantic Tradition* by Edwin Eigner (Princeton U.P., 1966), p. 230.

chiefly concerned. Duality and delinquency, of the kind that has made household names of a line of hypocrites, burgher-burglars, necromancers, necrophiles and noctambules, did not enter the life that turned on its axis of Bonaly Tower and Charlotte Square. Both his selves were bright. Both were, in important respects, virtuous and benign. I think, however, that it is worth inquiring into the phenomenon of Scottish duality, to find out whether there is any common ground between the experience of its leading exemplars and the accommodations which Cockburn effected between the rival forces of an authentically divided nature. It is worth trying to find out why, in the later years of his life, between 1820 and 1840, the theme of the double life was eagerly cultivated by certain Northern writers. Earlier, the exploits of notorious hypocrite-heroes had been marvelled at: now the double life was to be vividly imagined and closely examined by writers of fiction—and by medical writers too. A British doctor was prepared to diagnose cases of disharmony between a patient's rival selves, and to declare that duality was natural, that it was generic and genetic, that each person has his doppelganger.

The literary vogue for dualities and doppelgangers was brought to Scotland by contemporaries of Cockburn with an interest, which he himself lacked, in the German Romantics of the later eighteenth century, and in Germany and Scotland the double nature of man is prominently displayed during the first half of the following century. These were countries which had been claimed, to different degrees, by the Reformation. They were comparatively authoritarian countries. They were also countries which, in the second half of the eighteenth century, were conscious of a comparatively recent acquaintance with civil war—that analogue and encourager of the dual personality. It is probably fair to say that the double life was favoured by the social circumstances which arose as a result of the Reformation: by the workings of the puritan conscience, and the importance attached to dictatorial fatherhood in the Protestant communities of Western Europe.

In Presbyterian Scotland, where Catholicism was stigmatized as a religion of the mother, fathers became a powerful instrument of social and religious control, whose effectiveness was little impaired by the laxities, and the widespread indifference to Presbyterian and Covenanting shibboleths, which were evident in many quarters in the course of the eighteenth century. The authority of fathers was confirmed, moreover, by the success of Evangelical religion, with its reassertion of the puritan virtues, in subsequent decades, during which fathers may well have been sterner than they had ever been. Stern fathers are apt to be resisted, and such resistance will seldom be simple-minded or single-minded. There will usually be reluctance, and compunction, and dilemmas. Concurrently, in the first half of the nineteenth century, the difficulties attendant on the possession of a dual nationality may have become more onerous than before, as the pressures towards compliance with the South, in institutional terms, grew stronger. The process of class estrangement which seems to have taken place at the same time is also likely to have had divisive consequences for some individuals, with social mobility suspending them between two selves. In literature, respectability could mean that certain subjects were better hidden, or 'closeted'. Respectability could also mean that a man's public and private lives were two very different things. All these factors may have contributed, directly or indirectly, to the emergence of an interest in the double life.

Puritanism has tended, historically, to exhibit a duality of its own. Submission to the deliverances of religious authority—and to the father in his role as mediator of the faith, the pharos of the true light—has gone together with rebellion, which was principally directed at the state, and with schism, whereby each sect repudiated its neighbour. Turning towards the hearth, and away from the state, and from ecclesiastical history, one might guess that, internalized within the individual and domesticated within the family, puritanism could eventually mean, for many, a simultaneous obedience and disobedience, a repudiation of the father combined with a residual acceptance of his beliefs. This is to speak very loosely about a complex matter, but it does afford one line of approach, not only to the conduct of the mutineer ministers of the Disruption, but to the case of Cockburn himself, who was as much patrician as puritan but who was not unaffected by the prevailing ethos, which came to incorporate new severities and a sanctioned and sanctified rebelliousness. In the case of the conscious deceiver or cheat, puritan standards operated by exacting lip-service: the hypocrite in question then combined this with a secret life which rejected and affronted these standards. There has long been plenty of that in Scotland. In 1840, William Tait remarked in his study of magdalenism: 'Hypocrisy is a charge which has frequently been brought against the Scottish nation.'[1] In view of the severities which that nation has embraced, this is not surprising.

Whited sepulchres and Holy Willies are only one variety of double life. And the influence of Romanticism, impinging upon established propensities, forced into currency some very different varieties. Romantic writers created a repertoire of insights, and a tribe of doppelgangers, which imparted a new inwardness about human nature, and a new sense of its instability. The self-consciousness which they paraded and enjoined called into being a second self which was capable of witnessing, and even of disavowing, the first.

[1] *Magdalenism*, p. 10.

It would be wrong to think that Cockburn's Romanticism was innocent of that kind of self-consciousness. But he did not know, and would not have credited, that he led a double life, any more, perhaps, than he would have thought himself capable of attacking his father.

He was not—as the word is now generally understood—an introspective man. The introspections which posterity may find in his pastoral poetry were invisible as such to Cockburn himself, who would have felt further-more, I think, that, closet writings though they were, 'childish' though they were, they were not undisclosable. They may not have belonged to the public domain as much as his *Memorials* and *Journal* did, but they did belong to a convention of nature poetry and were the kind of thing that a gentleman might easily own up to practising at weekends, though modesty or delicacy might dissuade him from publication. In his published prose and manuscript verse alike, the important self-disclosures often seem involuntary. A writer's journal has come to be the receptacle of his self-consciousness: it was not so for Cockburn. He did not play upon his diary as on the romantic instrument that the diary increasingly became, calling for a confessional bravura, together with a pretence and parade of confidentiality and privacy. In his poems, he was an inadvertent Romantic, where he was one at all. Romantic individualism, where self-consciousness has involved the affirma-tion of a separate and special identity on the writer's part, was not for him: his sublime was rarely egotistical.

The most bizarre of Scotland's double lives was enacted in the heroic heyday of puritanism. The semi-legendary Major Weir was both a Presby-terian elder of conspicuous piety and a wizard. He was both a Covenanting soldier—who distinguished himself by his contemptuous treatment of Montrose when he escorted him to the scaffold—and a man whom it was necessary to burn at the stake for his sorceries and obscenities. As a saint, he was held to be outstandingly 'demure'—a word which was used by Hogg, in the *Confessions*, to characterize a godly demeanour, and which, by that time, could often be used to mean hypocritical—and earned the name of 'Angelical Thomas'. As a sinner, he was pure magic. This Covenanter, and his witch sister, ran a coven. The blasphemies committed by his secret self were quite unlike the home life of Lord Cockburn at Bonaly. But there are certain affinities. It will be remembered that Cockburn the Solicitor-General was 'demure' and that his double, Cocky, was 'frivolous'.

Major Weir was the owner of a magic walking-stick with a life of its own: it writhed in the flames which destroyed him and took a long time to sur-render—*nec tamen consumebatur*. In Cockburn's day, such stories concern-ing Weir were current, and were told, for example, by Scott in his *Letters*

*on Demonology and Witchcraft*. Weir's house still stood, an object of horror.
One of the stories has it that, being a wizard, he was unable to cross a
running stream: at Liberton, out towards the Pentlands, he suffered dis-
comfiture on that score. So it would seem that part of the imagery which
furnished Cockburn's paradise—the paternal stick and the maternal streams
—was pre-empted by this sorcerer. The wizard's wand, the witch's dildo-
stick—these have, of course, been reputed to be pagan properties which
survived in Christian societies. Milton's Satan has his wand, and when
Young Goodman Brown, in Nathaniel Hawthorne's story, takes to the forest
and discovers a coven of American double-dealers—the minister, a deacon
and so on—the Devil whom they worship wields a stick in the likeness of a
snake. Black magic was highly ecumenical: the witches of Salem share a
decor with Major Weir and his sister, and Cockburn's more than patriarchal
staff begins to seem less than respectable.

Stevenson was well-versed in Edinburgh's demoniacal and pious past, and,
as his friend W. E. Henley confirmed, his imagination dwelt from his
youth on the story of Major Weir. It is important, I think, that he chose to
call his heavy father by the wizard's name. The legend of Major Weir,
*Weir of Hermiston* and the life of Lord Cockburn all present situations in
which authority is simultaneously displayed and denied. Cockburn and the
two Weirs were all public men, wielders of the stick, and in this company
Cockburn stands revealed as a resister of the wizard he was afterwards to
become, rather as, in rebellion, Archie Weir took up his father's stick. The
wizard's wand—which is also the hereditary symbol of public eminence and
masculine predominance—passes into the hands of a judge. This is a baton
which runs a strange race. Simultaneously diabolical and patriarchal,
mutinous and punitive, this is a stick which has two selves.

Scotland had other wizards, other sticks. Chief among the wizards of the
North was the loyal and wholesome Scott: the 'Chaldee Manuscript' refers
to him as 'that great magician which hath his dwelling in the old fastness
hard by the river Jordan, which is by the Border', and this description seems
to have been picked up in the pamphlet of 1821 against the Pittites.[1]
Scott's stick does not symbolize—as some of those I have been talking
about do, in a manner not inappropriate to a seditious country—a combination of leadership and revolt. But even Scott's wizardry, self-avowed on
occasion, has a smack of the double life by virtue of his role as the Great
Unknown, the anonymous author of *Waverley*, and by virtue of his hidden
investment in the publishing house which ruined him—and his stick says
as much. At the time of his ruin, he wrote of himself: 'The magic wand of

[1] 'Chaldee Manuscript', Chapter Three, Verse 27, This was published in *Blackwood's* in 1817.

the Unknown is shiverd in his grasp. He must henceforth be termd the Too well Known.'[1]

Another case of duplicity which, while based on historical fact, soon turned into a legend and a byword is that of Deacon Brodie at the end of the eighteenth century. By day a solid citizen, Deacon of the Wrights and Masons, Brodie performed daring burglaries by night, and was caught and tried in 1788. Low-life, nocturnal Edinburgh, which, in Tait's time, provided fifty-two brothels in the short distance between the Castle Hill and the top of the Canongate, was fused, in the person of Brodie, with the respectability of its daylight hours. Stevenson, with Henley, wrote a play on the subject, *Deacon Brodie, or The Double Life*. When burgher Brodie dons his burglar's clothes, he cries: 'On with the new coat and into the new life! Down with the Deacon and up with the robber!'[2] It will be recalled that Cockburn the Lord of Session said much the same—'Off goes the grey jacket and on the black coat'—when he descended from the Pentlands and resumed his public life. Both in this play and in his later play *The Hanging Judge*, Stevenson indulges a taste for what might be called oedipal embezzlements: the double life consists of actions whereby the respectable are robbed and their bedrooms rifled, whereby the forbidden place is penetrated and profaned.

Brodie's feats are represented in the play as thrilling, and he is awarded his moments of Faustian (or Marlovian) rhetoric. But the play is mostly Edinburgh-pious and mundane, and reads like a cautionary tale designed to dissuade people from burglary. 'I loved pleasure,' says this housebreaker, 'I was weak.'[3] It has no doubt proved entirely comprehensible to a city which values property and which values propriety, while knowing that the second of these will sometimes be shown up as false and frail. The latest unmasking is that of George Pottinger, the senior civil servant who went to jail for corruption in 1974.

Mr Pottinger told the court that tried him: 'I think it is possible to separate one's public and private lives.' If he can be said to have led a double life, then it was by virtue of a simultaneous adherence, in his public capacity, to the standards of the Civil Service and to those of the wealthy and glamorous friends that he made in the course of his duties. His testimony, at a number of points, touched chords that brought to mind the double lives of nineteenth-century fiction. He said he informed his Permanent Under-Secretary that 'he had first met the architect during planning for the Aviemore project

---

[1] *Journal of Sir Walter Scott*, p. 40: 18 December 1825.
[2] *Deacon Brodie* (Tusitala edition, 1924), p. 19: Act One, Tableau One, Scene Nine.
[3] Ibid., p. 80: Act Five, Tableau Eight, Scene Five.

and Mr Poulson had since become an old friend of him and his family'. This is very much the kind of instantaneous old friend who appears in the literature of duality. The old friends in that literature may play the part of the princely tempter, and this is a part that Poulson could play too. Pottinger explained that he accompanied Poulson on a Hellenic cruise, and remarked: 'He marched across the Plains of Troy like an emperor, a much more Napoleonic figure than you see now.' Some while after I first thought of Pottinger in this connection I learnt that he had once lived in Bonaly Tower, which has been converted into flats. An interest in duality gives you a tendency to see double, which can prove deceptive. It also gives you an eye for coincidence, by which I trust I have not been misled.[1]

Not long before his trial, Pottinger, a man of parts and versatility, published the history of a local golf-course, *Muirfield and the Honourable Company*. Among the club's ancestors is John Gray, who is mentioned, as Pottinger points out, in the *Memorials*, where he is said to have been 'famous for drinking punch, holding his tongue, and doing jobs quietly'. A capacity for stealthy deals and favours scarcely constituted a double life at that time: but Pottinger's invocation of Gray and Cockburn is a reminder that the Edinburgh ethos has been that of a fairly small world, and a rather narrowly conditioned one, where the same bywords and allusions, the same types of predicament and cautionary instance, frequently recur. The same devils seduce the same deacons. The same golfers come to grief. The honourable company of worthies and old friends from time to time dishonours itself. So perhaps it is no less in keeping with the place that Pottinger should invoke Cockburn's worshipful John Gray than that two of its wizards should be called Weir. *Floreat Edina*.

A further fusion of high and low life occurred in the circumstances of the Burke and Hare scandal of 1828, which brought Cockburn into court as counsel for the defence. Robert Knox, the renowned anatomist, was denounced by Scott and others as the confederate of resurrection-men and murderers, as a trader in human flesh. Three years after Cockburn's death, the double life of Madeleine Smith burst upon the Empire: respectability was revealed as secretly rebellious and lascivious, and much of the Empire was persuaded—though the jury were not—that Madeleine Smith, whose father owned an estate, and a turreted mock-medieval country house, near Glasgow, had stooped to poisoning the lower-class French lover whom she used to meet in a corner of that paradise (Stevenson's great man, John Inglis, eventually Lord Glencorse, defended her). She has received more

[1] These extracts from Mr Pottinger's testimony are taken from *The Times* of 29 January 1974, 28 November 1973 and 22 January 1974.

attention than any other of Scotland's secret sinners. This is a category unknown to the Scottish courts. It can be seen to contain many subdivisions, and it belongs as much to the hearsay as it does to the history of these courts: does it include the respectable undertakers of recent years who have been caught practising chicaneries in the matter of coffins? At all events, it seems to have gone on delivering its quota of prisoners at the bar. The annals of Scottish crime continue to relish tales of hypocrisy—of criminal condescension, as it might be called, on the part of those of superior standing. Such is the hearsay of a society in which the word 'low' has often signified both the dishonest and the poor.

In the course of Cockburn's adult life, the theme of divided identity may be observed to have undergone a process of revision and extension. It was admitted to the literature of the country when Scotsmen began to direct their attention to certain elements in Continental Romanticism. The works in which the theme was treated came from the camp of his political opponents, from the wits of *Blackwood's Magazine* and of *Fraser's* in London, and the most impressive of these works was Hogg's *Confessions of a Justified Sinner*. The *Confessions* of 1824 is often seen as a picture of raging sanctimoniousness, of a type of madness which is encountered in a community made anxious by its religion. It is thought to issue warnings about the dangers of Antinomian Calvinism, of the conviction that a person of the elect can do no wrong, being assured, once and for all, of God's grace, and predestined to be saved. To the just, all things are just. The just man may be permitted to make a sore stumble. The hypocrisy of Hogg's sinner is unlike the more or less conscious deceit of a Tartuffe or a Holy Willie. Only 'objectively' can it be considered hypocrisy at all. He does not practise frauds: he is the victim of delusions. This illustrious person is also a kind of outcast.

The novel is also thought to contrast the confidence of the elect with the kind and merry ways of the country's social élite, and with the dictates of an Augustan rationalism and common sense, according to which superstition or enthusiasm was low and reprehensible. An examination of the novel in the light of the contemporary literature of duality, however, makes it appear less polemical than the conventional account suggests. It becomes a dynamic and intractable work which deals, not in competing prerogatives or points of view, but in the contrasts and quandaries that may be contained within the bounds of a single sensibility. It seems to be saying that a person may be predestined to suffer the confusions and contradictions of his own nature.

Hogg could look like an affable, sensible Tory. But his lesser writings reveal a stock-in-trade of peasant superstition, and, more to the point, he was not without first-hand experience of the double life. He had a pseudo-self or phantom of his own in the persona of the Ettrick Shepherd which enlivened the *Noctes Ambrosianae* of *Blackwood's Magazine*. The *Noctes* were mainly written by John Wilson ('Christopher North'), but Hogg contributed a vein of self-parody to the speeches assigned to him in the symposia. Cockburn's 'animated rustic', the droll, drunken, self-taught, scarcely house-trained spellbinder of the *Noctes*, with his spate of magnificent Scots, accords well enough with the charming and disgraceful Hogg who was an Edinburgh byword: but an animated rustic and boon companion could never have written the *Confessions*, and there is evidence that the historical Hogg was alternately enthralled and disquieted by this second self of his, which took on a life of its own and had been haunting him for some two years when the *Confessions* was published. His relationship with his *Maga* friends—who used him, condescended to him, and derided him in 1821 with the charge that his parodies of Wordsworth and others had been written by Byron—is sure to have been unsettling, with its mingling of gratification and pain. As John Carey notes in the introduction to his 1969 edition of the *Confessions*, Hogg spoke of Wilson and Lockhart, his *Blackwood's* colleagues, as 'two devils', and Wilson wrote of the 'Mephistopheles tricks' he had played on Hogg.

Hogg's novel is a feast of doubleness, and a hall of mirrors, affording a surreal perspective of likenesses and distortions. And as so often in this literature, the illusionist, the author of these tricks, the begetter of these twins, is the Devil. A laird's handsome and generous son, George Colwan, has a half-brother, Robert Wringhim, the justified sinner. Robert is led into crime by the Devil in the guise of a distinguished stranger, Gil-Martin, whom he takes to be Czar Peter of Russia, and who persuades him (with a version of his own Antinomian doctrines) that his soul is safe, that he can do no wrong, and that he has been allowed to perform a 'great work' of vengeance among the unworthy. These persuasions turn him into 'an accomplished vagabond, hypocrite, and sensualist',[1] and indeed into a murderer. George and Robert sometimes seem to represent the warring halves of the one nature, and Gil-Martin can seem like Robert's second self in the shape of his own worst enemy. Robert is also capable of supposing that he is two persons, one of whom is his brother and the other Gil-Martin: so that the latter, who can also resemble George on occasion, might be regarded as a tripleganger, at least. The story, moreover, is twice-told: first, by an editor, and then by the sinner himself. The novel was published anonymously: anonymities and pseudonyms, like those donned by Hogg and Scott, can appear to be

---

[1] *Confessions of a Justified Sinner* (1969 edition), p. 174.

an aspect of the dualities and devilish incognitos of the time. It seems possible to say, therefore, that the self that speaks to one in the *Confessions* is a succession of selves, or that it proliferates in a series of versions or 'clonings'.

Gil-Martin is very much a Gothic Devil. Doubles and devils seem to be bound together by a connection which reaches back through etymology—in some languages, the two words virtually coalesce—to ancient fears: fears which preceded, and survived, the Reformation. In the tall tales of the hallu-cinatory-Gothic mode, the second self may be the Devil, or it may be created by the Devil. It may be a scourge or a scapegoat. It may be a better half—a helpmeet or conscience. In general, it tends to be an evil genius, sophisticated and sarcastic, and to look like a projection of the individual's pride and uncertainty. Whenever the second self arrives, ironies ensue, and so, very often, do fatalities: the possessor of a second self is apt to be 'fey'.

As for Robert Wringhim, he is one of the eighteenth-century unco guid, and his fate, as Stevenson's mother observed in a letter of 1880 to her son,[1] 'sums up the evils of self-righteous phariseeism'. In Hogg's and Cockburn's day, and in Stevenson's, there were plenty of such pharisees in Scotland. The term 'elect', and Hogg's talk of reprobation and regeneration, would hardly have struck Cockburn as anachronistic, as outlandish or *outré*, at a time when the Evangelicals were talking, with fresh confidence, about these very things. Hypocrisy, moreover, was to become a popular reproach against Britain's Evangelicals: they were wolves in sheep's clothing. There is much to indicate that hypocrisy, secrecy and disguise were among the great preoccupations of his society, and puritanism seems to have been one of the several conditioning factors for the phenomena in question. Politics and party rancour were another, and so, with its subterfuges, bold fronts and brave faces, was insolvency. In a speech at the Pantheon meeting of 1820, Cockburn announced, to the accompaniment of hear-hears and laughter, that spying—of the Richmond variety—had grown to be a trade, perhaps the only one where there had been no bankruptcies (*Blackwood's* used to publish a list of Scotch and English Bankruptcies, and there were certainly many more debtors in the land than spies).[2] Another factor was anonymity, which provided golden opportunities for the hypocrite and the double-dealer, as well as for the pure in heart. For Cockburn, while the secret smears of Sir Alexander Boswell were beyond excuse, the anonymous

---

[1] The letter is dated 29 June 1880, and is now in a Yale University manuscript collection.

[2] 'Report of the Proceedings at the General Meeting of the Inhabitants of Edinburgh, December 16 1820', published in that year.

stealth of the *Edinburgh Review*—what the *Memorials* call its 'concealed authorship'—was benign.

Cockburn was, in fact, to become judicially acquainted with a justified sinner. The *Circuit Journeys* has an account of a case of demonic possession —or manic depression. On 17 April 1838 he writes at Huntly:

> The only curious case was that of Malcolm McLean, a fisherman from Lewis, who is doomed to die upon the 11th of May, for the murder of his wife. He admitted that he killed her, and intentionally, but the defence by his counsel was that he was mad at the time. There was not the slightest foundation for this, for though he was often under the influence of an odd mixture of wild religious speculation, and of terrified superstition, he had no illusion, and in all the affairs of life, including all his own feelings and concerns, was always dealt with as a sound practical man. One part of his pretended craziness was said to consist in his making machinery to attain the perpetual motion, and his believing that he had succeeded. . . .
>
> This man's declaration, which told the whole truth with anxious candour, contained a curious and fearful description of the feelings of a man about to commit a deliberate murder. He had taken it into his head that his wife was unkind, and perhaps faithless to him, and even meant to kill him, and therefore he thought it better, upon the whole, to prevent this by killing her, which accordingly, on a particular day, he was determined to do. He went to work on a piece of ground in the morning, thinking, all the time he was working, of going into the house and doing the deed, but was unwilling and infirm. However, he at last resolved, went in, sat down, she at the opposite side of the fire, the children in and out, but still he could not, and went to work again. After reasoning and dreaming of the great deed of the day, he went to the house again, but still could not, and came out; and this alternate resolving and wavering, this impulse of passion, and this recoiling of nature recurred most part of the day, till at last, sitting opposite to her again, he made a sudden plunge at her throat, and scientifically Burked her by compressing the mouth and nose, after which a sore fit of sated fury succeeded, which gave way, when people began to come in, to an access of terror and cunning, which made him do everything possible for his own safety, till tired of wandering about, and haunted by some of his religious notions, he went towards Stornoway to redeliver himself (for he had been previously taken, but escaped), when he was discovered. He is now low and resigned, and says he has not been so comfortable for years, because he has got the better of the Devil at last, and is sure of defying him on the 11th of May.

It is difficult to agree with the sound practical Cockburn (who could never bring himself to enter a madhouse) that this 'pretender' or malingerer, with the attendant Devil in whom he continued to believe, was responsible for his actions, that he was not, as it were, McNaghten-mad: we shall find, incidentally, that a distant relation of Cockburn's was to play a part in the devising of the McNaghten rules for the determination of madness in court. On the other hand, Cockburn's account does enter into the spirit of the thing, and in so doing enters into the spirit of the *Confessions*: 'the great deed of the day' is pure Hogg. These great deeds can be considered an element in the Scottish heritage.

Hogg's Wringhim, however, is not just a demented pharisee. No matter how he may yield to his worse self, he is also, like the other leading figures in the literature of doubleness, a type of the Romantic hero—as much so as Byron's guilty Manfred—and a representative of the writer's own first person singular, or plural. This may have helped to make Hogg's book a puzzle to its early readers, who may have wondered at this attack on religious zeal from a praiser of the Covenanters, and who may not have found it wholly convenient to think of Wringhim as a Romantic hero.

Readers have wondered, anyway, how such a work could have come from a single-handed human equivalent of the bucolic pseudo-self of *Blackwood's*. In her letter of 1880, Stevenson's mother wrote: 'Some people suppose that it was written by the Ettrick Shepherd but papa thinks it is better than he could have done. I am surprised that there could be any doubt about the author of such a clever book.' Snobbish theories about supplementary authorship—the second self as literary ghost—took a long time to expire. Such doubts may well have been felt in the 1820s, but even if they weren't, the book could hardly have escaped seeming exotic. It was an exotic book because it was a German book. Scotland's best novel, if that is what it is, owes its existence to German Romanticism. Scotsmen such as Scott and Richardson were already keenly interested in German culture at the end of the previous century, but in the 1820s the German-Gothic taste for doubleness was still a comparatively recent development as far as Scotland was concerned, and doppelgangers were no ordinary thing in Princes Street. Those in the know would have known about Hogg's debt to Germany, but it appears quite soon to have been forgotten.

In the last few years, resemblances have been observed between the *Confessions* and E. T. A. Hoffmann's *Die Elixiere des Teufels*. A translation of the Hoffmann tale appeared in the same month as the *Confessions*, and the translator was a close friend of Hogg's, R. P. Gillies. Gillies was a man of 'cosmopolite notions', a conduit for the German fantasy and philosophy that entered Scotland, and a desperate and interminable debtor, who dunned Scott at the time of his own misfortunes. Scott had a certain regard for him, while thinking him hopeless and a poetical bore. He wrote an article on Hoffmann for a magazine of his, and had been correcting the proofs at Abbotsford in May 1827 when the Ettrick Shepherd called to see him: perhaps, or perhaps not, there was some discussion of a debt to Hoffmann. In consequence of the same financial 'panic' that brought Scott low and shivered his wizard's wand, Gillies fell from respectability and became a 'Shadow', like one of those in the Gothic fiction he served: all this is explained in his *Memoirs of a Literary Veteran*. Display and debt were something of a vocation for many landowners in the years that followed the Napoleonic Wars, but lesser mortals could contrive to glitter and come to grief with scarcely less éclat, and Gillies's experiences very nearly deserve to rank with Micawber's. His life, as he tells it, using those very words, was that of a pariah, and was compounded of pandemonium and asylum.[1]

The hero and narrator of Hoffmann's tale, Medardus, conceives himself to be one of the elect, and predestination also plays a part. So does a doppelganger—the hero's—who thinks that his personality is 'split into two hostile and contending powers',[2] and so does an imposing stranger in foreign dress who is suspected of being the Devil. Medardus, who is given to drinking a strange elixir, explains his situation in these words: 'Like the fabulous knight, who fought with his DOUBLE in the dark forest, I am at variance, and combating with myself.'[3] The novel is about religious-mania and justified sinning, with Medardus persuading himself that he is St Anthony. (Hogg makes a point of mentioning the St Anthony's chapel and well at the foot of Arthur's Seat, a spot passed by both Robert and George when they set out separately towards their combat on the summit, but it may be that we have geography, rather than German literature, to thank for that.) Like Hogg's sinner, Medardus is an outcast and semi-orphan: it is apparent that orphans may belong to an elect, and there are literary works which cause one to wonder whether Scottish orphans should not be included among the self-electing oligarchies of the age.

The novel is not only about salvation, and delusions of salvation, but about ambition and aggression, and the power that may be gained over others by means of an individual's ability to contemplate and manipulate his own personality. Equally, it is about what he cannot help being, while also dreaming himself to be free and omnipotent. An awareness both of destiny and of heredity accompanies Medardus's sense of mission. Myriads and multiplication and succession are a feature of his perceptions; and he is a victim of kinship. It is as if duplication were to be fastened to genetic replication to afford some Gothic model of DNA. Hoffmann's novel has that sly wit which is present in many a Gothic tale. There are tales where its presence can suggest that the writer lacks the courage of his absurdities, but this is not one of them. For all its fabulousness, *The Devil's Elixir* is an exciting and winning work. Its confusions are lifelike, and are filled with pain. As with Hogg's novel, the reader feels for its monster, and both books are humanely explanatory of madness—and of other states—seen as a form

---

[1] See *Memoirs of a Literary Veteran* (3 vols, 1851), vol. III, pp. 138, 148, 285, 288 and *passim*.
[2] *The Devil's Elixir* by E. T. A. Hoffmann, translated by R. P. Gillies (2 vols, 1824), vol. II, p. 299.
[3] Ibid., vol. I, p. 138.

of compulsion. It should also be said that the Hogg is no replica of the Hoffmann, and that what we have to do with is something very different from plagiarism.

The resemblances between the two books do not end there. Hoffmann's dualism was influenced by Mesmerist theory, by Animal Magnetism, while Hogg's Wringhim is told by Gil-Martin: 'I am drawn towards you as by magnetism.'[1] For his portrayal of Scots infallibility and morbidity, Hogg was drawn, in this respect, towards an exotic notation which was becoming less exotic. In the Edinburgh of the 1820s and later, Gillies and others were intrigued by Animal Magnetism, though it was also scoffed at, and seems to have made fewer converts than the allied 'science' of Phrenology or Craniology.

Hoffmann was not the only German Romantic who was attracted to the idea of multiple personality, and to Mesmerism, and the Germans were also attracted to the adjacent idea of Metempsychosis, or the transmigration of souls. In taking up the Faust legend, Goethe was dealing with a double life of sorts which ended in damnation, and his Faust famously exclaims as if on behalf of generations of the distracted: *Zwei Seelen wohnen, ach! in meiner Brust.* The self-consciousness, and the preoccupation with questions of identity and sincerity, which procured, and was procured by, self-duplication remained strong in Europe. So far from being a mere literary game, some of these cosmopolite notions appear to have led on to the scientific psychologies attempted later in the nineteenth century, with Faust, as who should say, giving place to Freud. International Mesmerism and international dualism were intimately linked: each suffered periods of disgrace, but Mesmerism was very influential in European literature for over a hundred years. The notion of the double mind was still available at the end of the century to scientists such as Charcot and Freud, and may well have lent something to the belief in a conscious and subconscious mind. By then, the old world of single minds had become archaic, and a fascination with dualities and a proliferation of pairs had long been rife. As if by magic, the very Church of Scotland had split in two! It is worth adding that Hoffmann's concern with the subject has been thought a product of his own experience as a judge by day, which he was for a while, and a coiner of fantasies by night; and that another creator of doppelgangers, Adelbert von Chamisso, was a Franco-German nobleman whose dual nationality was a source of pain and embarrassment during the Napoleonic Wars.

After the *Confessions*, Hogg remained interested in the German subject-matter, and continued to explore it in his writings. It was also explored in

[1] *Confessions of a Justified Sinner*, p. 229.

the writings of a fellow contributor to *Blackwood's* and *Fraser's*, who was once quite well known and has since virtually disappeared from view. This man is Robert Macnish. Hogg was aware of Macnish, it would seem, and Macnish was very much aware of Hogg.

Born in Glasgow in 1802, Macnish became a doctor and a believer in Phrenology. During his twenties, he spent a year in Paris, where he met Dr Gall, one of Phrenology's great men. He also knew another, Dr Spurzheim. His thesis for the University of Glasgow was 'On the Anatomy of Drunkenness': published as a book, this ran into a number of editions. A later treatise was entitled *The Philosophy of Sleep*.[1] In both cases, his approach to the subject was that not only of a scientist but of a connoisseur of dreams and hallucinations: of the expansion of consciousness, to use the term that has been popular with the drug adepts of recent years. In addition, he wrote stories and poems. A story of his, 'The Metempsychosis', was published in 1826 in *Blackwood's*, to which it had been submitted under a pseudonym. With this, he made his mark as a writer. In 1838, a friend, the *Blackwood's* writer, D. M. Moir, pen-named Delta, brought out a collection of his tales: they occupy the second of two volumes, the first of which consists of a memoir of Macnish by Moir, and which are called *The Modern Pythagorean*. Macnish was a Pythagorean, or Metempsychosist, by virtue of his humorous or fanciful use of Pythagoras's doctrine of the transmigration of souls, a doctrine which could accommodate conjectures about the double nature of man. There are indications that he also took seriously Animal Magnetism and homoeopathy. Moir has this to say: 'The wit and humour of these sketches and stories are much more of the German than of the English school; and the writer's mind seems to have been deeply imbued at this time with the tone of freedom and freshness pervading the best prose fiction writers of Allemagne.'[2] The stories are full of diablerie and double identity, students and pedants, grotesquely long noses and vast mouths—vaster even than any owned by Cockburn's hulking Outer House monsters, vast enough, indeed, to swallow the Advocates' Library. This is a carnival of Gothic, and exotic, fun. The tone is polite and worldly, rather than other-worldly: the stories were unlikely to win converts to the teachings of Pythagoras, 'the sage of Samos'.[3]

Macnish sent a cast of his head—preserving its anonymity for the time being—to the foremost British phrenologist, George Combe, two of whose colleagues assessed its bumps. Macnish's qualities, as listed on the score-

---

[1] A fourth edition of *The Anatomy of Drunkenness* appeared in 1832. *The Philosophy of Sleep* was published in 1830.
[2] *The Modern Pythagorean*, vol. I, p. 45.     [3] Ibid., vol. II, p. 55.

card drawn up by one of these men, included 'Amativeness, very large'—20 points, 'Adhesiveness, large'—18 points, and 'Combativeness, enormous' —22 points. The amative Macnish never married; the combative Macnish does seem to have engaged in at least one futile quarrel; as for adhesiveness, he remained a phrenologist to the end of his days. Combe's colleague reported, in the guarded manner of consultants in general, that the subject 'has that combination of faculties which should make him rank himself on the side of the Whigs, if interest, family connexions, or some such cause, have not otherwise biassed his mind'.[1] Combe himself was a Scotsman.

Moir thought of his friend as a Tory, and Macnish thought of himself as a recreant Tory. Moir grants that both he and his friend felt, before Reform, that the representation of the people needed correction—but only because the Catholic Emancipation Bill, which they had opposed, had been passed against the wishes of the majority. Macnish went back to Paris in 1834 and noted that Louis Philippe was 'perfectly popular with the wealth and intelligence of the country':[2] a Reform Whig formulation. But he considered that the Whig Parliamentarians were inept. Clearly, neither of them was Cockburn's kind of reformer, and their literary leanings aligned them with the Tories. Moir admired 'the *fantasia* spirit' of Coleridge, and perceived a similarity between Coleridge's verse and that of Macnish: but the similarity exists mainly in the eye, or the bump, of the beholder, and 'The Nun of Lindisferne' is closer to Scott's brand of romantic medievalism than it is to 'Christabel'.[3]

1831 was a year of crises. Those afraid of the impending Reform Bill were also scared by the cholera epidemic. In a verse squib in *Fraser's* (February 1832) Hogg spoke of a time of 'Burking, Bill and Cholera', the first of these visitations being the Burke and Hare murders of a little earlier, on which Macnish published an ironic piece, also in *Fraser's*. Moir, who practised as a doctor in Musselburgh, wrote a pamphlet on cholera. The disease, which, let it be said, had come from Germany, crept up the coast from Sunderland to Musselburgh, and then infected the cities: Cockburn noted that it was the ragged and ill-fed who seemed to be catching it. In due course, Macnish, whose health was never very robust, went down with the preliminary symptoms. In 1835, a Continental tour took him to Germany—the Allemagne on which his imagination had fed—and two years later, after bringing out an *Introduction to Phrenology*, he died of typhus.

Two of Macnish's tales are of particular interest here: 'The Metempsychosis' of 1826 and the 'Confessions of an Unexecuted Feminicide', which appeared anonymously the following year. The first is set in the University

[1] Ibid., vol. I, pp. 274, 275.     [2] Ibid., vol. I, p. 327.     [3] Ibid., vol. I, p. 392.

of Göttingen, presided over by Doctor Dedimus Dunderhead. The narrator finds he has assumed the bodily likeness of another man, a profligate in whose person he proceeds to commit crimes. While labouring under his metempsychosis, he is waited upon by a quaint giggling old gentleman, with a wooden leg, tortoise-shell spectacles and a scarlet waistcoat, greatly given to derision and to snuff. Out of his waistcoat, with a reference to Phrenology, he produces, like a conjurer, a series of busts: they are those of sages and magicians—Socrates, Zoroaster, Paracelsus and so on—and among them is the head of Pythagoras, of whose system he is an adherent. The old man presses on the narrator a hellish contract according to which he is to sell his soul in exchange for an abrogation of the identity-switch from which he is suffering. He manages to avoid the Devil's snares and resumes his body, after being buried alive and rescued by resurrectionists attached to the university. His 'transmogrification' is over, but he ends a convinced Pythagorean. The nature of the deals that go with these beliefs is such that the writer would have done well to append a caveat. As for Macnish's 'Confessions', they are those of a whited sepulchre who murders a woman he has made pregnant. Both tales are treatments of the double life, and both seem to be responding to Hogg's recently published *Confessions* and to the German subject-matter which it helped to domicile in Scotland.

'Phrenology,' wrote Macnish, 'can alone account for such men as Hogg. Certain of his organs are splendidly developed, and others as miserably. This explains the fine imagination, and lamentable want of sense, which this strange compound of genius and imbecility—of strength and weakness—so oddly exhibits.'[1] It would appear that the organ of Imitativeness was highly developed in both men, and that each was fleetingly the other's double. Macnish claimed to have used 'James Hogg' as a *nom de guerre* for an article, and he reckoned that Hogg had imitated him. And in these two tales he himself to some degree imitated Hogg. In the case of his 'Confessions', the debt extends beyond the title, theme and treatment to the way in which the tale is offered to the reader—anonymously, and with an epigraph announcing it as 'No Fiction'. He had misgivings about the trick thus played on the public, with whom, Moir says, the tale 'took to a miracle'.[2] But if the two tales point back to Hogg, they also point forward to subsequent reworkings of the theme of double identity, and especially to Stevenson's *Jekyll and Hyde* and Wilde's *Dorian Gray*. The unexecuted feminicide describes himself:

My stature and appearance were good, better indeed than those of the generality of men. I was well formed, strongly knit, and altogether a person who might be denomi-

[1] Ibid., vol. I, p. 330: from a letter to Moir of 2 October 1834.     [2] Ibid., vol. I, p. 51.

nated handsome. But then my face! Had a countenance been sought for in which all the evil passions were pourtrayed, one would have been found in mine.[1]

How far did Hogg return the compliment and copy Macnish? It could be said that not only did he impersonate Macnish: he impersonated himself. The stories published in *Fraser's* during his last years rehearse or glance at the themes of doubles, devils, impostors and counterfeits, and show him as his own double as well as Macnish's. The 'Strange Letter of a Lunatic', published in December 1830, purports to be addressed to James Hogg of Mount Benger. The writer of the letter, James Beatman of Drumloning, meets, on the Castle Hill of Edinburgh, a 'little crooked gentleman' with a gold snuff-box. This 'old warlock', no very distant cousin to Macnish's tempter while also a predictable feature of any Gothic fable, traps him in a 'strange enchantment' whereby he enters into dealings with 'my whimsical namesake and second self'. His double lands him in painful embarrassments, chiefly of a scandalous or sexual kind. Beatman tells his double: 'You are one of the most notorious impostors that ever lived. A most unaccountable and impalpable being, who has taken a fancy to personate me, and to cross and confound me in every relation of life.' And Beatman is told by his double: 'You must be perfectly sensible that you are acting a part that is not your own. That you are either a rank counterfeit, or, what I rather begin to suspect, the devil in my likeness.'

Such is the badinage of doubles. Hogg is trying to be polite and worldly, in the manner of Macnish. For all its shocks and marvels, the tale has no real terrors. 'How could a person shoot game while in a state of uncertainty whether he was the devil or not?' Beatman is wounded in a duel with his double, and later dies. This lunatic, it is hinted, was really an alcoholic: such hints recur in the Scottish Gothic. But he himself asserts, in the terms by now conventional to the genre, that he has been 'turned into two men, acting on various and distinct principles'. Hogg's decision to write the 'Strange Letter of a Lunatic'—which has been almost completely ignored by critics, as has the whole German dimension of his work—is twice as extraordinary as the marvels it relates. Only a strange compound of genius and imbecility would have followed the *Confessions of a Justified Sinner* with a *reprise* of this calibre, in which the conventions and mechanics of the genre are left awkwardly exposed in the midst of a display of urbanity. In this story, he can sometimes seem to be re-doing the material of his *Confessions* in the light of the subject-matter of doubleness as it had developed in the six years since that novel appeared, and, in particular, as it had figured in the work of someone who could almost be called his disciple.

[1] Ibid., vol. II, p. 71.

A year later, in December 1831, Hogg published in *Fraser's* a Pythagorean piece 'On the Separate Existence of the Soul', in which a shepherd is 'transmogrified to a laird'. An atheistical improver, who has been in the habit of arguing about religion with his shepherd, undergoes, to his mortification, an exchange of bodies with the other man: social mobility with a difference. Not unnaturally, in the disputes between the two men Hogg sides with the shepherd, with the devout 'old changeling'. These transmogrifications could well have been assisted by memories of Macnish's 'Metempsychosis'.

Few of his cultivated contemporaries were further in outlook from Cockburn than Hogg and Macnish, who belonged to a kind of avant-garde, with the daftness of an avant-garde, and with its characteristic deference to foreign models, to 'the tone of freedom and freshness' accessible in certain foreign writers. To distinguish what this coterie represented, and to compare it with what Cockburn and his clan represented, is perhaps to gain a better understanding of Cockburn's piety towards the past, of his 'reactionary' character as a latter-day Augustan virtuoso and the qualified approver of an *ancien régime*. This, of course, is only one aspect of Cockburn, but the civilization which he wished to preserve, while seeking innovations and reforms, was one which respected common sense and practicality, and the skills and customs of a professional class and of a patriciate, and was very different from what was comprehended in Hogg's esteem for the 'traditionary'. Not that Hogg himself is to be understood solely in terms of an unconditional regard for the superstitions of the countryside: as I say, the agrestic Hogg was also a member of an avant-garde.

For all his double life, Cockburn can often seem to inhabit the world of the single mind, where the established certainties concerning character and conduct were unshaken. Hogg's 'states of uncertainty' did not belong there. It can seem that, for Cockburn, men were either mad, sane or pretenders, and were either innocent or guilty. Excellence, eminence and respectability contended in his world with a multitude of sins, by which they themselves were seldom tainted. A sense of sinfulness—traditionary enough, one may feel—and a certain fatalism were projected in many of the dualities of his opponents, whereas Cockburn, at the outset of his life at least, took a relatively optimistic view of human nature and hoped for improvements in the habits and institutions of his fellow men. The ideas of his opponents— farouche and faddish and incredible as some of these were—conveyed at their best a genuine sense of the variety and vulnerability of the human mind: Cockburn, by contrast, wanted invulnerability, mastery. If he had romantic inclinations, and he had, then they are rarely very difficult to distinguish from those of his opponents. And the 'fantasia' spirit of German transcendentalism, which meant so much to Coleridge and his admirers, had no appeal to him whatever. He was no friend to Animal Magnetism, to Phrenology or to Pythagoras. He would not have thought it possible that he or anyone else might labour under a metempsychosis. In 1841, the *Circuit Journeys* observes that the personally excellent George Combe, 'Writer to the Signet, and now the Apostle of Phrenology', is visiting Germany: 'In a land where thousands have faith in animal magnetism, and where mysticism and craze seem to be indigenous, lecturing on phrenology, he cannot fail.'[1] The contributors to *Blackwood's* and *Fraser's* were the enemies of much that Cockburn held dear, both privately and politically. These were Tories and magicians, devotees of the expansion of consciousness, fanciers of doubles and devils, brownies and bogles. Edinburgh harboured a coven of wizards, and *Blackwood's* was their stick, with which their own contributor was beaten: *Maga* was magical, and offensive alike to the outlook of the *Edinburgh Review* and to the view from the Pentlands. Cockburn may be known by those whom he did not wish to resemble.

And yet he did, in certain ways, resemble these opponents, and the subject of his leisure encourages one to ask about the literature produced by these opponents. His was a different doubleness from that imagined by exploiters of the vogue for doppelgangers. But it may be that his dreams and double life were formed by experiences similar to some of those which disposed people to accept the vogue, and which enabled the Gothic to grow, and grow luxuriantly, in Scotland. This is a question that will be considered in the next chapter.

---

[1] *Circuit Journeys*, p. 147.

# Chapter Twelve

# *Caledonia's Orphans*

Something more requires to be said about the adversary Gothic culture which confronted the Edinburgh Reviewers and those who agreed with them, and about the influence exercised by that culture in later years. If its exponents were magicians and metaphysicians, this did not mean that they lacked scientific support. It is true that the science which supported them was the pseudo-science, or meta-medicine, of Mesmerism, in partnership with Phrenology and at times with Metempsychosism. But in these years Mesmerism and Phrenology were by no means beyond the pale of scientific orthodoxy: Macnish was not the only doctor who believed in either or both.

The relationship between this type of science and this type of Romantic literature furnishes an instance of the way in which medicine and other scientific pursuits have been assisted, and even engendered, by external vogues and superstitions. If the interest in duality contributed to the development of modern psychology, a good deal of what it contributed was inherently unsound, and it also contributed lavishly to the development of modern credulity. Mesmer's impalpable Universal Fluid and Magnetic bucket, for example, prefigured Wilhelm Reich's cosmic energy and orgone box: box and bucket were intended to heal the world. The relationship illustrates, too, the way in which scientific progress has harboured commitments to the Occult. Recent scholarship has dealt with such commitments in relation to early science, and scholars have now moved into the nineteenth century: strange stories are promised of the trespass within the bounds of orthodox science of arcane or hermetic allegiances. Such allegiances went to the making of Mesmerism, which, in turn, through the theory and practice of Hypnotism, went to the making of, among other things, psychoanalysis, whose family tree has wizards in it as well, let's say, as Associationists.

When the ancient notion of the double mind was revived during the eighteenth century—long before Hogg and Macnish cast their spells, and long before there was any rumour that there might be something Scottish about such a thing—Mesmer himself was one of those responsible. He held that in each person there were two selves, magnetically fused, and that states of trance or somnambulism were capable of releasing the second self. This can be regarded as an attempt to make the double mind scientifically respectable, and other attempts ensued. Much later, post if not propter the adventures of such men as Hogg and Macnish, came *The Duality of the Mind* by A. L. Wigan, which was published in London in 1844, with Goethe's *Zwei Seelen* as an epigraph. Wigan was alive to the advanced ideas of the period, and spoke of them in a vocabulary which occasionally, like Cockburn's and Grahame's, seems to unite the old with the new and the proleptically modern. He refers like a McLuhan to the days when 'the theories of Dr Gall yet slept in his own sensorium'. He also cites Macnish's *Philosophy of Sleep*—for the De Quincey-like hallucinations, recounted there, which the author experienced during an attack of fever. He emphasizes that religious mania was a phenomenon of Protestant countries, where weak minds were undone by the agitation of abstruse theological points. Catholicism, by contrast, was 'a tranquillizing faith'.[1]

Wigan took the view, as did other advanced members of the medical profession, that the methods of coercion and punishment used in the treatment of insanity were brutal and misconceived. Cockburn thought likewise: in the *Circuit Journeys*, he tells of a conversation with a Dumfries boy who informed him that the local asylum had someone called the Breaker—'the man that *breaks* the daft folk'.[2] Neither Cockburn nor Wigan believed in breaking. Together with a condign stress on the importance of controlling the passions, Wigan argued for a new model of the brain, and in so doing tried, in effect, to physiologize the two 'distinct principles' which vied with one another in Hogg's lunatic and in other Romantic heroes. He has been dismissed, subsequently, as a crank, but I notice that some doctors have started to speak once more in a quite Wiganish way, and there may be people who would claim to have proved his theory on their pulses and nerve-endings.

*The Duality of the Mind* talks of the hemispheres of the single brain as the two cerebra, and undertakes to prove a number of propositions, among them the following:

1. That each cerebrum is a distinct and perfect whole, as an organ of thought.
2. That a separate and distinct process of thinking or ratiocination may be carried on in each cerebrum simultaneously.

[1] *The Duality of the Mind*, pp. 38, 429.     [2] *Circuit Journeys*, 21 September 1839.

8

3. That each cerebrum is capable of a distinct and separate volition, and that these are very often opposing volitions.
4. That, in the healthy brain, one of the cerebra is almost always superior in power to the other, and capable of exercising control over the volitions of its fellow, and of preventing them from passing into acts, or from being manifested to others. . . .
7. That when the disease or disorder of one cerebrum becomes sufficiently aggravated to defy the control of the other, the case is then one of the commonest forms of mental derangement or insanity; and that a lesser degree of discrepancy between the functions of the two cerebra constitutes the state of conscious delusion.

Wigan's 20th proposition runs:

20. That every man is, in his own person, conscious of two volitions, and very often conflicting volitions, quite distinct from the government of the passions by the intellect; a consciousness so universal, that it enters into all figurative language on the moral feelings and sentiments, has been enlisted into the service of every religion, and forms the basis of some of them, as the Manichaean.[1]

There is a passage in the book in which Wigan might appear to be giving a medical account of the plots and presuppositions of the Romantic literature of duality:

When one brain wills what is lawful and right, consistent with the duties a man owes to himself and others, and with the form of society existing at the time in the country he lives in, and the other brain suggests a process of ratiocination to justify or palliate some vicious or criminal act, the latter is sometimes attributed to 'the instigation of the devil'. On the approach of insanity, the patient is often found to be holding a conversation, as it may be called, between his two brains, conversing with himself.[2]

Here we have the two selves, one of which is dedicated to vicious acts. Here, in so many words, we have the justified sinner—Wigan's words being those of a secular explanation of his plight. And the Devil is seen at his old work of taking the hindmost of the two selves, instigating the vicious acts and prompting their rationalization. Wigan also includes the sketch of an intelligent and amiable man of his acquaintance laughing at his 'double', who laughs back in concert.[3]

It is a short journey from the magic of duality as practised by these writers and by this doctor to Stevenson's *The Strange Case of Dr Jekyll and Mr Hyde*, although some forty years elapse between the period we have now reached and the arrival of his tale. Born in the last years of Cockburn's life, he was himself a double-liver in the more or less benign sense that Cockburn was, and he was engrossed by the subject from childhood onwards. His fiction swarms with doubles, just as it does with orphans: a

[1] *The Duality of the Mind*, pp. 26–30.  [2] Ibid., p. 36.  [3] Ibid., p. 126.

joint presence which is expressive not only of Stevenson but of other
Scottish heretics and sensitives, both in books and in life. He thought of
himself as an orphan. In point of fact, he was rather the opposite at first, a
parents' pet, and yet he was not altogether lucky, either, in his Edinburgh,
or in his upbringing. 'O Caledonia! stern and wild,' sang Scott: 'Meet
nurse for a poetic child!'¹ This octosyllabic couplet has given satisfaction in
Scotland, and has become almost proverbial. When we think of some
Scottish orphans, both real and self-made, it has a grim cogency.

Stevenson once said that he meant to write a story 'about a fellow who
was two fellows', and apropos of *Jekyll and Hyde*, he invoked 'that strong
sense of man's double being which must at times come in upon and over-
whelm the mind of every thinking creature'². This confession of Stevenson's,
while hardly as arresting as that of some unexecuted feminicide, deserves
to be taken fairly seriously. Like Cockburn, he could feel that he was two
fellows, and he could feel that everyone else was too. It isn't everyone,
however, even in Scotland, who has been prepared to say these things.
Such confessions have been few and far between. He explained, on the second
of these occasions, that scenes in the novel were conceived in a dream: such
an explanation may be considered part of the literary tradition in which he
was working, but it may also say something about his life.

Among the tales of doubleness which Stevenson knew appears to have
been Bulwer-Lytton's *A Strange Story*, which was beholden to Mesmerism.
Another was Edgar Allan Poe's 'William Wilson', in which a fellow murders
his better self. Poe's *Tales of the Grotesque and Arabesque*, in which the
theme of doubleness is prominent, were being written in the 1830s, shortly
after the flights of Hogg and Macnish. Poe was drawn to Animal Magnetism,
and was prepared to pose as a Metempsychosist. Poe and Stevenson were
both of them estranged and ailing: each was a *moriturus*. And the odour of
Magnetism and Magdalenism, and of alcohol and opium, which was ascribed
to Poe's bohemianism would not have offended the young Stevenson, who
was choking on the odour of sanctity: in censorious societies, drugs and
prostitutes were the obvious vehicle for the double life which drew the line
at murder.

At all events, *Jekyll and Hyde* rests upon the lore of the Gothic Romanticism of fifty years before and on the magical psychology which animated it.
Stevenson thought of the tale as Gothic, and the use of the word 'strange' in
the title advertises the tradition. 'Henry Jekyll's Full Statement of the Case',

¹ *The Lay of the Last Minstrel*, Canto Six, lines 17 and 18.
² The 'two fellows' formulation is reported by Andrew Lang in his introduction to the Swanston
edition of Stevenson's works (1911–1912); the other is from 'A Chapter on Dreams' in *Across the
Plains* (edition of 1905), p. 166.

in which he confesses what he has been doing to himself with his powders
and his transcendental medicine, starts off in the following way:

> I was born in the year 18— to a large fortune, endowed besides with excellent parts,
> inclined by nature to industry, fond of the respect of the wise and good among my
> fellow-men, and thus, as might have been supposed, with every guarantee of an
> honourable and distinguished future. And indeed the worst of my faults was a certain
> impatient gaiety of disposition, such as has made the happiness of many, but such as
> I found it hard to reconcile with my imperious desire to carry my head high, and
> wear a more than commonly grave countenance before the public. Hence it came
> about that I concealed my pleasures; and that when I reached years of reflection, and
> began to look round me and take stock of my progress and position in the world, I
> stood already committed to a profound duplicity of life. Many a man would have even
> blazoned such irregularities as I was guilty of; but from the high views that I had set
> before me, I regarded and hid them with an almost morbid sense of shame. It was
> thus rather the exacting nature of my aspirations than any particular degradation in
> my faults, that made me what I was and, with even a deeper trench than in the
> majority of men, severed in me those provinces of good and ill which divide and com-
> pound man's dual nature. In this case, I was driven to reflect deeply and inveterately
> on that hard law of life, which lies at the root of religion and is one of the most plenti-
> ful springs of distress. Though so profound a double-dealer, I was in no sense a
> hypocrite; both sides of me were in dead earnest; I was no more myself when I laid
> aside restraint and plunged in shame, than when I laboured, in the eye of day, at the
> furtherance of knowledge or the relief of sorrow and suffering. And it chanced that
> the direction of my scientific studies, which led wholly towards the mystic and the
> transcendental, reacted and shed a strong light on this consciousness of the perennial
> war among my members. With every day, and from both sides of my intelligence,
> the moral and the intellectual, I thus drew steadily nearer to that truth, by whose
> partial discovery I have been doomed to such a dreadful shipwreck: that man is not
> truly one, but truly two. I say two, because the state of my own knowledge does not
> pass beyond that point. Others will follow, others will outstrip me on the same lines;
> and I hazard the guess that man will be ultimately known for a mere polity of multi-
> farious, incongruous and independent denizens. I for my part, from the nature of my
> life, advanced infallibly in one direction and in one direction only. It was on the moral
> side, and in my own person, that I learned to recognise the thorough and primitive
> duality of man; I saw that, of the two natures that contended in the field of my
> consciousness, even if I could rightly be said to be either, it was only because I was
> radically both; and from an early date, even before the course of my scientific dis-
> coveries had begun to suggest the most naked possibility of such a miracle, I had
> learned to dwell with pleasure, as a beloved daydream, on the thought of the separa-
> tion of these elements.[1]

The vicious acts and criminal appetites farmed out by the respectable
physician to a monstrous alter ego, with Hyde's *deteriora sequor* as an un-
assailable alibi, are like those diagnosed by Wigan and suffered by the
changeling in Macnish's 'Metempsychosis'. The style in which Jekyll
conducts his experiment on his own contending natures resembles that of
some Faustian alchemist deploying his alembics and abracadabra. He

[1] *Jekyll and Hyde* (first edition, 1886), pp. 106–9.

behaves like a magician: there is even a whisk of the conjurer's cape. But he is also meant to be a kind of scientist. The tale is scientific as well as Gothic.

Stevenson kept company with scientists when he was young, in a city that was proud of its medical men—the great wizards of what had become its leading profession. One of his early friends was Simpson, the inventor of chloroform, the suppressor of consciousness, a man who can be said, in a sense, to have worked in a more respectable corner of the same field as Macnish. Consciousness became an issue in Edinburgh, that is to say, on more sides than one. All his life Stevenson remained a student of psychology and of psychical research, and it is clear that there were medical, as well as literary, influences at work when he wrote the tale, though I doubt whether Wigan was consulted. Like Mesmerism itself, the tale was not devoid of scientific meaning. It is really quite fitting that the salt contained in Jekyll's transmogrifying draught may remind one of the lithium salts now used in the treatment of manic depression to effect a change of mind.

If Jekyll's Statement conjures up memories of Macnish, Hogg and Hoffmann, of an earlier mumbo-jumbo, it also conjures up a man who was opposed to mumbo-jumbo: Cockburn. Some of the words used by Jekyll to describe his condition are the words which are put to work in the *Memorials* and the *Journal*. The allusions to gravity and gaiety, to a decorum of bearing and behaviour, and to concealment, may seem to point to the reconciliations which Cockburn succeeded in making between duty and pleasure, and to the paradox of his being a witty and gregarious and poetic judge and an imperious pleasure-lover. He did not *conceal* his pleasures: but he certainly 'separated' them off, farming them out to Bonaly. 'What I was,' according to Jekyll, is not what Cockburn was. But there is at least a fugitive likeness between the two, a likeness which might lead us to wonder whether Cockburn's two minds and Stevenson's may not represent converging responses to the same environment: one of strict fathers, public decency, a stern sense of duty, and a driving desire for respectability and solid nests. This was the environment which made plausible and exciting the fantasies about duality which were projected during Cockburn's lifetime, together with Stevenson's clinching recapitulation of the subject-matter later in the century.

The notion of the split mind has enjoyed a remarkable popularity in Scotland—in certain quarters at least—and has been turned into a kind of patriotic slogan. If only by literary critics and their readership, it has come to be cautiously accepted that to be Scottish is to labour under, to be bedevilled by, transmogrified by, exalted by, tensions and contradictions. The true Scotsman sees double, is beside himself, is his own distinguished stranger. The true Scotsman can be comprehended in an oxymoron. It

would seem that the case of Madeleine Smith has been interpreted to mean
that the true Scotswoman has not been immune from this condition either,
and it can scarcely be necessary to think otherwise, though the way in which
the condition is usually discussed in Scotland might suggest that it is peculiar
to males. (In Russia, the poet Anna Akhmatova professed herself surrounded
by second selves, and in America lately, another poet, Sylvia Plath, affirmed
her doubleness, related it to her experience of a masterful father and of
acute mental suffering, and wrote a doctoral thesis on the double in Dos-
toevsky. These lives remind one that doubleness can appear to be an intensely literary state, and in the case of Akhmatova, it appears to have been
a state that depended on the invention and conscious cultivation of roles
and poses compatible with the literature of the subject. Their lives might
even suggest that it is a state peculiar to writers.)

The acceptance of this notion in Scotland has been assisted by an awareness of some of the books I have been examining, though not of others,
Macnish's stories, for instance, having long since sunk from view. The
nature of the contradictions in question has varied, as has the slogan itself,
and perhaps this was bound to happen, given the dream-like and drunken
character of the experiences postulated in these books. Alcohol is frequently mentioned in these books, and in books that take after them, usually
as a 'reason' for what has happened, and this is not surprising either, since
alcohol has been the country's staple expander of consciousness, the draught
that has produced more double minds than any other. Hugh MacDiarmid's
poem *A Drunk Man Looks at the Thistle* is a late example and critique of the
outlook I am discussing. This thistle is Gothic and phantasmagoric, the
poem has a dialogue of body and mind, it reels and lurches through a maze
of contrasts and opposites, and—to adapt Drummond of Hawthornden's
description of Ben Jonson—drink is the element in which it lives. But
despite the impact of the Gothic tradition, and despite its recrudescence in
MacDiarmid's poem and in other works of modern times, literature is
unlikely to have been solely responsible for the acknowledgement of a
Scottish split and for the mentalities to which it refers, in so far as these have
existed. Other influences are likely to have played a part, and to have been
caught and confirmed in the literature of the past hundred and fifty years.

It has become conventional to say that nineteenth-century Scotsmen were
often torn between past and present (a beguiling past and a present composed of opportunities and problems), romance and practicality, the heart
and the head, the hearth and the market-place, religion and sexuality. These
opposites are obviously related to certain of the opposites to which I have
called attention in the case of Cockburn, and the tensions to which they gave

rise are commonly seen to have been chiefly experienced—as they may have been in Cockburn's case—within the family. The quarrel between father and son, in particular, has seemed to act as a means of expression for the contradictions of Scottish life.

In recent years, from time to time, this has been seen to be the case. Earlier, however, in 1936, Edwin Muir's *Scott and Scotland* defined these contradictions differently: there they were a matter of the possession of a dual nationality and of two languages. In an essay which reads like an attempt to disabuse the Lallans writers and literary nationalists of the period, Muir asserts that there is a 'division in the Scottish consciousness': 'Scotsmen feel in one language and think in another.'[1] At the time of the Reformation, Scotland ceased to be an organic society. The riven Scotland that survived was then rent by further changes—principally, the acquisition of a double tongue. Muir picks up the phrase, 'the Caledonian Antisyzygy', which had been launched by G. Gregory Smith as a name for certain of the operations of the Scottish split mind, and places it at the service of his arguments.

In 1919, in *Scottish Literature: Character and Influence*, Gregory Smith claimed that this literature 'becomes, under the stress of foreign influence and native division and reaction, almost a zigzag of contradictions. The antithesis need not, however, disconcert us. Perhaps in the very combination of opposites—what either of the two Sir Thomases, of Norwich and Cromarty, might have been willing to call "the Caledonian antisyzygy"—we have a reflection of the contrasts which the Scot shows at every turn.'[2] The literature is pulled to and fro between the romantic and the prosaic, between fantasy and observation. Like the young Jekyll, it is at once grim and gay. Muir's gloss on this claim consists of suggesting that the 'high culture of the feelings as well as of the mind' which existed at the end of the pre-Reformation period was effaced by Calvinism, and that 'what took its place was either simple irresponsible feeling side by side with arid intellect, or else that reciprocally destructive confrontation of both for which Gregory Smith found the name of "the Caledonian Antisyzygy": a recognition that they are irreconcilable, and that Scottish life is split in two beyond remedy'.[3] At this and other points, Muir may also be thought to be glossing Eliot's doctrine of the dissociation of sensibility.

In his essay of 1921 on the Metaphysical poets, Eliot says that a dissociation of sensibility set in the seventeenth century, and lays stress on the notion of a lost wholeness. The prelapsarian poet, so to speak, was able to unite disparate experiences so that a thought could be felt, or even smelt.

[1] *Scott and Scotland*, pp. 22, 21.    [2] *Scottish Literature*, p. 4.    [3] *Scott and Scotland*, p. 61.

A dissociation of sensibility is very like a double mind, and Muir's version of the Scottish double mind seems to hark back to Eliot's doctrine. Muir argues that thought and feeling are dissociated in the Scot, and imagines for him a lost wholeness. And this appears to be related to the wholeness, also lost, of the organic community, an idea by which Eliot, too, was impressed later in his career. As it happens, Eliot reviewed Gregory Smith's book in the *Athenaeum* of 1 August 1919 under the heading 'Was there a Scottish literature?' Scottish literature is looked at 'in the light of eternity', as the review puts it; and, as the heading warns, the review is no less sceptical of the existence of that literature, in later times, than Muir's essay of 1936 was to be, though the grounds for Eliot's scepticism, as they figure in the review, are different from those expressed by Muir: there is no urging of dissociations or splits.

'To most of us who were born and brought up in Scotland,' Muir writes, 'dialect Scots is associated with childhood, and English with maturity.' To revert to dialect in adult life, like the Lallans poets, is to 'plunge in spite of ourselves into the simple world of childhood, with its emotions untouched by thought, its sanctioned irresponsibility and endless false hopes'.[1] In Cockburn's day, people already associated broad Scots with their childhood, and were malleable, irresponsible, in the hands of advocates, like Cockburn, who could exploit this fact. Yet Cockburn's own poetic regression to childhood took place without the aid of the Doric: it was Scott-like (and Lakeish) rather than Scots-speaking. This may serve to remind one that the poetry of all languages—not just dialect Scots—has found room for feelings of nostalgia and the desire to escape, for child's play and sanctioned irresponsibility.

Muir's essay seems at many points like a true bill, but it is, in fact, very sweeping. The Scottish Enlightenment of the eighteenth century tumbles into the void of his dissociation of sensibility, and the Edinburgh of the time is pictured as no place at all. While appearing to remonstrate with the literary nationalists of the 'Thirties, the essay is itself nationalistic, in that it gives the impression of pining for an age when Scotland was Scotland, and still a nation: an age long gone, and it could be retorted that Scotland was no more of a nation then than it was an organic community. The truth is that any literary English is apt to be very different from the language spoken by the artist in childhood, though it will incorporate his childhood: and that definitive contributions have been made to the literature of the English language by Americans and South Africans and West Indians whose first speech was remote from, though successfully subsumed in, that of their

[1] Ibid., p. 71.

fiction. Thomas Carlyle and Norman Mailer started with languages that were equally remote from the current metropolitan politeness or correctness: they moved to highly idiosyncratic prose styles (those of the *Reminiscences*, say, and of *Advertisements for Myself*) which have, nevertheless, much in common, which simultaneously are and are not like speech, and which are difficult to object to on the basis of doctrines concerning the relationship between speech and style. Admittedly, bilingualism, or the need to choose between two dialects of the one language, is likely to be a source of doubleness benign or otherwise. No doubt, too, it has given writers a good deal of trouble, producing a distracted or desiccated, a stilted or wilful prose, as well as swathes of Stevensonian purple (purple, perhaps, is orphan's wear). But this is far from inevitable or invariable: bilingualism is not a doom or a chronic disability. Muir's thesis would leave Scottish writers speechless or childish, unable to do as many have done and reconcile the irreconcilable: and there is a large amount of evidence to the contrary, including Cockburn's narrative prose. This has neither stammer nor split. There is no sense of strain. The English prose of this Scots-speaker was a sweet and seamless garment: conversational, idiomatic and at ease. It does not encourage one to believe in the predicament discussed by Muir.

But no more has to be said about Muir's thesis in this context. I have spoken of Gregory Smith and Muir because here was a new way of uttering the old cry about the double mind. Hogg, Macnish and Stevenson, with their German antecedents, had announced that human beings were split: Gregory Smith and Muir were announcing that Scottish human beings were split. Both these writers may possibly have reckoned with the nineteenth-century literature of duality, and with the Scottish corner of it. At one stage, indeed, Gregory Smith is 'content to say that Stevenson was a paradox. And, further, that his is the paradox of the Scot.'[1] He has in mind the contradiction between the Presbyterian that survived in Stevenson and the lyrical or bohemian side of his nature. In making pronouncements about a *Scottish* split, however, neither writer would have been well-advised to rely on the old doctrines of duality, since these, properly understood, and with due allowance made for the profusion of witnesses on a confusing subject, would have had to be perceived as international and universal in character. Edwin Muir, in addition, made surmises whose connection with the old dualities is somewhat indistinct: in writing of a Scottish split, that is to say, he also invoked the modern magic which believes in a time of unified sensibilities and organic communities. This magic works no wonders for the study of Henry Cockburn, but it may be worth noticing that the Paradise Lost of

[1] *Scottish Literature*, p. 288.

Muir and Eliot was a place where minds were single and a thought was an experience, whereas Cockburn's paradise was a place to which he could penetrate only through the acquisition of a double mind.

In the first half of the nineteenth century, the various theories of division were felt to apply to human nature in general—from China to Peru. A hundred years later, theories of division were used in accounts of Scottish life which saw it as inherently and especially split. I am inclined to suppose that the second set of theories was partly evolved from the first, or at least that it can hardly have failed to owe something to 'a century of dualistic thought'. One thing they had in common is that they belonged almost entirely to the imaginative literature of the country and to commentaries on it—the fuse ran from tale to tale, and in the end ignited some literary criticism— and that there was very little appeal to historical fact or autobiographical testimony. It was as if only literature, or literary criticism, could deal with such matters. No divided Scotsman started up, in the early days, to tell of strange conversations with his double—though such men as the justified sinner doomed at Huntly, Malcolm McLean of Lewis, should not be over-looked. Then came Stevenson, who said he was split and strange: but despite its obvious basis in experience, his saying so seems to belong almost as much to literature as the true confessions of Hogg's lunatic do. Later interpretations of the divisions in question have likewise been primarily concerned with literature, but in recent years, as I have already indicated, there has been a tendency to edge closer to the social realities. The images of authoritarian fatherhood in Scottish nineteenth-century fiction have been pondered, and so has their relation to the dualities which also appear there. One critic, incidentally, has been content to regard certain of these dualities as constituting a dissociation of sensibility.[1]

In 1946, another critic, J. D. Scott, glanced at the Scottish split in an interesting essay on *Weir of Hermiston* and George Douglas Brown's *The House with the Green Shutters*: the latter was published five years after Stevenson's novel, in 1901, and its grimness is sometimes thought to have put paid to Kailyard sentimentalism. Scott makes the by now more or less customary allusion to the co-existence in Scotland of dourness and fantastical gaiety: 'What is, I think, to some extent peculiar to Scotland is the presence of these two very different qualities in what we call "one person". It is a fusion, or it might be more accurate to say, a clash between them, which is at the root of the Braxfield touch.'[2] J. D. Scott is intent on explaining how the Scots-speaking coarseness and candour and energy that made a

---

[1] See Douglas Gifford's introduction to his selection of *Scottish Short Stories 1800–1900* (1971).
[2] 'R. L. Stevenson and G. D. Brown: The Myth of Lord Braxfield', *Horizon*, May 1946.

byword of Lord Braxfield were presently overlaid by the gentility, hypocrisy and repressive puritanism which accompanied the Scottish *embourgeoise-ment* of the nineteenth century. He also makes connections between this process and the patriarchal-parricidal strain evident in the two novels he is writing about. He points out that in the plan for *Weir of Hermiston* the stern father, wigged and gowned, was eventually to sit in judgment on the rebellious son, and that in *The House with the Green Shutters* the son puts his brutal father to death. Struck by the hand that had promised to save.

It is on the concurrences between these two works, and on the theme of filial disobedience, that his discussion should come to rest. My conclusion is that the Scottish double mind is at once a phantom and a reality: a con-clusion nicely in accord with the subject-matter in hand. Edgar Allan Poe wrote that 'if in many of my productions terror has been the thesis, I main-tain that terror is not of Germany, but of the soul.[1] By 'Germany', of course, Poe meant the Gothic: the mode which had fascinated certain susceptible and 'advanced' Scottish writers in the 1820s. The splits and doubles on show in these Scottish productions, the German terror that reigned there as virulently as the French had reigned in the fears and anathemas of Baron Cockburn's drawing-room, may have appealed to the Caledonian soul, but they cannot be considered peculiarly Scottish. These works represent a transmigration of the German soul to Scotland, a literary metempsychosis. Equally, the Caledonian Antisyzygy must in part be considered German, Gothic and Mesmeric: in part, too, it must be considered as chimerical as Wigan's two brains. Those later patriots who found a proud wound in the antithetical Scottishness exhibited in these productions, and who wore it and bore it ever after, have been deluding themselves.

But why Germany? Why Scotland? And why is it right, if it *is* right, to refer to the case of the anti-German Cockburn in asking why certain Allemagniacal Scotsmen preached a gospel of division? *Homo duplex*—the name is Buffon's—set foot in several European countries at this time, such as France and Russia. But it was in Germany and Scotland, together with England and America, that the gospel seems to have taken its strongest hold. These were Protestant countries, where duty and severity and respectability were, after various types of convulsion, much to the fore—not that they were invisible elsewhere. Scotland was the country of that 'priest-like father'—with his 'admonitions' and 'solemn air'—who is celebrated in 'The Cotter's Saturday Night'. In Scotland, the faith which was reborn at the time when Hogg and Macnish were writing was not of a tranquillizing kind:

[1] In a preface to his *Tales of the Grotesque and Arabesque* (2 vols, Philadelphia, 1840).

the Protestant ethic was refurbished then, if it would not be nearer the mark to say that it was invented then, and its impact on domestic life was to prove very formidable indeed. In such circumstances, resistance to the father is likely, and some of the resisters will belong to the species, *Homo duplex*.

The son who resists his father may feel guilty, and may accept his father's authority while also repudiating it. He may seek to be close to his mother, or to escape, lifting his eyes to the Pentland Hills. But he is likely, at the same time, to become, in some measure, the father he has resisted, and to be resisted in his turn. These are experiences of division and fragmentation, and it may on occasion be fair to say of him that he is split beyond remedy. But despite the fact that many of the believers in a double mind took an interest in lunacy, it cannot be said of him that he is likely to go mad.

Pathological instances of multiple personality are very often linked, in modern psychology, with repressive parenthood and with religious or quasi-religious sanctions fiercely enforced in childhood: two terrors that have yet to leave the land, for all our recent liberations. But it would be wrong to think of the range of divisions manifested in the fact and fiction of the subject as mainly a matter of pathology. In the last few years, rightly or wrongly, madness has sometimes been seen less as a form of illness or incapacity than as a solution to the problems of the family, and the double life can be seen as a solution too, and to some of the same problems. Double lives of one sort or other are almost as common as mixed feelings, distracting and disabling and devilish though they may, in certain cases, turn out to be. It can now seem that to be human, as well as to be domestic, is to be double. In any Western society where it is not thought very surprising that a prominent politician should take bribes while preaching about law and order, and where there's the kind of public spirit which takes pride in the society's work ethic while causing it to serve as an excuse for rapacity, the two faces of hypocrisy will seldom be thought the kind of condition which should be treated in a hospital. Double lives—so-called and by many another name— are normal. And they are apt to acquire the character of solutions. They may involve strategies of respite or escape, retributions, declarations of independence. They may involve vicious acts. But they may also involve courses of action which are intrinsically satisfying and which may even be inspiriting and salutary.

If duality provides solutions, it is likely that these will be solutions to more than one type of problem: and it is likely that there will be more than one type of double life. There certainly appear to be grounds for applying the term, by extension, to certain varieties of behaviour which cannot readily be described as mutinous, morbid, illicit or *outré*. In relation to the varieties of behaviour which do deserve to be so described, and to which the term is usually understood to refer, there is, moreover, a clear distinction to be drawn between the historical double life—in so far as this has ever been confessed or witnessed, in so far as it has been induced to desert its native secrecy—and the hypothetical double life of the Gothic tales, which were greatly constrained by the pursuit of theatrical effect and of a fashionable subject-matter, and which set out to amaze their readers by portraying expansions of consciousness and states of uncertainty. The Gothic tales imply that it is abnormal and strange to be split, despite the presence in the background of doctrines implying the opposite: that this is the human condition. The elasticity of most conceptions of doubleness is evident at quite an early stage of their history.

The phenomena of doubleness may range from the relatively simple expedients or dodges of some hypocrites and night-hawks to behaviour which is complex, rather than duplex, and deeply meditated, from the capitulations to the wicked and vengeful self which are deplored in melodramatic and meta-medical treatments of the subject to Milton's mixed feelings about the defiant Satan and Cockburn's about his public life. Neither Cockburn nor Milton—sinister though Milton may sometimes seem—was distracted or delinquent or damned or mad. Yet this is what we still expect of doubleness, reared as we are beyond remedy on Gothic sensationalism and on narrow notions of probity. There is still a superstitious fear of doubleness, and a superstitious awe of wholeness and integrity. But it may also be true to say that the old magic of wholeness has been joined by the glamour which may now attach to the divided self and the disturbed mind. For whatever reason, there are now those who feel that some states of doubleness are equally states of wholeness, and who might agree that doubleness may be held to include *Paradise Lost* and the Reform Bill as well as the acts and intimations of feminicide, fratricide and parricide delivered to an impressionable public by the Gothic writers of Scotland.

The double life—in the customary, as indeed in the extended, sense of the term—may often look like a consequence of the rules and rigours and restraints of an exacting society. Where much is forbidden, the tribute that vice pays to virtue will be paid without stint, and much will be done in secret. Secrecy and stealth may be worshipped, and may become sexually attractive: the prohibition of sex, and the imagination of sex as disobedience, has caused this to happen, and has persuaded the impressionable, in the words of the playwright Webster, that 'love mix'd with fear is sweetest'.[1] When the clandestine has come to seem beautiful, the hours of darkness, the streets of a

---

[1] *The Duchess of Malfi*, Act Three, Scene Two.

city at night as Doré might have engraved them or as Hyde might prowl them, or as the unsuspected criminal of American films might drive them, will come to seem beautiful too. Such a society will not be a tranquil one. Some of its rules will be thought right by those who break them.

The rules and rigours and restraints of an exacting society may be expressed and ordained in the authority of fathers. The sternness of fathers, or of their society, may produce the sternness of sons, some of whom may feel impelled to lead double lives. Some of them may turn into self-styled orphans or stepchildren: this is a role which a certain type of rebel may embrace; it is an important aspect of the interest in orphans and estrangement which is widespread in the literature of the first half of the nineteenth century, and which was shared by Cockburn's circle; and it corresponds to fantasies which, according to Freud, are typical of the 'family romance'. The orphan may dream himself attended by a distinguished domino'd stranger, a mighty prince pseudonymous or incognito: this is a role played by the second self in Gothic fiction, and, in Freudian terms, it represents an image of the father, though it could equally well, one might suppose, be an image of the father-supplanter. And the orphan may dream of a paradise which represents an image of the mother. In these and other ways, the double life may coincide with, or recapitulate, the prior oedipal conflicts predicated by Freud, and it seems possible that these first conflicts are capable of energizing the quarrels which may erupt in adolescence.

The real and the self-made orphans who figure in nineteenth-century literature, and who helped to write it, were drawn not only to the double life but to opium. In discussing these tendencies, Baudelaire offers the most musical and evocative of all affirmations of duality: *Qui parmi nous n'est pas un* homo duplex? *Je veux parler de ceux dont l'esprit a été dès l'enfance* touched with pensiveness; *toujours double, action et intention, rêve et réalité; toujours l'un nuisant à l'autre, l'un usurpant la part de l'autre.*[1] Here is the sensibility, the music, of the self-made orphan. And here, too, every bit as much as in Jekyll's Statement, may be sensed the ghost of Cockburn. Like a sparrow rustling among leaves, his poetic second self is present in the phrase, 'touched with pensiveness'. His poems are full of pensiveness, and make pointed use of the word itself. The phrase in question is that of the orphaned De Quincey, whose *Confessions of an English Opium-Eater*, together with the *Suspiria de Profundis*, was presented to a French audience by Baudelaire in his *Paradis Artificiels*. *Les Paradis Artificiels* is about the expansion of consciousness, and it provides an inventory of the possibilities:

---

[1] From Baudelaire's discussion of *La Double Vie* by Charles Asselineau, first published in *l'Artiste*, 9 January 1859, and reprinted in the Pléiade edition of his works (1961), p. 658.

it is an anatomy of consciousness comparable—at a higher level of consciousness, so to speak—with the inquiries undertaken by Macnish. De Quincey's *Confessions* were published a matter of months before Hogg's, the two men later came to know each other well, and De Quincey was a member of the *Blackwood's* set: and the impact of his *Confessions* gives fresh grounds for thinking that this was an avant-garde whose ideas found favour with a variety of artists in other places. Confessions are the opposite of Memorials, and 'confessions' was very much a word of the age: it was an age in which Rousseau had not been forgotten. De Quincey's *Confessions* contributed to the critique of consciousness which was developed in Edinburgh, and they also contributed, as other confessions have done, to the art of the orphan. Opium was the opium of the orphan (as well as of the people) during much of Cockburn's adult life. Along with alcohol, it may be ranked with the artificial paradises to which the literal or artificial waif retreated. Cockburn's eminent semi-orphaned Sir James Mackintosh retreated there.

De Quincey's *Confessions* and Hogg's were written, as I have said, about the same time—which was also the time when Cockburn began to write the *Memorials*—and there is a point at which the two works coincide. When the Justified Sinner flees 'forlorn' towards Edinburgh and then towards Dalkeith, and when De Quincey stands in London's stony-hearted Oxford Street looking north and longing for the Lakes, where he was to sit in his cottage with a book of German metaphysics placed beside his quart of ruby-coloured laudanum, both books utter the same cry, the cry of the orphan and the outcast: 'O that I had the wings of a dove!'[1] Early in 1834, at his most Lakeish, Francis Jeffrey uttered the cry. Returning to Westminster after a spell of Scottish rustication, he longed to fly from the cares of official life. During the previous year, the government of which this despondent Jeffrey was a member had emancipated both the West Indian slaves and the Scottish burghs: few Parliamentary orphans can have done a better year's work.[2] In 1875, as we have seen, Stevenson also uttered the cry.

The Gothic themes of doubles and orphans could be adopted by writers otherwise indifferent to the genre, and they are nowhere easy to interpret. Like the secrets and anonymities which were cherished in the same society, however, they can sometimes seem to signify a resistance to the father or to authority, at a time when the demands made by the family had become severe, when religion and respectability were enjoined as the only refuge in a world which was full of disease and shame, and full, for that

---

[1] *Confessions of a Justified Sinner*, pp. 219, 224. *Confessions of an English Opium-Eater* (Penguin edition, 1971), p. 69.
[2] JLC: 6 February 1834.

matter, of authentic orphans: the strengthening of family life coincided with a gathering clan of those who had no family to resist. Some of those who quarrelled with their fathers, or with God the Father, or who chose to disobey the society's bans and behests as these were enforced in the context of family life, who refused to behave consistently 'with the duties a man owes to himself and others, and with the form of society existing at the time in the country he lived in', as Wigan puts it, might lead double lives and dream themselves bereaved. The imaginary orphan could embrace the double life, in the capacity of author or delinquent, or he could do what the real orphan could do: take opium and escape into reveries of the mother, of Heaven, and of the world's pariahs. In Scotland's lower depths, where respectability was less of an issue and there were plenty of pariahs, such behaviour was no doubt comparatively rare.

The orphans, outcasts, urchins, vagabonds, elixirs, princely strangers, sensualities and wild and unnatural crimes which presage and bear witness to the arrival of the double and the Devil in the Gothic tales attracted a considerable following, and *Blackwood's Magazine* was to a large degree responsible for the vogue. Madeleine Smith read it in its later and less reckless days, and so did her lover,who appears to have been an opium-eater and an arsenic-eater (*Blackwood's* published news of both elixirs). As children, the Brontës pored over the back-numbers of *Blackwood's*, over Hogg's fairy stories, over Scott and Scots lore generally. Branwell said that he turned to opium after reading De Quincey, and it may be that *Wuthering Heights* owes something, if not to a reading of Hogg's *Confessions*, then to the mentions of that novel (and to the extracts from Hoffmann's) in the magazine. During these years, Hogg's very title, one might think, was capable of inspiring—of speaking volumes. Emily Brontë used to knead the dough with a German book propped in front of her. Her novel has its moments of duplication, and Heathcliff, the devilish outcast and orphan, is pronounced fit to be 'a prince in disguise',[1] whose father may have been the Emperor of China. Cockburn once imagined himself that very dignitary, and he and Heathcliff have in common pugnacity and an ostracized pride. But if he was an emperor in Edinburgh, and at home, he was an orphan on the Pentlands: one who

[1] *Wuthering Heights* (Travellers' Library edition, 1926), p. 65. Wilkie Collins's *The Moonstone* (1868) is a prize confection of Gothic ingredients: secrecy, hypocrisy, princes, an orphan lad who is a Mesmeric subject, and a hero on whom opium confers a double. 'How soon may our own evil passions prove to be Oriental noblemen who pounce on us unawares?' (Penguin edition, 1966, p. 241). Collins is one of eight writers discussed by Alethea Hayter in her *Opium and the Romantic Imagination* (1968), which examines their work for influences specific to the use of the drug, and in which the opium-eater's dream of bliss and terror and of the pariah is described. The hallucinogens and anodynes favoured by certain Romantics have acquired a formidable bibliography, and pharmacology, in recent years.

was comforted there, and in raptures. He was a lion, and he was a lamb. Cockburn suffered from delusions neither of grandeur nor of destitution. But some of the cries, and some of the roles and recourses, which communicate the theme of alienation in Romantic literature may also be found to have formed part of the private life of His Majesty's Solicitor-General.

The double life may depend, even in those who imagine themselves to be orphans, upon aggression: it is pugnacious sons who are likely to embrace it. Stevenson seems to have known this. He seems to have known that it may depend upon an aggression, not only against the father's code, but against the father himself. So, at any rate, one may think when the incestuous burglaries of his plays are studied in conjunction with the parricidal drift of *Jekyll and Hyde*. Hyde's clothes, which are those of his second self and ought perhaps to fit, are in fact too small. This is eloquent, and poignant. It matters that Hyde should at times seem like Jekyll's disobedient son, and that his 'ape-like' tricks should embody insults directed at the memory of Jekyll's father, which include the burning of his letters.[1] Perhaps it matters, too, that the libidinous Hyde should be allowed by the author of his exploits, by which I mean Stevenson, to take pleasure only in cruelty.

Both Cockburn and Stevenson fell out with their fathers. Both were drawn to older women, and married motherly ones. Each led two lives, which united virtue and pleasure, respectability and retreat. Each solved his contradictions, in some sense: no doubt the goodly words available to a Naphtali enabled them to do so. Each fled from worldly goods to the maternal Pentland Hills: their joint Arcadia afforded a range of edifying pleasures, but for the youthful Stevenson it also included visits to the Victorian underworld.

Stevenson helped to prolong the Gothic vogue for dual personality, by whose tricks and elixirs Cockburn would have been repelled. At its worst, in the manner of a detective story, it treated human identity as a conundrum or tease, and it did not have much to do, in its doctrinal aspects, with any-thing peculiarly Scottish. Nevertheless, the popularity and persistence of this literature suggest that Gothic duplication found congenial soil in Scotland, and the divided lives of Cockburn and Stevenson suggest why this should have been so.

Cockburn was capable of imagining that he was two fellows, just as he was capable of imagining two Broughams—Cockburn's and Sir James Mack-intosh's. He was also capable of using the Gothic vocabulary—of referring to poor Otho Herman Wemyss's second self. His two lives did not amount to a double life, in the Romantic fashion which was current from the 1820s

---

[1] *Jekyll and Hyde*, p. 138.

onwards, and which was suffused with a sense of delinquency and sin, but he could use the language of duality, and he could use it to describe himself. Here we have intimations of a German Cockburn—a yielding to the Gothic account of human nature. In his recurrent light use of these romantic words the divisions apparent in his own nature are expressed, and perhaps the fight with his father can be seen there too. It seems that the last of the old Scotch gentlemen can be considered an example of the modern Scot as certain modern Scots have conceived him.

Much of the secret of Cockburn lies in the character of that interest in secrecy which was retained by a man whose life was charged with publicity. It was solitude rather than secrecy that he was after at Bonaly: and his secrecy in other matters was partly a consequence of the decorum of behaviour to which he and his friends believed that all gentlemen and public men should adhere. For all his frivolity-masking demureness, he was no pharisee or secret sinner. For all his paradise, he was no pariah. For all his 'parricide', he became a patriarchal public man. In the same way, the duplicity of which he was publicly accused was that of a lawyer, rather than a liar: the 'lies' he was blamed for seem largely to have been of the kind that is to be expected when the skills of the orator and the raconteur are addressed to the tasks of the advocate. Yet he possessed a second self—sequestered and serene—which wrote verse on 'secret' subjects and which may well have been invisible at suppers or on circuit. And there are moments in the Gothic literature of duality when Cockburn might almost seem to be intended, or impending. Hogg's hero addresses a reprobate on the mysterious ways of the Almighty, and it is as if both the pugnacious and the paradisal Cockburn were being evoked: 'Hath he not builded his stories in the heavens, and laid the foundations thereof in the earth, and how can a being like thee judge between good and evil, that are both subjected to the workings of his hand; or of the opposing principles in the soul of man, correcting, modifying, and refining one another?'[1]

The terror and pleasure of the twin self are not only of Germany, not only a literary fashion or 'rage'. They are of the soul, too. And it may be that the souls of Protestant-ethical sons (and daughters) have been especially exposed to these assaults and seductions. But, of course, these assaults and seductions must be very ancient. All societies, perhaps, are more or less puritanical, and all fathers more or less pugnacious. Think of Shakespeare's Prospero, the magician father with his staff and strong will: pre-Gothic and effectively pre-Protestant. Who more fitted to obey than Miranda? Who more sullen than Caliban? To the extent that they are the figments of

---

[1] *Confessions of a Justified Sinner*, p. 101.

Prospero's pugnacious imagination, which is what they feel like, they are a symbiosis. Pent in the one self, they would make an exquisite double life in the Gothic mode. All fathers are magicians, and one of their tricks is to split the rock of the human personality, doing to it what the wizard Michael Scott did to the Eildon Hills. The pugnacity of fathers is as old as these hills, and very like that of Almighty God, as many of those whom it has expelled from Paradise would agree.

The pugnacity of mothers is no doubt an equally important theme. But it does not suit this book. Here it has been necessary to say: *le père de famille est capable de tout.*

# Chapter Thirteen

# *Cockburn Law*

Cockburn Law is the name of the hill in Berwickshire beneath which the Cockburns began. It might also be a name for the opinions concerning the Scots legal system which were expressed by Henry Cockburn in the *Edinburgh Review*, in the *Sedition Trials* and in his writings at large, and for his career at the bar, his behaviour on the bench and on circuit, and his work as a legislator. He could plead like an angel. He walked in procession through remote royal burghs. He punished the riotous and disorderly. He pressed for changes in the law, both of substance and procedure. And in 1830 he drafted the Scotch Reform Bill.

The majesty of the Scots law was a higher hill, an Alp, on whose slopes he was content to graze—while seeking, as was sometimes charged, their sunny side. Though he pressed for changes, he revered the Scottish system, and thought it in several respects superior to the English. It was politically necessary for him, when he wrote in the *Edinburgh Review*, to protect himself against accusations of reckless Anglophilia by making much of the merits of the Scottish system, but it is certain that he believed in these merits. An article of April 1830 in the *Review* contains this paean of praise to the civil law of his native country:

It pleased the barons of England to reject the Roman law; and it is the fashion to praise them for having done so. They thought that they could not maintain their liberty otherwise; and if this was the case, they were right. But we are most thankful that no such necessity was imposed upon the barons of Scotland. At an age far beyond authentic history, the civil law percolated through the canon courts into every part of our system; and we can scarcely conceive a circumstance more fortunate for a people, than that, in the very dawning of their civilisation, they should have been led to adopt a code so deeply founded in natural equity, so applicable to so many transactions and relations, so beautifully unfolded, and so intimately connected with general philosophy and literature. Besides introducing a rational system of law, the collateral benefit arose, of connecting our lawyers and legislators with those of other countries. While the English, according to the image of Bacon, when speaking of goodness, were, by their exclusive addiction to their own ways, an 'island separated from other lands', we were 'a continent that joined them'. A residence at the great continental schools of law was, for centuries, an established part of the education, not only of professional lawyers, but of liberally educated gentlemen. Hence our laws may be said to have arisen under the tuition of all the jurists of Europe, who were appealed to, freely and familiarly, both in Parliament and in our courts. The minds of our own lawyers, moreover, were kept open. They were saved from that slavery to whatever *is*, which sometimes makes professional lawyers such miserable legislators, especially in matters of law.

This is the face of the Cockburn who did not think that 'whatever is' should be let alone. But by the end of the article he is proposing that the legal system be let alone after a few final corrective touches have been applied. Many reforms had been put through in past years, and it is as if all that remained to be done was for obsolete usages and offices to be pruned and for civil jury trial to be lodged securely in the Court of Session (both changes were impending), and for the question of appeals to the House of Lords to be re-examined. Scottish lawyers are praised here for their open-mindedness. Later in the article, not altogether consistently, he mentions two main sources of dissatisfaction with Scottish justice, one of which is the postponement of reforms (the other is the appointment of judges on extra-judicial grounds). He himself was shortly to be denounced, by opponents, as a miserable legislator. They said that the Scottish Reform Bill had been drafted by men who had no practical acquaintance with Scotland. As we have seen, this is a criticism which has been renewed in recent years.

Between 1808 and 1825, various innovations and experiments were carried out in relation to the structure and procedures of the Scottish courts. The country's highest courts consists of the civil Court of Session and the criminal Court of Justiciary. The judges of the first court are called the Senators of the College of Justice, and some of their number serve on the second court. Before 1808, the President of the Court of Session and his fourteen judges did their work as a single body in the Inner House. Each of the judges, except for the President, took turns to sit for a week at a time as Lord Ordinary in the Outer House, where the Richardson parody was set: his decisions might then be reviewed by his colleagues. The judges had to deal with written or printed pleadings, and were gravelled by the resultant paperwork. Towards the end of the eighteenth century, there were numerous complaints about congestion and delay; and, in civil causes, Scotland was distinguishing itself by the volume and inconvenience of its appeals to the House of Lords. The mainly Whig Ministry of All the Talents tried to bring order to the situation by dividing the Court of Session into three chambers and creating a Court of Review, and also wished to institute jury

trial in civil causes. The Ministry soon collapsed, but in 1808 the returning
Tories separated the Court of Session into two divisions under the Lord
President and the Lord Justice-Clerk respectively. In 1810, judges were
taken from both divisions to act as permanent Lords Ordinary. In 1814,
an oral emphasis was introduced with regard to pleadings, which became
more pronounced in 1825.

In 1815, a civil Jury Court was established. Civil juries were a conten-
tious notion, being seen as an adjustment to English practice. But, in time,
they were also seen to work, and were later embodied in the Court of Session:
they are still employed, in a restricted capacity. In the 1820s, the criminal
jury was reformed in order to admit a right of peremptory challenge (a
challenge that could be made without assigning reasons for it) on the part
of the defendant, and in 1825 a right of ballot was introduced by the second
Lord Melville. Both these measures had been argued for in Parliament by
Kennedy of Dunure, with Cockburn's assistance. Previously, judges had
been able to pick, and pack, their juries.

The reshaping of the Court of Session helped to open up a split between
the older Scottish Whigs, some of whom gained office in Grenville's Ministry
of All the Talents, and the young Turks of the *Edinburgh Review*, who
inspired jealousy when they came into their own. Much though they
esteemed the estimable Henry Erskine, the leader and exemplar of the
Northern Whigs in times when they had often had to lie low and take to the
hills, the younger Whigs saw their elders as over-protective of the aristocratic
interest, and saw themselves as moderates in relation to the Grenville
measures. The successful civil-jury Bill of 1815 was due to Lord Eldon
in London, who, as Lord Chancellor, was set on stemming the flow of
Scotch appeals, and in supporting Eldon's Bill in the Faculty of Advocates,
Jeffrey was at odds with the veterans of the party. Civil juries were therefore
the occasion for a trial of strength within its ranks. Cockburn was keenly in
favour of having them, and he called the Act of 1815 'the greatest step in our
judicial history':[1] he was seldom nervous of superlatives. Of the advocates
of the time, he and Jeffrey were easily the most skilful with juries, and in
that sense were the Bill's main beneficiaries. With the country still more or
less unrepresented in Parliament, there were no doubt those for whom the
case for new jurymen had rather the colour of the case for more voters.

In considering some of these matters in the *Edinburgh Review*, Cockburn's

[1] *ER*, April, 1830. The attribution to Cockburn of anonymous articles in the *Edinburgh Review*
is based on the findings of the *Wellesley Index to Victorian Periodicals* and on acknowledgements
contained in his own writings. The article of August 1825 which is referred to in this chapter is
given conjecturally to Cockburn in the *Wellesley Index*. It expresses his opinions, and is likely to
have been by him.

stance can be one of reassuring his readers that only a little more needs to be done to get the Scottish judicial system right, and of avoiding the suspicion of truckling to Southern precedent. In an article of October 1821, he addresses himself to the question of the 'Nomination of Scottish Juries' in criminal cases. The article is ostensibly a review of Bentham's *The Elements of the Art of Packing, as applied to Special Juries*, but explains that 'we have borrowed the title of it merely—as a peg on which to hang a discussion of a more local and domestic nature' (it is not for nothing that this journal has been reckoned an ancestor of the kind of literary journalism practised in Britain to this day). He provides an arresting, if rather distant example of jury-packing—dating from 1752, when Stewart of Ardshiel was tried at Inveraray for the murder of Campbell of Glenure:

> There had long been an almost deadly feud between the Stewarts and the Campbells. The Duke of Argyle, the head of the Campbells, was Lord Justice-General—a nominal office, which did not require him to act at all. But he chose to act; and the way in which he acted was this. There were many persons within the district who were qualified to be Jurors, who belonged neither to the one clan nor to the other. Indeed, an entire and unexceptionable Jury might have been obtained, without taking a single man from the country where the feud subsisted, or the crime was said to be committed. But there were put (whether by him or not, we cannot say), into the list of forty-five, no fewer than *twenty-five Campbells*; and of the remaining twenty, *only three were Stewarts*. Still the whole of both clans might have been left out of the Jury of fifteen, and there were enough to make an Assize. But when the trial began, his Grace named *eleven Campbells*, all from Argyleshire, as part of the Jury. Of the remaining four, *not one* was a Stewart. The result was what might have been expected.

The article concludes with an effort to scotch any impression that the use of a ballot and the creation of a right to challenge jurors meant tampering with the essential structure of criminal jurisprudence. He first mentions certain adjacent features of the law, among them the following:

> The authority of a court of law to declare acts, never before challenged as criminal, to be offences—to fix the proper punishments for these—and to do this by irreversible sentences, seems scarcely consistent with an accurate regard to the proper limits of judicial and legislative power; and to leave any man or any faction who may hereafter have an unconstitutional predominance in the State, too little to change in our judicial institutions, if the re-establishment of arbitrary power be their object.
>
> But we repeat, that we wish to be understood as stating these things merely as *facts*, and not as reasoning about their merits or demerits. The only conclusions that we can draw from them, as applicable to the measure particularly in question, are, in the *first* place, that this measure has no such connexion with them as makes it right to introduce them into this discussion at all; but, in the *second* place, that if these matters are to be forced into the consideration of this Bill, then, so far from the proposed alteration being superseded and rendered unnecessary by the other peculiarities of our law, it is precisely in the law of any country where such peculiarities may happen

to exist, that this Bill is peculiarly useful. For though these things might not in themselves be alarmingly questionable, yet when they are combined with an absolute nomination of the Jury, by Judges who are not only named, but are liable to be promoted, by the Crown, the whole system assumes a different appearance. It is for this very reason, that everyone who understands the right application of the principle, that old institutions are not to be rashly touched, must be friendly to the success of this simple and yet renovating measure. By adopting it, everything else may stand. The good that remains cannot possibly be hurt, and what is bad or doubtful must be corrected and improved.

This is a soft answer intended to pacify readers who felt, as he himself often felt, that old institutions should not be rashly touched, and should as far as possible be let alone; and it hints at the existence, on the part of his readership and beyond that pale too, of some very lively fears for the future of Scottish customs and traditions. Having suggested that the custom whereby criminal judges could make new law, by an exercise of their 'native vigour', was irrelevant to the proposed arrangements for criminal juries, he then goes on to demonstrate its relevance. He himself regarded this custom as 'alarmingly questionable', and did not want it to stand, and its bearing on the proposed rules is plain enough. Judges who could make law could also pick juries. Since he held that neither of these prerogatives belonged to a satisfactory criminal jurisprudence, he would have done better to admit here that both deserved to fall.

In the *Edinburgh Review* for February 1823, he looks at the situation after half of what he has been arguing for has become law: a right of challenge has been obtained for prisoner and prosecution, and the Court of Justiciary has lost its right to name the forty-five people from whom the jury was empanelled. He shows that in certain respects half a loaf is worse than no bread: the authority of judges is threatened if there is a right of challenge while judges continue to nominate. But he also says that Scottish criminal jurisprudence has not been harmed: 'To our eyes, the fabric seems far more venerable than ever.' If the judge's selection of the jury had ceased, 'it would have been nearly as perfect as mere regulation can make it'. Shortly afterwards his will was done, and his civil-jury millennium ensued.

Two years later, in the *Edinburgh Review* for January 1825, he returned to the matter of the alarmingly questionable power of the criminal courts to make new law: to the matter of the Justiciary's 'native vigour'. Scottish judges had made plenty of law in the eighteenth century, but for a great deal of his life he was to press his case against certain of their later initiatives. In 1845, he wrote to Macvey Napier about a piece he was preparing on the subject.[1] In common, it seemed, with most other Scotsmen, Napier had no

[1] 25 October 1845: British Museum MSS. The piece in question (*ER*, January 1846) was a review of a Supplement to Baron Hume's *Commentaries*.

idea what 'native vigour' meant. 'May you never feel it!' said Cockburn, and enlightened him. 'It is the power claimed, *and actually exercised*, by the Justiciary, of declaring any act that it pleases to be a crime—i.e., of indicting and transporting you for editing the *Edinburgh Review*, or me for having large nails in my shoes.' By the exercise of this power, as Cockburn saw it, trade-union combination, without striking, had been declared a crime— indictable at common law—in the years that led up to Bonnymuir. A few years after that, however, Parliament had taken a different view.

Cockburn's insistence on the distinction between the judicial and legislative functions should itself be distinguished from the positions taken by members of his party, in earlier years, on the judges' equitable and common-law jurisdictions: certain Whigs thought there should be a separation between the two. Such a separation was, at that time, 'English', though England was later to make a fusion: it was a feature of the Continental tradition that the two were united, and they have remained united in Scotland. And Cockburn does not appear to have desired a separation. His arguments concerning the 'native vigour' are best understood, I think, in relation to the progress of political reform and to the coming of a world in which Parliament would exercise rather more native vigour of its own in respect of social legislation. His stand on the legislative activities of the criminal judiciary is certainly consistent with his efforts to secure an improved political representation, responsive to the needs of the intelligent and the independent, and with his case that Scotland should partake to the full of the British freedoms. Native vigour may perhaps be regarded as involving a Northern reaction to the failure of past Parliaments to pay proper attention to this part of the Empire. No doubt, too, a devolutionary patriotism entered into it. The name itself says as much: it was the next thing to calling it Scottish Virr or Smeddum—that quality of which Cockburn enjoyed his fair share. Native vigour may have been an affirmation of their independence by the Scottish courts which could be said not to square with the British Constitution. It may not have been as sinister as Cockburn, wearing his Anglophile hat, made out: he admitted, indeed, that it had once been necessary.

In the article of January 1825 (as in another of August of that year, which was accompanied by an article by Macaulay on Milton and by one by Brougham on what may pardonably be described as the *Edinburgh Review*'s new university in London), he spoke with approval of the role of the Lord Advocate as public prosecutor, a role that England lacked. For a while he felt that the Lord Advocate's prosecutorial powers should, in effect, be restrained by the provision of grand juries on the English model, but this opinion was retracted. The responsibilities of the post of Lord Advocate struck him as excessive—even before Jeffrey groaned beneath them. The post combined the duties, in England, of the Home Secretary and the Attorney-General, and he reckoned there was a case for having something like a Secretary of State for Scotland: a post that Kennedy, then a Treasury Lord, could have filled when Jeffrey was Lord Advocate. These arguments of his are steeped in the Northern political history of the period. The performance of the Lord Advocate's duties had been compromised in the past by party obligations: this thought also informs some of his previous arguments on the manipulation of petty juries by those in authority. The Lord Advocates Maconochie and Rae were widely held to have acted stupidly and highly politically: Maconochie in relation to the business of seditious oaths just before Bonnymuir, when the prosecution suffered a fiasco, and Rae in relation to the question of Government involvement in the Sir Alexander Boswell libel case and the chicaneries that were linked to that.

The Scottish 'manager' of the past had often been Lord Advocate, and the problem of how Scotland should be managed was one which preoccupied Cockburn and his friends in the later 1820s. Perhaps it should be run by someone quite outside the party situation in the North, who would work through the departments of state—rather than through kinship and friendship as the old proconsuls had done, lording it over their province? Better an Englishman as Scottish Manager than a native jobbing Scot. Before long, the old arrangements were dying out with the advent of Reform. We know the kind of man whom Cockburn thought suitable for high responsibility in general: an early piece of his[1] is devoted to praising the executive abilities of the fair-minded Duncan Forbes, who ran the North, and stilled its rancours, after what Cockburn saw as the rather sordid 'Forty-Five.

In this same article of January 1825, Cockburn also calls for a curtailment of the 'almost unlimited' powers of review available to judges in the case of civil verdicts, while asking for powers of review and revision, for consultation with colleagues, and for a right of appeal to a superior tribunal, to be instituted in the case of criminal verdicts: the latter were the 'irreversible sentences' referred to in his article of October 1821.

In 1826, he wrote about entails in the *Edinburgh Review:* one of the last areas, as it must often have seemed, where feudalism was due to be dismantled. Entails had originally been sought by landowners as a safeguard, in troubled or tyrannous times, against the chances of forfeiture. Cockburn believed that for a century and a half almost three-quarters of Scotland could not be sold or attached for debt, and he gives a figure of 1,591 for the number of entails executed since the Stuarts—since a statute of 1685: this in

[1] *ER*, February 1816.

itself (for there were very few before that) provides a comment on the small number of people who owned the country. Since 1805, the rate of execution. had been stepped up, but entails were now resented by landowners who were gasping to sell and could not do so. Capital was clamouring to go where the law would not let it. Two statutes had tried, and failed, to ease this pain. Cockburn suggests that entails be allowed for a limited length of time (and he also suggests that entails are for upstarts rather than the old blood). In 1848, Rutherfurd was Lord Advocate, and a Bill of his was passed which Cockburn greeted with satisfaction in some of the best prose which a legal matter can ever have elicited:

> The great improvement will consist in the obliteration of those distressed and humiliating Esquires of great places, whose rural grandeur is entirely nominal, and who, with sounding titles, are known hereditary bankrupts. Some of these, owing to the want of consents, may drown on; but their own comfort, joined to the power given by the new law to creditors, will induce many heirs rather to be the true owners of a little, than the holders for creditors of a great deal. So that, on the whole, though some of our old fixed stars may disappear, our sky may still sparkle by a due number of moving ones.
>
> But the favourite Perpetuity dreams of our forefathers are at an end. The powers of the recent statute may sometimes be allowed to sleep; and some entails may be maintained in spite of the Act, as some estates have been long preserved without entails. But this is no longer *certain*, and certainty was the charm. Not only big feudal lords, but every petty tradesman who had converted the till into acres, used to live and to die proudly complacent in the undisturbed conviction that eternity was but a type of his entail. Every entailer and every heir now knows that at the very best his greatest security is not greater than the pleasure of the heir in possession and certain consenters.[1]

Certainty had its charm for the writer himself. The man who could be said to be 'immovable on the Pentlands' was, in his own way, an expert on eternity. So was the ally of those English Reformers who wanted 'finality'. And so was the Harry Cockburn (or Cocky) who advised the Rev. Charles Anderson: 'Better be the certain owner of a field of neeps, than the precarious expectant of a Venus.'[2] Cockburn was not wholly untouched by 'yird hunger' (landed desires), or by the wish to laird it on an estate: he had, moreover, sailed close to bankruptcy in recent months. None of this seems to have done anything to prevent his ironies at the expense of the immortal longings of others. He was hardly nature's entailer, but he was acquainted with the perils of perpetuity.

Further stands taken by Cockburn should also be mentioned. While generally considerate of the rights of the accused before trial, he was critical of the rule which laid down that the prosecutor had to present him with a

[1] *J* II, pp. 220, 221.   [2] 6 December 1818.

copy of his indictment fifteen days before the trial. This enabled the accused to spring a special defence which placed the prosecutor at a disadvantage by denying him the chance to gather evidence to meet this defence, and which could therefore force him to respond with a new indictment: muddles and delays resulted. Cockburn was doubtful of the Scottish verdict of not proven: it could confer an unwarranted stigma on a prisoner who had been successfully defended, and it could distract jurymen from the evidence while allowing them to soothe their consciences.

Another cause he took up was the abolition of relationship, or kinship and affinity, as an objection to a witness's competency, except in the case of husband and wife. He seems to have believed[1] that the arrival of civilization in Scotland had meant that certain classes of witness became credible, and if women, servants and paupers could be trusted, why not sons? In criminal cases, he disliked a comparatively recent arrangement called 'the option' whereby parents and children were allowed to choose whether or not to testify in relation to each other: this interfered with the processes of justice by excluding what would often be indispensable evidence, and it treated the monster who wanted to hang his parent as a trustworthy witness. On the subject of witnesses, as on the selection of criminal juries, Cockburn's will was done. In 1840, a change was made of a kind that suited him, with Ruther-furd again responsible. Relationship, as an objection, was quashed. At the same time, changes, which Cockburn also supported, were made in the rules of evidence: procedures for charging witnesses and admitting testimony were simplified and relaxed.

Cockburn did not wish to repudiate the appellate jurisdiction of the House of Lords, but at the time of the Reform Bill he was drawn to the idea of a supplementary Scottish Court of Review, somewhat on the lines of the one mooted by the Grenville Government of 1806. The damming of the southward flow of Scottish appeals was still a desideratum, and so, for some, was a curtailment in the interventions of English lawyers. But such a court, said Cockburn, would be 'agreeable to the analogy of England'.[2]

In his last years, Cockburn would have been entitled to comfort himself with the reflection that much of what he had argued for with the improve-ment, or perfection, of the Scottish system in mind had come about. The development of the law in relation to sedition was a comfort in itself. He took the view—expressed *passim* in the *Sedition Trials*—that the old concept was dangerously vague, and he was keen that in this matter Scots law should be neither less liberal nor less articulate than English. In the course of his lifetime, the dubious power, as he saw it, of transportation for 14 years or for

[1] *ER*, April 1833.  [2] *ER*, April 1830.

life, in cases of sedition, was removed by Parliament. The lesser power of banishment was then retained in Scotland longer than in England—till 1837, when Cockburn helped to write the Bill removing it. High treason came to be treated, not only in a manner agreeable to the analogy of England, but in terms of English law.

The most enduringly controversial aspect of Cockburn's commentaries on the laws and legal system of his country is likely to be his opinions on the statutory relief of poverty. The position he took on the poor was not one which most people now would expect of a reformer, though there was no incongruity in its being taken by a Whig Reformer. Two important dates are 1824 and 1845. In 1824, Kennedy prepared a Bill which Cockburn praises in an article on the 'Poor Laws of Scotland' in the *Edinburgh Review* for October of that year. Kennedy's Bill failed. Then in 1845 an Act was passed whereby the oversight of the Kirk was replaced by the system of supervisory boards which the Utilitarian bureaucrats had introduced into English local government. As a result, the number of parishes where heritors were assessed for poor relief rose from 230 to 420. Cockburn's article of 1824 had tried to protect the lairds: in it, assessment is bitterly decried. But the lairds had blocked Kennedy's Bill.

The guiding principle urged in Cockburn's article is that 'a compulsory provision for the poor, *as a regular and established measure,* is not only pernicious, but has a direct and necessary tendency to increase the very evil which it is meant to cure'. Assessment is seen as itself an evil, as a kind oi cholera creeping up from the Merse, where the authorities had been tainted by proximity to English procedures, and breaking out all over the hardy North in loathsome patches. In England, assessment was widespread, and the poor tended to receive more in the way of assistance, both absolutely and in terms of assessment: in 1840, when the population of England was $15\frac{1}{2}$ and that of Scotland $2\frac{1}{2}$ million, the law relieved $7\frac{3}{4}$ per cent of the people in England, as against $3\frac{1}{6}$ per cent of those in Scotland.[1] For Cockburn, the poor were like flies buzzing round the carcase of compulsory provision. What chiefly offends him is the thought of a transfer of money from the rich to the able-bodied poor, and his attitude appears to have been shaped, not only by a reluctance to concuss the propertied classes, but by the doctrines of Adam Smith and of Malthus, who was a friend of Jeffrey's. Assessment was bad for the poor, who should fend for themselves and be encouraged to save, though whether it was possible to save on the five shillings a week which was a common wage at the time is not a question by which he was sufficiently detained.

[1] Figures given in Saunders's *Scottish Democracy*, p. 198.

The distinction between the able-bodied poor and the impotent poor ('quhilks of necessitie, mon live be almes,' quotes Cockburn) was a traditional one, and the fiction prevailed in Scotland that the able-bodied poor had not been relieved in the past. A second fiction declared that scarcely any parishes had been assessed before 1700. Recent work by Rosalind Mitchison has shown that contemporary assumptions about the perfection of past arrangements were wishful thinking.[1] The Kirk administered poor relief, with the co-operation, in town and country respectively, of the magistrates and heritors, and about the middle of the eighteenth century, at the time when Moderatism began in the Church on a footing of respect for the state and for the law, and of support for patronage, heritors asserted a claim to the control of the parochial funds for the poor. The claim was upheld by the Court of Session—under the guidance, it seems, of Lord President Dundas, Henry Dundas's father. Those liable to be 'stented' for poor relief—that is to say, the heritors of the parish—were apt to disapprove of stenting, or assessment. We can conclude that Cockburn took the part of the landlords over assessment, while quarrelling with them over patronage.

The Kirk was to some degree opposed to Kennedy's Bill. Five presbyteries, including Edinburgh, petitioned against it. These opponents were concerned about the right of the pauper to appeal from the kirk session to a secular court: Kennedy's Bill forbade this. The poor, Cockburn states, should have no legal right to relief: 'Whenever the notion of a right to relief prevails, the modesty of charity is extinguished, and the poor take perfectly good care of themselves.' They could not be counted on to remain ignorant of their rights. When times were bad—and he witnessed several such times—people became shamelessly interested in survival.

Cockburn's article extols the beauty of an experiment by Chalmers in his parish of St John's in Glasgow which was designed to prove the practical value of the virtue of self-help, and which lasted from 1819 to 1823. 'In substance and effect,' Cockburn writes, 'it was the poor who maintained the poor.' This was a stock view, if not a stock formulation.[2] As a result of the regime set up by the future leader of the Disruption, the poor made ends meet by relying on voluntary funds and by helping one another. That was

---

[1] 'The Making of the Old Scottish Poor Law', *Past and Present*, May 1974.

[2] Ibid. Mrs Mitchison writes that the nineteenth-century legal position is prefigured in a statement of 1781: 'In that year James Anderson of Monkshill, near Aberdeen, writer on agricultural matters and political economy, sent a description of the Scottish law to the Earl of Shelburne. This gives the full system: no relief except to those permanently disabled; little use of assessment; non-resident heritors do not contribute unless assessed, with the result, as he remarks with approval, that "the Poor are supported by the Poor".' Of Chalmers she writes: 'Under Chalmers the church sanctified the refusal of the landowners of the 18th century to work the poor law as laid down by Parliament and Privy Council or as created by the parish communities of the 17th century.'

the beauty of he thing. The poor were let alone, as Lord Melbourne prescribed—except, of course, that they were not, since they were assisted
from voluntary funds. Chalmers took pride in the small amount of time that
the deacons of St John's needed to spend on relief. Public charity, he thought,
was wrong, apart from support for education and hospitals, and Cockburn
agreed. St John's was not, in fact, a particularly poor parish, and Chalmers
does not appear to have ascertained the true extent of the need that existed
there. Some of the deserving appear to have been deterred from seeking
relief by the inquisitorial character of the proceedings to which they were
subjected. And it was possible to apply for help to neighbouring parishes
where assessment operated, and also to Dissenting congregations.

In his social policies, Chalmers stood like a tower for the family, and for a
self-reliance which leant, when it had to, on the paternalism of the larger
family of the parish. He showed a distaste for what urban life had now become, and he wanted to fight the ills and evils of the cities by fostering there
the peasant virtues and pastoral responsibilities of the rural parish. He also
stood for Malthusianism and laissez-faire. Rank and class were not to be
thrown down. Business was virtuous, or could be so: he sympathetically
expounded an ethics of business practice. He believed that, after a strike, an
employer might justifiably refuse to give work to the ringleaders, and might
tax the wages of those whom he did take on again. So assessment had its
uses, after all.

Cockburn's article is unpleasant—a distant prospect of the poor, seen
from the great height of gentlemanliness, and from Bonaly's ivory tower—
and it is particularly unpleasant, perhaps, when he talks about those who
were worse-off than the poorest natives: that is to say, those who had sailed
across the sea from the green island of Miletus.

Glasgow is much infested by Irish of the lowest description; and as there is no law of
removal in Scotland, but everyone acquires a settlement merely by three years' continued residence in any parish he may happen to go to, it is impossible to get rid of
these persons, when they fall, as they very generally do, after the three years are out,
into a state of what is reckoned destitution in this country, but which, when relieved
by poors-rates, is paradise to an Irish beggar. In order to check the premium thus held
out to the daily arrival of hosts of locusts, a general resolution was adopted by the
heritors and kirk-session of the Barony parish of that city, that no Irishman should be
admitted upon the poors-roll. Whether this was a fair or judicious resolution, is quite
immaterial. It was one which they held that they were just as well entitled to form, as
to exclude persons of bad character, or to exercise their discretion in any other way
that was satisfactory to their own minds. They accordingly rejected the claim of an
applicant, because he was a native of Ireland. On this the claimant brought their
opinion under the review of the Court of Session.

The rejected claimant was an old Irishman named Higgins, a member of the 'impotent' or disabled poor who had lived in the parish for seventeen years: a long time, but for Cockburn, what was to be done about the Irish was associated with what was to be done about persons of bad character. The Barony Kirk Session argued that their power in these matters was in the nature of a power of taxation, which meant that relief was for natives only. rather than residents, and that the decisions of the parish were technically immune from review by a court of law. The Court of Session had lately ruled, first, that it was entitled to rule on the decisions of heritors and kirk sessions with regard to such claims, and secondly, that on this occasion the heritors and kirk session of the Barony parish had acted illegally. The criterion for relief was affirmed to be one of residence, not birth. The Court, in its vigour, had made it law that the beggar should stand as a creditor in relation to a fund of which the heritors and kirk session were the trustees: this is what Cockburn took the ruling to mean, and he thought it a grave error. Meanwhile Higgins continued to inhabit his paradise.

Sixteen years went by, in the course of which clergymen seem to have come increasingly to share Chalmers's horror of assessment. In 1840, however, the debate was convulsed by the pronouncements of a public-health specialist, Dr W. P. Alison. He was the brother of Sir Archibald Alison the historian, who was a *Blackwood's* Tory and a legal colleague and courtroom opponent of Cockburn's: so that there were three Alisons who mattered to him. W. P. Alison's pamphlet 'On the Management of the Poor in Scotland' strongly criticized the propertied classes and exposed the realities of working-class life in an era when population had soared and industrial communities lay at the mercy of endemic and epidemic disease and of sharp fluctuations in earnings due to a very volatile trade cycle. A Royal Commission, put in hand shortly afterwards, pointed to the defects of the Scottish Poor Law, and noted that, in any case, it was not being carried out. The Act of 1845 was based on the Commission's findings. The unpopular Benthamite English Poor Law of 1834, which was directed against the 'Speenhamland' practice of using the rates to support wages, had ordained that, to obtain relief, the able-bodied had to enter the workhouse. In Scotland, a Board of Supervision was now created to induce parishes to do what was needed, even if assessment was what was needed, a legal right to relief was instituted, and there was an increase in medical aid. Rosalind Mitchison has observed that the Act was 'vitiated by the old Scottish principle that the only qualification for relief must be disability added to destitution'.[1] Eventually, though, the Board had some success in encouraging parishes to relieve the able-bodied, and its

[1] *A History of Scotland* p. 388.

doctors were concerned to stress the connection between destitution and disability. At the end of the century the Act was still in operation, and imperfectly applied. Access to its loopholes no doubt helped to preserve the moral fibre of the Scots.

Cockburn was impressed, despite himself, by Alison's pamphlet. He was dissuaded from rejecting it, as he confides to his *Journal*,[1] by 'first, the increase of Dissenters, who contribute nothing at the Church doors; and, secondly, the whole populations that are now thrown idle at once by periodical stagnations of trade. But notwithstanding this, I adhere as yet to my old faith in the necessary and progressive tendency of compulsory provision to increase the appetite of pauperism by what it feeds on. Still, however, poors-rates are convenient in the first instance, and have been steadily advancing for many years, and my belief is that they will at last, and soon, cover the whole land.' The cholera would triumph. When the Royal Commission was set up, he was still adhering to the principles of the old system *'if they be rightly applied'*.[2] But they never had been rightly applied, and there were no grounds for supposing, as many besides Cockburn had done, that they could cope with the problems of a swelling, swarming, locust-infested Scotland. At this point in the *Journal*, the question of the management of the poor vanishes in a cloud of forebodings about demagogues and manufactures. Britain's industrial monopoly in the world was no more. *Troja fuit*. As long as it remained 'a nation of manufacturers', there would be trouble from trade fluctuations. As long as there was such trouble, the pristine virtues of Scotland's self-supporting poverty would be at risk. The experiment of St John's must have started to seem like an idyllic dream.

On 15 August 1845, he writes at length in the *Journal* about the new statute. He summarizes the virtues of the old system, until recently 'the perfection of wisdom', and then remarks:

> Dr Alison startled people by questioning all this about three years ago, and now the whole system is extinguished in a single month by the Legislature. The old heritors and kirk-sessions *as such* are superseded. The claim of the poor for relief as a legal right is established. New local authorities are created, and the whole system is put under the control of Commissioners. It is a Poor-Law revolution; one of the many examples of the precariousness of everything that really deserves to be changed. Our Poor-Law, if it had not been administered with disgraceful shabbiness, was excellent. The interjection of the Commissioners between the pauper and the Court of Session, which it is the most fashionable thing to abuse, seems to me to be one of the very best parts of the new scheme.

The passage conveys the weakness of his residual attachment to the traditional arrangements, though he is now more disposed to cast doubt on these

[1] *J* I, pp. 258, 259.  [2] *J* II, p. 1.

arrangements. It is a strange kind of excellent law which permits wholesale disregard of its provisions.

The *Journal* entry for 8 November 1848 predicts the arrival of statutory relief for the able-bodied as a result of the Act, and an end to the old song of Scottish self-help. A footnote dated 8 March 1849 reports that his prediction (that of a Court of Session judge) had proved pessimistic. The judges 'have decided that the law of Scotland provides no legal relief by assessment, either to the able-bodied or to their children—a merciful judgment for the country: but it will probably be reviewed by English judges steeped in their old system; and if they adhere, our system will be fortunate if it escapes being Anglified in Parliament.' So, at the last, he proved unregenerate on pauperism, and hostile to the assessments of the South. His pronouncements on the subject show him as less of an Anglifier, and less of a reformer, than is usually supposed.

When Cockburn thought of the Ragged Schools, he thought of guilt. The guilt which had given birth to these children. When he thought of the poor, he thought of greed. The greed of the poor. Yet this is a man who played at orphans on the Pentland Hills, a man who was considered amiable by many of those who knew him, high and low. What appears to have excluded a more promising approach on his part to the problem of poverty was an ingrained deference to the economic interests of his kind or class—this, together with the hectic and unfamiliar character which the problem had assumed. His position agreed with what may be called the Malthusiasm of the age, and with the new fanaticism in religion: he recognized, I think, that such a thing had come to exist, and found it both appealing and un-appealing. In the nineteenth century, neither the old system of poor relief nor the new was honoured in the parishes, and neither system worked. Certainly the tender-hearted Whigs of Cockburn's circle could not manage—and could not manage to behave decently towards—'the murmuring poor, who will not fast in peace', as Crabbe calls them in his poem 'The News-paper'. The Whig notion of civil liberty could be used as a way of constrain-ing the liberties of most of the population, and the pioneering Cockburn cannot be considered a pioneer of the welfare state.

It is time to turn from his opinions on the law to his performance as an advocate and judge. He was thought to be a great pleader. He and Jeffrey excelled with juries, and he many a time melted the heart of Midlothian. His most celebrated performances were his opening speech, in 1821, for Stuart of Dunearn, who had killed Sir Alexander Boswell in a duel, and his defence of Helen MacDougal in the Burke and Hare body-snatching trial seven years later. Stuart undertook his duel without ever having handled a pistol: his opponent fired in the air. Previously libelled in another paper, he had, in a gentleman-like way, caned the printer in the street. Cockburn sometimes speaks of him as if he were a hero and a victim. The Burke and Hare trial was a very different occasion, which opened a door on the Edinburgh underworld. The 'dying sounds' of an old woman they murdered had been described by one witness, said Cockburn in court, as 'the stifled moans of an animal suffocating'.[1] The Enlightenment science of anatomy needed such sounds, and the Edinburgh poor supplied them: Burke and Hare procured corpses for Knox the surgeon, and took at least fifteen lives—rather less than able bodies, for the most part—in the furtherance of their trade. 'Except that he murdered, Burke was a sensible, and what might be called a respectable, man,' say the *Memorials*, perceiving the Edinburgh virtues where they might not be expected. Helen MacDougal was Burke's woman, and Cockburn got her off with his closing speech one grey winter morning. The acquittal was delivered in the customary language: 'The Lords assoilzie the panel Helen MacDougal, *simpliciter*, and dismiss her from the bar.' Often he spoke for those who were poor and who badly needed defending, like this woman, and like the weavers of the West accused of subversion or combination.

Cockburn defended a second duellist, David Landale, who was tried at Perth in 1826 for killing a man after severe provocation. In a manuscript note,[2] Cockburn remarks that this was the first case in which the judge decided that the jury was to take the whole matter into their own hands. Lord Gillies said that, in a case of murder, 'there must be legal malice', that 'the fact of killing was only a presumption of the existence of this necessary element, but did not exclude other evidence', that 'this other evidence consisted of the whole circumstances—of which the jury were the judge'. This charge of Gillies's to the jury, favourable as it was to Cockburn's own view of the case, is characterized as 'very sensible, but very illegal'. About the same time came a case involving dark questions of respectability and anonymity. Cockburn appeared for a man named Watson who, having been blackballed from a club of gentlemen, was accused of uttering obscene letters by a well-known Glasgow joker named Kingham, a dubious figure who seems to have won the jury's sympathy.

According to Lockhart in his *Peter's Letters to His Kinsfolk*, though you would not guess it from the transcripts of his speeches on behalf of Stuart and Helen MacDougal, Cockburn's relationship with a jury ran to romantic ardours and a stylized eroticism. If the Town Council was impenetrable to the aspiring Whig lawyer, juries were not. Lockhart says that Cockburn's

[1] From a shorthand transcript of the trial published in 1829.    [2] NLS Cockburn MSS.

skull displayed its biggest bump in the phrenological region of veneration, but that he had 'a pair of eyes that seem to be as keen as those of a falcon'. Juries were his prey: 'He sees their breasts lie bare to his weapon, and he will make no thrust in vain.' When facts failed him, pathos took over: 'His lips quivered, and his tongue faultered, and a large drop gathered slowly under his eyelids, through which the swimming pupil shot faint and languid rays, that were more eloquent than words.' It is as if he reserved his emotions and his extravagance for the bar—rather as some Scotsmen have done with the other kind of bar. Words seldom seem to have failed him, if facts sometimes did, and these words were homely: 'It is not his ambition to be admired: he wishes only to be trusted.' Lockhart proceeds: 'After he has been allowed to tell his story in his own way, for ten minutes, I would defy Diogenes himself to doubt it.' I suppose this is a way of saying he was a bit of a liar. 'He uses the Scottish dialect—always its music, and not unfrequently its words,' Lockhart points out. This was the speech 'to whose music the ears around him had been taught to thrill in infancy', and it could beguile them from listening carefully to a defective argument.[1]

There is a pornography of grief—a romantic art practised in Henry Mackenzie's *Man of Feeling*. Lockhart's account possesses, and describes, a pornographic quality, but it also seems to bask in a possible fraudulence on Cockburn's part, and it may have been meant to make readers suspicious of a leading Scottish Whig. This paragon of trust and tears, of histrionics and calculation, might well excite suspicion—but of the sort that is generally excited by pornographers rather than Whigs. Cockburn himself was inclined to suspect the accuracy of *Peter's Letters*, but I would imagine that this particular account can be credited with a grain of truth. Here in full flight, authentically enough, are Cockburn and his double—the Roman and the romantic, the calculator and the man of feeling. He could shed tears—in the arms, for instance, of old Eliza Fletcher—and he undoubtedly had a healthy respect for them. In a letter to Kennedy he commended Stuart's bearing in court: 'He behaved beautifully, uniformly firm and calm, but made amiable by some occasional bursts of tears.'[2] There is no reason to decide that Cockburn's blandishments—his shows of sensibility, which may have been as shrewd as they were sincere—did any harm. The sense and humanity of his best writings, and his record at the bar, indicate that the trust he inspired so theatrically was not misplaced.

The trust that Stuart inspired in Cockburn, however, does appear to have been a little misplaced. Cockburn can make him seem like a Scottish

[1] *Peter's Letter's to His Kinsfolk* (3 vols, third edition, 1819), vol. II, pp. 65–72.
[2] *Letters to Kennedy*, p. 51.

orphan, but in 1828 word came that made him seem like a Scottish orphan who had made free with the mites of Scottish widows. While holding the office of collector for the widows' fund of the Writers to the Signet, he fell into debt through speculation and absconded to America. Cockburn told Macvey Napier[1] that those who knew Stuart would 'resort to any fancy rather than yield to the belief that one they thought so pure and firm can have imitated the paltriness of common debtors'. Their connection with him was a 'bright track of happiness', but his flight was a terrible example of how precarious human happiness was. Stuart subsequently righted himself, becoming a London newspaper editor and an inspector of factories.

Cockburn took an appreciative interest in lawyers' ways, in their glories and absurdities, but this did not prevent him from seeing, and from frequently specifying, the error of those ways. In the *Sedition Trials* he refers to Jeffrey's 'soft heart' and 'disease of complimenting'. An old minister, Neil Douglas, was charged in 1817 with sedition, having allegedly compared George III to Nebuchadnezzar in a sermon, and Jeffrey, in defending him, had been lavishing his compliments on the prosecution. Cockburn protests that Jeffrey's ' "*learned and honourable friend*" was a person with whom he had not even any personal acquaintance, and knew only professionally; and his *candour* and *liberality* consisted in his making a most cruel and unhandsome attempt to hurt the character of an old man against whom he had preferred a groundless charge. He should have been excoriated.' It is a pity he did not include this incident, which made his very wig stand on end, in his *Life of Lord Jeffrey*, where it would have lightened the load of Cockburnian compliment.[2]

His record as a judge and as a legal light is fraught with Scottish disparagement. It seems that Cockburn, come to judgment, has been thought deficient, a dilettante, particularly in civil law: he was no feudalist. Jeffrey was anxious, when his friend benchified, that he should make a point of exhibiting the learning, patience, veneration of the law, which he was

[1] In a letter of 5 July 1828: British Museum MSS.
[2] *Sedition Trials*, vol. II, p. 201. A further example of the interest taken by Cockburn in lawyers' ways—which is also an example of the interest he took in the ways of politicians—is provided by a 'Report' he published in 1817 of a case decided in the House of Lords on 16 May of that year. According to a hand-written note of his on the flyleaf of the British Museum copy, he compiled the report 'voluntarily' and in 'pure indignation', being unconnected with the case. Two generals, a Whig and a Tory, Maitland and Campbell of Monzie, had contested a seat: the district of burghs to which Inverkeithing belonged. Having helped to persuade the Town Clerk of Inverkeithing, David Black, to exercise his discretion as to the legality of the votes cast for the delegate due to take part in the election of the Member, Campbell prevailed on the Court of Session to fine Black for disallowing two of the votes, but the House of Lords reversed the interlocutor. Campbell had got in anyway, but wanted to punish the returning officer: and the Court of Session had smiled on his suit.

suspected to lack, that, rather like justice itself, he should be seen to be judicial and to take pains, and that he should curb his quickness of mind. It seems that Cockburn was not always able to follow this advice. Discussing the *Memorials* soon after Cockburn's death in an article in the *North British Review* which has already been mentioned, Patrick Fraser complained that he was too lucid, and asserted: 'The utterly untechnical character of his mind made his judgments read in the eyes of a foreign lawyer with a force not due to their intrinsic merits.' Masterfully sour. This was the same writer who reproved him for his 'indolence' and 'love of enjoyment'. By 'foreign lawyer' is meant the House of Lords, which upheld certain civil judgments of the Anglophile Cockburn reversed by his colleagues of the Court of Session.

Sir Archibald Alison felt much the same way about Cockburn's performance as a barrister as Fraser felt about his performance as a judge: 'I often experienced that in criminal cases, especially those involving the life of the prisoner, which I conducted on the circuits, and he was generally the leading counsel on the other side, he seldom failed on such occasions to so move the jury that in the face of the clearest evidence they brought in the verdict, "By plurality not proven". He was indolent, and averse to *continued* labour, though none by fits and starts could make greater efforts.'[1] The conceptions of labour and technique which are brought to bear on Cockburn's intermittences by Fraser and Alison are plain enough: in their own way, they were no doubt very exacting. Alison's words also help one to understand Cockburn's misgivings about the verdict of not proven.

In 1838, Cockburn had a brush with some of his colleagues on the bench: First Division judges who, he thought, were out of sympathy with jury trial in civil causes, which had been in force for some time, and were prepared to administer stealthy snubs and checks to Outer House judges who felt differently. As Lord Ordinary in Glasgow, Cockburn had heard the case of Collins against Hamilton, which concerned the alleged pollution of a river by a dyeworks. His verdict was appealed against to the Inner House, and the appeal was upheld on what he thought were spurious grounds. Nothing loath, Cockburn published a pamphlet of protest, dated 17 February 1838, and addressed to the President of the Court of Session, Charles Hope: with the generous, choleric Hope, he had long been, and continued to be, publicly friendly, but there is reason to think, as we have seen, that he had reservations about him of a kind that had to be withheld from the tribute accorded in the *Memorials*. Cockburn reasoned that the judge who heard the case in the first place should be heard by the appeal judges: 'The entire isolation of

[1] *Some Account of My Life and Writings* (2 vols, 1883), vol. I, p. 279.

the judge who tries from the Court that reviews, is incompatible with Trial by Jury.' William Adam, the retired Lord Chief Commissioner of the Jury Court and the man who had originally seen to the introduction of civil jury trial, took Cockburn's side and fought the battle from that point on. Cockburn later noted that Adam's victory 'has been complete'. A fair amount of heat appears to have been generated in the land of Avizandum—which is to say the Court of Session—and the episode affords a ripe example of Cockburn's pugnacity. It also affords the not unattractive spectacle of a judge publicly criticizing his fellows—or semi-publicly, since the pamphlet does not seem to have been made generally available.

Cockburn, then, was a somewhat controversial judge. And we have looked previously at the criticisms that were made at the time, and have been made again in recent years, of his work as a legislator. All this talk of his fits and starts and indolence, all these disparagements, some of which came from men who were his ideological enemies, should not be taken to mean that Cockburn was a worm. He and Jeffrey did a great deal to expose the defects and disgraces of the established legal and political system, even if they made mistakes when they set themselves to mend it. By virtue of their adversary roles, their contribution to the Reform Bill and the leadership they gave to the unrepresented and the unequivocally oppressed, they lent impetus to a process of adjustment which eventually brought a more satisfactory system: the same cannot be said of the great Henry Dundas, whom Cockburn's detractors at times admire. As we have seen, Cockburn played a pugnacious part in effecting various changes in the law, some of which certainly deserved to be made. His love-affair with juries was enhanced by the new arrangements in the civil and criminal fields, but there were good reasons of a public kind for him to argue as he did. The verdict on this ambitious lawyer would seem to be that his skills were those of a barrister and of a critic of the laws and courtroom practice of his society, and of the performance of its legal lights: as a legislator, and in the more abstruse and altogether less blissful regions of the law, he did no better than it would be safe to expect of a reformer.

There is one 'foreign lawyer' who resembles Cockburn, and who was indeed his remote kinsman. If we hadn't had perhaps a bit too much about doubles, it might have been tempting to claim a further instance here. Sir Alexander Cockburn, a small man, some twenty years younger, became Lord Chief Justice of England. This Cockburn was reckoned to be very much an advocate, and he made an excellent *nisi prius* judge. His reputation was that of a man liberal in his views and a little testy—a man of keen application, but not free from fits and starts. He was a close friend of Dickens, a valued critic of his public readings, and himself a raconteur. He successfully defended Daniel McNaghten, who murdered Peel's secretary: insanity was pleaded, and as a result of that trial the McNaghten rules were devised for the purpose of regulating the forensic approach to insanity—a subject on which, as his remarks at Huntly about his justified sinner make clear, Henry Cockburn's views were not of the soundest. I have not come across a syllable about the Lord Chief Justice anywhere in Cockburn's published or unpublished works. A strange omission. Nor is there anything about another kinsman of his from the Langton branch of the family, the admiral Sir George Cockburn, who captured the town of Washington in 1813 and escorted Napoleon to St Helena.

Cockburn's behaviour on the bench can be studied not only in the reports of his trials but in his own *Circuit Journeys*. This book contains reflections on 'Trades Unions and the guilt that is apt to adhere to combinations':[1] these reflections, recorded after the trial in Edinburgh of the Glasgow cotton-spinners in 1838, might suggest that his best work as a judge was done in an area to which the disparagers of his judicial career seem to have paid little attention. The Cotton-Spinners' Association, among whose antagonists was Sir Archibald Alison, had long been implicated in charges of murder, fire-raising and vitriol-throwing, and the trial in Edinburgh drew threatening crowds. In Glasgow, Cockburn tried a cotton-spinner of the time named Thomas Riddle, and he writes that his address from the bench, 'while it pointed out the criminality of violence', 'judicially acknowledged the innocence of mere combination, and thus removed the imputation that the Courts did not do justice to workmen'. Riddle was transported for breaking into the house of a fellow worker in order to force him to go on strike, and injuring a woman of the house. He was told by Cockburn in his address:

> The Indictment sets forth that you had struck work. But this is not your crime—it is not even a part of it. The law now entitles you, and every man, to strike work when he pleases. Your labour is your own, and you may sell it as you please. So may every other man, by law. Whether there be certain persons who won't let this law be acted on, we shall see immediately. The Indictment also states, that you struck in concert with a number of other Operative Cotton-Spinners. But this is no part of your crime either. The law not only allows every man to demand what wages he pleases, and to refuse working if he does not get them, but it allows him to arrange, and combine with others, in order that by concerted strikes they may make their joint demands more effectual. Masters may combine against workmen, and workmen against masters. By law, the market of labour, like that of capital, is free. Would that the workmen of this country had always shown themselves worthy of the recent removal of the old restrictions on the power of demanding what wages they chose, and of uniting to enforce this demand!

[1] *Circuit Journeys*, pp. 8, 9.

His crime was not combination but concussion. He had invaded the house of someone who was willing to take lower wages. Riddle enjoyed the liberty to sell his labour as he pleased, but he had tried to deny the same liberty to another.

> For this crime—and for its attendant circumstances—you are to be transported for seven years. If you think this punishment severe, this can only be because you choose to shut your eyes to the wickedness, and to the plain consequences, of what you and others have been doing. The labour of a poor man is his principal property; and he who robs him of this makes him a beggar. Yet there are masses of people who set themselves up as the dictators of the market of labour, and who have the audacity to band themselves together in defence of this tyranny. These persons not only abstain from working themselves—which the law leaves them at liberty to do—but they proclaim that nobody else shall work for less: and if their insolent mandate be disregarded, they enforce it by violence; and then declare themselves the friends of free trade. How anything so iniquitous and absurd should ever enter the minds of the educated people of Scotland, has always appeared to me incomprehensible.[1]

Trade unionism has been in various ways concussive from the beginning. Cockburn's judgment could hardly have been expected to acknowledge that concussion had been necessary, and few people would now say that his judgment was unambiguously favourable to working-class interests. Nevertheless, it firmly supported mere combination at a time when this still needed supporting, though it had, in fact, been legally recognized in Britain since 1824.

When they were the King's Ministers, Cockburn and Jeffrey put down 'an alarming confederacy' of calico printers, as Cockburn terms it in his notes to the Jeffrey letters.[2] The calico printers were attempting to 'controul their masters, and their fellow workmen', and the military were called in. The military had been called in in Baron Cockburn's day too, but this was a different case: this contained sedition of opinion. John MacFarlane—designated 'apostolic' in the *Memorials* despite his German tastes—published a letter of advice to the calico printers, which Jeffrey mentions, and Cockburn's notes have this to say about its author:

> John MacFarlane of Kirkton, a retired advocate. A remarkable person; who wrote several admirable short addresses to the working classes—*most admirable*! The one here referred to was on Trades unions and strikes. He is a strong Whig, all his life devoted to the people, yet firm against their injustice; deeply pious, and a strict observer of the Sabbath, yet resolute against all compulsory respect to it. His style was as plain and clear as Cobbett's, his thoughts as human and enlightened as Fénelon's.

[1] *Report of the Trial of Thomas Hunter, Peter Hacket, Richard McNeil, James Gibb and William McLean* by Archibald Swinton (1838), p. 30. Riddle's trial followed this one.
[2] JLC: Cockburn's notes to Jeffrey's letters of 6 and 18 February 1834.
9*

Here is another exquisite portrait of a Scottish Whig. This is the kind of Whig that Cockburn was himself: he was, by temperament, an 'addresser of the lower orders', as the *Journal* describes the activity, as well as an up-braider of his fellow Lords of Session. And the style he praises here is like his own. (It is evident that, for Cockburn, there were two Cobbetts: one plain and clear, and the other contemptible.) There's a certain subdued Braxfieldian heat in the notes at this point which is suitably absent from his pronouncements from the bench on the same subject, which belong to the same period of his life, and we can be sure that this was a subject on which, in private, he was not always judicially calm.

On the bench, Braxfield not only made his political sentiments plain: he also made them law, by the exercise of his own native vigour. Cockburn did not make his political sentiments law, but he was willing to disclose them on the bench. Some men were tried in 1837, the year before the cotton-spinners' trial, for rioting at Hawick during the elections to the Reformed Parliament which were held at the accession of Victoria. 'I do not know if there are many people who have a stronger sympathy than I have, with the formation and expression of popular political opinion,' said Cockburn. 'But it is just because I am a friend to popular election, and grateful for the possession of the existing law, that I must, even independently of the place where I sit, be a determined enemy to all election violence.'[1] The *'vis medicatrix* of reform[2]—a phrase of Cockburn's from another context—should not be tainted by the kind of thing that happened at Hawick. Whether it was stage-managed in the style of the English hustings, or more a piece of Border horseplay, this was classifiable as Whig violence, which was then given to using the name of the Queen and to proclaiming its loyalty, and a Whig Minister, Lord Minto, was present during the poll, when eleven electors were seized and stripped, and three of them made to run naked through the town. The one-time Reformer Sir James Graham, who had defected to Peel and who appears to have been preoccupied with worries about a riotous working class, was shocked by these symptoms of a *vis populi* in Roxburgh-shire. This was the mobbish county which, six years before, had threatened to burke Sir Walter.

The *Circuit Journeys* also contain reflections on crime and punishment which reveal traces of the 'ruggedness' he disapproved of in the excoriated Braxfield. There is a gallows humour, and a taste for dooms and misde-meanours, which might indicate that he had acquired certain of the less culpable attributes of the ogres of his youth. One of his murderers asked:

[1] *Report of the Trial of Cairns, Turnbull, Smith and Lamb* by Archibald Swinton (1838), p. 38.
[2] *Sedition Trials*, vol. I, p. 36.

'If they hang me, what will they do wi' ma claes?' At this mention of his clothes, there was 'some horror and a little mirth' in court.[1] This is the kind of incident by which Archie Weir would have been moved—as he was moved by Duncan Jopp's sore throat. Cockburn is less compunctious.

He tells (twice—in the *Circuit Journeys* and more sedately in the *Journal*) the story of Mrs Mackinnon, who kept a brothel and was hanged for murder, but was for all that, it seems, a woman of the better sort. She was defended by Jeffrey and himself. On the gallows she ate one half of an orange, the other half of which was eaten, at the same time, by her 'only earthly friend', an English Jew, 'who looked like a gentleman, on the outside at least'. She died cheered by this ceremony, and left all her money to her only earthly friend. 'He took the legacy, *but refused to pay the costs of her defence*, which her agent only screwed out of him by an action.'[2]

Cockburn robustly believed in capital punishment, and elsewhere in the *Circuit Journeys* he remarks that 'the suppression of the gallows deprives modern Courts of half their charm'.[3] He has in mind the falling into disuse of capital punishment for cases of theft (the last such execution occurred in 1833, though the law was not changed till 1877): this had flooded the courts with boring and inglorious habitual offenders. Heiton even credits him with answering petitioners on behalf of an old man he'd sentenced to death for murder with the words (which certainly sound in character): 'It is better to be hanged at 81 than at 18.'[4] A reminder, this, of his unfilial or irreverent vein: but there is no need to suspect a phobia about old men, and it is as well to remember his concern for Neil Douglas. It is as well to remember, too, that there is nothing very strange about this ruggedness. I think we can understand and live with a certain roughness and concussiveness in lawyers and doctors: he delivered a vast number of sentences in his time, and he belonged, as Braxfield did, to an age in which you could be transported for stealing an overcoat. Cockburn transported a man at Dumfries for that very offence, and thought it a small matter.

The murderer who was worried about his clothes was Cockburn's last case. When it was over, he walked down to the seashore at the bay of Ayr, a beautiful and peaceful scene. He was 75. This old man watched the white-skinned boys bathing. Anglers dozed. 'They caught nothing, and said that they would not till it should rain, which it had not done for six weeks. So the very fishes were at rest too.'[5] The next day he fell ill. Soon he would be at rest himself.

The law meant much to Cockburn. But certain other things mattered no

---

[1] *Circuit Journeys*, p. 404.  [2] Ibid., pp. 339-41.  [3] Ibid., p. 222.
[4] *The Castes of Edinburgh*, p. 54.  [5] *Circuit Journeys*, pp. 404, 405.

less—literature, his friends and family, his hills. A few months before he died, he wrote a letter,[1] from his new town house in Manor Place, to Mrs Trotter of Dreghorn, near the Parnassian Pentlands. Mrs Trotter was the granddaughter of Henry Dundas, was married to the son of Alexander Trotter, who had played a part in the financial transactions which caused Dundas's impeachment, and was related by marriage to a Coutts Trotter (which was also her son's name) who had played a part in opposing the Reform Bill: it would not have been easy for Cockburn to forget the past even if he had wanted to. Cockburn tells her, with reference to Lord Fullerton's finances, that the 'public imputation' of imprudence 'is very bitter to be obliged to submit to', and he also tells her: 'I never see the Pentlands now nearer than from this street.' He may have felt that it was time to die.

[1] 13 December 1853.

# Chapter Fourteen

## *Kirk and Country*

'Set not thy trust in parsons,' wrote Cockburn once to Rutherfurd.[1] He was quite prepared to criticize the Kirk and the cloth, and he was not the type to suffer gladly the bletheraciousness of the Lord's anointed. His published works show a certain reserve on such subjects, however, and his sharpest words appear in a manuscript letter of 28 July 1853 to an unknown recipient. The letter is in the nature of a blackball. One of his 'lengthy bores' ought to be banned from a club for being a lengthy bore: the club seems to have been the Academical Club, to which former pupils of Edinburgh Academy belonged—the University's Academical Society was long since defunct. 'Let me advise you to set a black mark at the name of that Reverend ass the minister of Muiravonside, with a view to his perpetual exclusion from our future Academic symposia. That conceited blockhead would have gone on preaching all night if we had not taken up our hats, and shown him that he would soon be left to be his own congregation. Horrid beast.'[2]

Was Cockburn a believing Christian? Would he have passed the tests imposed by any of the orthodoxies? His rather lordly attitude towards ministers, his impatience with their long-windedness, and his impatience with a concussive attitude towards the Sabbath, do not mean that he was a pagan. The pantheism expressed in his worship of the Pentlands does not mean this either (though 'paradise' is not a word that quite belongs to the vocabulary of Presbyterianism, and his millennium was not like the kind spoken of by Evangelicals). It would not do to read an enormous amount into an early letter to Richardson in which he says of an encounter with his brother-in-law, a Presbyterian minister: 'Dined with Dr Davidson who deplored that I had given up even my religious *profession*.'[3] But it is impossible to mistake the importance of a letter of 17 March 1846 to John Hill

---

[1] 24 June 1839.    [2] Signet Library MSS.
[3] *Some Letters of Lord Cockburn*, p. 9. On paper watermarked 1806.

Burton, author of a life of David Hume, the philosopher. Cockburn was
reluctant, when asked, to eulogize David Hume the lawyer, in a public
speech, though his tact proved equal to the occasion. But he was not reluctant to eulogize the lawyer's uncle. In this letter, he writes: 'The humane
purity of David's life, and the almost divine tranquillity of his death, have
done more in favour of true religion, than all that his speculative doubts
have ever done against it. The real question is, whether, *religion and his
speculations being properly understood*, these two be at all inconsistant.' An
epitaph is quoted:

> Within this circular idea,
> Called commonly a tomb,
> Th'impressions and ideas lie,
> That constituted Hume.

No one who could suggest that Hume's impressions and ideas might be a
service to religion was likely to sit entirely at ease in a Presbyterian pew, and
he may well have been, for a while, in the first flush of the rebelliousness of
his youth, a renegade from the faith of his fathers. Nevertheless, he seems to
have believed in a true religion, with a personal God—a God who walked
and could be worshipped on the Pentland Hills. This, perhaps, was the God
whom he asked, in his last testament, at the time of his worst trials, to bless
his family.

Not many months after his giving up his religious profession had been
deplored at dinner, he dispatched a letter to Grahame in Bath which was
unquestionably devout, though we may wish to make some small allowances
for an element of encouraging courtesy extended to a gloomy friend who
had given up the legal profession: Grahame had once patrolled the now
reconditioned Outer House.[1] 'Having betaken yourself to the Gospel, I
presume you have no interest in the Law, and therefore I need recall to your
quiet, perfumed parish the din and odour of the outer house. The ghosts
that flit or solemnly stalk along it are in every respect as they were—the
building, inside and out, is so completely changed that you would not know
it. No improvement has taken place which ought to make you regret having
bidden it adieu; or wish that your feet, instead of reposing on the hearths of
the simple and the pious, should struggle to maintain a hard-earned, precarious and not more honourable place, which a peculiar disposition only
can render valuable once it is got.' Cockburn warms to his theme: 'The
contrast is strange between a hard blackiron lawyer—if not a bachelor,

[1] 18 September 1809.

wedded to his cook—advanced at the age of 70 to a bench which has only the advantage of making his income less and his dotage more visible—and at last dying, with no question asked but who is to succeed him?—and a clergyman whose life has been passed among occupations and people to which he has all along been connected by no tie but that of religion—a relation which strengthens while every other decays—and at last consigns his bones to the hallowed respect that becomes the death-given exaltation of his Soul.' Perhaps this is the voice of his true religion. And on this occasion parsons are taken very seriously, with no more than a passing hint of irreverence.

He was also interested—though not speculatively, and well this side of idolatry and insanity—in the religion of his country, which was probably another thing again. He cared about the traditional Presbyterian pieties. At the same time, he cared about toleration, and religious bigotry could produce some of his most memorable revulsions. The *Journal*'s account of the oratories and strategies that led to the Disruption enabled him to say what he wanted to say, publicly and memorially, about religion and the state. The Disruption was both parricidal and respectful: it was something old and something new, representing both the past and the abolition of the past. As I have said before, this must have appealed to an aggressive and compunctious nature. It was not something which needed to be discussed in terms of competing theologies. During the years that precede the Disruption, the Court of Session is sometimes seen by Cockburn to assert a rightful claim in respect of temporalities, patronage being the law of the land and an aspect of property, manses and livings being, in that sense, the Court's business: but it is also seen to overreach itself.

While still an advocate, in 1821, he had acted against the prerogatives asserted by the Kirk in the field of education when he befriended a Schoolmasters' Committee, composed of parochial teachers, who were pressing (in vain) for higher salaries to be met out of national taxes. He gave it as his opinion that, in law, the right of the local presbytery to dismiss a dominie was an extremely restricted one. The dominies wanted, and got, greater security of tenure in relation to presbyteries, and the Court of Session was to assert for itself a right of redress in respect of failure to comply with the law. The Kirk and the Court were rivals once more, as they had been in the past over the control of parish funds. Cockburn was concerned, and felt that his own dominies were insufficiently concerned, about intellectual standards in schools: he felt that the dominies had weakened their case by failing to keep abreast of educational advances from which the private schools had profited. He did not feel that the oversight forthcoming from presbyteries could ever effectively guarantee that due standards would be maintained:

and later in life he thought it tyrannous to insist that state subvention should only go to schools connected with the Established Church. The affair of the schoolmasters' claims, which ran its course in the 1820s,[1] was not calculated to produce a major struggle between the Kirk and the Court. But such a struggle eventually came, as a result of the long exposure of the institution of patronage to demands for 'popular election' in the kirks. As Cockburn recognized, these demands were, broadly speaking, democratic in character.

While knowing it to be 'unpopular', Cockburn can at times appear to favour patronage, as did those English Whigs in Ministerial office who were forced to think about the affairs of the Venerable. In the years before the Reform Bill, however, many Scotsmen considered it a worse evil than the general political subjection of which it formed part, and many country people were prepared to support Parliamentary Reform in the hope that democracy in the kirks would follow. It might be assumed, therefore, that Cockburn's capacity to pick and choose in this way among the main reforming initiatives—a wider franchise, more and fairer juries, an elected clergy— and to bring a lesser pugnacity to the last of these, is a further example of his gift for the reconciliation of contrasting views. But as a Lord of Session, with a vote, he sided with the Kirk in its contentions with the Justiciary on this issue. He was in two minds about patronage, but he may be said to have made them up, though he did not do so without hesitations and second thoughts.

At one point, the *Journal* offers a plain enough statement of his attitude towards the 'intrusion' of ministers, though it is necessary to add that the opinions expressed, for the 1830s, in the notes to his volumes of Jeffrey's letters are rather more ardently anti-intrusionist, and indicate, indeed, an important complicity between himself and Moncreiff, as judges, on the one hand, and Chalmers, the leader of the Wild, on the other. A *Journal* entry for 1840[2] mentions his dislike of the Evangelical 'wildness of the dominant Church', but speaks of persons, 'among whom I place Jeffrey and myself, whom it is rather odd to find on the Church's side, because these persons are no devotees of ecclesiastical establishments, and are thoroughly aware of the offensive errors of our present Church, and for their own tastes would prefer patronage to popular election; but then, though there would probably be no Established Church in our Utopia, it seems to us to be little short of lunacy to try to pull down the one we have got in Scotland; and though patronage may not be so unpalatable to our taste as any substitute for it, yet perhaps their whole history shows that it is nauseous to the taste of Scotch-men, and we can see no right that we have to compel the people to receive

---

[1] It is dealt with in Saunders's *Scottish Democracy*, pp. 283–87.          [2] *J* I, pp. 254, 255.

the thing that of all others they and their fathers have particularly abhorred.' 'Nauseous' had been, in earlier days, a distinctively Presbyterian word, as 'savoury' had once been. Popular election in the kirks had long been savoury to the devout Scots fathers by whom the religion of the country was transmitted: Cockburn was therefore prepared to set his preferences aside.

The 'Ten Years' Conflict', as it was called, which came to a climax in the Disruption may be dated from the passing of the Catholic Emancipation Act of 1829. Fearing political pressure on behalf of an established Catholic Church in Ireland, numerous Dissenters argued for the disestablishment of the Scottish Church: this was Voluntaryism, a position which placed the Evangelicals in a quandary, and which causes the *Journal* to cry: 'A plague on both your Houses!' The bitterest episodes in the Disruption quarrel were often between the Voluntaries and the Evangelicals, who could not afford to be outdone in their opposition to Erastianism and intrusion. Neither the Wild party in the Scottish Church nor the eventual Free Church was in favour of disestablishment. Early in the 1830s, the Wild party managed, in the General Assembly, to pass the Veto Act, which allowed the absolute rejection of a presentee to a living on the basis of objections, without reasons, from a majority of male heads of families, and the Chapel Act, which allowed the ministers of chapels of ease (or *quoad sacra* or extension churches) to sit in church courts. Such chapels were outwith the patronage system, were free from the kind of property considerations which affected the kirks, and were an attempt to tackle the problem of those areas of population growth where Established ministers were scarce, and where their Dissenting rivals had built up a damaging predominance. Both the Veto Act, which showed signs of working quite well in the parishes, and the Chapel Act were nauseous to the Moderates and intrusionists in the General Assembly, and the Moderate leader John Hope—the screaming, sweating and gesticulating 'high-pressure' Dean of the Faculty of Advocates, as the *Journal* depicts him, whose authority lost nothing by the fact that his father, Charles Hope, was President of the Court of Session—arranged for test cases in order to defeat the church ordinances in law. These test cases helped to produce, in the years that followed, a series of *causes célèbres*.

The first was Auchterarder in 1834, where a rejected presentee tried to get the presbytery's decision reversed by means of an action before the Court of Session. The Auchterarder case was really two cases: the first resulted in the Court's finding the Veto Act illegal on the grounds that it infringed a patron's civil rights; in the second case, the Court said it could control a presbytery in respect of an illegal refusal, on the presbytery's part, to act ecclesiastically. 'Saint Andrew' Rutherfurd defended the presbytery which had been complained of: 'When I say that the Church of Scotland is dependent on the State, I do not mean to speak of the Church of Scotland in a spiritual sense, as forming part of that universal Church which consists of all the elect in every age and climate, and under all denominations. . . .'[1] Auchterarder trailed on till 1838: by the end of it the Court of Session had affirmed that the Church of Scotland was subject to statute, and had no powers save those conferred by Act of Parliament. Taking the people's side, Cockburn voted with the minority of five judges, who included Jeffrey and Moncreiff. The Voluntaries were amply satisfied with the outcome, since they, too, were capable of desiring a plague on both houses, and the Evangelicals mustered their strength to ward off from the Church the assaults of the state. Meanwhile, in 1837, the case of Marnoch in Strathbogie had begun. A minister who had been vetoed objected to a second candidate put forward by the patron, and the objection was sustained by the Court of Session. A majority of the presbytery, seven ministers in all, accepted the Court of Session ruling. The General Assembly suspended the Strathbogie seven, and the Court interdicted the proclamation of the suspension in the presbytery. Again Cockburn voted with the minority of the judges. At one point the House of Lords declared the Veto Act illegal.

The Lethendy case, in which a vetoed presentee obtained a Court of Session decree preventing the induction of a second candidate, was decided in 1839. Here Cockburn voted with the majority. A *Journal* entry[2] says that he had changed his mind about the Auchterarder verdict, and now held that both in that and the Lethendy case there was 'sufficient civil matter involved' to justify the Court's intervention on behalf of the rejected presentee. A footnote to the entry, however, indicates that he had second thoughts about this opinion four years later, at the time of the Stewarton case. And the entry itself goes on to remark that the Court's Lethendy judgment is a 'deep cut into the nervous system of the Church; for if we can order a presbytery not to induct, I don't see how we have not power to bid it induct, and after this where is the peculiar power of the Church; especially if this authority of ours be connected with Brougham's opinion in the Lords, the doctrine of which (shallow and presumptuous though his speech be) was, when I stated it in my Lethendy opinion, adopted by all the Judges who had formed the majority in Auchterarder. This doctrine is—that except in deciding on the presentee's orthodoxy, morals, and learning, and in performing the strictly spiritual act of ordaining, the Church has *no power whatever*; and in particu-

[1] *The Lord Advocates of Scotland: Second Series* (1914), p. 55. Rutherfurd may have been alluding to Milton's words about the elect in the *De Doctrina Christiana* (Book One, Chapter 24), discovered and translated a few years before.

[2] *J* 1, pp. 227–9.

lar that intrusion and unfitness for the particular parish were things with which the Church had nothing to do.' Cockburn did not want the power of the Church to be taken away: and yet he concurred in the Lethendy judgment. He did not think much of Brougham's doctrine: and yet he cited it in his Lethendy opinion.

Early in 1843 came the Stewarton case, which concerned the creation of a *quoad sacra* parish for the benefit of some Seceders who wished to rejoin the Church: this was opposed by the local heritors. With Cockburn and four other judges dissenting, the Court ruled that it was entitled to control the Church in ecclesiastical matters, and the Chapel Act was pronounced *ultra vires*. In 1843, the expoundings of the minority on the bench (Cockburn, Jeffrey, Moncreiff, Fullerton and Ivory) were published in a book called *The Law of the Land regarding the Independent Jurisdiction of the Church of Scotland*. Cockburn found that the presbytery had acted legally, and that, even if it had not, the Court had no jurisdiction to control it, or to correct its mistake, in the way that was sought: the Church was entitled to set up its Chapel of Ease, and he saw very little civil matter in its actions. He also held that the Court of Session had no ecclesiastical jurisdiction, and no authority, so to speak, to make a new Church of Scotland. Having previously thought the Court right to interfere in the Lethendy case, he had now changed his mind, and was convinced that he had expressed himself much too strongly.

The Stewarton judgment was discussed by Cockburn in his *Journal* on 26 January: the Court had 'again maimed the Church by another most effective slash'. This cut was to prove, in a sense, the *coup de grâce*. The Church of Scotland was to be disqualified from taking essential steps to protect its own interests in relation to the rival Churches, and chapel ministers would no longer have full ministerial status. With the exclusion of the *quoad sacra* representation, the Evangelicals would no longer be dominant in the General Assembly. When this was recognized, the Disruption took place. On 18 May some two hundred ministers and elders, almost the whole of the left side of the house, quit the General Assembly, and walked in procession down the hill to Hanover Street and the New Town, and down again to the asylum of a hall hired in Canonmills. Onward Christian soldiers. Downward rebel angels. But if these were mutineers, they did not think of themselves as such. Here, on the march, was the true Church.

Some time before, the Assembly had denounced patronage, Parliament and the Court of Session in the Claim of Right, which asserted the authority of the Kirk over the Court, not merely *quoad spiritualia*, but in respect of its property also. After the Disruption, patronage was not long in dying, though it was a matter of decades before the Kirk felt able to bury it.

During these contentions, the Whigs showed neither the energy nor the ingenuity which might have assisted a settlement. As for the Tories, their appeal was not enhanced by the Ten Years' Conflict either, nor by the disposition of landowners to behave vindictively towards the outed ministers of the Free Church and their flocks. The Free Church was refused ground for its churches—not entirely to its displeasure, it might appear—and Cockburn writes:

> In some places, where whole parishes are the property of one man, and he a tyrant, the people, denied a spot of ground even to stand upon, and not allowed to obstruct the high road, have been obliged to assemble for the worship of God in the way that their consciences approve of on the sea-shore, between low and high water-mark. Modern Scotland has exhibited no such examples of the extent to which persecution would be carried if not prevented by law, and this even by otherwise amiable men.[1]

These amiable men fostered a Free Church electorate which voted solidly for the Liberals for the next forty years, and put the Tories out of the running in many parts of Scotland.

In wielding the flaming sword of the state which drove the ministers from their paradise, Cockburn sympathized with their rebellion, though he did not do so completely or consistently, retaining a certain partiality for intrusion. And the reasons why he took this line may have had more to do with patriotism than with piety. The 'Scotticism' of the secession appealed deeply to Cockburn and Jeffrey. There is a telling passage in the *Journal*[2] about the lamentations of the women of Portmoak, who protested to the presbytery of Kirkcaldy about the minister intruded on these 'few defenceless sheep': 'We weep in secret at the prospect of being forced to leave this sacred edifice, in which we and our fathers have worshipped God and shown forth the Lord's death with great delight; yea, her very dust to us is dear.' While it may have some of the pleader's unctuousness poured out by the younger Cockburn (the tears in question were scarcely secret), the eloquence of the women of Portmoak is moving, and Cockburn was undoubtedly moved by it. 'These things may be sneered at, but no one who knows this country can be ignorant that these views and feelings, and even the phrases, constitute the very soul of Scotch Presbytery.' Cockburn's piety did not sneer at, and was not remote from, the piety of Portmoak, and there are times when his piety can look very like patriotism.

His piety deserves to be included among his dreams. For him, Presby-

---

[1] *J* II, pp. 48, 49.
[2] *J* II, p. 75. The year is 1844. These women have not yet left the Established Church, but their language is that of Evangelicals. The 'remonstrance', as Cockburn calls it, has in it both supplication and secession.

terianism was romantic. It was romantic because, in his eyes, it was very old, though he, or the 'progressive' in him, might have been privately relieved had he felt that it was dying, or that its current fanaticism would not last. It was romantic because it was Scottish. And it was romantic because it had proved mutinous and intransigent. These, I would say, are the reasons for his sympathy with the Disruption—a sympathy that might appear uncharacteristic or incongruous: another of the Cockburn anomalies. His tastes, after all, were Roman and rational. His main anomalies were to be a classical romantic and a patrician democrat or *aristocrat roturier*. And in neither capacity did he admire the faith of the Evangelicals, with their doctrines of grace and of exclusion from grace—despite his love for Sir Harry Moncreiff and his veneration of the towering, charitable Chalmers. Except in the realm of Reform, Cockburn was no Covenanter. And yet he was moved by the heirs and emulators of the Covenanters—of those whom the Enlightenment had regarded as the fanatics of old. The theocratic pretensions of old, to the extent that these were once more entertained, could not be countenanced by a judge: but he could not help marvelling at the spectacle of a kind of apostolic succession, and conceding the more sober of the contemporary claims. I do not think that he fully explains in the *Journal* why he sided with the departing ministers. But his explanation makes it clear that—to draw on the language he once used of Jeffrey's political conversion—his position can't be accounted for in terms of a conviction of the soundness of their opinions on religious matters. He praises them as men of honour and as patriots. It was the 'chivalry' of the Church which had left it.

The ardent patriotism which informs his awareness of the Disruption drama is in evidence everywhere in his works, and perhaps this patriotism should also be included among his dreams—in the sense that his works pay homage to a separate Scotland whose impairment he accepted as inevitable. The Corryvreckan of industrialization and large cities was exerting its pull throughout the fastnesses of the country, and there was a second Corry- vreckan which enjoined a conformity with the South: the advantages of a common market, and of belonging to an enterprising Great Britain, and the need for an improved political system to be achieved together with the South, were bound to injure and attenuate many of the Scottish singularities he loved, but these were forces which could not be denied. Scott feared that the future lay with an unscotched and democratic Scotland: Cockburn feared that a regenerate and enterprising Scotland, in which there was politics, commerce and a middle-class public, would mean an unscotched Scotland. The Scots tongue, he supposed, could not last much longer, and

Jeffrey's unnatural English dialect, scorned by Braxfield, might have seemed a portent of the accommodations and affectations that were in store. Braxfield was reputed to have said of Jeffrey's speech: 'The laddie has clean tint'—lost—'his Scotch, and found nae English'. But here Cockburn was wrong: the Scots tongue has survived being shed by this or that public man.

Cockburn felt himself to be, and was, Scottish, rather than British. And he went on speaking Scots till the end of his days. His children spoke it much less, if at all. It was partly his own fault, in the case of his sons, for sending them to Edinburgh Academy, where they were taught to forswear their native language. On 11 August 1844, he wrote in his *Journal*: 'English has made no encroachment on me; yet, though I speak more Scotch than English throughout the day, and read Burns aloud, and recommend him, I cannot get even my own children to do more than pick up a queer word of him here and there. Scotch has ceased to be the vernacular language of the upper classes.' The protesting vigour of his Scottishness, and his protective attitude towards his mother tongue, take on a Braxfieldian growl in a letter to a friend, John Marshall, written in the last few weeks of his life.[1] He is attacking the use of the word *Scots* rather than *Scotch* (still a point of honour in Scotland with the ignorant and the genteel): 'Scots is the affected pronunciation and spelling of a paltry, lisping, puppy Englishman. A *good* Caledonian calls himself a *Skotcchman*. Even the Suthrons don't call themselves *Englismen*. They keep their H, but won't give us ours!' Cockburn was a good Caledonian.

'Lockhart the Snake'—which was how he figured in the bestiary conferred on themselves by the *Blackwood's* writers—hissed that Cockburn could not write English. But he could. The English prose of this semi-English-speaker has none of the straining after correctness to be found in the productions of a number of the earlier literati, and none of the inarticulateness, caused by an all but medically detectable divorce of thought and feeling, which was predicated by certain devotees of the Scottish split mind. He writes what could be called a rational prose, but it is one which can treat points of law with feeling, and which can breathe life—his memorial and epistolary writings manage it better than his poems—into various dry doctrines including the Alisonian pathetic fallacy: nor is it some sort of genetic fallacy to suppose that in this respect, and in respect of its short, simple, souple, plain-spoken, elegant, injurious sentences, it is like the pithy prose of Evelyn Waugh, who is not held to suffer from any hereditary aphasia.

Correctness came naturally to Cockburn, as did many shades of tact. This is a poised, deliberate public utterance which keeps some of its secrets,

---

[1] 25 March 1854: Signet Library MSS.

and remains aloof—or aloft—from the reader. It is an eloquence that is almost taciturn, though its accumulated mass is formidable, threatening to efface a way of life, to demolish the towers of Troy. Yet it can also be vehement and mordant: 'The two most extraordinary revelations to the people of Edinburgh' in the second volume of Lockhart's biography of Scott were 'that John Irving had once a particle of literary taste, and that there was a time when Lady Scott was pretty and agreeable.'[1] This aside about Lady Scott says something about the life of Scott which can well be believed but which the biographies have been unable to admit. These are among the most outspoken words in nineteenth-century Scottish literature.

Cockburn's writings are hardly innocent of the desire to charm and to persuade, but they have none of the familiarity and cajoling that were reported to mark his style as an advocate, and his style as an annalist contrasts fiercely with the prose of Carlyle's *Reminiscences*. Carlyle delivers himself without reserve. He stands very close to the reader, plying him with intimacies and home truths, offering an interminable smoking syntax of admissions and disclosures. Confessions, rather than memorials. Entrails, indeed.

It is perhaps incongruous, and a concession to the times, as well as to his love of enjoyment and to his low view of lengthy bores, that he should have preferred the journal form for the later stages of what are, after all, Classical commentaries. Classical commentaries are not usually made up of impromptus, of 'things as they arose', of occasions that compelled an immediate response—not that the *Journal* is lacking in perspective or premeditation. At the time, 'memorials' was a conventional word for some form of record or report, for an act of commemoration, for a petition, and for an autobiography or biography which dealt in a dignified way with public events and personal achievements and with the building of a reputation: it also signified, in Scots law, a type of advocate's deposition or brief. With its Latin air and origin, it is a fitting word for what Cockburn wrote, although the title of his best-known book does not appear to have been this. Whereas the Romantic writers provided confessions, the Roman Cockburn, in his forbearance, provided memorials.

In doing so, he was conscious of Tacitus, I think, above all other Classical writers. The two have much in common, and there is a degree of temperamental affinity. The prose of both writers relies on a structural use of epigram. Both were well-connected public men (the father-in-law of Tacitus was the general Agricola), both were actors in their own dramas, and both resort to tact and taciturnity. Both of them go in for eulogies of the famous

---

[1] *J* I, p. 134.

dead and of famous relatives. For Roman reasons, then, Cockburn's autobiography is structured in terms of eulogy and epigram, and there is a
touch of the funeral oration of ancient days. There is also a touch, in its
sly jokes and professional anecdotes, of the immemorial lawyer's after-
dinner speech. Of all British historians, the one closest to Cockburn, in
respect of technique and in other respects besides, is Clarendon, whose
account of his rebellion—with its 'characters' of the vicious and virtuous
Cromwell and the rest—gained much from Tacitus and other Classical
models, and from the historian's participation in the events he is describing.
Clarendon's events and his have something in common, and were of a kind
that could inspire divided sympathies even on the part of those who were
by no means neutral. Cockburn, too, is writing about civil war—a civil war
of Whig and Tory, church and state, past and present.

Cockburn's eulogies are far from uniformly favourable, and there is a
structural use of insult to consider as well. But he does have a tendency to
over-praise, which produces, for instance, the discrepancy between the lark-
like, concupiscent Jeffrey of the manuscript letters and the statuesque
Jeffrey of the published works. When Jeffrey died, Cockburn completed
his eulogy of him in the *Journal* by granting that this 'gives no more idea
than a statue does of a living man'.[1] A second statue of Jeffrey was also
erected—this time in stone, and in the Outer House. Cockburn had wanted it
in the open air, but was out-voted by less sensible men. His own statue was
later to stand near that of his partner and second self (Richardson being his
second second self). There in the Outer House they remain, a pair of vertical
crusaders, David and Jonathan lauded in perpetuity.

The eulogy with which the *Journal* greets the death of Graham Speirs,
Sheriff of Midlothian and the Free Kirk's 'weightiest layman', is very divert-
ing. Speirs was 'sensible without what could be called talent'. Is there some
insinuation here, or has Speirs been inadvertently diminished? This can
scarcely be the left-handed compliment of a latent enemy. But it is not
altogether easy to decide whether Cockburn is being insidious, or merely
invidious, when he writes: 'I don't think I ever knew a layman (Lord
Moncreiff not excepted) to whom such religious authority attached in virtue
of mere solemnity of character and gravity of manner.'[2] Cockburn says that
Speirs was like one of Cromwell's colonels, but he ends up seeming more like
one of Muirfield's golfers. Eulogy is a treacherous art.

Cockburn's methods of composition, his fits and starts, seem to have
involved storing and copying favourite passages, and this led to some repeti-
tion in the published works, and to rival versions of the same passage. The

---

[1] *J* II, p. 255.  [2] *J* II, pp. 205, 206.

versions in the *Circuit Journeys* can be funnier and more outspoken than their counterparts. In the description there of the judges tippling on the bench, noses get 'a little redder', and Cockburn writes:

> The strong-headed ones stood it tolerably well. Bacchus had never an easy victory over Braxfield. But it told, plainly enough, upon the feeble or the twaddling, such as Eskgrove and Craig. Not that the ermine was absolutely intoxicated. But it was certainly very muzzy.[1]

These tenderly disrespectful sentences are sadly softened and abridged in the *Memorials*, which adduce a Latin dignity, and name no names. The *Memorials'* sheriff editors, concerned to prune Cockburn's insults and displays of pugnacity, would appear to have intervened here. This passage comes from the 'recollections of old circuits' which fill the entries in the *Circuit Journeys* for the autumn of 1847: when his money troubles were upon him, he turned —both in this book and in the *Journal*—towards the past.

There is no better evocation of Cockburn's Scottishness than Carlyle's. When John Wilson of *Blackwood's Magazine* died, Carlyle wrote in his journal:

> A few days later (Wednesday last) there died also at Edinburgh Lord Cockburn, a figure from my early years: Jeffrey's biographer and friend; in all respects the converse or contrast of Wilson—rustic Scotch sense, sincerity, and humour, all of the practical Scotch type, *versus* the *Neo-poetical* Wordsworthian, Coleridgean, extremely chaotic 'Church of the Future', if Calvary, Parnassus, and whisky punch can ever be supposed capable of growing into anything but a dungheap of the future or past. Cockburn, small, solid, and genuine, was by much the wholesomer product; a bright, cheery-voiced, hazel-eyed man; a Scotch dialect with plenty of good logic in it, and of practical sagacity. Veracious, too. A gentleman, I should say, and perfectly in the Scotch type, perhaps the very last of that peculiar species.[2]

The word 'Scotch' can never have occurred so frequently within the space of a single paragraph. Wholesome and homely, Cockburn is perceived as the very embodiment of the old Scots virtues of practical sagacity and the rest, and is contrasted with his opposite in the shape of one of the foremost of Edinburgh's metaphysical Tories. This portrait may be thought to supplement the definitive portrait of Cocky—the domestic, demotic, Doric Cockburn—which is given in his letter of 1833 to Dick Lauder. Cocky is not only his better half: he is also his homelier and more Scottish half.

Even when he was being Cockburn rather than Cocky, even when he was 'arrayed in solemn black', as he puts it in his letter of 1833, and when he

---

[1] *Circuit Journeys*, p. 328.

[2] The passage from the journal is quoted in *Thomas Carlyle: A History of his Life in London, 1834–1881* by J. A. Froude (2 vols, 1884), vol. II, p. 158.

was addressing himself in print to public themes, he was often homely as well as aloof. On solemn subjects, this homeliness became the 'practical sagacity' commended by Carlyle. His homeliness, like Scott's, seems to embody a response to the growth of trusting readerships and electorates: leaders had turned into pleaders, and pleasers, and used blandishments. Homeliness had become a Scottish quality, and these two members of the upper classes were respected for exhibiting it.

Scott's homeliness is caught in a story told in the *Circuit Journeys* about that twaddling judge, Lord Craig, a great fearer of the French Revolution, who was once muzzy enough to bare his sensibility to Scott and Cockburn. Craig was 'driven from the paradise of Barskimming where he had retreated for nature and romance, by looking out on a dewy morning and seeing the brute (as he called him) of a butcher killing a calf on the lawn. "Would not you have fled too, Mr Sheriff Scott?" "No, my Lord, I would have consoled myself by thinking of a good veal cutlet." ' Cockburn, who led a 'steadily muttonised life', is later able to cap the allusion to that veal cutlet with some sustained lyricism about a leg of mutton which 'left its savour on the palate, like the savour of a good deed on the heart'.[1]

Cockburn's relation to Scott—a matter to which any account of his life continually has to revert—was not the least ambiguous thing about him. Given that Scott, a lifelong friend of the Dundases, stood for an allegiance towards those whom Cockburn had originally offended, and that Scott could seriously be supposed to have died of the demise of their political hegemony, it is possible to imagine that here again, in being both like and unlike Scott, Cockburn was re-enacting early experiences of a cleft or equivocal character. It was chiefly, if not exclusively, on politics that they differed. They were, in fact, sufficiently friendly, and had enough in common, including some close friends (Scott attended the christening of John Richardson's son, Henry Cockburn Richardson), to revive the thought that there was much in Cockburn's life to complicate his political intent as this declared itself, popularly and philanthropically, in his youth. In middle age, his experience of Whig politics was, naturally enough, less hopeful and less conspiratorial than it was in the days when Richardson played his orphan's flute and wrote his democratic songs, and when there was talk of sudden change. And his days, too, as a zealous Pantheon Foxite were numbered—in the sense that, after the Reform Bill, he settled into sagacity, satisfied with what had been done and anxious for order. I have tried to convey that doubts concerning his earlier political intent may have been implicit in Cockburn's fits and feats of retrospect: these, at any rate, would certainly not have been dis-

[1] *Circuit Journeys*, pp. 54, 397.

pleasing to Scott. One way of looking at Cockburn's politics would be to say that they were amended or arrested by his patriotism and by his gentleman's dislike of the mob, and to the extent that this was so, or became so, it may appear that he was not entirely hostile to Scott even politically. What they chiefly shared was a love of the old Scotland, some degree of responsibility for its destruction, and some degree of responsibility for the Scotland that lay ahead.

On matters of literature and the arts, Scott and Cockburn often concurred. From opposite ends of the party spectrum, they coincided in the desire for a rural fief, complete with castellation: Bonaly is, after all, a feudal tower, distinctly baronial for a friend of the people. Evelyn Waugh writes that the 'pretty, sham castle' of Bonaly was built 'in emulation of' Abbotsford.[1] These were rather different havens or hermitages, but they have their resemblances: among them, the fact that each of these Gothic piles was a dangerous seduction which contributed to a financial disaster. Cockburn thought more highly of Scott's sense than he did of his genius, but he also thought that his sense was not infallible. Look at Abbotsford, he seems to say, and he did not like what he saw. Scott's greatly credited infallibility was indeed to leave him almost as forlorn as the Justified Sinner. But then Cockburn himself looked at Bonaly with something other than a sensible eye, and he gives no sign of regarding it as a risk or a seduction. For him, Bonaly was beyond sense (as Abbotsford was for Scott, perhaps), and his attitude to it was well on the far side of idolatry. Cockburn's Abbotsford is without the pretentiousness of Scott's country seat. Standing up straight and true and comparatively homely in the lee of the Pentlands, it is none the less emblematic of a loyalty on Cockburn's part, which is seldom otherwise confessed, to his feudal kindred. Part of his paradise was designed as their memorial.

If Scott and Cockburn were often domestic and homely, they were often the reverse. Cockburn was hardly less romantic than Scott on those occasions when it is right to think of him as romantic, and in this respect, I believe, his tastes were schooled by an awareness of Scott. Lord Craig's pursuit of nature and romance was far outdistanced by their own. This practical pair were keen on old buildings and old days, and on Highland landscapes—on the 'bothies, precipices, unchangeable natural features, adventure, and heather'[2] relished on Cockburn's circuit journeys. Generations of Scotsmen were to lift up their eyes unto the hills in the same way, and to pass into a sentimental dream of adventure and heather, as a refuge from the opposing Cockburn (and Whig) category of 'wealth and sense'. Wealth and sense took

[1] *A Little Learning*, p. 11.    [2] *Circuit Journeys*, p. 32.

notice of such pursuits, and there was tourism. During Cockburn's adult life it was flourishing, and indeed the rough Highlands were already becoming fashionable, and picturesque, when he was a boy. Eventually, too, homeliness became a sentimental dream, and something very different from sagacity.

Cockburn said that he could see Bannockburn in a latter-day Lochaber axe. The calotype pictures of a Bonaly balustrade, together with wraith-like Cockburns and retainers, appeal to the same faculty and offer premonitions of Balmoral: they began building that castle the year before his death. They also offer premonitions of Victoria, off to the hills on horseback in her borrowed tartans, attended by John Brown. Bonaly and Abbotsford heralded a thousand Highland hotels and hostels, and encouraged the Scottish-Baronial boom. Tourism, at first, was Gothic and Romantic. To those Boy Scouts who traverse the Pentlands in his firm footsteps Cockburn has bequeathed his long pole, and that long pole has also become a million golf clubs. I like to think that the Scottish tourist industry, and many of the country's recreations, owe their origin, in some measure, to Lord Cockburn's oedipal dreams.

# Chapter Fifteen

# *Objections to the Heavenly Whigs*

Carlyle mentioned the hazel eyes of Cockburn and Jeffrey in setting down his thoughts about them, while also mentioning that Jeffrey's were bright black. Lockhart reports that Cockburn's eyes were 'a rich clear brown', and this is confirmed in the portraits.[1] They were a shade of amber, rather like the stone tigereye; and he was also thought to have the eye of a hawk, as Dante's Caesar has in the *Inferno*. But the human eye is very much in the eye of the beholder, and it is tempting to take advantage of Carlyle's poetic licence and dream that Cockburn and Jeffrey gazed on the world with eyes of hazel, or of a true Pentland blue.

These small hazel-eyed millennial Whigs, and the heavenly city of their desire, are capable of arousing distrust. Carlyle seems to have thought that the Scotch reviewers were not profound enough, not German enough (though he did not think much of their quasi-German adversaries in Edinburgh). Some citizens seem to have felt that Cockburn was not boring enough. And it is possible to feel at times that he and his friends were self-satisfied and cocksure (that last word is as hard to resist as his nickname Cocky must have been—and it deserves to be pronounced 'co'sure', as in 'brochure'). Their contemporary Sir Archibald Alison felt this way about them.

Alison was a Tory historian who refused to worship the Dagon of Liberalism, and as Sheriff of Lanarkshire he was a stalwart queller of riots. For Cockburn in the *Journal*, Jeffrey was 'our sun'—that is to say, Edinburgh's sun—while Alison, elsewhere in the *Journal*, is 'the Sun of the West'. What we have here is a case of solar opposites, and Alison was of the opinion that the Scottish Whigs of this generation 'were too exclusive'. In a reverberating phrase, he speaks of their 'withering self-sufficiency.'[2]

[1] See p. 267, Carlyle's *Reminiscences*, pp. 313, 340, and *Peter's Letters*, vol. II, p. 67.
[2] *Some Account of My Life and Writings*, vol. I, pp. 126, 129.

Those readers now who would agree with Alison would wish to dwell, one may suppose, on the limits of the compassion to which Cockburn laid claim. They are likely to see in him a man who was happy because he was privileged and safe, and they might well take as their text—perhaps ignoring the irony to be found in it—the recipe for iced lemon punch which he sent to a friend just before his debts came to a crisis, and which contains this:

> The criterion of success is to have nothing sticking out in the broust. If there be a plain edge of sweetness, or of sourness, or of rumminess, quash it, and produce a vague, general homogeneity, a gentle harmony, a steady, mild, well-poised fusion of contrarieties, like the British Constitution—hit that, and you hit the thing. The general composition should resemble a calm temper, a soft sunset, a quiet conscience, a well-balanced, complete argument, an easy untroubled long vacation, a peaceful country holyday in the summer session, a gentle slumber under a roaracious sermon.
>
> And to any elements and rules must be added the exquisite tact, the delicate sensibility, the profound experience, of the Finished Punchifex Maximus. A rash, rough, ignorant and conceited hand may easily throw in the ingredients. A sow may mix, as a sow may drink. But it is not thus that the Poetry of Potation is to be produced. It is by nicety of hand, fine taste, deep thought, and long reflective practice. . . .
>
> Iced Punch is the final end of the West Indies. What pious eye can avoid seeing that it was for this product that islands of rum, of sugar, and of lemons, are scattered over the ocean. It is the chief use of each. 'Spirits are not finely touched, but to fine Issues.'[1]

The irony is certainly there: Cockburn is affecting an outrageous complacency. But the recipe reads like a piece of roguish twentieth-century advertising copy, and the closing quotation from *Measure for Measure* is perhaps the worst of it. Fancying the West Indies to be a cluster of uninhabited islands dedicated to pleasing the palates of the Edinburgh literati was all too near the knuckle: no doubt that made it all the more of a joke.

This objectionable passage does, however, have the interest of resembling a self-portrait of Cockburn at his most composed, at his most successful and serene. He can himself appear to be a well-poised fusion, a well-tempered brew, of contrarieties, and I have tried, in earlier chapters, to give the recipe for this harmonious condition, and to account for its sweetness and sourness. In doing so, I have been aware that, for some political people, this Cockburn will seem to be, like the British Constitution, a flowing bowl of hypocrisy, duplicity and complacent self-deception. For such people, it will seem a welcome coincidence that the Cockburn family should since have become famous for the manufacture of port—the drink of the merry dons and country gentlemen (as well as the working-class matriarchs) of a later time.

[1] From a letter to John Marshall of 22 July 1847: Signet Library MSS. The recipe is also given in *Some Letters of Lord Cockburn* ((pp. 58, 59), with the adjective 'roaracious' conspicuously absent.

If there *is* such a thing as a stealthy smugness, then Cockburn did not
have it, and in so far as this view of him may be taken to mean that he disguised—from himself or from others—his belief in hierarchies and élites,
and in birth and breeding, it is undoubtedly false. But there are other
objections, of a related kind, to Cockburn and his friends which may have
substance, and I shall suggest what I think they are.

It is possible to study Cockburn's portraits of his genial or irascible
panjandrums, the succession of omnipotent alcoholics and strolling sages,
among whom to be sensible without talent constituted distinction, and to find
them, at times, unwholesome and bizarre. It is possible to respond to these
paragons with the revulsion felt by Roquentin in Sartre's *La Nausée* when he
walks round a provincial art gallery studying the portraits of the megalo-
maniac French worthies.[1] Sartre writes, ironically: 'They were entitled to
everything: to life, to work, to wealth, to authority, to respect, and finally
to immortality.' Cockburn's worthies are 'entitled' to these things too, as we
have seen. They are 'entitled' to immortality, and his books have helped to
confer it. Bouville's 'affable' bourgeois élite is not very different from that of
Cockburn's Edinburgh: both places have their gentleman-like leaders. One
of the subjects of the portraits in *La Nausée* had, in his day, 'evoked memories
and told anecdotes, drawing an amusing and profound moral from each'.
There is more than a hint of Cockburn here, and of his subjects. 'This un-
pretentious savant put people at their ease straight away. If it hadn't been
for the spirituality of his gaze you would even have taken him for a very
ordinary man.' Homely Graham Speirs was like that.

Did Cockburn tell the truth about his paragons and panjandrums? Can
we believe his *de mortuis*? It would not be reasonable to expect the whole
truth from works which were, in part, a contribution to their greater glory,
and which were received by their successors, the panjandrums of a later
Pandemonium, the paragons of the law in later times, as a dimension of their
corporate self-esteem. And yet, as Carlyle observed, Cockburn was unquestionably veracious. Civic or legal history, in its more formal modes, is
never strong on candour as far as reputations are concerned, and such sources
do not seem to subject these episodes in Cockburn to all that much in the way
of corroboration or disproof. In the circumstances, it may be worth consulting John Heiton's Apocrypha, *The Castes of Edinburgh*, for further light on
the terrestrial city, overworld and underworld alike, which co-existed with
the heavenly city imagined by these Whigs.

Heiton is a hostile witness: hostile to several of those he remembers, and
to Cockburn in particular. He violates the secrecy which Cockburn had

---

[1] *La Nausée*, pp. 122–8.

preserved on the point by announcing that his Lordship was constantly in debt. He also claims that 'the laziness attributed to Cockburn was co-ordinate with a carelessness of obligation and a certain want of sympathy with the wants and feelings of those beyond his own fireside or circle of friendship.'[1] Cockburn was pugnacious enough, and, in due course, patriar-chal enough, and sufficient of a devoted friend and of a political partisan, for this to seem plausible. And yet the opposite was true of him too: he defied the fireside, after all, in response to a kind of *noblesse oblige*. His work as a Reformer can't be represented as careless of his obligations to those outside the circle of his family and friends, unless the circle is widened to include the community of wealth and sense beyond whom the franchise did not pass, and it might once have been represented as careless of his obligations to his family, as a fouling of his own solid nest. Here, as so often, the contrarieties in Cockburn produce a situation in which the opposite of the truth can also be seen to be true (it was Heiton who reported that he was no romantic). It may, of course, be that no elaborate explanations are called for in respect of Heiton's comment: it may simply have been Cockburn's success, his sceptical style and his antipathy to humbug which caused the censorious to pursue this particular line of gossip.

Heiton was a reckless anecdotalist of the sort that furnished a genre of Scottish writing in the nineteenth century. This genre, or an aspect of it, has been described as 'Anecdotal Biography',[2] and it is one which the *Memorials* served to encourage: Dean Ramsay's *Reminiscences* were its main adornment, and it appears to have lapsed into drivel and ended in the Kailyard. An un-confirmed Heiton story cannot unreservedly be believed. But much of what he says about Cockburn can in fact be confirmed, and it requires an effort of will to reject outright the story he tells about Cockburn's colleague of an older generation, the Whig lawyer and politician, John Clerk. It has, at the very least, a definite imaginative power, which can only with difficulty be distinguished from the brute force of probability.

An angry, ugly, humorous, gifted cripple, Clerk is a notable figure in the *Memorials*, as he was in the Edinburgh of his time. He was the son of John Clerk of Eldin, an eminent naval tactician, and he made his name at the bar as counsel for one of double-living Deacon Brodie's gang of burglars. According to Scott's *Letters on Demonology and Witchcraft*, an ancestor of his was among the first to decline to act as a commissioner for the trial of a witch, 'alleging, drily, that he did not feel himself warlock (that is, conjurer)

---

[1] *The Castes of Edinburgh*, p. 54.

[2] The phrase is used in the introductory material to *Kay's Edinburgh Portraits* by James Paterson, edited by James Maidment (1885). This is a book of engravings—which portray many of the Edinburgh worthies of Cockburn's early life—by the excellent John Kay.

sufficient to be a judge upon such an adjudication'.[1] Cockburn's Clerk was sufficient of a warlock to turn himself into a byword for eccentricity and rage. He was a not very competent Solicitor-General in the Whig Administration of 1806, an artist, and a collector of etchings and of cats. When, after his death, his pictures were being sold off at his house, the floor collapsed, injuring some of 'the principal people here', in Cockburn's phrase:[2] it may have seemed like a 'judgment'.

In his life of Jeffrey, Cockburn writes of Clerk: 'Honest, warm-hearted, generous, and simple, he was a steady friend, and of the most touching affection in all the domestic relations.'[3] But the *Journal* talks of his 'crazy fierceness', and a letter of December 1803, mentioned earlier, talks of his 'illiberal' and 'despicable celebrity' (a type of celebrity shared with Charles Hope). Heiton has this to say about the same man:

> One night he was interrupted in his studies by the rumbling entry of two Gilmerton carters. John turned up his gray eye, and as the men seemed inclined to hang about the door, he rose and hirpled up to them. 'My cart's broken, sir,' said one. 'My horse dee'd last nicht,' said the other. 'And what have I to do with that, ye bitches?' 'You're my faither, sir,' said one, taking his front-lock in his hand and bowing. 'You're my faither, sir,' said the other, with the same sign. 'And wha was your mither?' inquired John. 'Twa mithers, sir,' replied the men at once. 'Twa mithers?' responded John. 'Ay, sir, we're cousins, and you're our faither, ye ken.' John meditated grimly, and grinningly drew out his purse. 'Weel, there's five pounds; and never let me see your ugly mugs again.' 'If they're no bonnie, they're your ain,' returned one of the carters. 'Weel, ye bitch, that's worth another five pounds'; and John, with a grin, handed him the money.[4]

I have replaced Heiton's 'b—s' with 'bitches', a favourite expletive of the lawyers of Clerk's day and before.

This hirpling sage, it appears, was himself one of those Scotsmen who led a double life, and one of those many fathers who, in one way or another, have lacked consideration. Cockburn would probably have heard the rumour —the 'sough', as he might himself have put it—which supplied the material for Heiton's anecdotal skills on this occasion. But Cockburn's writings obey the general 'Wheesht!' of Edinburgh respectability on such matters. His *pudeur* would have suppressed any story of the warm-hearted Clerk which tended to assimilate his domestic relations to those of that latter-day collector of etchings who has also become a byword, and this kind of story was recorded less and less as the century went on. Yet the relationships exposed in Heiton's story persisted till recent years in Edinburgh and its

---

[1] *Letters on Demonology and Witchcraft* (Morley's Universal Library, 1898), p. 268.
[2] The phrase is from a note of Cockburn's in reference to a letter of Jeffrey's of 20 March 1833 (JLC).
[3] *Life of Jeffrey*, vol. I, p. 200.    [4] *The Castes of Edinburgh*, p. 57.

industrial and agricultural vicinity, and not just in its underworld, though they would rarely have been noticed except by those who knew the area well enough to be able to penetrate its secret life. I remember a story told in my own family of two miners who lived in their village near the Pentlands, and who had long been in the habit of drinking together. One day in the pub, the younger man said quietly to his companion: 'Ye'll be ma faither.'

In Cockburn's day, the civilization that had come to Scotland disowned such relationships. They were barbarous. 'The principal people here' and those whom he called, in the *Memorials*, 'the worthy of this place' were unwilling to mention them in public (and it must be remembered that these people *were* the public), though I imagine that, among themselves, the upper classes spoke about them fairly freely. Those well below the respectability line—the sizeable caste of bastards, carters, miners, whores and Helen MacDougals—are barely visible in the literature of that time except when they can be used as picturesque or Ramsayesque material, as an occasion for drollery or severity, or when a convulsion like the Burke and Hare trial flings them into the open.

Heiton's story reminds one that High Whigs could be as seigneurial as High Tories, and nothing that is known about this society leads one to doubt that its class divisions were sharp and sheer enough for a wealthy man to behave as Clerk was reputed to have done and still be considered warm-hearted. In the same way, it is a measure of the political bitterness which prevailed at the start of the nineteenth century that one man could threaten another with commercial ruin for party reasons, as happened at Peebles, and still be considered to have an 'amiable' disposition. And amiable land-owners could be tyrants enough to compel Free Church congregations to worship on the seashore. Social and political differences were very firmly entrenched, and permitted frequent recourse to a double standard. Here, perhaps, was the most common form of double life in Scotland, though it was not one that lent itself to Gothic theatricality. In the interests of respectability, at all events, amiability was repeatedly obliged to restrain itself.

Cockburn himself was as amiable as he was veracious. His veracity was not such that he was incapable of error or exaggeration: it meant that he had a strong desire for the truth and a nervous distaste for fraudulence and pretence. Equally, his amiability was consistent, not only with pugnacity and a love of insult—'the landlord here is a living dunghill'[1]—but with occasional, and on certain subjects systematic, harshness. His amiability was restricted by the conventions of his time and place to the extent, in particular, that he shared a class outlook which insisted on the protection

---

[1] At Beatock: *Circuit Journeys*, p. 57.

of wealth and property and which valued self-reliance and individual liberty. In the field of poor relief, the charity he argued for was tantamount to cruelty—given the condition of the working class during periods of unemployment, and the known accessibility of alternative arrangements. The shibboleths of his class were used as shillelaghs.

During his lifetime, the presence in the society of an increasing number of people able and anxious to be respectable appears to have generated an increased hostility towards the poor and towards inferiors, a hostility which was felt not only by the opponent of change but by the patrician people's friend, and even by the 'Felon's Friend', Francis Jeffrey.[1] Heiton's story may have been meant to make his reader smile or sneer at Clerk, at a seigneurial act by someone who had taken the people's side, if only notionally: but I don't believe that the story was meant to make his readers deplore a lack of human or parental feeling, though it may enable the modern reader to sympathize a little with the crime of parricide. It is more than likely that by the end of Cockburn's life, when Heiton was writing, what might once have seemed seigneurial in John Clerk (a grander, grosser example of the kind of 'ducal contempt' imputed to the Duke of Buccleuch in the *Memorials*' disquisition on the etiquette of toasts) had come to seem like common prudence: something any amiable or respectable person might have done, though embarrassing for a High Whig.

The *Memorials* is an optimistic book. The *Journal* is austere, and has less in the way of 'Cockiness'. It is acquainted with, and alive to, some of the developments that were to bring about the worst miseries of Scottish working-class life in the hundred years that followed Cockburn's death. A man named Bill Douglas has made two very impressive films, which will form part of a trilogy, about the miseries in question: *My Childhood* and *My Ain Folk*. These are the memorials of his own youth, at the time of the Second World War, in the mining village of Newcraighall, where Cockburn's paradise of Niddrie used to stand, and a mile or so from the mining village of Gilmerton, where the Richardsons were feuars, where John Clerk's carters came from, and where, quitting the foothills of the Pentlands at an early age, I grew up myself. It is only a few miles, too, from the great house of Arniston, where the Dundases lived, and from Melville Castle, where they also lived and where Scott spent many happy days.

Seen from near Newcraighall, at a point not far from where Scott experienced his ecstatic vision of the Pentlands, the bing or slag heap of

---

[1] *Reminiscences*, p. 313. Carlyle is speaking of Jeffrey's conduct as an advocate, not as a Lord Advocate: this, according to Carlyle, is what satirists might have called him. Satirists might have called the advocate Cockburn by the same name.

Gilmerton pit appears to provide these hills with a further peak, its surly slate-blue flanking their paradisal azure. The Gilmerton workings, now abandoned, are said to date back at least to the Reformation. Turning from these contrarieties, these ancient Scottish ups and downs, paradise and pit, asylum and pandemonium, you look towards the city and think of the tall structures—the stakes or sticks thrust down into the Edinburgh earth—by which the contentions I have been writing about are commemorated: Henry Dundas, stylites on his soaring stone column in St Andrew's Square in the New Town, Scott capsuled in his rocketing Gothic spire, with the two Tory mausoleums flanked by the rival Martyrs' Monument.

The shape of Duty, reflects Scott in his *Journal*,[1] is rectangular (though the concept is often female there—Mrs Duty). In Edinburgh, the shape of Duty is perpendicular. Both the Tories and the Grumbletonians, as Braxfield called the protesters of his time, were, in their different ways, dutiful, and powerful, and it is right that their respective memorials should stand up straight together in rectilinear rectitude, affirming a common cockiness. It is right, too, that Cockburn Street should climb romantically—convoluted, uterine—in the direction of the dark and dirty dens of the Old Town. This most literal of cities is also among the most metaphoric, being, more than most, a map of its own history. The appearance of the place, town and surrounding countryside alike, still enacts a variety of old conflicts. It still salutes the Grumbletonians and Gilmertonians of the past, together with their adversaries, the lords of the earth.

In the eighteenth century, the Lothian miners were, as the *Memorials* explain, hereditary slaves or serfs. They were heritable property. Children were bound to the pits by oaths of uncertain but unchallenged legality. While the law was changed during Cockburn's lifetime (thanks to Henry Dundas in 1799), the character of these communities changed very little. Lived in, according to Cockburn, by 'black scoundrels', 'hereditary blackguards' and 'underground gypsies', such villages belonged to the verges of society and were, in more senses than one, Midlothian's other underworld. The first of these insults refers to the arrival of miners in an unspoilt corner of Ayrshire. In the *Circuit Journeys* he finds them 'lying snoring, and, I presume, drunk, on many indignant knolls': it is like him to pity the knolls.[2] The other insults are from the *Memorials*.

James Grant writes in his *Old and New Edinburgh*: 'Gilmerton was long characterized simply as a village of colliers of a peculiarly degraded and brutal nature, as ferocious and unprincipled as a gang of desperadoes, who rendered all the adjacent roads unsafe after nightfall, and whose long

---

[1] *Journal of Sir Walter Scott*, p. 291.    [2] *Circuit Journeys*, p. 332.

career of atrocities culminated in the execution of two of them for a singularly brutal murder in 1831.'[1] When I was a boy, stories of this kind, of
carters' rapes and other crimes, were still being told. Such is the infernal
history of Gilmerton. The place must have looked quite familiar to Hogg's
Gil-Martin when he passed by it on the way to Dalkeith, in pursuit of his
sinner.

Scott wrote a ballad, set in Gilmerton, about a medieval crime which was
committed there, and for which no black scoundrel was to blame. A prefatory note of his tells the story on which 'The Gray Brother' is loosely
based,[2] and which was related to him by John Clerk's father, the naval
tactician, who 'taught the Genius of Britain to concentrate her thunders,
and to launch them against her foes with an unerring aim'. Scott also explains, no less characteristically, that 'the barony of Gilmerton belonged, of
yore, to a gentleman named Heron, who had one beautiful daughter.' This
daughter entered into a love-affair with the Abbot of nearby Newbattle.
Having found out about their 'guilty intercourse', says Scott, Heron caught
them at a tryst and burned them to death. The ballad looks at the summit
of Carnethy, and at 'Pentland's mountains blue', and it sings the praises of
Midlothian:

> Who knows not Melville's beechy grove,
>   And Roslin's rocky glen,
> Dalkeith, which all the virtues love,
>   And classic Hawthornden?

There is a second poem about Gilmerton. Out of the local sandstone
(the carters used to carry yellow sand, as well as coal), a blacksmith named
George Paterson carved an underground dwelling for himself in the 1720s.
There was a smithy and other apartments, and he lived there blissfully for
eleven years. This retreat, which still exists, was one of the wonders of
Midlothian, and judges would come and drink with him in his stone parlour.
Over the entrance were inscribed these lines, written by Alexander Pennicuik,
'the burgess-bard of Edinburgh':

> Upon the earth there's villany and woe,
> But happiness and I do dwell below;
> My hands hewed out this rock into a cell,
> Wherein from din of life I safely dwell:
> On Jacob's pillow nightly lies my head,

---

[1] *Cassell's Old and New Edinburgh* by James Grant (3 vols, 1880–3), vol. III, p. 346.
[2] *Minstrelsy of the Scottish Border* (1931 edition, edited by Thomas Henderson), p. 699.

My house when living and my grave when dead:
Inscribe upon it, when I'm dead and gone,
'I lived and died within my mother's womb.'[1]

There was a good deal in the Gilmerton of the time from which the orphan blacksmith did well to escape, and his feat was a subterranean equivalent of Cockburn's pastoral quest: this judge sought his mother's womb 800 feet above sea level, on Pentland's mountains blue.

The people in Bill Douglas's films are the descendants of the Lothian desperadoes of old. His two boys, Jamie and a cousin, are orphans. They are unhappy and poor, they live on bread and milk, and they would have been none the worse for an underground den. They are like the lad that loused the cravats, and their situation is like that of Clerk's carters, in that they appear to be illegitimate and have been abandoned by their fathers. *My Ain Folk* is a coldly ironic title: these are films about kinship in which kinship scarcely exists except as a succession of puzzles and threats like those met in nightmares or in nightmarish fairy-tales. Jamie's mother is in a mental home. His grandmother does what she can for him. Dressed in solemn black like some Sicilian widow, she sits out her last hours by the fire—gleanings from the bing—her only speech an incoherent grief, which is closer to 'the stifled moans of an animal suffocating' than to the eloquence of the women of Portmoak. That eloquence is absent from Newcraighall. Religion is absent too, though it is clear that the teachings of the past have helped to create a place which is virtually without play or pleasure. It is as if the love of enjoyment had died out in Scotland.

Douglas is keen to show what the most desperate lives were like in these communities in the 1940s. This was an especially bad time, as indeed was the preceding decade, though it was also a time when, in response to the war, social policies were devised which led to widespread improvements. It is true, moreover, that there is a certain sense of dedication to misfortune in the films. But I don't believe they are inaccurate. Such places, at their worst, had exactly this terminal grimness, relieved by feats of patience and submission (the bitter end of the old Scots sagacity—speechless now, its face turned to the wall), and of hostility and disparagement: vicious resentments break out in the house over a canary. The canary gives the orphans something to play with and to think about: it is a little bit of cultural life, as canaries could be in such places. But eventually it is killed. One of the boys finds a friend, his 'only earthly friend', in a German prisoner-of-war, and loses him when the war is over.

[1] *Cassell's Old and New Edinburgh*, vol. III, p. 345.

Here, in a corner of the Lothian coalfields, after decades of democracy and universal suffrage, was a different kind of pandemonium from Cockburn's, and a different kind of asylum—the doubtful safety of the mother's mental home—from the one he imagined. Cockburn's much more efficacious mental home, the Pentlands, might seem to belong, not only to another century and another class, but to another world. The hazel-eyed millennial Whigs cannot be held responsible for the continuing hardship and nullity of certain sectors of Scottish life, and we may be entitled to guess that the aftermath would have been worse still without the political momentum which they set going, however compunctiously or reluctantly. But the political attitudes of Cockburn's earlier days, and of the first Reformers in general, do not display a comprehension of the difficulties that lay in store, though they can be glimpsed in his terminal forebodings. And I think we are also entitled to say that, despite the powerful efforts that were made by medical men and others, Cockburn's Millennium was followed by the endemic diseases of bronchitis, tuberculosis and alcoholism, by some of the worst housing, and perhaps the worst teeth, in Europe, and by the Pandemonium of Newcraighall.

'Newcraighall' was the world of my mother's childhood and adolescence, and I got to know it myself when I was young. I remember thinking about it one evening as I sat by my mother's bed in another Edinburgh hospital. From here, too, the Pentlands could be seen. They rose up sudden and celestial, and seemed to be beside me, as Mont Blanc seemed to be beside Cockburn. Cockburn the Pentlandizer rose up before me too, and I thought of the city he lived in, and of what became of it. Newcraighall became of it. I don't offer my mother as an objection to Cockburn, or to the Scotland that succeeded him. But it did very little to make her happy, and it may be that one can say that the delight he took in the Edinburgh of his time, and the diligence with which he tried to improve it, deserved a better outcome.

The hospital is part of a medical complex, spread about the district, which includes an old people's home and a mental hospital. One building is a great shapeless baronial-gothic pile dating from the later years of the last century, and full of what I took to be twin wards and staircases and other bewildering duplications. A doctor told me—unless I dreamt it— that it was designed by a psychiatric patient in order to house members of the landed gentry. I have made it sound insupportably confessional in the Gothic mode, but it has, in fact, few terrors. Not far off there's a clinic named after Andrew Duncan, a distinguished doctor lauded, and laughed at, in the *Memorials*: 'He was the promoter and the president of more innocent and foolish clubs and societies than perhaps any man in the world, and the author of pamphlets, jokes, poems, and epitaphs, sufficient to stock the nation.' The truth is that the *Memorials* do not do justice to Duncan. He worked in the City Bedlam, where the poet Robert Fergusson died, and Fergusson's last sufferings made a deep impression on him. He argued for humanity in the treatment of the mentally ill, and established the first public lunatic asylum in Edinburgh at the start of the nineteenth century: he did so with the aid of Henry Erskine and, it seems, with funds derived from the forfeited Jacobite estates. The Bedlamites moved there, and this is where the medical complex now stands.

There has been no bright track of happiness, such as Cockburn and his subjects pursued, for my mother. Sometimes she could fall into a track of suspicions and resentments, and with old age and illness she had found it harder to escape from this. Her father sailed across the sea from Miletus, but she herself has scarcely stirred from Midlothian. The Depression of the early 'Thirties helped to break her marriage, and explains her politics, which could seem punitive and full of a sad animus (not unlike that attributed to the Whigs by the ailing Scott). I had never lived with her, and I had never done enough to help her: each of us had lacked consideration. Sitting by her bed, I admired her, and felt for her. Her angers can be exhilarating. She can seem sour in the style of one of Cockburn's termagants—such as Miss Menie Trotter, who dreamt that she went to heaven and was encompassed by thousands upon thousands of stark-naked children: 'That wad be a dreadfu' thing! for ye ken I ne'er could bide bairns a' my days!' My mother has never had the least taste of eminence or success, unlike Cockburn. But she had, and has kept, what Cockburn had: a fighting wit.

Later I went for a walk with her, and with a woman friend of hers from the hospital. We sat in the grounds drinking in the summer evening, which was almost as glorious as the best of those enjoyed at Bonaly—not far from where my mother used to live on the Lanark Road. Blackbirds came and went, and I heard myself foolishly saying that Macbeth might be expected in the corridors of so baronial a hospital. 'Banquo's more our line,' said the friend. And my mother said: 'We've got Napoleon.' I thought of those second-self emperors who march across the Plains of Troy, and of how, from his Rhenish rock, on his Continental tour, Cockburn had shouted 'Napoleon!' and other doubtful sentiments. Here in the hospital was a pugnacity like his, and a native vigour like his. Here, too, were comedy, and the courage that comedy can show.

Cockburn's Edinburgh was no paradise lost. But it has to be regarded as a place of the very greatest interest and appeal, even if we admit that the interest of his accounts is due to this magician of an observer, this Prospero, as well as to the objects of his pugnacious attention. Cockburn was the Emperor of Edinburgh—rather than China—in the scarcely trivial sense that no one can have taken more pleasure in it, or evoked it so well. Edinburgh, he explained in 1809[1] to the Bath-bound Grahame, is 'solitude in summer, and riott in winter'—he means the riot of social life, not the Canonmills kind: with 'the wise enjoying in growing rapture the views of the blue Firth, the well-placed hills, and the romantic town; and the unworthy, when the decent part of the family is in bed, hastening away to large literary stupid dinner-crammed parties at supper, talking about the review and Scott, and all saying in the morning that this life is nonsense, but all repeating it, till God in pity prolongs the days so much that candle light is absurd, and it is made fashionable to go to the country'.

On 2 April 1819, not long before he started on his commemorations of the past in the *Memorials*, he wrote from Bonaly to Mrs Richardson about the Edinburgh hinterland: 'The sun never descended more sweetly than he did two hours ago. I went up to Torphin hill and saw him casting his last splendour on all the western windows over the land, amidst the songs of two or three mavises who were perched on full-blown broom bushes. A number of people were prolonging their field labours by sowing long after six—the smoke, symptomatic of rural porridge, ascended from the low-laying Colington and various other villages—the first lambs were beginning to appear on the hills—it was so calm that the wheels of the solitary carts were heard on the Lanark road.' The Alpine sunset at Geneva which was in store can have meant no more to him. He is sad to think of the people of these glens and hills who are now gone, but the places where they once lived are dear to him because of the ghosts that walk there. His native town possessed a radiant past as well as a radiant present, and in that past lay Cockburn's peace.

The *Memorials* depict an age of ceremonies and hilarities and holidays, succeeded by a discussing age, in which the intellectual standards of the earlier Enlightenment were in some measure maintained, and in which a mounting desire to protest and make progress was allied to a fondness for monuments and to a quite Venetian fondness for processions. Both were drinking ages, and dining ages. In the days of his youth, the cognoscenti—or the literati, or the eaterati, as Ramsay of Ochtertyre entitled them—made merry in their boisterous Edinburgh Eden. This was, in certain respects, undoubtedly a state of bliss. The Flood of humanity had yet to cover the face of the earth. Politically, the people had yet to arise. The dinners of the literati were not yet troubled by the congested, cannibalistic world, the

---

[1] 18 September.

infinitely quarrelsome world, which he predicted in the sombreness of his
*Journal*. Young and old, however, he took part in the pleasures of the town,
entering his reservations, and his predictions, in his notebooks.

He suffered eventually from lumbago, but for the cold winds, coughs and
sore stomachs which afflicted his circle and which are not ignored in his
correspondence, he had a sovereign remedy: he believed that a man should
be mindful of his viscera and should be Bacchanalian at least once a week. A
letter of 1840[1] implies a partial explanation of the drinking habits of his
native land:

> The worst of Teetotalism is its cold. One freezes all night, even between eiderdown.
> An icicle in flannel is a type of me. Were it not for the glow at the heart, the blood
> would be solid.

He was clear that the potations of his set avoided excess, but Bonaly was a
paradise which required its ambrosias, though these did not include the
drowsy syrups, dull opiates and transmogrifying powders taken by his
Romantic contemporaries—and by Sir James Mackintosh. The paradise of
the opium-eater was not in favour there, and the heaviest opiate known to
Cockburn—when he was old and on circuit—seems to have been a copy of
the *Edinburgh Review*.

Wealth, sense and adventure are celebrated in his writings. He loved
enjoyment, and roses, primroses and hyacinths, and a flower new to Scotland, the dahlia. He hated greatcoats and umbrellas. He would career down
children's slides on the icy streets of the city, defying the police. But the
face that we see in the photographs is not that of a merry diner or a dilettante
or a frivolous dog or a Boy Scout: it is the face of his very darkest thoughts.

While he called himself a happy man, he had dark thoughts about the
'precariousness' of human life: it is a word he constantly uses. His need
to look for serenity and security and certainty may be felt to commemorate
not only the pleasures of childhood and the nursery but their terrors, too.
This is one of the ways in which this resolute public man with his Bacchanalian advice can make the reader think of the sick and sensitive Stevenson,
and the sick and sensitive Proust. As we have seen, the bright track of
happiness which he followed could lead down at times into the bitterest
shadows. Even the Whigs' great triumph of 1832 proved precarious,
Pyrrhic. By the end of his days the Whig Party was dead.

He lived at a time when a more sophisticated sense of the self, a new
self-consciousness, began to be communicated, and when, for the first time
in her history, Scotland began to experience a political life in which more

[1] To Mrs Rutherfurd, 14 May.

than a small number of special people took part, and in which the paternalism of 'philanthropy'—that at least—began to legislate on social matters. He responded and contributed to these developments, while remaining, in many respects, a man of the old world. He remained suspicious, for example, of new forms of state action. He did not quarrel with his society, which invested him with some of the 'old excessive Edinburgh Hero-worship' referred to in Carlyle's *Reminscences*.[1] There was nothing solitary or idiosyncratic about his dissenting politics earlier in his career: they were common enough—and he saved his solitariness for the Pentlands. He criticized his society, however, for all he was worth and for the whole of his life, and it can be said that many of the objects for which he worked do him honour. Contemptuous and compassionate, demure and frivolous, eminent and vagrant, an iconoclast who revered the past, to which, as to his hills, he turned for refuge, he was the kind of man without whom the best societies would never come about, and without whom they would die.

The old Scotland of heritors and their property, of superiors and vassals, patrons and pariahs, leaders and orphans, was changed by Cockburn and his friends. But it did not disappear. In September 1974, the Land Tenure Reform (Scotland) Act was passed, which proposed a method—based on a recourse to Government stock—whereby Scottish property-owners may redeem their holdings from the feu-duties payable by them, as vassals, to their superiors. It seems that escalating feu-duties on new houses are a problem. The practices in question have run for a thousand years, and by this and other means they are to be brought to an end. It is, the Lord Advocate has said, 'goodbye to the feudal system'. He may have spoken too soon, as his predecessor Jeffrey did when he addressed the House of Commons on Parliamentary Reform in 1831 and 'gloried in making the avowal that no shred or rag, no jot or tittle of the old system was to be left'.[2]

Cockburn's imagination dwelt on departures from Paradise and on the return to it. His chivalrous ministers leave the Heaven of the Church, as he himself had left his kin. Lairds are bribed and bullied from their Edens by the railways and the 'modern Huns' who speculate in furious communication. Reform takes the Scots out of Egypt, and leads them towards their Goshen or Millennium, and he himself enjoys his promised land—his Beulah—of Bonaly. These are the images which Cockburn employs or invites. They are the images of a man who was both fierce and calm, and who was sometimes to contradict himself. And yet they give a sense of

[1] *Reminiscences*, p. 328.
[2] House of Commons, 23 September 1831: quoted by William Ferguson (*Scottish Historical Review*, April 1966). The Lord Advocate who has said a further goodbye to the feudal system is Ronald King Murray (*The Times*, 3 September 1974).

capacity, rather than incapacity, of order, rather than disorder. They appear
to express a state of mind which was established at the start of his experience,
and which proved equal to its later occasions. There is war there, and peace:
both descriptions are true of him. There is contradiction and division, and
there is singleness and composure.

His contradictory attitudes and impulses did not distract or frustrate him,
or make him miserable: it is as if they were able to serve the happiness of
which he so often speaks. Amid Scotland's storms, with their shrinking
orphans, Cockburn's port, with its lighthouse, its cries of relief, its cordials
and other comforts, may seem too good to be true. But his avowals of happiness cannot be disbelieved, though they may be seen in part as anxiously
attesting to something very different. The anxieties and dilemmas which
he suffered were the anxieties and dilemmas of a contented and decisive
man, who used his talents to the full. His state of mind may be called a
victory for the imagination, a work of art, in that it could not have been
achieved without his dreams.

It may even be said that Cockburn's contradictions were the life of him.
The Roman god Janus, the god of doorways, whose two faces looked before
him and behind, may be felt to have rated a shrine at Bonaly, among the
dryads and the roses. He was a man who wanted to be King, and who
wanted there to be no more kings. At the time of the Reform Bill, he wrote
to Kennedy: 'My old regal desire has been very strong of late.' Three years
previously, he had informed him: 'I should like to see the world without
kings, bishops, or standing armies, and with a new house at Bonaly.'[1]
In 1830,[2] he declared he would 'eat my heart' if he and his associates did
not achieve their political ends, and—to abide by the metaphor—it may be
he had already taken a bite from his father's. The *Almanach des Gourmands*,
whose tomes the *Edinburgh Review* did not disdain to notice, once praised a
certain sauce: with such a sauce, *on mangerait son père*. And this, after a
fashion, for Reform's sake, is what he did. But he was also a man who kept
his taste for the solid fare of the unregenerate Scotland, an enemy of the
lairds who was never to leave their ranks. It was given out in China that the
late, disgraced Lin Piao had been a bourgeois careerist, and socialism here,
with all the cogency of a half-truth, would no doubt say the same of 'Linn'
Cockburn, who fancied himself the emperor of that country.

But if he was two-faced—running with the hare and hunting with the
hounds—both faces were largely benign. He was a benign force, a kindly
though concussive light. The *Edinburgh Review*'s review of the *Memorials*
manages to evoke that benignity, together with the truce he established

[1] *Letters to Kennedy*, pp. 348, 203.    [2] *Ibid.*, p. 245.

between his pugnacious politics and his dreams of the past and of the Pentlands. It remarks of Bonaly: 'Those romantic grounds which he had reclaimed from the rugged Pentlands, he threw open to every holiday wanderer who loved fresh air and nature like himself. So would he have had it with all the political and social good which this world affords.' Here is the art of eulogy again. These are the words of a friend, of the later Lord Moncreiff, and Cockburn was not a communist. But few who read his books and study his life will dismiss the words as valedictory rhetoric.

Cockburn was not as rashly hospitable, either, as Moncreiff suggests. On 28 October 1847, when his financial troubles were galling him, he wrote this letter from Bonaly to James Ballantine, the 'Gaberlunzie' poet, who piled up a little Pentland of poems about Bonaly and its people, including one called 'The Gaberlunzie to the Wee Raggit Laddie'. Cockburn pretends here that Ballantine and the Gaberlunzie are two fellows:

If you happen to be acquainted with a Gaberlunzie who goes about with a wallet full of scraps of meat and verse, I wish you would thank him, in my name, for some very good, and very complimentary, lines which he, or somebody in his person, has lately published about this humble spot and its humble master.

I am really grateful for the man's good opinion; especially as I am conscious that, to him at least, I have done very little to deserve it.

But I suspect that he feels that I have been negligent of him, and takes this method of punishing me, and an effectual punishment it is. Because from the moment he announced that my yett was open to all, I have been unable to call my own my own. There were successive hordes of roaming and roaring dogs out today—who positively took possession, and looked damnation to my eyes when I dared humbly to submit to them that property was property. One fellow's only answer was always by a loud stave of a song. The wee raggit laddies I don't object to, nor to anyone, male or female, who really enjoys the hills in decorum. But there is a species of riottous, devil may care, half-and-half genteel blackguards that are very odious. Odious to others of their fellow creatures—to mavises—to burns—to roses—to cows—sunsets—lambs, and everything reasonable. Therefore I mean to put up a placard saying—'*No passage this way without leave from the Gaberlunzie!!*' And if the Body can turn a penny, or fill his bag with heuk banes, for selling indulgences, like the Pope, I shall be very glad. Without some such check, a popular yett is a very inconvenient thing near a large town.

The Raggit Laddie is quite wrong, though, about Blackford. The first 25 years of my life were passed near—I may almost say upon—that Hill; and tho', like other open ground, it was certainly roamed over freely enough, this was always understood to be by tollerance. All my boyish holydays were spent amidst the whins, the rocks and the views of that delightful eminence; but I used to be often turned back; and the best thrashing I ever got in my life was for not instantly obeying. The move against shutters up is most meritorious, but nothing can be worse for their cause than their being defeated upon unjust claims. Nor would anything be better for it than their succeeding in a single claim that was just.

They will do no good, however, by merely resolving and roaring. They must subscribe. I read many heroic speeches, but never hear the clink of a guinea. Do they suppose that the silent, steady, constant tenacity of a Laird is to be relaxed by wind!

Cockburn also says: 'This season is done, and in a few days I am a townsman again.' In a few days he would resume his other self: 'somebody in his person', incidentally, is very Gothic. This is the last of his letters that I shall quote, and it is characteristic of him. That hill, those burns, those raggit laddies, those blackguards odious to sunsets—together with his being both for and against property! Any one who reads Cockburn, as I have said before, is likely to be struck by an early awareness of such subjects as 'pollution' and 'communication': in the light of this letter, it also seems that he can be credited with a foreknowledge of what was to happen in the field of 'publicity'. The terrors of publicity—in the restricted sense of the word which is now current—had already started to shake the Scotsman in his castle, though not, as yet, the black Gilmertonian scoundrel at his gate.

According to Cockburn, Ballantine's collection of prose and verse, *The Gaberlunzie's Wallet*, was 'a work which Burns would not have been anxious to have disowned'.[1] This seems excessive, and so does Ballantine himself. His verse overflows with sentimental and patriotic feelings, though some of his things have charm and verve. His *Poems*, which were published in 1856, are dedicated to Jeffrey's friend and his own, Charles Dickens—to the creator, one thinks of adding, of Little Nell. In 'The Wee Raggit Laddie to the Laird of Blackford Hill', the laird is asked to 'open Blackford Hill ance mair': a request to which Cockburn alludes in his letter. And 'The Gaberlunzie to the Wee Raggit Laddie' strikes a paradisal note:

> Nae rude expulsion need we fear
> Frae sweet Bonaly.

> Bonaly's laird is dear to a',
> His yett stands open to the wa',
> An' oh! he's pleased to get a ca'
> Frae rich or poor;
> Nae hungry bairnie wins awa'
> Frae Cockburn's door.

The reader was to believe that the laird of Bonaly invited the world to come and gaze from the Pentlands, and this indeed is what the laird sometimes seemed to be doing. But when the world came, Cockburn wanted it warned off—except for the raggit laddies—and behaved as if Revolution had scaled Carnethy.

---

[1] *Life of Jeffrey*, vol. I, p. 396. *The Gaberlunzie's Wallet* appeared in 1843.

Ballantine was the orphan's bard. He wrote 'A Chant for Ragged Schools', 'Naebody's Bairn', 'The Outcast', 'The Orphan's Hymn', and 'The Orphan Wanderer':

> I'm fatherless! motherless! weary and worn,
> Dejected, forsaken, sad, sad, and forlorn!

Who could expel someone in this condition? Certainly not the kind of man who took an interest in the fate of the forlorn Charles Cotier and William Macbean. Ballantine thought of the Pentlands as holy gound, and they were a place where his orphans might repair. He also has a poem on a Gilmerton carter, 'Coal Jock':

> King o' the coal mine, dingy Knicht,
> Wi' phiz sae grim, an' ee sae bricht . . .

Late in Cockburn's life, Ballantine produced some 'Lines suggested by a small but beautiful bouquet of flowers received by the Author at Bonaly, August, 1850':[1]

> Fair Edina woos the eye;
> Pentland's summits tower on high,
> Grandeur grace, and beauty reign
> O'er Bonaly's rare domain.

The lines contain fleeting similarities to Cockburn's own verse, and to 'Geraldine' in particular:

> Memory conjures up the scene,
> Holy, beauteous, and serene.
> Mountain streamlet, sparkling clear . . .

Some of Ballantine's celebratory verse could be called gushing, or purling, and there is an air of *de bas en haut*.

The Gothic writers knew how to be popular, and elves and fairies entered the literature. As winsome, wholesome and homely a specimen as the Gothic imagination has ever yielded, 'Bonnie Bonaly' salutes the objects and associations treasured by Bonaly's resident gnome. It makes one want to say that Cockburn was scarcely a plausible elf, and that the Gaberlunzie was Cockburn's goblin: a dainty version of the man who thought about orphans and had romantic leanings, and the kind of gnome who was later to stand about stonily in suburban gardens. The poem reads:

---

[1] NLS Ballantine MSS. A text of this poem is included in the *Poems* of 1856, and the volume also has the other poems of his from which quotations are given.

Bonnie Bonaly's wee fairy-led stream
Murmurs and sobs like a child in a dream;
Falling where silver light gleams on its breast,
Gliding through nooks where the dark shadows rest,
Flooding with music its own tiny valley,
Dances in gladness the stream o' Bonaly.

Proudly Bonaly's grey-browed Castle towers,
Bounded by mountains, and bedded in flowers;
Here hangs the blue bell, and there waves the broom;
Nurtured by art, rarest garden sweets bloom.
Heather and thyme scent the breezes that dally,
Playing amang the green knolls o' Bonaly.

Pentland's high hills raise their heather-crowned crest,
Peerless Edina expands her white breast,
Beauty and grandeur are blent in the scene,
Bonnie Bonaly lies smiling between.
Nature and art, like fair twins, wander gaily;
Friendship and love dwell in bonnie Bonaly.

Contrary to Cockburn's law that the name should rhyme with 'daily', Bonaly is rhymed with 'dally'. But it is also rhymed with 'gaily', and it seems in keeping that the name should furnish alternative sets of rhymes. When his friend and patron died, Ballantine wrote 'Bonaly's Lament for Lord Cockburn':

Ye clouds encircling Pentland high,
Whether in orient robes ye fly,
Or in grey wreaths o' vapour lie,
Enshrouding a',
Dissolve in tears, and frae the sky,
In torrents fa'.

Mercifully perhaps, Cockburn's books are left unsung by the Gaber-lunzie. And if this merciful, it is also apt. The *Memorials* apart, these books have been left virtually unstudied in Scotland, together with many other elements, early and late, of the Scottish Enlightenment. Cockburn himself has been mainly regarded as a charming dispenser of anecdotes and memories. This is unfortunate. It is not enough to think of him with nostalgia, in the manner that has become customary, as something resembling a municipal pet: as a personification of the old Edinburgh, torn between the 'heavenly

Hanoverianism', in Burns's phrase,[1] of its New Town and the heaven of his own creation in the hills, between dailying and dallying, Pantheonizing and Pentlandizing. He did not wish to enter Parliament, and he felt it was foolish for anyone to set up as a professional writer. But he was not shy about doing what he wished in several other fields. While he cannot be accounted an important political thinker, he was an important politician and social critic, a famous orator, a lawyer of consequence, and a narrative historian of genius. His youthful ambition to contribute to the literature of his country was achieved. It is not enough to think of him reading Tacitus all summer long in a cleft of the Pentlands—on the sunny side of the hill. He is the Tacitus of Scotland.

[1] The phrase is used in another connection, with 'Jacobite' sarcasm, in a letter to Mrs Dunlop of 13 November 1788.

*Cockburn's Poems*

## The Linn
### First Version

Thou source of the stream where my infancy flew!
Long dreamt of in fondness, and vainly explored;
Discovered at last amidst friendships so true,
Oh hallowed retreat, be thou ever adored!

How purely thy rill from its old rocks descends;
Amusing the ear by its breeze-varied sound,
And fixing the eye, on the arches it bends,
Unheeding the wildness that watches around.

How long have these mosses gleamed rich in thy dew;
This Elm, thy companion, thrown o'er thee its shade;
The wonder-struck Pilgrim stood still at thy view;
And the Sun shone in peace on thy lonely cascade.

What bosoms forgotten have drawn at thy shrine
The Spirit that blessed them thro' life's weary day.
How many a lover of nature and thine
Have here mused their sorrows and fancies away.

In some moment of rapture, their aims high and pure,
And fearing to lose the enobling emotion,
One seed did they give to this cliff ever sure,
And bade it attest all their hopes and devotion.

But the vow-planted Elm is now doomed to decline;
And thy Genius prophetic seems, rising, to mourn
That Spring shall awaken no foliage of thine,
Nor Autumn's sad splendour thy fountain adorn.

Yes! gratefully mingling their visions with ours,
But led to thy haunts by still holier calls,
These seedlings, devoted to thy sacred powers,
Shall soften thy rocks, and embower thy falls.

By us then at seasons the world resigning,
But remembering all that has passed at this spot,
Under our own planted branches reclining,
Be all but the Past and the Future forgot.

Should the Present, with views uncongenial, intrude,
Thy Spirit shall say, 'Trust thy heart and be still!
As these hills, that a prospect too splendid exclude,
But deepen the relish of this secret rill.

Disturb not thy quiet with thoughts that must perish.
These branches shall flourish, untouched by decay,
And Nature for ages their energy cherish,
But the Flower of Mortality passes away!

Nor sigh that it passes! while here taught to die,
These shades stretch around thee to soothe all thy woes;
And thy soul takes its colour from yon placid sky;
And thy Form 'neath its often pressed turf shall repose.

This Bower then enduring, all peaceful as Heaven,
Shall bid other votaries be calm and be blest;
And thy Piety thus to earth shall have given
One Porch that conducts to the mansions of rest.'

## The Linn
### Second Version

Thou Source of the stream where my Infancy flew,
Long dreamt of in fondness, now ever adored,
Since known to me only with friendships so true,
The past may be hallowed, but never deplored!

How purely thy rill from its old rocks descends,
Amusing the ear by its breeze-varied sound!
And fixing the eye on the arches it bends
Unheeding the Wildness that watches around!

How long have these mosses gleamed rich in thy dew!
This Elm, thy companion, thrown o'er thee its shade!
The wonder-struck Pilgrim stood still at thy view!
And the Sun shone in peace on thy lonely cascade!

What bosoms forgotten have drawn at thy shrine
The Spirit that blessed them thro' life's weary day;
And endeared to each lover of nature's and thine
The spot where reposes thy unnoticed clay.

In some moment of rapture, their aims high and pure,
But fearing to part with the noble emotion,
They have given one seed to this cliff ever sure
And bade it remember their hopes and devotion!

But the vow-planted Elm at last follows their doom;
And thy Genius, Prophetic, seems, rising, to mourn,
That its stream soon deserted must flow from a tomb,
And the scene of their visions be marked by an urn!

No never! For mingling their visions with ours,
But led to thy haunt by still holier calls,
These seedlings, devoted to thy sacred powers,
Shall soften thy cliffs and embower thy falls.

Thy Temple thus reared upon this solemn ground,
Not unhonoured hereafter thy fountain shall flow,
While the Spirits of Nature, attracted around,
To thee and the source of their valley shall bow.

By us too, at seasons, the world resigning,
But remembering all that has past at this spot,
Under our own planted branches reclining,
Be all but the past and the future forgot!

Should the present with views uncongenial intrude,
Thy Genius shall say—'Trust thy heart and be still!
As these Hills, that a prospect too splendid exclude,
But deepen the relish of this secret rill.

Disturb not thy quiet with thoughts that must perish!
These branches shall darken, untouched by decay,
And nature for ages their energies cherish,
But the flower of mortality passes away!

Nor sigh that it passes, while here taught to die,
These shades rise around thee to soothe not upbraid;
And thy soul takes its colour from yon placid sky,
And thy form 'neath its often pressed moss shall be laid.

This Bower then remaining, all peaceful as Heaven!
Shall bid other votarys be calm and be blest;
And thy piety thus to Earth shall have given
One Porch that conducts to the Mansion of Rest.'

---

*Içi Repose*
*Charles Cotier, De*
*Dunkerque*
*Né* * *
*Mort* * *

---

And here hast thou perished, oh! Desolate stranger,
Nor given thy dust to thy own garden grave!
But sunk amidst objects thy memory knew not,
And struck by the hand that had promised to save!

Thy ambition still proud with its youthful designs!
And exile, endearing the freedom to be!
And the scene of thy infancy kept all unchanged,
By a mother beholding an Image of thee!

The image is broken! For never again
Shall the Spirit of Morning revisit thy breast!
Or the tales of thy exile be heard in the Bower
Now silent alike with this home of thy rest!

(*Caetera Desunt*)

Notes

1. Line 27. The manuscript has no comma after 'seedlings'.
2. Line 39. The manuscript has no comma after 'exclude'.
3. Line 46. The manuscript has 'upraid'.
4. Line 52. The second version has no closing quotation-mark after 'Rest'. The Genius of the Linn has presumably ceased to speak at this point, as in the first version, so that the requiem for the desolate stranger is that of Cockburn himself.
5. Line 61. The manuscript has a comma after 'never'.
6. Line 62. The manuscript has a comma after 'Morning'.

*The Holy Grove*
or, *Geraldine*

Oh! quiet scene! so oft admired!
So tranquil, solemn and retired!
Where is the Peace you once inspired?
　'Tis fled, alas, with Geraldine!

No vernal Morn, nor Summer glare—
But only Autumn's thoughtful air
Serenes the Winter of Despair
　Here left by thee, my Geraldine.

The prospects I believed so true,
And felt so blessed, while Love and You
Touched all life's scen'ry to my view
　With Hope's own Pencil, Geraldine,

Are dark for ever! And the rays
Which sometimes gleam, of favrite days
But leave the past in sadder haze
　To Pensive Memory, Geraldine.

Yet thence the Soul assumes a cast,
Too sacred while our pleasures last,
But more than every transport past
　Revered in Silence, Geraldine!

For it can make our sorrows dear;
And life's few days it well may cheer
By whispering ever 'Thou art here'
   To soothe my Spirit, Geraldine!

Thus Hallowed Spot! thou still canst please!
Here tears may flow—all murmurs cease!
For thro' thy path I'm led to Peace!
   And led by thee, my Geraldine!

The lovely scenes that heaven designed
A solace to the anguish'd mind,
To me are pictures to the blind,
   Bereft of thee, my Geraldine.

The dawn of morn, the noontide glare,
Nor evening's mild and soothing air,
Can chase this midnight of despair,
   Bereft of thee, my Geraldine.

The dream of life so bright and new
That witch'd my soul when love and you
Gave charms resistless to my view
   And waked fond hopes, my Geraldine,

Is fled for ay, and in its stead
A weary waste of joys all dead
Where'er I turn my eyes is spread,
   Bereft of thee, my Geraldine.

## Notes

1. The manuscript is under-punctuated throughout, and further punctuation has been added, such as the inverted commas round 'Thou art here'.
2. The verses from the eighth to the end are in a different and unknown hand. From this point on in the manuscript the lavish use of capital letters and exclamation-marks is no longer in evidence: this change has been preserved.

## How solemn the close . . .

How solemn the close of this last Autumn day!
And how still the repose of this ever-loved vale!
Hark! What sound but yon brook as it murmurs away,
And that poor red-breast's note are now heard in the dale.

How sublimely yon woods bend their hermitage o'er!
We follow the leaf as it drops from its tree;
While yon rock by its grandeur reminds us the more
Of the weakness of every thing else that we see.

Yet thou Blessed Relic! here still dost repose!
The frail being that placed thee once visits again!
On thy shrine Winter gently has laid his sad snows,
And the feet of th'unhallowed passed near thee in vain.

Thou Hope of the future and Pledge of the past!
Revered be the hour, tho' in childhood forgot,
When something foreboding that Youth would not last,
I vowed to revive it in this lovely spot!

For the vows of our childhood in Heaven are sealed!
And lest ever the virtue they sprung from expire,
In our favourite haunt to our bosoms revealed,
The Spirit that breathed them rekindles their fire.

### Notes

1. Line 7. The manuscript has a comma after 'rock' and 'more'.
2. Line 20. The manuscript has a comma after 'them'.

## Relugas

When wakeful in the night profound,
The fearful pulses of my heart I hear,
And long for some external sound,
Relugas! be thy whispers near!

The stirring of thy foliaged hills,
As fitful breezes o'er them float;
Hushed into silence, like thy rills,
By owlet's strange and solemn note;

And over all, the softened roar
Of rocky Findhorn's gullied stream;
Suggesting his romantic shore,
And soothing more than sweetest dream

What pictures rise! The granite ridge,
The broomy glade, the cavern cool,
Primeval Dulsie's savage bridge,
And Sluie's dark and eddying pool,

The grey and ghostly dotard oaks,
Altnari's sunless, shattered, dell,
And yon recess of wood and rocks
Where the sacred herons dwell.

Ye winged sages! Feathered Gods!
How calm your social city rests;
While ye, within your old abodes,
Sagacious watch your solid nests.

To fancy's eye, each favourite spot
Returns again in stronger light.
The very dead, by day forgot,
Come back in visionary night.

Ah Gordon! long shalt thou pervade
Haunts to thy living spirit dear.
In every scene thy graceful shade,
Recurring, claims the pensive tear.

How bright arose thy early dawn,
By friendship and by science hailed!
How soon o'er splendid hopes was drawn
The cloud of night, and death prevailed!

Yet still the eye thy form will see,
Still o'er the heart thy virtues come.
Day wants its sunshine without thee,
And evening's gentle voice is dumb.

Thus oft may night's inspiring gloom
Remove Oblivion's time-wove pall!
Unlock the treasures of the tomb,
And dear Relugas days recall!

## Notes

1. Line 16. 'Sluie' is the usual spelling of the name. Cockburn's manuscript has 'Sluy's'.
2. Line 18. The Altnarie is a burn which runs into the Findhorn, and which was known at one time for its romantic falls and deep wooded glen.
3. Line 24. A cancelled version of this line reads: 'Like burghers watch your solid nests.'
4. Line 29. Dr John Gordon died in 1818. He is discussed in Chapters Two and Four.
5. Line 37. A cancelled version of the tenth verse reads:

> Yet still the eye thy form will see,
> Thy virtues still the heart inspire.
> Day wants its sunshine without thee,
> Less brightly sparkling evening's fire.

### On losing a staff from a gig

Adieu! my tall, my chestnut staff.
Maitland and his wife may laugh,
But missing thee, my heart is sad;
I curs'd the Gig—they thought me mad.
Companion of my mountain hour
Who ten long years thro' blast and show'r
With me didst brave—with what delight
As Law each session clos'd his fight,
And gave me to myself once more,
I flew to thee, and turned thee o'er
And ere one ramble had begun
Display'd thee to the well-pleas'd Sun!
How often have we climbed the hill,
How often searched the secret rill!
How oft beheld the morning dawn

And day's declining light withdrawn!
While crossed upon thy tawny side,
My imps enjoyed their fancied ride,
And thou partookst in seeming play
Bonaly's constant holiday.
In distant soil a seedling placed,
Some far-off scenes thy umbrage graced,
Some Spanish brook thy fibres laved,
In Spain's rich gale thy foliage waved.
And hence when borne to Scotia's shore,
By me as foreign prized the more.
And oft I thought, when coming age
Should bid these sports no more engage,
I still might find thy faithful stem
(Respectable, with mounted gem)
Reposing in thy untouched nook
And blest with thee, and thoughtful book,
Might still step forth on level walk
By beechen hedge to read or talk.
And when at last that prop shall fail
And time o'er my frail leaf prevail,
I still had hopes these playful boys
Might share with thee their mountain joys,
And tenderly for many a year,
The old paternal staff revere.
But oh that Gig! and him who drove
Through Morton's mean and rutted grove!
They gave to some unconscious hand
A more than patriarchal wand,
And left these arms without a friend
In danger's hour who could not bend.

## Notes

1. Line 1. The manuscript has a comma after 'staff'.
2. Line 2. Thomas Maitland, his brother-in-law, and a judge.
3. Line 9. Cockburn has an exclamation-mark after 'more'.
4. Line 21. The manuscript has no punctuation at the end of this line.
5. Line 23. The manuscript has no punctuation at the end of this line.

*Cockburn's Memorial
of the Outer House*

Writing at Bridge of Tilt in the *Circuit Journeys*, on 11 April 1845, Cockburn says that he does not propose to describe, on this occasion, his old North Circuit route. 'Not that I'm at all tired of it; but, for the nonce, I am tired of describing it.' At this point in the *Circuit Journeys* the Bridge of Tilt entry ceases. But his manuscript proceeds, as follows, to elucidate Richardson's 'Helvellyn' parody.

Then what am I to do? For the Circuit Journal can't be given up; and intermitting and giving up are nearly the same. And it must be legal, or connected with legal matter. Various schemes have occurred to me: an account of some curious trials, of the illustrious lawyers of my day, of some, even already, incredible legal customs, which, tho' now exploded and incomprehensible, were ingrained into people's ideas of what was indispensible within the last 40 years. But a doze in the carriage, near Kinross, was irradiated by a vision of Otho Wemyss and the other heroes of Richardson's 'Helvellyn'; and I settled that while posterity is surfeited by details about the great and distinguished, it is wrong that no record is ever preserved of the vulgar and unsuccessful, who, however, had courage to be remarkable by oddity or even black-guardism. Richardson thought it worth while to *allude* to certain persons about 40 years ago, in verses which are sought after still; but in a very few years more, not a person will be alive who can tell what the allusions mean.

The verses were a parody on Scott's 'Helvellyn'. They were published, *for the first time*, about two years ago, in a contemptible compilation of bad trash called *The Court of Session Garland*. It is there stated in one place that the parody was the joint composition of Lord Jeffrey, Lord Murray, Lord Cockburn and Mr Richardson; and in another place this error is corrected by another, where it is said that, except one *line* by Lord Jeffrey, it was all Richardson's. Both statements are inaccurate, and the explanatory notes are meagre and incorrect. Neither Murray, nor Cranstoun, nor I, wrote, or suggested, one word or idea of it. Jeffrey wrote most of the second stanza. All the rest, and the general idea even of this stanza, was Richardson's alone.

The parody was written, and privately shown, in MSS, within a few weeks of the appearance of the original—which, I think, was in 1804. Nobody was more diverted by it than Scott, between whom and Richardson there was always a cordial and unbroken friendship. Like all good men, Richardson has always been flirting with the Muses. Few laborious men of business, and certainly no Scotch London solicitor, have written more verse. Amiableness and elegance are its character, and some of his songs are extremely beautiful.

Ludicrous ressemblance is generally the only object, or pleasure, of parody. This one has some greater interest from its graphic touches of the old Outer House, and of some of its old characters. It evokes men and scenes once far more talked of than more important things.

So, first, here, for the sake of reference, come the lines.

I climbed the High Street as the ninth bell was ringing;
   The Macer to three of his roll had got on;[1]
And eager each clerk to his counsel was springing;
   Save on thee, luckless lawyer, who fee had got none![2]

On the right Nicodemus his leg was extending;[3]
O'er the stove Johny Wright his brown visage was bending,[4]
And a huge brainless judge the Fore-Bar was ascending,[5]
    When I marked thee, Poor Otho! stand briefless alone![2]

Dark brown was the spot by thy love still distinguished,
    Twixt the stove and the Side-Bar, where oft thou didst stray;[6]
Like the ghost of a lawyer, by hunger extinguished,
    Who walks a sad warning to crowds at bright day!
Yet not quite deserted, tho' poorly attended;
For see Virgin Smith his right hand hath extended;[7]
And Haggart's strong breath thy retreat hath defended,[8]
    And chased the vain wits and loud scoffers away!

How eager thou look'st as the agents rush past thee!
    How oft as the Macer bawls loud dost thou start![9]
Alas! thy thin wig not much longer will last thee![10]
    And no fee will the hard-hearted agent impart!
And Oh! is it meet that a student of Leyden
Should hardly have whole coat or breeches to stride in[11]
While home-breds and blockheads their carriages ride in,
    Who can't tell where Leyden is placed on the chart!

When Balmuto or Banny the bench hath ascended,
    The former to bellow, the latter to sleep;[12]
Or Hermand, as fierce as a Tyger offended,
    Is mutt'ring his curses, not loudly but deep;[13]
Then are all the fee'd lawyers most anxiously waiting.
Some ready to proze, and all ready for prating;
While some for delay are most nobly debating,[14]
    Lamenting a cause thro' their fingers should slip!

But meeter for thee with old Thomas Macgrugar,[15]
    Thy heart's dearest friend, in condolence to sigh!
And to some moral question in words sweet as sugar,
    To urge in soft answer a gentle reply!
Far meeter, I ween, than for gowns idly hoping,
With the Corsican faery thy way darkly groping,[16]
To spend the gay hours in John Dowie's, deep toping,
    And sup on salt herrings and hot mutton pies![17]

And here comes what it's all about.

1. The Outer House met then, as now, at nine; and therefore as nine was still ringing, the Macer, in calling out his list of causes, should not have been at No 3. But this is a sneer at an abuse, then far from uncommon, arising from the practice of paying the Judges' clerks partly by fees on enrolments. The more causes that were called in people's absence, the better for the clerk, for it made a new enrollment necessary. It is one of the things now incredible, but nevertheless quite true, that some of the Judges *shared in their clerks' fees*, which was called 'Riding the Clerk'—

and of course had no objection to facilitate tricks, by taking their seats suddenly, when nobody was expecting them. Eskgrove was a notorious and shameless delinquent in this way.

2. This *'luckless lawyer', 'Poor Otho'*, was an Advocate, who can't at least be said to have made no figure at the bar; because for about forty years he was an absolute target for Parliament House jokes. His familiar title was Otho Wemyss, which James Grahame, the Author of *The Sabbath*, used to enrage him by translating *O quamvis parvula puella*. But his full and respectful address was Otho *Herman* Wemyss; for he had been sent to study Civil Law in his youth at Leyden, and testified his gratitude to his master, on coming away, by inserting his name between the two parts of his own; being the only fee that the learned Dutchman was supposed to have got. At his first appearance, Otho was thought intelligent and clever; and twice or thrice he certainly did write good papers; and he was always kindly. I have been told that he used even to be talked of as the probable rival of Cranstoun. But this was when Cranstoun was scarcely a visible star.

These predictions, however, were all vain. He was doomed always to be laughed at, and never to rise—a fate sufficiently accounted for by his appearance and his pretension. An air of conscious gentility contrasted ludicrously with very poor, tho' ambitious raiment, and a yellow, hungry look. His modest assumption of superiority, from what he called Foreign Travel—which meant having been a year at Leyden— might perhaps have been offensive, if this had not been avoided by the absurdity of his elegant and patronising politeness. And his graces and virtues had their 'soft verdure' gradually worn off by whiskey—which in his case, as in that of his chums, was the parent, as well as the child, of poverty.

Always thin, dry, and of a sort of palish saffron hue, he at last fell, literally, into the sere and yellow leaf, for he had become perfectly withered. Time, and hunger, and liquor, and most elaborate politeness, had 'shrunk his thin essence'. When in this state, and considerably doited, Whiggery marked him for its own, and he finished off, at above three score, as Sherriff Substitute of Selkirkshire. But a narrow-minded burgh thought his judicial habits somewhat incorrect; and this, forsooth, merely because he combined them with a little of that attention to the Fair which became a man of elegance and foreign travel. And he evinced his innocence by being above all hypocricy: tho' this, no doubt, had its inconveniences, for he was at least twice soused with pails of water, by the Nereids of the Public well, for over-familiarity. After dispensing local justice for about two years, whiskey prevailed; and he died, after all, rather liked.

3. *Nicodemus* was Edward Maccormick, Advocate; why so nicknamed I do not know, unless it was that, being Assessor to the town of Leith, he was 'a ruler of the Jews'. Large and stately—one leg, with a black silk stocking on it, and a huge foot and a silver buckle at the end of it, was always projected before him—and there he stood, with his great bland countenance, as if for the world to worship. President Blair used to say that if a man's intellectual power could be judged of by mere look and air, Nicodemus would be the greatest of men. But in spite of his pompous con-descension, vast presence, and slow grand sentences, he was a profound formal blockhead, an utter ass.

4. *John Wright*—Advocate; a curious species of man, if indeed he belonged to this genus. Short, stumpy, and as brown as deep-tanned leather; a large head; a huge mouth, which gaped to its utmost possible wideness whenever cogitation, or liquor, or wonder, made the enormous chin drop. He must have sat to the framer of the first

Dutch nutcracker. There is a portrait of him in Kay's Edinburgh caricatures, which, outrageous as it may appear, owes its only unlikeness to its being so little caricatured. Had the hole called a mouth been a great deal larger, the ressemblance, very considerable tho' it be, would have been still greater.

The whole professional practice of a long life was said to have consisted of one cause; and it about a trunk. But he professed to teach Civil Law—a form for begging a guinea, which several people gave him yearly, for what he termed his Course. No less a person than Francis Horner did so once. Horner told me that, on first meeting, the class, consisting of seven or eight, sat round a table in what the learned lecturer announced as the parlour—a small, smoky place down a close; and that Johny seemed to be in the throes, before he began, and took the cube-shaped Corpus between his hands, and squeezed, and turned, and dandled it affectionately, and then proceeded—'Gentle Men, this wee bit bookie conteens the hail Ceevil Law!' The first lecture generally ended the course.

It was a worthy creature—miserably poor, in so much that it was fed and slaked at last almost entirely on charity; much addicted to golf; and not at all bigotted against strong drink, tho' in its general habits rather temperate and philosophical. The dark ochre of its thick, filthy hide, its cavern of a mouth, its large, staring white eye, the general sturdiness of its structure, and the slowness of its gait and speech, exposed it to many adventures. For instance, he was believed to have been once fired at for a seal when bathing. The first shot missed, because he had ducked; and on preparing for a second fire, the sportsman was petrified by hearing the fish grunt, as soon as its head was up, 'Stop Sir! I'm a man—and not a beast!' which last was certainly not true, but the pious fraud probably saved a life. Biography has also asserted that sleeping, naked and drunk, in the travellers' room of an inn, he was lifted one dark morning, and strapped on the back of a chaise, for a hair trunk.

5. The '*Huge brainless Judge*' was not meant by Richardson as a Generic, but was intended to describe William Baillie, Lord Polkemmet; a good man, but huge and brainless, certainly. In voice, stare, manner and intellect, not much above an idiot; but respectable from bulk, good nature, broad Scotch, and slow, gracious stupidity.

6. '*Twixt the stove and the Side-Bar*'. This was a well-known spot, very accurately laid down in the parodist's geography. It was towards the south-west end of the Outer House. There were no *permanent* Lords Ordinary in those days; only one Lord Ordinary for the week, whose throne was called the *Fore*-Bar. The other Ordinaries came out from the Inner House, apparently according to no rule or system except their own pleasure, and sat on what were termed *Side*-Bars. Now there was a Side-Bar and a stove on the west side of the House; and between these two was the 'dark brown spot'—a cosy, dingy recess, of about a dozen of feet or so, which the junior counsel were too fine, and the senior too dignified, to enter, but it was the favourite Howf of some unemployed middle-aged disreputables of the Faculty. They used to be called 'The Itch Club'. Wemyss, Wright, Haggart, Macgregor and Hutcheson were the predominating members. Hutcheson is not honoured by Richardson. So I have nothing to do with him. Only, he was that Gilbert who has bequeathed himself to the law of Scotland in the book called Hutcheson's *Justice of Peace*.

7. 'Virgin Smith' was John Smith Esq of Balquharron, Advocate. He obtained, and kept, the title here given to him by his timid, blushing modesty. Downcast eyes, pink cheeks, a low voice and retired air, perfect respectability, and comfortable circumstances, make him a good deal out of place in the company he here stands in. But the explanation is that he did sometimes do the very thing Richardson says—*extended*

*his hand*—by way of disarming the coarse jeers of these fellows at his gentle diffidence. But he never did more. He was no member of their craft. I think I see him—shrinking past the dark brown spot, detecting a gibe coming, for his trying to pass, pausing for an instant and deprecating it, sometimes successfully, by a momentary extension of the hand, and, after shuddering at the recognition, pass on. His being obliged occasionally to shake their hands is meant as a proof of the power of their Free Masonry over weak sensitiveness.

8. '*Haggart's strong breath*'—John Haggart, originally of nothing, at last of a small place, to which, merely in order to annoy his neighbour Mackenzie of Delvin, he gave the rival name of Glendelvin. He too was an Advocate, and it may be doubted if so famous and peculiar a beast ever shone at any other bar.

He was the only one of the eminent Low here immortalised who got any fees—the wages for degrading his profession by the ardent patronage of any villainy, against any worth. John Haggart was Blackguardism's standing counsel. In so much that on one occasion which I myself witnessed, when a rogue who had never seen or employed him, but knew him, as all scoundrels did, by reputation, was suddenly ordered by the court to be taken by the neck, he no sooner felt the Macer's hand upon him than he exclaimed instinctively 'Gude God! Whare's Maister Haggart?'

It was not native and original rascality that led him into this line, tho' the nature was certainly never high. He owed the bad eminence to the success of a few efforts of vulgar pettyfogging and coarseness. These ruined him for respectable practice, after which he was obliged to adhere to the only walk in which he had any chance; which was further recommended to him by the certainty that he would have the monopoly of it. Woe be on any man with an humble competency, a decent character, a head liable to be misled, and a generous neighbour; or a violent Laird on the march beside a noble and liberal proprietor; or a foolish tennant in arrear of his rent to an indulgent landlord; or an apprentice or servant rebellious and ungrateful towards a valuable master—if any of them came in Haggart's way! The Devil did not put more mischief into the ear of Eve than Haggart blew into the brains and hearts of these confiding and abused fools. Being his clients, they were all sure to be beggared at last. But still, the long, obstinate, reckless battle that he fought before striking, joined to two or three pieces of accidental success, the cordial brotherliness of his zeal in defence of all low iniquity, and the purposed impudence with which he irritated and nauseated the court, made him the natural champion of offensive and desperate litigousness. With just enough of vulgar common sense and readiness to be able to state his case, either verbally or in writing, but with no talent or learning, and little jocularity, and with an ill-favoured appearance and a disgusting manner, it was impossible to mistake the cause of his importance, or to ascribe it to anything except sheer persevering, coarse, regardless impudence.

This would have extinguished him sooner than it did, had it not been for the occasional indiscretion of his opponents, and particularly the Judges. They were too apt to lose their tempers. This gave him importance. They used to make him the subject of a tone of indignation of which he was quite unworthy, and greatly enjoyed. Indeed, in spite of its abominableness, it was not always possible for a spectator to avoid smiling at the success with which his slow, quiet, impervious impudence assailed high-placed propriety. Catch him losing his temper. Not that he kept it from policy. He was one of the thick-skinned beasts, and never felt any temptation to lose it. And he could stand any amount of kicking. Nothing that disturbed others was any annoyance to him. Because they were silly enough to be discomposed by him, this fellow annoyed the court, and his Grace of Athole, and the Perthshire gentry, for above thirty years. This power of vexing gave him, in his palmy state, a considerable tail of low agents, fraudulent bankrupts, self-ruined tennants, litigious heritors, over-mortgaged Lairds, disreputable clergymen, and other pests of the law—a constituency which elevated its representative into something like public station. He was not directly dishonest—that is, he did not plainly cheat, at least he was never detected. And there were two, or at the most three, half-understood occurrences which made a few weak people fancy that he could even be generous. If they were right, this makes his case only the more singular. For it leaves him a man blasted individually by pure personal blackguardism, and professionally, by the voluntary bottle-holdership of every base legal knave who tempted his taste by having a respectable opponent.

Whiskey was the most refined of his pleasures. Then came gross language, grosser acts, grossest thoughts. Yet he pillaged the litigious poor less than he might have done if avarice had been his besetting sin. Brougham used to assert that, in the vacation, Haggart used to hold what he called Beds of Justice, which consisted in his sitting on a knoll, in Perthshire, surrounded by a crowd of rustic admirers, whose disputes he settled—his fee being, first, Money—which failing, Whiskey—which failing, Meal—which all failing, the liberty of insulting their daughters. It was he who carried on the action of damages against the Lord President (Hope) in which it was settled that no supreme Judge was civilly responsible for words judicially spoken. The stinking monster was once, on business, in the presence of Romily. Nature probably never produced such a contrast. He astounded that lofty Purist by some memorable, but unrepeatable, remarks.

Over the carcase of this wretch, there stands, as I am told, in the beautiful churchyard of Capputh, a monument, with an inscription recording his virtues.

9. '*The Macer bawled loud*'. I wonder if there be any other court where counsel, instead of being obliged to wait on for their causes, within earshot of the Judge, lounge as they list, being sure to be summoned by a brazen-throated Herald, whose strong, swinging voice makes their names resound wherever they may be lurking, so as to startle them in their own ears. It is a very gentlemanlike institution, and greatly promotes legal ignorance. For no one need attend a moment longer than he pleases; and therefore, having the Library and Outer House at his command, the practice is for each Barrister to be in court when his own affair is under discussion, and never to listen to the proceedings merely for the sake of learning his profession. Hence we have more jokers, and poets, and philosophers, than lawyers. I wish one of the poets would give us an Ode on the First Call after the long Vacation. Jeffrey compared it to the first note of Spring. It recalls, in one moment, all the associations of the place. A rush of counsel, like 'Eagles to the prey', to which Peter Peebles compared it, always follows the proclamation of each case. How many a good talk have these proclamations dissipated! How often robbed us of Erskine's wit! of Scott's story! of Jeffrey's speculation!

10. The 'hard-hearted agent' persisted in imparting no fee. But the 'thin wig' survived its owner. However, the report may possibly be true that, after being a Judge, Otho clouted it. It was a very curious article. He had bought it at second hand, so that its original colour was lost in Antiquity. But time and smoke (he lived in the Canongate) had made it a sandy yellow. It was certainly thin, for it seemed in some places as if it had been scratched through—probably by the indignant claws of the Canongate ladies. And the ochrey hairs, tho' carefully combed so as to make each particular quill hide a frail part, were so sparse that the inner framework was visible. The ground had been scourged till the subsoil was bare. Yet such is the force of inborn elegance that it had really an air of gentility, even in its dotage.

11. 'Should hardly have whole coat or breeches to stride in'. The '*hardly*' expresses the very thing. There were no slits, or tatters, in the worthy gentleman's integuments —a thing his feelings could not have endured. But his garments, tho' still entire, were so abraded that it seemed as if one other rub would be dangerous. And a few auxiliary threads that had been added to close rivetts up might be seen lurking in the confidence of retired nooks. Still Gentility prevailed. I see him! There he goes! with the bright, cobbled shoes, the brown, gold-headed cane, the antique, often-pawned ring, the black silk stockings—their frailities hid beneath faded gaiters—the snuff and the dust of his Session black, or vacation brown, suit, swept, in visible streaks, by a brush worn to the stump, an air of pensive, ill-fed, self-satisfied fashionableness, the downward aspect, as if of a poor gentleman thinking, but truly surveying the progress of decay in his general man, and inwardly indignant at the world's neglect of talent and foreign travel.

12. *Balmuto and Banny*—'The former to bellow, the latter to sleep'. These were two of the Judges.

The first was Claud Boswell of Balmuto—entitled Lord Balmuto. A very worthy man, but a horrible Judge. As huge and strong as a cart horse, and nearly as illiterate; his language broad Scotch, in its poorest and most vulgar diction. A coarse Ogre to those who did not know his real kindness. Nature required to have made no other change, except by supplying two additional legs, to have made the shafts of a dung cart his proper place in this world.

The other was McLeod Bannatyne, Lord Bannatyne—a nice, merry old Celtic gentleman; the greatest public sleeper, and the most successful compounder of incoherent Interlocutors, that ever tried these Arts. His judicial slumber was owing to an inhuman practice of rising at four or five in the morning. And he rose thus early apparently for the sake of the nap on the bench. The nodding used to set his wig awry, and nothing could be more ludicrous than his good-natured stare when, on awakening suddenly, he found himself in court, and everybody laughing. But he soon relieved himself by another nod, after which they might laugh as they pleased for him. His Interlocutors were like a Song by a person of Quality. Cranstoun's imitation, in his 'Diamond Beetle', is no caricature. Nevertheless, Banny was a Gentleman, and popular; with all the warmth of the Highland heart, and all the defects of the Highland understanding.

13. 'Or Hermand, as fierce as a Tyger offended'. Lord Hermand was George Fergusson, the son of Kilkerran. He was my uncle by affinity, and therefore I shall only say that tho' he certainly had very often the appearance of being a Tyger in public, he was never anything but a Lamb in private. Richardson did not know him when he wrote these two lines. They were great friends afterwards, and the lines were retained just because they had been written.

14. 'And some for delay were most loudly debating.' In the old state of the court, where almost nothing was peremptory, it is absolutely beyond belief how many wrangles there were for delay. The loudness of debate was never so conspicuous as in roaring for, or against, procrastination.

15. 'But meeter for thee with old Thomas Macgrugar'—Macgrugar was an Advocate, and, except in elegance, the second self of Otho! They were alike in the indication of early talent, and in subsequent failure; in whiskey and apparent poverty; but most unlike in this, that after Macgrugar was dead, it was discovered, to everybody's surprize, that he was worth three or four thousand pounds. While alive, he had

the look, and appearance, and habits, of a famished beggar. He was a good lawyer, and a skillful writing pleader—in so much that some of the great guns of the profession got considerable praise for successful shots which Macgrugar had loaded and pointed for them. And he published a supplement to the Dictionary, tho' I am not sure that his name was at it.

I cannot therefore make a theory for his failure—which was complete. But it probably was owing to a shabby, scarecrow appearance, and the fragrance of whiskey. He had, to be sure, a horrid, begrutten, lousy look. It was a common joke in those days to describe people by the titles in the Dictionary. Macgrugar was *Squalor Carceris.*

Otho and he were inseparable. Amidst the tumult of the Outer House, the faithful pair were sequestered in what a General Assembly Orator lately called 'Proud Humility'. They did seem 'in condolence to sigh'. But, when dying, Macgrugar, as if ashamed of his friend, sent a note by his lass (they were all Batchelors) requesting a reputable, but long forgotten acquaintance 'to take the trouble of laying my head in the grave'. The gentleman was not fond of the task, but did it.

16. *'The Corsican Faery'.* Not Napoleon, but Mr George Sandy. He was once secretary, or something, to the first Lord Minto, when that nobleman was something in Corsica, and got his title from his huge, hairy grey bulk, very like a human baboon. He still afflicts the Bank of Scotland as one of its secretaries.

17. *'John Dowie's'*—Fired at the sound! John was the last of his class in Edinburgh. He kept a mean, but respectably conducted tavern in Forresters Wynd. It was nearly empty the whole day, till about nine at night, when crowds of parties, composed chiefly of young men belonging to some of the departments of the law, went to sup. There can be no doubt, since Richardson, who knew the haunt well, says so, that they got (red) herrings and mutton pies, but there can be just as little doubt that toasted cheese and ale were the staple. John's terms were so moderate that no poor gentleman, or humble lad, could have any compunction in visiting his den. Sawney not being gregarious, there was no common room. Each party was put into a small low-roofed chamber, with a sanded floor, a little fireplace, a strong, well scrubbed, and well dinted, fir table—decent, however, in a pure white cloth—and two tallow candles, set in bright brass candlesticks. The tabernacle was full of these pidgeon holes.

There being very little variety of eats or drinks, the hive was easily managed. The Queen bee took a general superintendance. She was aided by one handmaid, the slave of the gridiron, who streaked the herrings, and warmed the pies, and toasted the cheese, expeditiously and quietly. John, a boy, and another lass, bustled at the call of all the little sharp bells, and drew the corks, and replenished the jugs with hot water, totally undistracted by the many important disputes, exquisite jokes and joyous songs going off all around them.

I was in a Manse, in Peebleshire, a few years ago. 'Was you ever in John Dowie's?' said the minister. I said I had. Instantly a little old woman, above eighty, for whose excitement the question had been put, said eagerly—'Lord bless ye, Sir! Hae ye been in oor hoose! *A'm John's widow!*' Her old heart warmed on getting a guest to talk to. It had been a decent establishment, and she was proud of its virtue. She had often seen a hundred people (she said) in it in one evening. 'And'—weeping—'no a fou cratur e'er gaed oot o' the hoose! Hoo could they? Ou shut at twall.'

But the worthy lady was liberal in construction both of time and temperature. For many a philosopher staggered across her threshold long after St Giles had called out twelve. And many a twopence, for many a page, did many an apprentice part with there. Many a studious day did young men bring to a close in that snuggery.

Many a night did the Itch Club quench its thirst in Johnie's ale. Many an hour of solitary, as well as of social, muzziness did even Otho drown amidst the fumes of that fragrant den.

## Notes

Cockburn's '1804' for the appearance of Scott's 'Helvellyn' is too early: Scott did not climb the mountain, and gain his theme, till the autumn of the following year. The pattern of line indentations in the Richardson parody is that of the text which appeared in the *North British Review* for 1864, which is that of the poem being parodied: that of the manuscript is slightly different. At three points, the *North British Review* text of the parody has been followed in preference to the manuscript reading. Line 23 of the manuscript text has 'home-bred', and lines 35 and 36 read:

> And some moral question, in words sweet as sugar,
> To urge in soft answer and gentle reply?

In the last sentence of Cockburn's section 12, the *North British Review*'s 'the' before 'Highland understanding' has been inserted.

# Index

*Index*